John W. H Porter

A Record of Events in Norfolk County, Virginia, from April 19th, 1861, to May 10th, 1862

With a History of the Soldiers and Sailors of Norfolk County

John W. H Porter

A Record of Events in Norfolk County, Virginia, from April 19th, 1861, to May 10th, 1862
With a History of the Soldiers and Sailors of Norfolk County

ISBN/EAN: 9783744778312

Printed in Europe, USA, Canada, Australia, Japan

Cover: Foto ©ninafisch / pixelio.de

More available books at **www.hansebooks.com**

A RECORD

OF

*EVENTS IN NORFOLK COUNTY, VIRGINIA, FROM APRIL 19th, 1861,
TO MAY 10th, 1862, WITH A HISTORY OF THE SOLDIERS
AND SAILORS OF NORFOLK COUNTY, NORFOLK CITY
AND PORTSMOUTH WHO SERVED IN THE
CONFEDERATE STATES ARMY OR NAVY.*

BY

JOHN W. H. PORTER,

A COMRADE OF STONEWALL CAMP, CONFEDERATE VETERANS,
OF PORTSMOUTH, VA.

PORTSMOUTH, VA.:
W. A. FISKE, PRINTER AND BOOKBINDER,
1892.

TO

LIEUTENANT-COLONEL WM. H. STEWART, FORMERLY OF NORFOLK COUNTY, BUT NOW A CITIZEN OF PORTSMOUTH, WHO SERVED FAITHFULLY THROUGH THE WAR FROM THE BEGINNING TO THE END, AS LIEUTENANT, CAPTAIN, MAJOR AND LIEUTENANT-COLONEL, AND TO WHOSE ASSISTANCE IS DUE THE COLLECTION OF MANY INTERESTING FACTS CONTAINED IN THIS VOLUME; TO STONEWALL CAMP, CONFEDERATE VETERANS, OF PORTSMOUTH, AT WHOSE SUGGESTION THIS WORK WAS BEGUN; TO PICKETT-BUCHANAN CAMP, OF NORFOLK, WHICH IS PERFORMING A GOOD TASK IN RELIEVING THE NECESSITIES OF MANY OLD COMRADES IN THE ARMY OF NORTHERN VIRGINIA, AND TO THE THIRTY-FOUR HUNDRED MEN OF NORFOLK COUNTY, NORFOLK CITY AND PORTSMOUTH, WHO BID ADIEU TO THEIR HOMES AND KINDRED ON THE 10TH OF MAY, 1862, AND MARCHED FORTH UNDER THE BANNERS OF THE SOUTH,

THIS BOOK IS RESPECTFULLY DEDICATED

BY

THE AUTHOR.

PREFACE.

Stonewall Camp, Confederate Veterans, of Portsmouth, being desirous of preserving the names of the Confederate soldiers and sailors of this county, appointed various historical committees; but slow progress was made, and each succeeding year rendered the task more difficult of accomplishment. Having been an eye-witness of some of the scenes herein related, and having become possessed of many authentic records and personal reminiscences, I have, by request, undertaken the work. I have collected the names of more than thirty-three hundred men who marched under the Southern flag, from their homes in Norfolk county on that memorable 10th of May, 1862, and have followed them through the smoke of battle, in the hospitals, and sometimes through prison walls, recording when and where they were wounded, or when and where they died. In a work of this character, the first which ever sought to tell the history of the private soldier in the ranks as well as the doings of the officer in command, and which must depend largely upon recollection, much of necessity, will be left out which should be made to appear; for memory, after a lapse of more than a quarter of a century, will sometimes fail to recall events just as they happened, and comrades who were associated with us then have passed out of mind, but much has been rescued from oblivion. The mistakes are more those of omission than of commission. I have not succeeded in getting the names of the Portsmouth men in the Navy Yard in Richmond who, like the Jews at the rebuilding of King Solomon's Temple, worked with their tools while their swords were by their sides ready to be taken up at a moment's notice. Those men were in the trenches around Richmond almost as much as they were employed in their workshops, and their names should appear in this book, but nearly all of the Confederate Navy Department records appear to have been destroyed. Most of the men were advanced in years and have "passed beyond the river."

I have ascertained and published the names of 1,018 men from Norfolk county, of whom 280 were killed or died during the war, 1,119 who enlisted in Norfolk city companies, of whom 176 were killed or died, and 1,242 from Portsmouth, of whom 199 were killed or died, making a total of 3,379 men, of whom 655 gave up their lives for the cause in which they enlisted, and hundreds of others were disabled from wounds. A number of Norfolk county men were in the Princess Anne Cavalry and in Company F, 3d Virginia Regiment, which was recruited principally in Nansemond county, and these will more than offset the Nansemond men in Company I, 9th Virginia Infantry. Tracing up these facts has required months of patient research and inquiry. If I have not given each man as extended a record as he deserves I hope he will consider the number of names in the book and the limitless bounds it would occupy if not condensed.

J. W. H. P.

CONTENTS.

CHAPTER.	PAGE.
I. The first year of the war in Portsmouth,	9
II. The Portsmouth Light Artillery.	38
III. The Dismal Swamp Rangers, Co. A, 3d Va.,	47
IV. The Virginia Riflemen, Co. B, 3d Va.,	52
V. The National Grays, Co. H, 3d Va.,	57
VI. The Third Virginia Regiment,	63
VII. Capt. Jno. H. Myers' Company, Co. E, 6th Va.,	70
VIII. The Virginia Artillery, Co. D, 9th Va.,	73
IX. The Portsmouth Rifles, Co. G, 9th Va.,	78
X. The Craney Island Artillery, Co. I, 9th Va.,	86
XI. The Old Dominion Guard, Co. K, 9th Va.,	93
XII. The Ninth Virginia Regiment,	101
XIII. The Virginia Defenders, Co. C, 16th Va.,	126
XIV. The St. Bride's Artillery, Co. I, 38th Va.,	132
XV. The Norfolk County Rifle Patriots, Co. F, 41st Va.,	136
XVI. The Jackson Grays, Co. A, 61st V.,	141
XVII. The Wilson Guard, Co. B, 61st Va.,	147
XVIII. The Blanchard Grays, Co. C, 61st Va.,	151
XIX. The Jackson Light Infantry, Co. D, 61st Va.,	154
XX. The Border Rifles, Co. E, 61st Va.,	157
XXI. The Virginia Rangers, Co. H, 61st Va.,	161
XXII. The Bilisoly Blues, Co. I, 61st Va.,	164
XXIII. Company K, 61st Va., Co. K, 61st Va.,	169
XXIV. The Sixty-First Virginia Regiment,	173
XXV. In Outside Commands,	200
XXVI. The St. Bride's Cavalry, Co. F, 15th Va. Cavalry,	206
XXVII. Field and Staff,	210
XXVIII. The Wise Light Dragoons,	220
XXIV. In the Navy—Portsmouth,	221
XXX. Operations Around Norfolk, 1861-2,	228
XXXI. Norfolk Light Artillery Blues,	247
XXXII. Norfolk Light Artillery. (Huger's Battery),	255
XXXIII. Company A, 6th Virginia Regiment,	259
XXXIV. Woodis Riflemen, Co. C, 6th Va.,	262
XXXV. The Norfolk Light Infantry, Co. D, 6th Va.,	266
XXXVI. Company F, Co. G, 6th Va.,	269
XXXVII. The Independent Grays, Co. H, 6th Va.,	276
XXXVIII. The Sixth Virginia Regiment,	279
XXXIX. The Norfolk Juniors, Co. H, 12th Va.,	288
XL. The Atlantic Artillery,	294
XLI. The United Artillery,	296
XLII. Young's Harbor Guard,	301
XLIII. The Signal Corps,	304
XLIV. Field and Staff,	306
XLV. In the Navy—Norfolk,	313
XLVI. In Other Commands,	324
XLVII. The First Iron-clad, the Virginia,	327
XLVIII. The Battle in Hampton Roads,	358

ERRATA.

Page 42, line 20, for July 14th read July 1st.
" 55, " 5, for 1884-5 read 1864-5.
" 55, " 49, for Five Forks read Appomattox.
" 74, " 37, for June, 1862, read June, 1863.
" 83, " 1, for Barton read Burton.
" 127, " 29, for Company G read Company C.
" 129, " 47, for September 30th read September 14th.
" 139, head line, for 61st Virginia read 41st.
" 175, line 38, for 1892 read 1862.
" 190, " 24, for Maj. J. T. Woodhouse, read Lieut. Col. R. O. Whitehead.
" 207, " 47, for Israel Eason read Isaac.
" 249, " 12, for Petersburg read Fredericksburg.
" 289, " 46, for May 19th–21st, '62, read '61.
" 348, " 8, for 1861 read 1862.

In Thos. Scott's Advertisement add Undertaking.

CHAPTER I.

THE FIRST YEAR OF THE WAR IN PORTSMOUTH.

Thirty-one years have gone by since the beginning of the struggle between the States which, raging for four years, reached nearly every portion of the South, from the Potomac to the Rio Grande, and left in its devastating track blazing homes and wasted fields. In no previous war in the history of the world's battles was there a greater display of bravery and fortitude than the people of the Southern States put forth in defence of those principles of self government which had been instilled in them from the foundation of the American Union, and no braver men served under the banners of the Southern Confederacy than those whom the City of Norfolk, the City of Portsmouth and County of Norfolk sent to the front when the Governor of Virginia issued his call for volunteers. They were brave men and courageous soldiers, fighting most of the time in defence of the homes and families of others, while their own homes and families were in the possession of the enemy, but, in the many struggles of that long and weary war, in the heroic charge of Pickett's Division at Gettysburg, in the determined rush of Mahone's Brigade at the "Crater," proving their devotion to Virginia and the metal that was in them.

Many of them fell upon the field of battle, or died from diseases contracted from exposure in the line of duty, and many returned home with a leg or an arm gone or with bones broken, and disabled, while those who survived the ordeal of battle and exposure are rapidly passing away.

The twenty-seven years since the last gun was fired and the last soldier of the South laid down his arms, have witnessed the funeral of many a survivor of "the Lost Cause," and while there are still enough left to tell the tale, and before memory becomes dimmed by age, it is proper that the names and deeds of those who, had success crowned their bravery and devotion, would have lived in history and in song as heroes and patriots should be collected and preserved.

The record of the men who marched from this county is one to which future generations of their children may recur with pride. From the General at the head of his brigade to the humblest soldier in the ranks, "Fame crowned their brows with an amaranthine wreath that will never fade," and the object of this modest volume is to collect and preserve this record.

The city of Portsmouth sent more men to the Confederate cause than there were voters in the city, and it has been said by one who has given the subject sufficient study to speak advisedly, that there was not an important battle fought east of the Mississippi river during the entire war in which there was not present a soldier from Portsmouth. At this late day memory cannot recall the names of all those brave men who, upon distant battle fields, so gallantly upheld the name and fame of the little city which gave them birth and sent them forth at the call of duty, hence many of them will necessarily be omitted from its pages; passed from memory as the years roll by!

I leave to the general historian the task of tracing out the progress of campaigns and describing the manoeuvres, the charges and the struggles when armies met in deadly combat, and will endeavor to tell, as well as I can, the part which Norfolk, Portsmouth and the county of Norfolk took in that great war. The history of one is the history of the other, for their companies stood shoulder to shoulder in the same regiments, marched to the tap of the same drums, sat by the same camp fires and fell upon the same battle fields.

In the year 1861 Portsmouth, the county seat of Norfolk county, was a city of about nine thousand inhabitants, of whom less than six thousand were white persons. Norfolk county, exclusive of the cities of Norfolk and Portsmouth, contained a population of about twelve thousand, of whom about seven thousand were white persons. The Gosport navy yard, the most important of the United States Naval Stations, was located at the southern extremity of the city, and, on account of the large amount of work done there by the Government, usually gave employment to from twelve hundred to fifteen hundred mechanics and laborers. The city was prosperous and contented, and when the question of seceding from the Federal Union came before the people on the 4th of February, 1861, in the form of an election for delegates to the State Convention, Portsmouth and Norfolk county, which together were entitled to two delegates, elected Dr. William White and Mr. James G. Holladay upon what was known as the Union ticket, by a large majority over Messrs. James Murdaugh and Samuel M. Wilson, who ran upon what was known as the Secession ticket. The Union sentiment predominated largely in the State Convention also, but, unfortunately, the sentiment of the men who controlled the North was in favor of forcing rather than persuading back into the Union the States which had already seceded, and, in obedience to that sentiment, President Lincoln issued his call for 75,000 troops, assigning to Virginia her proportionate share. Then it became evident that Virginia would not be permitted to hold a neutral position but would be compelled to fight with or against the other Southern States, and the convention underwent a change of opinion. It was held that it would be better to stand or fall with those States than to take up arms against them, and men who were elected as Union delegates voted to submit to the people, for ratification or rejection, the Ordinance of Secession. This resolution was passed April 17th, 1861, and was to be submitted to a vote of the people on the fourth Thursday in May following, but the State was virtually out of the Union from the day the convention adopted the ordinance.

It will not avail anything to discuss the right of a State to secede from the Federal Union, for, whether the right existed or not, under the Constitution, it has been stamped out under the feet of more than a million of soldiers, but six years after that date the Congress of the United States, which denied the right of the States to go out of the Union of their own accord, claimed for itself the right and authority to put them out, and the Southern States became territories, under military governors, and, after going through a course of reconstruction prescribed by act of Congress, were readmitted into the Union as States, with their constitutions radically altered to suit the views of the majority in Congress. As a prerequisite to their readmission into the Union, they were required to vote to ratify certain amendments to the Constitution of the United States; hence those amendments were adopted and became the law of the land by the aid of the votes of States which were out of the Union, by act of Congress, and under military government. But this discussion is foreign to the object for which this work is being written. Virginia, by virtue of a reservation in the resolution by which her Legislature ratified the Constitution of the United States and consented to become a State in the Federal Union, always claimed the right to withdraw therefrom. In that resolution she said:

"The powers granted under the Constitution, being derived from the people of the United States, may be resumed by them whensoever the same may be perverted to their injury or oppression."

And the State Convention, believing the time had arrived when the powers conferred upon the General Government were being perverted to the injury of the people of Virginia, and that the State had the legal and constitutional right to do so, decided to withdraw from that compact.

The State Convention passed the ordinance of secession on the 17th of April, 1861, but it was not made public immediately. On the night of the 18th General William B. Taliaferro arrived in Norfolk with authority from Governor Letcher to take command of the Virginia forces in that city, and on the same day Lieutenants Robert B. Pegram and Catesby Ap. R. Jones, who had resigned from the United States Navy, were appointed by the Governor captains in the Virginia Navy, with orders to take command of the naval station and organize naval defences.

General Taliaferro was accompanied by Major Nathaniel Tyler

and Captain Henry Heth as his staff, and the Virginia military forces in the vicinity consisted of the Norfolk Juniors, Independent Grays, Woodis Rifles, Company F, and the Light Artillery Blues of Norfolk City; the Portsmouth Rifles, Old Dominion Guard, National Grays, Marion Rifles and Portsmouth Light Artillery, of Portsmouth, and the Dismal Swamp Rangers, of Deep Creek, and the Rifle Patriots, of Great Bridge, Norfolk county, the twelve companies numbering probably eight hundred and fifty men, but without any ammunition. The two artillery companies had each four light guns. The naval forces at the disposal of Captain Pegram consisted of absolutely nothing. There was also in Norfolk county a small cavalry company, the Wise Light Dragoons.

The Navy Yard was under the command of Commodore McCauley, who, under the very peculiar circumstances which surrounded him, was uncertain how to act, and the Navy Department at Washington left him without instructions. He had received orders on the 16th from the Department to immediately fit out the Merrimac, to put her guns on her without loss of time (they had been taken ashore), and to send her, with the other vessels capable of being moved, together with the ordnance, stores, &c., beyond the reach of seizure.

Commodore McCauley construed the order to mean a desire on the part of the Navy Department to abandon the station, and did not feel authorized to disobey the order to the extent of bringing on hostilities by maintaining possession of the Navy Yard and firing upon the City of Portsmouth, more especially as the United States Government had made no hostile demonstration against the State of Virginia.

There were at the Navy Yard at that time, the sloop-of-war Cumberland, 22 guns, in commission, with a full complement of officers and men on board; the sloops-of-war Plymouth, 22 guns, and Germantown, 22 guns, and the brig Dolphin, 6 guns, almost ready for sea; the steam frigate Merrimac, 40 guns, almost ready for sea and undergoing repairs; the line of battle ship Pennsylvania, 120 guns, in commission as a receiving ship, with a considerable crew on board, and the 74-gun ships Delaware and Columbus, and the frigates Raritan, Columbia and United States, dismantled and in ordinary. The force of sailors and marines on the various vessels and at the Navy Yard was probably about 600, well armed and abundantly supplied with ammunition. The Plymouth, Germantown, Dolphin and Merrimac were lying alongside the wharves and men were working on them. The Delaware and Columbus were at a wharf at the southern end of the yard, and might have been considered as in "Rotten Row," a term applied to vessels for which the Government no longer has any use.

Commodore McCauley might have held the Navy Yard for a

considerable time against any forces at the disposal of the State of Virginia. The Cumberland and Pennsylvania could have swept it with their guns, and he has been considerably censured for not doing so, but there was another side to the question. The Pennsylvania might have been considered as stationary. She was supposed to have been fast in the mud, and could easily have been enfiladed by batteries on shore, in such a position that her broadside could not be brought to bear on them, and furthermore, it would have been possible, shut up in a close harbor as those two vessels were, to have captured them by a determined attack by boarders at night, just as General Magruder, later in the war, captured the steamer Harriet Lane in Galveston harbor. By the erection of batteries on the St. Helena side of the river, opposite the Navy Yard, the Cumberland could have been driven away or destroyed. She would have been compelled to have relied upon her sails for motive power. It is true the State of Virginia had nothing heavier than twelve-pounder howitzers with which to man those batteries, but Commodore McCauley was not familiar with the resources of the State, and therefore, in the light of the last orders he had received from Washington, determined to leave with what he could take with him and destroy the remainder. His determination was quickened by reports which reached him that the Virginia forces were sinking obstructions in the river below Fort Norfolk and erecting batteries. He was deceived also by the continued moving of trains on the Norfolk and Petersburg Railroad within hearing of the Navy Yard, and thought they were bringing troops to Norfolk. This was done by General Mahone, who was then president of the railroad company, for the purpose of creating just such an impression.

The work of destruction began a little before noon on the 20th, and the frigate Merrimac was the first object of the destroyers. Carpenters and machinists were at work on her at the time. The carpenter of the Cumberland, with a small squad of sailors to assist him, opened her bilge cocks and she filled with water and settled quietly until she rested on the bottom. Owing to her great draft of water she did not settle far.

After the 12 o'clock bell was rung for the workmen to knock off for dinner, the gates of the Navy Yard were closed, and no one was permitted to enter without the approval of the Commodore. The work of destruction then proceeded very rapidly. The standing rigging of the Germantown was cut away and the guys which held the heavy masting shears were cut in two, so that the shears fell across her and she was broken and sunk. The Plymouth and Dolphin also were scuttled, as were also the 74-gun ships Delaware and Columbus, but on account of their great depth they were not submerged.

During the afternoon it became generally known in Portsmouth that the vessels and stores in the Navy Yard were being destroyed and a rumor became prevalent that it was the intention of Commodore McCauley to set the buildings on fire. This, it was feared, would cause serious damage in the city, as it was separated from the yard only by the width of Lincoln street, which was but sixty feet wide, and a meeting of citizens was held, at which Messrs. Samuel Watts, James Murdaugh and William H. Peters were appointed a committee to wait upon Commodore McCauley to endeavor to persuade him to reconsider that purpose, if he really entertained it, but the Commodore refused to see them and they were denied admission into the yard.

About dusk the sloop-of-war Pawnee, under Captain Paulding, steamed up to the Navy Yard, and her crew were added to the wrecking force. It is said the torch was applied by the orders of Captain Paulding. The long building on the north front of the yard, facing Lincoln street, and in which was the main entrance, was set on fire and totally destroyed. This building, among other things, contained the armory of the yard, and its hundreds of rifles, carbines, pistols, cutlasses, and other ordnance stores, besides ropes, canvas, &c. The two large ship houses, A and B, were also fired. Ship house A had in it, on the stocks, the 74-gun ship New York, completely framed, with her deck beams, carlines and knees completed, and partially planked, inside and out, and her decks partially laid.

The fire from the ship houses communicated to the Merrimac, Plymouth, Germantown and Dolphin, and all of them that was above the water was consumed. The Pennsylvania, Raritan and Columbia, which were anchored out in the stream, shared the fate of the ship houses. They were set on fire and burned almost down to their keels. Several buildings, containing stores of various kinds, were fired and, together with their valuable contents, totally destroyed.

An effort was made to destroy the usefulness of the heavy cannon, hundreds of which were in the yard, by breaking off their trunions with mauls, but this was successful in only a few instances. There was a large quantity of liquor in the spirit room in the naval store house, and the sailors, getting possession of this liquor, filled themselves so full of it that they were unable to keep up the work of destruction. They spiked a number of the cannon with nails, but these were easily gotten out subsequently by the Confederates.

History says an attempt was made to blow up the large stone dry dock but that it was discovered by the Confederates in time to prevent its successful accomplishment, but history is at fault in this instance, as in many others. The true reason why the dock was not blown up has never before been published, and the proof of it seems conclusive. On the morning of the 21st, about daybreak, detachments from the Portsmouth military companies which had been under arms all night, marched into the Navy Yard and took possession of it, and Privates David A. Williams, of the Old Dominion Guard, and Joseph F. Weaver, of the Portsmouth Rifle Company, attracted by curiosity, strolled down to the dry dock, and, looking down into it, noticed a train of loose powder, leading down to the culvert at the northeast corner. Mr. Williams immediately ran down into the dock and broke the connection by kicking one of the planks down. They then hunted for the fuse or slow match, but did not succeed in finding it, and concluded that after the train was laid the orders to blow it up had been countermanded, or that there had been some other hitch in the proceedings. Soon afterwards the wicket gate was opened by the Confederates and the water turned into the dock. This caused about thirty barrels of powder to float out of the culvert.

The cause of the failure to ignite the train of powder remained a mystery until the following February, when it was discovered by a singular coincidence. Mr. Weaver had, in the meantime, been appointed a carpenter in the Confederate States Navy, and was attached to the steamer Seabird in the fight at Roanoke Island February 7th, 1862, between the small fleet of small steamers under Commodore Lynch, and the greatly superior force of United States vessels. The Island fell into the hands of the Federals on the 8th, and Commodore Lynch's fleet, having fired away all of its ammunition, fell back to Elizabeth City for a new supply, but did not succeed in obtaining any. On the 9th the Federal fleet arrived before Elizabeth City, and the tugs Raleigh and Beaufort escaped though the Dismal Swamp Canal, but the Seabird and Fanny were too wide to get through the locks. The Seabird was sunk by a 9-inch Columbiad and her crew were captured.

While a prisoner on board a Federal gunboat Mr. Weaver formed the acquaintance of a master's mate, with whose mess he obtained his meals, and the mate, finding out that he was from Portsmouth, told him about the attempt to blow up the dry dock at the Navy Yard. He said he had charge of a party of sailors, with orders to destroy it; that he put the powder in, and he described to Mr. Weaver the arrangement of the planks to hold the train, just as Mr. Weaver had seen it on the morning of the 21st of April; that after the powder had been placed in the culvert and the train was laid to it, he sent the sailors to their boat, lighted the fuse, and then, instead of placing it where it would ignite the powder, threw it overboard. He gave as a reason for doing so, that he had a number of friends living in Portsmouth near the Navy Yard, who had been very kind to him; that the quantity of powder with which the dock was mined was sufficient to have blown some of the stone beyond the Navy Yard wall, and, in falling, it might have crushed in some of the houses and killed some of the women and children in the city, and he did not care to be the instrument to take their lives. He said he lighted the match so that he would be able to report that he had done so, and he had no apprehension that any of the officers or men would go back to the dock to see if it was burning.

His account tallies exactly with what Mr. Williams and Mr. Weaver saw when they went to the dock that morning, and as they were the first to go there, there is no reason to doubt its correctness. He could not have so accurately described the situation unless he had seen it. One plank extended from the gate chain to the side of the dock, and from the middle of this plank another plank extended into the culvert, thus forming the letter T, and the train was laid along those two planks. It will be remembered that Messrs. Weaver and Williams searched carefully for the fuse, but did not succeed in finding it, nor was it subsequently found. Had it been lighted and gone out of its own accord, the remains would have been found there. The failure to destroy the dock was due, therefore, to the humanity of the man who was ordered to do the work, and not to the sagacity of the Confederate officials. At this writing, May 27th, 1892, Messrs. Williams and Weaver are both living in Portsmouth. Mr. Williams is in the employment of the Seaboard and Roanoke Railroad Company as section master, and Mr. Weaver is keeping a drug store on South street.

But, to return to the Navy Yard and its destruction. The old frigate United States, around which clustered so many memories of brave deeds and gallant victories, was the only vessel which was spared in the general devastation, and that night of the 20th of April was a night of anxiety in Portsmouth. The immense ship houses, with their millions of feet of timber, were seathing volcanos of flames, and the huge ship Pennsylvania was a pyramid of fire, while the burning Merrimac, Dolphin, Germantown, Plymouth, Raritan and Columbia and the large store houses added to the conflagration and lighted up the heavens with a lurid glare that was seen for thirty miles. To add to the dangers of the night the dwelling houses on the north side of Lincoln street in Portsmouth caught fire, and the whole city was threatened with destruction, which was only averted by a change of the direction of the wind. Occasionally one of the guns of the Pennsylvania, which had been left loaded by her crew, would be discharged as it became hot enough from the fire to ignite the powder, but, fortunately, no one was hurt by them, and amid all of this crackling of flames, booming of guns and deluge of falling sparks, the cry arose that the Pawnee was about to bombard the city.

A correspondence had taken place between General Taliaferro and Commodore McCauley in which the General proposed to the

Commodore that if he put a stop to the work of destruction the Pawnee and Cumberland would be permitted to leave the Navy Yard and the port in safety. He had no means to prevent them from leaving, and in fact was very anxious to have them go, but Commodore McCauley was not aware of that and accepted the proposal. Accordingly, about midnight the Pawnee left the yard with the Cumberland in tow. Captain Paulding returned an answer to General Taliaferro threatening severe retaliation in case they were molested. This was construed to mean the bombardment of the two cities, and probably gave rise to the rumor which was prevalent in Portsmouth.

During "the reign of terror" which existed in the city on the 20th, an order was received from the Governor calling out the military companies of Portsmouth and Norfolk county. They assembled about 2 o'clock in the afternoon of that day, and were in continual service from then until the surrender of General Lee's army at Appomattox Court House on the 9th of April, 1865. Those companies composed the Third Virginia Volunteers, and were as follows:

Portsmouth Rifle Company, Captain John C. Owens;

Old Dominion Guard, Captain Edward Kearns;

The National Grays, Captain John E. Deans;

The Marion Rifles, Captain Johannis Watson;

The Dismal Swamp Rangers, Captain James C. Choat of Deep Creek, Norfolk county; and,

The Portsmouth Light Artillery, Captain Cary F. Grimes, four guns.

The Union Guard, a company composed exclusively of our Irish-American citizens, was formerly in the Third Regiment, but was disbanded about a year before the war broke out from lack of interest among its members.

The Regiment was under command of the following field and staff officers:

Colonel, James G. Hodges; Lieutenant Colonel, David J. Godwin; Major, William C. Wingfield; Adjutant, John W. H. Wrenn; Commissary, C. W. Murdaugh; Quartermaster, John Hobday; Surgeon, H. F. Butt; Assistant Surgeon, V. B. Bilisoly.

On the night of the 20th the men slept on their arms in the Court House and City Hall, and at day break on the 21st one-half were sent to the Navy Yard and the other to the Naval Hospital point to assist in building an earthwork. After the Military entered the yard Lieutenant C. F. M. Spotwood of the Virginia Navy went in, and, hoisting a State flag upon the flag staff, took formal possession in the name of the Commonwealth of Virginia, and Captain Robert B. Pegram assumed command. He was relieved on the 22d by Commodore French Forrest, who arrived under orders from Governor Letcher. Captain Pegram was subsequently ordered to the command of the post at Pig Point, at the mouth of the Nansemond river, and had command of the battery there on the 5th of June, when the United States steamer Harriett Lane was driven off by the Portsmouth Rifle Company.

Later in the day of the 21st the military, with the exception of the National Grays, were marched from the Navy Yard to the Naval Hospital Point, and the Regiment became re-united. A very strong earthwork was thrown up there and manned with guns from the Navy Yard. Obstructions were placed in the harbor so as to narrow the channel, and guns were mounted at Fort Norfolk, so that it would have been difficult if not impossible for the Pawnee and Cumberland to have returned, had they desired to do so. On the 21st the Norfolk County Rifle Patriots took possession of the Government ordnance depot at St. Helena, opposite the Navy Yard. The officers of the Third Regiment had hardly gotten warmed in their quarters when Governor Letcher, in pursuance of the policy of placing in command of the volunteer troops, field officers with whom they had not been familiarly associated before they were mustered into service, removed Colonel Hodges, Lieutenant Colonel Godwin and Major Wingfield from their commands and appointed in their stead Colonel Roger A. Pryor, Lieutenant Colonel Joseph Mayo, Jr., and Major Joseph V. Scott, whereupon the staff officers of the Regiment tendered their resignations and entered the service in other positions.

Colonel Hodges and Lieutenant Colonel Godwin were assigned to the Fourteenth Virginia Regiment, Major Wingfield became Major and Commissary of Mahone's Brigade and afterwards of the Division, Doctors Butt and Bilisoly were appointed Surgeons, and Messrs. Murdaugh and Hobday were elected Lieutenants in the Bilisoly Blues, afterwards Company I, Sixty-first Virginia, a company which was shortly afterwards organized. Adjutant Wrenn was elected Captain of the Virginia Rifles of Portsmouth.

After remaining at the Hospital Point about a week or ten days the Portsmouth Rifle Company was detached from the Third Regiment and ordered to Pig Point and the Old Dominion Guard was detached and ordered to Pinner's Point to take charge of fortifications, and in June were organized with the Ninth Virginia Regiment as Companies G and K, respectively.

After the State seceded from the Union and hostilities had actually commenced the military fever ran high in the city and county, notwithstanding their strong Union sentiments. Their love for Virginia was stronger than their love for the Union. They believed in the opinions which were held by the men who founded the American Government, the fathers of the Revolution, that their allegiance was due, first to their State and afterwards to the General Government, and that it was due to the

General Government only so long as the State was a part of it. New companies were organized rapidly. In the city these were:

The Virginia Defenders, Captain Edward Blamire, afterwards Co. C, 16th Va. Regiment, infantry.

The Virginia Artillery, Captain James H. Richardson, afterwards Co. D, 9th Va. Infantry.

Captain John H. Myers' Company, attached as Co. E to the 6th Va. Regiment.

The Bilisoly Blues, afterwards changed to the Rebel Grays, Captain Charles R. McAlpine, Co. I, 61st Va. Infantry.

The Jackson Artillery, Captain V. O. Cassell, which was attached to the 61st Va. Infantry as Co. D.

The Bilisoly Blues contained a number of men from the Bowers' Hill section of Norfolk county.

Thus there were mustered into the Confederate service from the city of Portsmouth one company of light artillery and nine companies of infantry, distributed as follows:

Two in the 3d Regiment, three in the 9th Regiment, one in the 16th Regiment, one in the 6th Regiment, two in the 61st Regiment.

The Virginia Rangers, Company H, 61st Regiment, was recruited partly from Portsmouth, though credited here to Norfolk county. All of its officers in active service were from the city.

All of those companies were large, and five of them, viz., the Portsmouth Rifle Company, Old Dominion Guard, National Grays, Jackson Artillery and Portsmouth Light Artillery, numbered over one hundred men each.

In addition to those companies there were two or three hundred Portsmouth men scattered among other commands. One commanded a North Carolina Brigade, four were field officers in North Carolina Regiments, one commanded an Alabama Regiment, ten were Surgeons in the Army, between forty and fifty were officers in the Navy, they were in full numbers in the Norfolk Light Artillery Blues, the Signal Corps and in the Navy, and every man who entered the service from this city was a volunteer. The city was evacuated by the Confederates before the conscript law was put into operation, and after it fell into the hands of the Federals, boys arriving at a sufficient age to do military duty made their escape through the Federal lines and joined their fathers and older brothers in the Confederate Army.

At the beginning of the war there were only two organized volunteer infantry companies in Norfolk county, one of which, the Dismal Swamp Rangers, Captain James C. Choat commanding, was raised in the vicinity of Deep Creek and was attached to the Third Regiment, and the Norfolk County Rifle Patriots, Captain William H. Etheredge, was raised in the Great Bridge section, it afterwards became Company F, Forty-first Regiment.

In the shifting of the companies composing the Third Regiment the Dismal Swamp Rangers became Company A. Like the men of Portsmouth, those of Norfolk county were none the less Virginians, though they had opposed the secession of the State, and when the tocsin of war was sounded, and the Governor called for volunteers to fight the battles of the Commonwealth, there was a general rush to arms, and young men and old ones responded to the call. The following companies were speedily organized and mustered into service and assigned to regiments in due course of time:

The Craney Island Artillery, Captain John T. Kilby, Co. I, 9th Va. Reg.

The St. Bride's Artillery, Captain George A. Martin, Co. I, 38th Va. Reg.

The St. Bride's Cavalry, Captain John Doyle, Co. F, 15th Va. Cavalry.

The Jackson Grays, Captain William H. Stewart, Co. A, 61st Va. Reg.

The Wilson Guard, Captain John W. M. Hopkins, Co. B, 61st Va. Reg.

The Blanchard Grays, Captain John G. Wallace, Co. C, 61st Va. Reg.

The Border Rifles, Captain Jetson Jett, Co. E, 61st Va. Reg.

The Virginia Rangers, Captain James C. Choat, Co. H, 61st Va. Reg.

——————, Captain Max Herbert, Co. K, 61st Va. Reg.

Quite a number of Norfolk county men living near the Princess Anne county line joined the Princess Anne cavalry, Captain Burroughs, Co. I, 15th Va. Cavalry, while many in the Western Branch section joined the Nansemond cavalry, which was attached to the 13th Regiment. The Tanner's Creek section contributed a large number of men to the various companies which were raised in Norfolk city. Thus it will be seen that Norfolk county contributed fully eleven companies to the Confederate Army. Co. H, 61st Regiment, was recruited partly in Portsmouth, and Co. B, 9th Va., was recruited partly in Norfolk county, in the vicinity of Craney Island. The eleven companies accredited to the county were thus distributed:

One in the 3d Regiment Infantry, one in the 9th Regiment Infantry, one in the 38th Regiment Infantry, one in the 41st Regiment Infantry, six in the 61st Regiment Infantry, one in the 15th Regiment Cavalry.

On the 23d of May, 1861, a very unfortunate occurrence took place at the Naval Hospital battery, owing to the hasty and inconsiderate action of Colonel Roger A. Pryor. The State Convention passed the Ordinance of Secession on the 17th of April and directed that it be submitted to a vote of the people on the

23d of May for ratification or rejection. The people were the final court to decide the question, and if a majority of them cast their votes in favor of the ratification of the ordinance the State would secede from the Union, but if the majority of votes should be the other way it would remain in the Union. The question for the people to decide was, therefore, whether or not the State should secede.

As has already been said, the Union sentiment was very strong in Portsmouth. It permeated all classes of her citizens, and when the vote was taken most of the members of the Marion Rifle Company voted against the ratification of the ordinance. Colonel Pryor, who was an ultra Secessionist, became so enraged at them for exercising a privilege which they had a perfect right to exercise, that he assembled the regiment, ordered the Marion Rifles to advance to the front and ground arms. He then made a bitter and offensive speech to them and disbanded the company, charging the men with disloyalty to Virginia. This action on his part was very uncalled for. Those men had acknowledged their allegiance to Virginia as superior to their allegiance to the United States, and had responded to the call of Governor Letcher for troops, even while the State was still in the Union, but when called upon at the election to declare whether they were in favor of the State going out of the Union or remaining in it, they voted as they thought best for themselves and the Commonwealth. The company reorganized under the name of Virginia Riflemen and was continued in the 3d Regiment as Co. B, and the men made good records for themselves as soldiers. It was a member of this company, Sergeant Robert A. Hutchings of Portsmouth, who planted the colors of the 3rd Regiment on the stone wall at Gettysburg when Pickett's Division made its famous and historic charge there. The company remained at the Hospital battery until June 7th, when they went to Burwell's Bay with the 3rd Regiment, but Colonel Pryor's ill advised and hasty action lost to the State the services of some of the old members, who would doubtless have made good soldiers, for the best soldiers were not necessarily those who had shouted loudest for Secession.

Immediately upon the evacuation of the Navy Yard the Confederates began pouring troops into this section. Several companies from Petersburg and the Richmond Grays were the first to arrive, and reached Norfolk on the 21st. Four companies from Georgia arrived in Portsmouth on the 22d. These were the Columbus Light Guard, of Columbus, the Macon Volunteers and Floyd Rifles, of Macon, and the Spaulding Grays, of Griffin, and in a very short time there were gathered for the defence of the harbor the following organizations:

The 3d, 6th, 9th, 12th, 41st and 61st Virginia Regiments.

The 3d, 4th and 22d Georgia Regiments and the 2ee heavy Battalion.

The 1st Louisiana Regiment and 3d Louisiana Battalion.
The 3d Alabama Regiment.
The 2d North Carolina Battalion, afterwards the 32d Regiment.
The Portsmouth Light Artillery; the Norfolk Light Artillery Blues, the United Artillery, the Atlantic Artillery and the Huger Battery, of Norfolk, the Salem Artillery, and the Louisiana Guard Artillery.

Burroughs' and Cooper's Calvary Companies 15th Virginia Cavalry, and two companies of cavalry from Nansemond county and one from Southampton county, in the 13th Virginia Cavalry Regiment.

There was also a North Carolina battalion stationed near Suffolk. Captain Martin's Company, of Norfolk county, and Captain Young's, of Norfolk city, were also on duty near here.

General Taliaferro was superseded in command by General W. Gwynn on the 23d of April, and he was relieved by General Huger on the 24th of May, with headquarters in Norfolk. General Blanchard commanded the troops on the Portsmouth side of the river. The Navy Yard was under the command of Commodore French Forrest, who had under him Captain and Executive Officer S. S. Lee; Captain A. B. Fairfax, ordnance officer; Naval Constructor John L. Porter; and Chief Engineer William P. Williamson, all of whom had resigned from the United States Navy.

Two days after the Navy Yard was burned by the United States forces Mr. William H. Peters, of Portsmouth, was appointed by Governor Letcher Paymaster in the Virginia Navy and assigned to duty there. Mr. Peters took an inventory of the stock and material left in the yard, which he reported to the Governor, who transmitted it to the State Convention then in session. Mr. Peters' report states that there were in the yard when it fell into the hands of the Confederates 1,085 heavy cannon of six, eight, nine and ten-inch bore. These were ready for service, with carriages, breeching, blocks and tackle complete, and their possession enabled the Confederates to prepare for defence against the attacks of their enemies.

There were also on hand in the yard, as per said report, 250,-000 pounds of powder, a large number of shells, stands of grape shot, and various other ordnance equipment stores, valued at $341,000. Also bread, beef, pork, flour, and other provisions, valued at $38,763. Also clothing, flannel, shirting, round jackets, &c., valued at $56,269. Also general naval supplies, such as timber, anchors, chains, copper, &c., valued at $1,448,223.

In a paper read before Stonewall Camp, Confederate Veterans, of ortsmouth, by Mr. Peters the latter part of 1891, he gave the and ity po which cannon were shipped from the Navy Yard from to July 1st, 1871, the date Virginia formally turned the Navy Yard over to the Confederate States Government. These were as follows. The six-inch guns were 32-pounders, and the seven-inch were 42s:

To battery at Naval Hospital, 13 six-inch and 2 eight inch guns.
" " " Craney Island, 12 six-inch, 10 eight-inch, 7 nine-inch and 1 ten-inch.
To battery at Fort Norfolk, 8 nine-inch guns.
" " " Boush's Bluff, 5 six-inch guns.
" " " Pinner's Point, 7 " "
" " " Pig Point, 12 six-inch and 2 eight inch guns.
" Richmond, 90 six-inch, 12 seven-inch, 10 eight inch and 24 nine inch.
To Charleston, 43 six-inch, 12 seven-inch and 3 old English cannon.
To Fredericksburg, 4 six-inch.
" Fort Powhatan, 6 six-inch.
" Kempsville, 1 twelve-pounder and 2 nine-pounder brass guns.
" Seaboard and Roanoke Railroad Co., 1 twenty-seven pounder.
" Savannah, 10 six-inch guns.
" Pensacola. " " "
" Captain Thomas, at Baltimore, 20 twenty-four pounders and 20 six-inch guns.
To Memphis, 5 six-inch guns.
" New Orleans, 13 six-inch, 8 eight-inch and 2 nine-inch guns.
" Tennessee, 32 six-inch guns.
" Lieutenant George T. Sinclair, for army South, 16 six-inch, 9 seven-inch, 8 eight-inch and 1 nine-inch.
To Norfolk city, 3 six-inch.
" battery at Seawell's Point, 8 six-inch and 6 nine-inch guns.
" " " Lambert's Point, 6 "
" " " Burwell's Bay, 5 "
" " " Pagan Creek, 4 "
" " " Powell's Point, 4 "
" " " City Point, 6 "
" General Gwynn and taken to North Carolina, 197 six-inch, 1 seven-inch, 11 eight-inch, and 4 twenty-four pounders.

All of those guns which were sent to General Gwynn shortly afterward were captured by the enemy, owing to the want of wisdom which prevailed in the management of affairs in Eastern North Carolina by the Confederate Government, coupled with the inefficiency and inexperience of some of the officers in immediate command.

The Federal forces had scarcely evacuated the Navy Yard before the active Virginia troops began erecting batteries at every available point in the harbor which would command the approaches by river to the city. Guns were sent over to Fort Norfolk from the Navy Yard and mounted there, and three heavy guns were placed in position at the Hospital Point on the morning of the 21st behind a temporary breastwork of cotton bales to keep the Pawnee and Cumberland back while a substantial breastwork was being built. This was so far completed by the end of the week as to have twelve heavy guns in position, and the experience of the naval officers was brought into requisition in drilling the men at the guns.

While the battery at the Naval Hospital was being constructed formidable works were going up at Pinner's Point under the supervision of Major F. W. Jett, of the engineers, Fort Norfolk, Boush's Bluff, Lambert's Point, Craney Island and Seawell's Point, so that, in less than ten days, the Confederates were able to bring about seventy-five or eighty guns to bear upon a vessel attempting to enter the harbor, and a fleet of wooden vessels could scarcely have run the gauntlet. These batteries were subsequently strengthened by the addition of rifled cannon, the heaviest fortifications being on Craney Island and Seawell's Point. The fortifications at Pinner's Point contained 12 six and eight-inch guns and four six-inch rifle guns, banded at the breech. One of the batteries was also roofed over and supposed to be bomb proof.

Pig Point, at the mouth of the Nansemond river, was also fortified. The battery there was manned by the Portsmouth Rifle Company, Captain John C. Owens, and the post was under command of Captain R. B. Pegram of the Navy. This battery had a small engagement with the United States cutter Harriett Lane on the 5th of June, which hauled off after an exchange of shots for about twenty minutes. No one was hurt in the battery, nor was the earthwork injured, though one of its guns, a 48-pounder, was disabled by a shot from the Lane. The batteries at Pinner's Point were under command of Captain George Harrison of the Navy, and the men at Craney Island were drilled at the guns by several Naval officers, chief of whom was Lieutenant Sharpe of Norfolk.

Captain A. B. Fairfax of the Navy was ordered to the Navy Yard in charge of the Ordnance Department, and was a man of practical ideas. Under his orders, with the approbation of Commodore Forrest, an experiment was made of rifling one of the 32-pounder Dahlgren guns which was left by the Federals when they made their hasty exit. An experienced mechanic was directed to supervise the work, and in order to strengthen the gun strong wrought iron bands were shrunk around it at the breech. The work was finished that summer and the gun was mounted on a small steam tug called the Harmony belonging to Captain James Brown of Portsmouth, and used for carrying freight between Portsmouth and Norfolk. Captain Fairfax took command of this little vessel of one gun, and, taking on board twenty-five shells, steamed down into Hampton Roads to engage the United States vessels which were anchored there. It was a repetition of the combat between David and Goliath. The frigate Savannah was the first object of the Harmony's attack. She was lying at the mouth of the James river, and the rifle gun from the little craft threw its shells over and into the big frigate, but the shots which were aimed at her in return fell far short of their mark. Captain Fairfax continued the engagement until he had fired away all of his ammunition.

This gun was a great advancement in the science of the manufacture of ordnance, and the inventor has not received the credit which is justly due him. It was the work of Mr. Thomas Carr of Portsmouth, who, at the time, was a foreman or quarterman in the Steam Engineering Department of the Gosport Navy Yard. Mr. James Flemming was Master Machinist and Chief Engineer William P. Williamson was in charge of the Department. Mr. Carr says he saw two Parrott guns in possession of the 3d Georgia Regiment, which was camped near the Navy Yard, and noticed the manner in which they were rifled and banded, and the thought occurred to him that it would be practicable to rifle and band the six-inch Dahlgren guns, and he got up a machine which could be attached to a lathe and with which the grooves might be cut in the guns. He made a small pencil sketch of it and submitted it to Chief Engineer Williamson, who at once saw its utility and sent for Captain Fairfax, to whom the machine and its objects were explained. Captain Fairfax approved of the idea and directed Mr. Carr to go ahead with it, to make his machine and experiment on one of the guns. Mr. George Maxwell of Portsmouth, an experienced machinist, operated the machine and did the mechanical part of the work, and its successful test was made in the engagement between the Harmony and Savannah. Mr. Carr was an humble mechanic, interested only in the success of the Southern cause, and not seeking to make either fame or fortune for himself out of the war, and has therefore not been mentioned in connection with this great experiment, but he claims that he is none the less entitled to all the credit which should attach to it. Hundreds of heavy cannon were rifled in the South after Mr. Carr's idea. Mr. Carr is alive at this writing and is still a citizen of Portsmouth.

Notwithstanding the fact that the Navy Yard was evacuated by the Federals on the 20th of April and the Confederates had fortified the harbor to prevent the return of the United States men of war, communication was kept up with Baltimore by the Bay Line steamers until the 30th, when the United States Government declared the port in a state of blockade. That day the steamer William Selden was permitted to come through with her mails and passengers but the Confederates seized her and refused to allow her to return. She brought down a large number of Baltimoreans who had taken part in the riot in that city on the 19th of April, when the Massachusetts troops were passing through. Upon their arrival here they organized themselves into a military company, were joined by a number of recruits from Southampton and Norfolk counties, and were assigned to the 9th Virginia Regiment as Company B, and were on duty on Craney Island until May 10th, 1862, when they marched off with the regiment at the evacuation of this section by the Confederates. The following were the officers of the company at Craney Island:

Captain, John D. Myrick of Norfolk.

First Lieutenant, John O'Donnell of Baltimore.

Second Lieutenant, —— Parker of Southampton county, Va.

Third Lieutenant, Benjamin F. Cason of Princess Anne county.

Among the defences of the harbor was the old frigate United States. This was the only vessel spared by Commodore McCauley when he burned the Navy Yard. The Confederates subsequently changed her name to the Confederate States, fitted her up with a battery, manned her, and anchored her near the bend in the channel just above Craney Island. The sunken vessels Merrimac, Plymouth, Germantown and Dolphin, which were lying alongside the wharves at the Navy Yard, were gotten up by the Baker Wrecking Company, under direction of the Confederate authorities, to get them out of the way, and some work was commenced on the last three with a view to fitting them out. The Merrimac was burned down to her water line, and it was not thought any use could be made of her beyond taking her machinery out of her, but subsequent events proved the fallacy of human predictions, for "the stone which the builders rejected became the key stone of the temple." But the Merrimac will be made the subject of another chapter, and many matters of local interest will be found in the short historical sketches of the various companies from Portsmouth and the county, which will follow later on in this work.

On the 7th of June, 1861, the companies of the 3d Regiment, under Colonel Roger A. Pryor, which had been on duty at the Naval Hospital batteries, were ordered to Burwell's Bay in Isle of Wight county, and the Hospital batteries were left in the care of the Elliott Grays, Captain Louis Bossieux, of Manchester, attached to the 12th Virginia Regiment, and the Jackson Grays, Captain William H. Stewart, of Norfolk county, afterwards Co. A, 61st Virginia Regiment. About the same time the Old Dominion Guard of Portsmouth was reinforced at Pinner's Point by the Craney Island Artillery of Norfolk county, Captain J. T. Kilby, and the Portsmouth Rifle Company at Pig Point was reinforced by Company H, 59th Virginia Regiment, Captain Niblett, of Lunenburg county.

Quite an active trade in sugar and fruit was carried on between Norfolk and the West India Islands, by way of Hatteras Inlet, through the agency of light draft schooners, and the steamer J. E. Coffer was converted into a gunboat, armed with one gun, and with her name changed to the Winslow, captured a number of prizes off Cape Hatteras, which she brought into the Carolina sounds. She was finally lost by running upon an obstruction or sunken wreck while going to the assistance of a French vessel which had gotten ashore on the coast near Ocracoke Inlet.

Had Secretary Mallory, of the Confederate States Navy, been possessed of a little foresight about this time, the affairs of the Southern Confederacy might not have turned out so disastrously. Naval Constructor John L. Porter, of Portsmouth, in June, 1861, while in Richmond on business connected with the conversion of the Merrimac into an iron-clad, urged upon Secretary Mallory the importance of importing at once from England steam engines and armor plates for gunboats to defend the Southern ports. Mr. Porter had been a Naval Constructor in the United States Navy, and upon the secession of Virginia resigned his commission and tendered his services to her. He was opposed to the war and to the secession of the State, but when she had decided to go out of the Union he cast his fortunes with her. He knew the resources of the United States and its ability to speedily fit out a large naval force, and called Secretary Mallory's attention to the fact that, while the South was rich in material out of which to build gunboats, it was deficient in means of building machinery for them and preparing armor plating to protect them. He further told the Secretary that it would not be long before the United States would have afloat a sufficient force to blockade the ports of the South and shut them up from the outside world, and urged that steps be taken at once to import engines and armor iron before it would be too late. Secretary Mallory replied that it was useless to go to all of that expense; that the war would be over in six months, and Mr. Porter could not convince him otherwise. Soon matters turned out just as Mr. Porter had predicted.

On the 29th of August a powerful Federal fleet attacked the forts at Hatteras Inlet, and they surrendered after a short but destructive bombardment. Lieutenant William H. Murdaugh, of the Navy, of Portsmouth, was severely wounded during the bombardment. The Confederates abandoned the fort at Oregon Inlet shortly afterwards, and on the 8th of February, 1862, Roanoke Island was captured, and the United States vessels held undisputed possession of the North Carolina sounds. The fleet of shells, which the Confederates gathered in the sounds and called gunboats, could afford no material resistance to the overwhelming force which was sent against them. Some were sunk at Roanoke Island, and the rest retreated to Elizabeth City, leaving the troops on Roanoke Island, to the number of 2,500, to their fate, which was not long doubtful. Newbern was captured on the 4th of March, and fifty-eight heavy guns and three hundred prisoners fell into the hands of the enemy. On the 12th of April Fort Pulaski, at the entrance to the Savannah river, surrendered after a short bombardment, and Fort Macon, at the entrance to the harbor of Beaufort, yielded on the 25th, so that on the whole Southern Atlantic coast only two ports, Wilmington and Charleston, were left to the Confederacy, and these were closely blockaded. Then, when it was too late, Secretary Mallory's eyes were opened, and he made contracts everywhere, and with every one, to build iron-clad gunboats. Old saw mills were robbed of their machinery to furnish motive power for them, while armor iron with which to cover them could not be obtained at any price. There was only one establishment in the South, the Tredegar Iron Works in Richmond, where it could be manufactured, and the capacity of that was very limited. While the Merrimac was being changed into an iron-clad at the Navy Yard here a half-dozen smaller and lighter draft vessels could have been built like the Richmond, had there been machinery and armor iron on hand for them. As it was, the work on the Merrimac was greatly delayed because the Tredegar Works could not furnish the iron fast enough, and others were wholly neglected.

After all of the ports had been closed Secretary Mallory developed an energy which, had it manifested itself earlier, might have saved the Southern Confederacy from destruction, and in May, 1863, according to an official report of Chief Constructor John L. Porter, there were fourteen vessels completed, as to their wood work, waiting for iron to cover them. The amount needed was 4,230 tons. Others were in course of construction, but the machinery with which to propel them was of the crudest kind. So scarce was iron in the Confederacy that, when Captain Cooke was superintending the building of the Albemarle on the Roanoke river, he went through the country blacksmith shops and gathered up every scrap and old bolt he could find. How different would matters have been had Secretary Mallory taken Mr. Porter's advice in 1861. Considerable money was expended in efforts to secure vessels abroad to cripple the enemy's commerce, but the defence of the home ports of the South was neglected.

Matters moved along smoothly in this vicinity after the Federal forces left until the attack upon Fort Hatteras, already alluded to. This, and the fall of Roanoke Island and the loss of its garrison of 2,500 men, who could have been saved had there been a vessel present to have taken them off, were severe blows to the Confederacy, as they opened the whole of Eastern North Carolina to the incursions of the enemy's gunboats and infantry supports, and forced the Confederates to guard hundreds of miles of territory in their uncertainty as to where the next blow would be struck. Hatteras and Oregon Inlets should have been better protected. The fall of Roanoke Island had an influence on the Confederate affairs about Portsmouth also, as it exposed the lines there to an attack from the rear, while the Federal force at Fortress Monroe was a constant menace from the front, and, in order to meet demonstrations from the enemy in that direction, the 3d Georgia, 1st Louisiana, 32d North Carolina, the Portsmouth Rifle Company and Grimes' Battery were sent to the vicinity of South Mills. The 3d Georgia had two engagements with the enemy before the arrival of the other troops, one at Chicamicomico, October 5th, 1861, and the other near South Mills, April 19th, 1862, and it was daily apprehended that the force which captured Newbern would make an attempt in the direction of Portsmouth. The bulk of this force, however, was subsequently sent to the Peninsula to reinforce General McClellan.

In the Navy Yard everything was activity. Hundreds of skilled mechanics who had enlisted in the army were detailed to work there. Work was commenced on the Merrimac on the 12th of July, 1861, and several other vessels were being built. The Richmond, an iron-clad, to carry four guns, built with slanting roof like the shield of the Merrimac, but with ends above the water line and protected like the shield, was launched, as were the Hampton and Nansemond, two two-gun gunboats, and the Escambia and Elizabeth, two light draft, iron-protected gunboats, to carry two guns each, were also commenced, and later another of the same character, called the Yadkin. Some work was done on the Germantown and Plymouth also, towards fitting them out. The machine shops and foundries were being run to their utmost capacity. Numerous thirty-two pound Dahlgren guns were rifled and banded, like the one with which Captain Fairfax so successfully contended against the frigate Savannah, and were sent to the different batteries around the harbor and to other localities. Some were sent to Seawell's Point, and a masked battery of them was constructed at the point nearest the Rip Raps, but was never unmasked. It was left there for the Federals when Norfolk was evacuated. Two were placed on the outer battery at Seawell's Point, and were manned by the Jackson Grays, of Norfolk county. Several were sent to Craney Island, four to Pinner's Point, and four to Naval Hospital Point, all of which were subsequently donated to the enemy.

During all these trying times the ladies of Portsmouth were not idle. The newly organized companies of Portsmouth and Norfolk county were mustered into service without uniforms, and many of the companies which came from further South were similarly conditioned, but the ladies organized sewing circles and made up hundreds of uniforms for them. They also made organized efforts to care for the sick soldiers in the camps and in the hospital, so that many a poor fellow who was stricken down by disease, in consequence of the exposure of camp life, had his fevered pulses cooled and his couch softened by the tender hands of the ladies of Portsmouth. Nor did their good works stop here, but they were untiring in their efforts to provide the soldiers with shoes, blankets, overcoats and everything else which would make them comfortable, while the families of those who were in the service were tenderly cared for. Nor was the City Council backward in aiding the cause in which the State of Virginia was engaged, as will be seen by glancing over the records of its proceedings from April, 1861, to May, 1862.

On the 18th of April, 1861, $1,500 was appropriated to purchase arms and ammunition for the defense of the city, and on the 3d of May the Council passed a resolution authorizing the Mayor to make provision for quartering and feeding the troops arriving in the city from the South. On the 15th of June the sum of $1,000 was appropriated for the relief of the families of Portsmouth soldiers who were in the field, and an appropriation of $500 was made to purchase sabre bayonets for the Portsmouth Rifle Company. On the 17th of July $500 was appropriated to the Portsmouth Artillery Company to procure side arms and $1,000 to the relief of the families of Portsmouth soldiers, and on the 14th of August $1,000 additional was appropriated for this purpose. That night a committee composed of Messrs. Arthur Emmerson, John S. Stubbs and David Griffith was appointed to consider the question of relief of the families of the military, and made their report on the 26th. The committee stated that they had ascertained that four hundred families were in need of assistance, and recommended that the sum of $5 per month be appropriated to each. The report of the committee was concurred in and the sum of $10,000 was appropriated to carry the recommendation into effect. The reports of the Relief Committee show that there was expended of this sum for August and September $2,690, and similar amounts thereafter. For April, 1862, the amount expended was $1,450, distributed among two hundred and ninety families.

On the 4th of May it became rumored that the Confederates intended evacuating the city and that it was the purpose of the authorities to burn the Navy Yard, and, at a meeting of the Council held that night a committee was appointed to wait upon Captain S. S. Lee, who had been Commandant of the Navy Yard since March 24th, to protest against setting the buildings on fire, as it would endanger the city, besides, if left standing, they would be serviceable to the Confederate Government after the close of the war. The Mayor was authorized to employ the watchmen in the Navy Yard after the evacuation to protect the property from incendiaries. The protest of the Council, however, did not avail anything, and the buildings were all burned.

On the 17th of March General McClellan began transferring his army from Manassas to Fortress Monroe for the purpose of trying to reach Richmond by the Peninsula route, instead of the overland route, upon which the Federal armies had been operating for the preceding year, and General Joseph E. Johnston, commander of the Confederate forces which had been operating in front of him at Manassas, followed him, and the opposing armies confronted each other near Yorktown. General Johnston was perhaps the most skillful general in conducting a retreat the world ever saw, and having decided some time in April that he would fall back near Richmond, communicated his plans to the Confederate authorities in that city, who approved of them. McClellan was getting ready to open a number of heavy batteries upon General Johnston's lines, and the Confederate commander felt apprehensive of the result of the bombardment, though subsequent events later in the war demonstrated the fact that earthworks could stand an unlimited amount of pounding without being materially injured. There does not seem to have been much ground for his apprehension, for the works at Yorktown prevented an expedition up York river to turn his left flank, and Swinton, in his "Army of the Potomac," says "the iron-plated Merrimac reigned mistress of Hampton Roads and prevented a turning expedition up James river." But General Johnston had determined to fall back, and did not desire to do it by piecemeal, therefore his plan included the evacuation of Norfolk and Portsmouth. Perhaps he wanted the 15,000 troops there to reinforce his army before Richmond, but, be that as it may, it was decided to evacuate Norfolk and Portsmouth, and to abandon the Navy Yard, with its valuable machinery and its facilities for building ships and casting cannon. It was the principal workshop in the South, and its loss was irreparable.

The latter part of April or the first of May, 1862, Secretary Mallory, of the Confederate States Navy, arrived in Portsmouth and informed Captain S. S. Lee, commanding the Navy Yard, that it was the intention of the Government to evacuate the city. He directed Captain Lee to remove such naval supplies as could be moved to Charlotte, North Carolina, and other points. Accordingly the work of evacuating commenced. Several train loads were sent off by rail, and a convoy of vessels started up James river for Richmond. Among them was the new iron-clad Richmond, then ready to receive her armor. These were loaded with such stores as were available, and taking advantage of the darkness of night, the vessels steamed or were towed past Newport News. The terror of the Merrimac's name kept that portion of Hampton Roads free from Federal vessels, therefore the expedition was not interfered with in its passage. Two new gunboats, the Nansemond and Hampton, built at the Navy Yard, also steamed up to Richmond.

Early in the morning of the 10th of May Captain James Byers commanding the tug J. B. White, of Norfolk, deserted with his tug to Old Point, and General Huger became very apprehensive that he would report the condition of affairs in Norfolk to the Federal authorities at Fortress Monroe, and that they would send an expedition to capture the two cities before the Confederates could get away. He therefore determined to leave at once, and hurried away with his splendid division of twelve or fifteen thousand troops, when no one pursued and thousands of dollars worth of valuable stores were burned in the haste with which the place was abandoned. The buildings in the Navy Yard were burned, as was also what was left of the Germantown and Plymouth. The Escambia and Elizabeth, which might have been towed to Richmond, had the attempt been made in time, were set on fire and destroyed, as was also the Yadkin, which was on the stocks. The dry dock, also, was somewhat injured. As the day advanced General Wool, commanding the forces at Fortress Monroe, noticed that the Confederate flag had been hauled down from the batteries at Seawell's Point, landed 6,000 men near the base of Willoughby's Spit and advanced towards Norfolk. He was met in the afternoon about half-past four o'clock near the entrenched camp by Mayor W. W. Lamb, of Norfolk, who informed him that the Confederate forces had left the city, and, as the representative of the civil authorities, he was ready to surrender it. The next day a force of Federals crossed over the river to Portsmouth and occupied that city. Later an expeditionary force was pushed out towards Suffolk.

The scenes at the evacuation of Portsmouth by the Confederates were peculiarly distressing. The soldiers bid adieu to their wives, mothers and little children with the full knowledge that, as the Southern Confederate authorities found themselves unable to hold the city while they had possession of it, they would never be able to recover possession until the close of the war, and in every man's mind was the natural dread and uncertainty as to what would become of their wives and helpless little ones, in the hands of the enemy, with no means of sustenance and no one to take care of them. Under these circumstances it required the highest amount of moral courage and the sublimest degree of patriotism for a man to turn his back upon his family and to march forth and encounter the dangers and uncertainties of the future which lay before him.

On the 10th of May, 1862, the last Confederate soldier marched out of Portsmouth, the Portsmouth Rifle Company bringing up the rear, and, looking back through the thirty years which have passed since then, the anxious countenances of the women and children who were left behind, as they thought of what the morrow would bring them, can be seen as vividly to-day as then. It was an impression which can never be erased from memory "while the mind holds sway in the seat of thought;" and of the twenty-two hundred men of Portsmouth and Norfolk county who marched away from their homes on that day nearly one-fourth fell upon the field of battle or died from disease contracted in the service, and three years after they bid adieu to their homes and families the remnant came back, broken in health, disabled from wounds, or their bodies enfeebled from seeds of diseases contracted in the loathsome prison camps of the enemy.

The batteries which had been erected around the harbor with so much care and labor, and the scores of heavy guns which had been placed in positions where, it was fondly hoped, they would keep the foe at bay forever, were abandoned without a struggle and in such haste that no effort was made to remove the guns.

Nearly all of the workmen who were employed in the Navy Yard followed the army to Richmond and took their families with them. These men were employed in the navy yard which was improvised in that city or sent to Charlotte to work on ordnance stores. Those who were retained in Richmond were organized into a battalion for local defence, and elected Martin Curlin, of Portsmouth, major. The battalion was frequently called into service defending the city against raiding parties of the enemy, and thus enabled the regular army to remain in front of the enemy's main army.

The names which follow in the histories of each company embrace those who marched away from the cities and county with their commands on the 10th of May, 1862, as far as they could be obtained. There may possibly have been a few others, but there were not many. Those lists have been very carefully prepared, and while possibly not absolutely correct, are very nearly so. Those who are marked as having been detailed in 1861 are believed to have followed the army to Richmond upon the evacuation. Some of them worked in the Navy Yard there or at other points in the South, but most of them rejoined the companies to which they were originally attached.

The lists of those who were killed or died in the service is believed to be correct, though, as the places at which they died were made up partially from memory by the survivors, it is possible that there may be a few errors in that particular feature. It is very certain, too, that quite a number of men were wounded but whose wounds were forgotten by those now living, and while the record is reliable as far as it goes, it is possible that some were wounded who are not so recorded. The work of gathering together these facts was postponed so long after the close of the scenes herein recorded, and so many of those who took part in them have died since they laid down their arms, that the wonder is, not that much has been omitted but that so much has been collected and preserved. The author has given it careful study, and no accessible source of information has been neglected. He hopes, therefore, his readers will approve what he has succeeded in rescuing from oblivion and not criticise him for not having done better.

While the Federal forces occupied the city of Portsmouth the citizens, whose sympathies were with the Southern Cause, experienced all of the rigors and oppressions of a conquered people. Not only were their personal liberties taken from them but their religious privileges were abridged. The Northern Methodist Church sent "missionaries" to the city, and by order of the Federal Commander of the post the old Dinwiddie Street Methodist Church was taken from its congregation and turned over to one of these imported preachers, for the purpose of conducting services therein. The order was issued one Saturday, and that night fires were made in the furnaces for the purpose of heating the building for the next day's services, but, on account of a defective flue, the building caught on fire and was burned to the ground. Then another order from the Military Commander gave St. John's Episcopal Church to the disappointed preacher, and that church was used by the Northern Methodists until after the close of the war, when its owners again obtained possession of it. Rev. John H. D. Wingfield, pastor of Trinity Episcopal Church was arrested and put to work on the streets with a ball and chain fastened to his leg and the church was taken possession of and converted into a hospital for negro troops.

Portsmouth had the honor of being represented in the very closing scenes of "the drama of the Lost Cause." A number of mechanics from the Gosport Navy Yard were taken to Charlotte, North Carolina, upon the evacuation of Portsmouth by the Confederates and were employed there by the Government in the manufacture of ordnance stores. These men were organized into a military battalion and were frequently called away from their work benches to repel raiding parties of the enemy. After the fall of Richmond President Davis started southward, and upon the arrival at Charlotte of the train bearing the specie which was in the Confederate Treasury volunteers were called for to escort it to the army of General Kirby Smith in the Trans-Mississippi Department, and sixty of these men volunteered for that service. The corps of midshipmen from the Confederate Naval Academy, under Captain W. H. Parker of the Navy, was with the train. At Chester, South Carolina, the party was joined by Mrs. Davis, wife of President Davis. She had with her her infant daughter, now Miss Winnie, and at that point the specie was transferred to wagons. On the march from Chester to Newberry Mrs. Davis became tired of riding in the wagon and got out to walk, carrying the baby in her arms, but Messrs. Charles T. Myers, C. W. Walker and Henry A. Tabb volunteered to relieve her of the burden, and took turns at carrying the little traveler. The company again took the cars at Newberry and proceeded as far as Abbeville, where the specie was again loaded in wagons and the escort pushed on to Augusta, Georgia, when news came that the Federal forces had taken possession of Macon and thus interposed between them and the Mississippi. The specie belonging to the Richmond banks was deposited in a bank in Augusta and the expedition then turned back and moved on to Abbeville, South Carolina, where they met President Davis and a part of his Cabinet, and the specie belonging to the Confederate Treasury was turned over to him. A bag of pennies was very generously given to the company. The men counted them and found there would be just $33\frac{1}{3}$ cents apiece and put them back in the bag and returned them with thanks. The corps of cadets were disbanded at Abbeville on the 2d of May. General Johnston's army had surrendered then, and the company of volunteers was ordered back to Charlotte. President Davis left them at Abbeville and pushed on until he was captured. The Captain of this company had a roll of its members, but, not appreciating the importance it might become as a matter of history, permitted it to become lost. This was, perhaps, the last organized body of Confederate troops east of the Mississippi river. It was composed of about forty-five Portsmouth men, five Washingtonians and ten North Carolinians from Charlotte. The following are all of the Portsmouth men whom memory can recall:

John Archer,	George Daougherty,	John Owins,
John Anderson,	J. W. Davis,	William Peed,
James Brown,	Alphons Dunham,	C. C. Peed,
Bartlett Brown,	Thomas H. Deans,	James Peed,
Henry C. Brown,	Richard Grimes.	Benj. Presson.
Thomas Baker,	Edward Lewis,	James Potter,
Wash. Bright,	Walter Mahoney,	Hugh Smith,
Samuel Butt,	Charles T. Myers.	Joshua Sykes,
Reuben Culpepper,	Cornelius Myers,	Wm. H. Turner,
William Culpepper,	Joseph Merchant,	Henry A. Tabb,
Robert Culpepper,	George Maxwell,	C. W. Walker,
John E. Deans,	Robert Myers,	Wm. Whitehurst,
Charles Davis,	Merritt Moore,	William J. Wood,
Thomas Dwyer,	Jerry Nichols.	Total, 41.

Lieutenant Thomas Gleason of Co. D, 9th Va. Regiment, and Privates William T. Edwards, Co. G, 9th Va., and Edward Grant of Co. C, 16th Va. Regiment, all of Portsmouth, were also with the party. They had been captured previously and paroled, but

had not been exchanged, and had not, therefore, rejoined their companies. The five men from Washington were:
William Clements,   William Thompson,   William Tucker,
George Thompson,   John Tucker.

After the war Major F. W. Jett, formerly of Hampton, removed to Portsmouth. He was a Civil Engineer in the Confederate army and superintended the construction of the earthworks at the Naval Hospital and at Pinner's Point in April, 1861. He also built a military road from the Western Branch to Nansemond river and a bridge across the Western Branch. Upon the evacuation of Portsmouth by the Confederates he became Chief of Engineers of Anderson's Division, afterwards Mahone's, and rendered very efficient service. He was specially complimented in General Anderson's official report of the part taken by his Division in the battle of Fredericksburg. It occurred to Major Jett that the Portsmouth and Norfolk county soldiers, who had won fame's immortal wreath in such battles as Gettysburg and the Crater, should have a monument erected to commemorate their courage and fortitude, and by his efforts a Monument Association was organized in 1875, with the following officers:

President—Adjutant James F. Crocker.

Vice Presidents—Major William H. Etheredge and Colonel William White.

Treasurer—Major George W. Grice.

Secretary—Corporal O. V. Smith.

Directors—Sergeant B. A. Armistead, Captain John T. Griffin, Major W. C. Wingfield, E. G. Ghio, Esq., Captain James H. Toomer, Colonel D. J. Godwin, Captain John H. Gayle, Captain C. W. Murdaugh, L. R. Watts, Esq., Sergeant Major Charles T. Phillips, Lieutenant Colonel William H. Stewart, Private Alonzo Ives, Captain Thomas M. Hodges and Captain Jetson Jett.

A design by Charles E. Cassell, Esq., architect, of Portsmouth, was selected for the monument, and the corner stone was laid December 14th, 1876, with Masonic ceremonies. The stone for the monument was presented to the Association by the Seaboard and Roanoke and Raleigh and Gaston railroad companies, and came from a granite quarry in North Carolina belonging to the Raleigh and Gaston company. The Monument Association paid the cost of quarrying it, and the two railroad companies hauled it to the city free of charge. Major Jett was untiring in his efforts to raise money to carry on the work, and but for his energy and determination it would undoubtedly have fallen through, but, after several delays and interruptions, Major Jett announced on the 12th of June, 1881, that the next day he would be prepared to swing the copestone in position and complete the monument proper. On the morning of the 13th the ladies of the Confederate Memorial Association of Portsmouth "manned" the arms of the capstan and raised the copestone in position. The site, on Court street in front of the Court House, was selected by a committee composed of Messrs. H. V. Niemeyer, Samuel Watts, F. W. Jett, James T. Borum and George M. Bain, Jr., and the City Council gave its consent.

The monument is of granite, fifty-five feet six inches high. The base is fifteen feet across and seven feet high, surmounted by a sub-base seven feet square and thirteen feet high. Four white metal statues, life size, one on each side of the base, represent the different branches of the service, infantry, cavalry, artillery and the sailors.

Major George W. Grice, who was elected treasurer of the Association, died in October, 1875, and was succeeded by Mr. William H. H. Hodges. Mr. Hodges died in January, 1880, and Mr. William V. H. Williams was elected treasurer and filled the position until the completion of the monument.

CHAPTER II.

THE PORTSMOUTH LIGHT ARTILLERY.

GRIMES' BATTERY.

This company dates its organization back to a period prior to the war of 1812 between the United States and Great Britain, in which it achieved an enviable record. The principal engagement in which it took part was the battle of Craney Island in 1814, where, under command of Captain Arthur Emmerson, it contributed materially to the repulse of the British, and in 1861, at the beginning of the war between the North and the South, it was the oldest artillery company in the State. The company in 1861 was equipped with four smooth bore iron field pieces, and the following were its officers:

Captain—Cary F. Grimes.
First Lieutenant—John H. Thompson.
Second Lieutenant—Bernard Fauth.

The company was ordered into service by Governor Letcher on the 20th of April, 1861, upon the secession of Virginia, and responded promptly. There were at that time about forty men on its rolls, but with the actual commencement of hostilities recruits rapidly joined its ranks until its membership exceeded a hundred. On the night of April 20th the United States naval authorities burned the Gosport Navy Yard and evacuated it. The company was on duty that night, with their battery parked at the intersection of High and Court streets, but without any ammunition.

On the 21st the company was marched to the Naval Hospital grounds, where it remained until May 16th, when it was ordered to Hoffler's creek to guard the shore of Hampton Roads from Craney Island to the mouth of Nansemond river.

On the 20th of July Private Richard Webb was elected Third Lieutenant, as under the Confederate Army regulations the company became entitled to another officer. While at Hoffler's creek the name of the company underwent an informal change, and instead of the Portsmouth Light Artillery it became known as "Grimes' Battery," and their camp at Hoffler's creek was named Camp Grimes.

On the 26th of March, 1862, there was a reorganization of the company, as the one year term of the original enlistment of the men was about to expire. This was nominally a reorganization but was really only a new election of officers, as the members of the company re-enlisted in a body "for three years or the war."

There were present for duty that day in camp ninety-nine men who answered to roll call. The following officers were elected:
Captain—Cary F. Grimes.
First Lieutenant—John H. Thompson.
Second Lieutenant—William T. Fentress.
Third Lieutenant—Thomas J. Oakham.

The next month Francis Russ was elected Fourth Lieutenant, as the size of the company and the number of guns in the battery entitled it to four Lieutenants.

In the early portion of 1862 the United States forces captured Roanoke Island and held undisputed possession of the waters of Albemarle Sound, and in April a brigade of troops under General Reno advanced from Elizabeth City towards South Mills, threatening the Dismal Swamp canal. General Huger ordered the 3d Georgia Regiment, one of the finest regiments in the Confederate army, and numbering fully a thousand men, under Colonel A. R. Wright, to check their advance, and on the 23d of April Grimes' Battery was ordered from Hoffler's creek to reinforce the Georgians. The 1st Louisiana and the Portsmouth Rifle Company, Co. G, 9th Virginia, were also sent with them, but the reinforcements arrived too late to take part in the action. Colonel Wright fought the enemy at Sawyer's lane, about three miles from South Mills, and drove them back to Camden Court House.

On the 2d of May, however, Grimes' Battery had a brush with the enemy on its own hook. One section, under Lieutenant Thompson, opened fire upon two United States gunboats in Pasquotank river, and, after a spirited engagement, forced them to drop down the stream, considerably damaged. The next day a countryman brought news into camp that one of them sank shortly after the engagement from the effects of the shot. The other section of the battery, under Captain Grimes' immediate command, was on the opposite side of the river from Lieutenant Thompson, but not being able to find an eligible position in which his pieces could be brought to bear upon the gunboats, it took no part in the action.

On the 5th of May the battery returned under orders to Portsmouth and was given two additional guns, making six in all with which it was equipped. It moved off with the Division of General Huger on the 10th, when Portsmouth was evacuated, and arrived in Petersburg on the 14th. On the 24th the battery was ordered to Drewry's Bluff, and on the 28th was marched to Richmond and became a part of the Army of Northern Virginia, which was then barring McClellan's way to Richmond.

Grimes' Battery never shirked a duty or shrunk from obeying an order because the execution thereof was attended with danger, and it soon became known throughout the army as a fighting battery. Captain Grimes' courage was proverbial, bordering even upon rashness, and on several occasions the battery received the commendation of General Anderson, to whose Division it was attached.

On the 25th of June, at the beginning of the seven days' battles around Richmond, during which General McClellan's army was driven from Mechanicsville to Harrison's Landing on James river, the battery had two guns engaged, shelling the enemy at rather long range, from 400 to 800 yards, and silenced two Federal guns, and at Malvern Hill on the 1st of July it behaved with distinguished gallantry, maintaining a fight at close range and unsupported against about eighty or one hundred Federal guns, which were sheltered by breastworks. Captain Grimes held his position for about two hours, until ordered to retire. He lost here three men killed, Walter A. Creekmore, John W. Matthews and William Swain, besides eight wounded, of whom E. T. W. Sumners and John Weymouth died. James H. Gaskins lost a leg here. Fifteen horses belonging to the battery were killed while getting into position.

On the 27th of July the battery was ordered to City Point for the purpose of firing upon the Federal transports in James river, and returned in time to join the army in its march to attack General Pope. It engaged in an artillery fight at Warrenton Springs on the 26th of August and had three men wounded there, one of whom died, and on the 30th reached the battle ground at Second Manassas. In this battle it added largely to the reputation it had already made in its previous encounters with the enemy, and charged in line with Mahone's Brigade in the final rush upon and defeat of the left wing of Pope's army.

It was with the army on its march to Maryland, took part in the battle at Crampton Gap September 14th, and, at Sharpsburg September 17th, 1862, lost its gallant commander, who was shot from his horse while directing the fire of his guns. Captain Grimes was in command of a battalion, composed of three companies, Grimes' Battery of Portsmouth, 4 guns, Huger's Battery of Norfolk, 4 guns, and Moorman's Battery of Lynchburg, 4 guns. The battalion was under command of Major Saunders, but that officer was absent at the time and Captain Grimes, as senior officer, was in charge. Lieutenant Thompson had immediate command of Grimes' Battery. The battle had wavered backward and forward on the left and center, where Jackson, after driving back Hooker's corps of the Federal army, had in turn been pushed back by the attack of Mansfield's corps. This in turn had been defeated by the assistance of fresh troops which arrived on the field from Harper's Ferry, and Sumner's corps of 20,000 men, coming to the assistance of their beaten comrades, was once more turning the tide of battle against the Confederates. At this critical moment Grimes' battalion arrived upon the battle field with

Anderson's Division and took post upon the Confederate left center, where the Federal attack had been most successful. The enemy were driven back, but the toll paid for the victory was heavy. Captain Grimes was struck from his horse by a wound in the thigh from a rifle ball, and as his men were bearing him off the field a second ball struck him in the groin and ended a military career which had given promise of a brilliant maturity.

The men of the battery buried him with heavy hearts, and marked his grave, so that after the war his remains were disinterred and brought back to the home and family, from which he parted just four months before he received his death wound. This brave soldier and kind friend was long lamented by the men in his command. His remains are interred in Oakwood Cemetery, near Portsmouth.

Upon the death of Captain Grimes Lieutenant John H. Thompson was promoted to captain, but was not destined to long wear his well-earned honors. Prior to the battle of Sharpsburg General Lee had decided upon a reorganization of the artillery arm of the service. Horses were becoming scarce, and there was too great a proportion of artillery in the army as compared with the infantry. Captain Grimes, as commander of the battalion, had received orders to recommend one of his companies to be disbanded and to divide the men among the other two, but as the order was not to be executed immediately, and he had facilities for keeping all three in the field, he decided to wait until after the close of the campaign to make the changes. Had he done so at once the Huger Battery would have been disbanded, as Captain Huger was the junior captain, but Captain Grimes' death made Captain Thompson the junior, hence, when, upon the return of the army to Virginia, and when near Winchester, General Lee's order was carried into effect, Grimes' Battery was disbanded and its men, about eighty in number, were divided between the two other companies in the battalion. This was part of General Order October 4th, 1862, and embraced twenty other batteries. Captain Thompson says he had perhaps as many men present for duty as the other two companies combined, and protested earnestly to General Lee against his company being disbanded, but General Lee explained to him the necessity for the movement in so kindly a manner that all of the sting was taken out of it.

The detachment which went with Moorman's battery subsequently became horse artillery and were attached to the cavalry arm of the service, Fitzhugh Lee's Division. They kept up, as far as possible, a separate organization in that battery under Sergeant William H. Hughes, and maintained their reputation until the close of the war. On the 11th of June, 1864, Sergeant Hughes was promoted to a lieutenancy in the Lee Battery of Light Artillery and Thomas J. D. White became sergeant. The detachment which was assigned to the Huger Battery also proved the metal that was in them, but, having passed out of existence as a separate organization, the brave deeds of the men in the battery brought credit to other places than their own beloved city, Portsmouth.

Upon the disbanding of the battery the officers were assigned to other fields of duty, and General Lee, in recognition of their great disappointment in being deprived of their battery, very kindly assigned them to positions which were agreeable to them.

The section which was assigned to Moorman's Battery distinguished itself in an engagement December 4th, 1862, on the Rappahannock river, near Port Royal, with four Federal gunboats, the Anacostia, the Cœur de Leon, Currituck and Jacob Bell. Sergeant Hughes had charge of a three-inch rifle gun, and George W. R. McDonell was gunner. The gunboats were driven down the river by Moorman's Battery with heavy loss. The battery had one man killed, Private Compton of Lynchburg.

MALVERN HILL.

Below will be found Captain Grimes' report of the work of the battery during the seven days' battles, ending at Malvern Hill July 14th, 1862:

CAMP NEAR FALLING CREEK, VA., July 21st, 1862.

Sir—Below please find a report of the movements of my battery from June 20th last, when I was ordered to report to Brigadier General Mahone, on the advanced lines, for the purpose of relieving Captain Moorman's battery.

After reporting to General Mahone we were expecting an engagement with the enemy every day, but had none until the 25th, on which day we discovered the enemy on the opposite side of French's farm, between the Charles City and Williamsburg roads, at which place I engaged them with one section of my battery at 850 yards distance, driving the enemy from his position. I afterwards moved one piece up to French's house, within 450 yards of his position, and opened on him, which was quickly replied to by him with a 12-pounder Parrott rifle gun; but I had the pleasure of driving him from his position, leaving his horses and guns behind; which fact I was not aware of until informed the next morning by Colonel Smith of the 49th Virginia and others. The enemy was then attacked by a portion of three regiments of General Mahone's Brigade, the 12th, 6th and 49th Virginia. The 4th Georgia and 28th North Carolina Regiments were also on the field. The enemy was driven from the field, making a complete stampede. I had the good luck on that day to lose neither man nor horse.

Nothing of importance occurred with my battery after the 25th until July 1st. On that day I was on the Charles City road with General Mahone's Brigade and was ordered back to Darbeytown road to report to Brigadier General Armistead, which I immediately did. When I arrived at that position and reported, General Armistead told me that a captain had just reported his battery to him for duty and directed me to report to the first general I saw, and, General Wright being the first, I reported to him, and while talking to General Wright General Armistead's aide came up, stating that General Armistead had become disgusted with the captain who had reported his battery to him and had driven him with his battery from the field and that he wished to see General Wright. General Wright asked me to ride with him, which I did. When we found General Armistead he told General Wright that the captain alluded to above had formed so many excuses about getting his battery on the field that he had driven him from the field, and that he wanted General Wright to send a battery that was willing to go in and engage the enemy. General Wright told him he had one, naming mine. General Armistead asked me if I could carry my battery on the hill. I told him if any battery in the world could go, mine could. He directed General Wright to show me the position to take, which he did. I found the enemy with their batteries planted and their infantry drawn up in line of battle at about 1,200 yards distant. I then went to the rear for my battery and carried it on the field. As soon as the battery entered the field the enemy opened fire on it, killing one man and wounding three, and killing one horse and wounding two before I fired a gun. I unlimbered and commenced firing as soon as possible, and with telling effect on the enemy.

I remained on the field about two hours. Lost three men killed outright and eight wounded, of whom two have since died. I lost ten public horses killed and seven wounded. My own private horse was killed, also my first lieutenant's horse.

My officers behaved very well, but I feel it my duty to speak more particularly of First Lieutenant John H. Thompson, who remained on the field with me until the last gun was taken off. I had so many horses killed and wounded that it took three trips to get all my guns off.

On the next day, the 2d, Colonel DeLagnel, chief of artillery, ordered me back to the old camp, near Richmond, to refit my battery. As soon as I completed it I was ordered by yourself to camp near Falling creek, on the Richmond and Petersburg turnpike, where I now am, with my battery complete and in good condition, ready and willing to meet the invaders of our soil at any time and anywhere. I have, General, the honor to be,

Very respectfully your obedient servant,
C. F. GRIMES,
Captain Field Battery, Virginia Volunteers.

Major General B. Huger.

General Armistead said: "No men could have behaved better than Captains Pegram and Grimes; they worked their guns after their men were cut down, and only retired when entirely disabled. What I wanted never arrived; that is, more guns and heavier ones."

The roster of the company, at the close of this chapter, is from the date of its being mustered into service. It was made up from memory, for the author, by some of the survivors, and it is possible some names may have escaped them during the lapse of twenty-seven years, since the close of the war. For many of the dates in this chapter the author is indebted to Mr. Thomas H. Virnelson, who kept a diary of the movements of the company until the second battle of Manassas.

Captain Cary F. Grimes, killed September 17th, 1862, at Sharpsburg.
Captain John H. Thompson, promoted captain.
Lieutenant Bernard Fauth, joined signal corps and killed 1864.
Lieutenant Richard Webb, transferred to cavalry, Thirteenth Virginia.
Lieutenant William T. Fentress.
Lieutenant Thomas J. Oakham.
Lieutenant Francis Russ.

PRIVATES.

Allen, M. W., severely wounded July 1st, 1862, Malvern Hill, and on the Petersburg lines 1864.
Ash, John W. (sergeant), surrendered at Appomattox.
Boyce, David, wounded at Chancellorsville May 3d, 1863, and at Warrenton August 28th, 1862.
Bohannon, Churchill.
Buchanan, W. H., wounded at Brandy Station.
Beaton, Edward E., wounded April 1st, 1865, on Hatcher's Run and died in hands of enemy.
Brownley, A. M.
Bell, W. H., died at Culpepper Court House 1862.
Bland, Thomas.
Brent, George W., wounded August 30th, 1862, Second Manassas, and transferred to Navy.
Backus, William T., Jr., died at hospital May, 1862.
Batten, William A.
Bright, William Jordan.
Boutwell, Richard M., killed April 1st, 1865, on Hatcher's Run.
Crismond, John W.
Crismond, George E.
Cummings, Southall.
Cutherell, William H.
Cherry, W. H., wounded September 17th, 1862, Sharpsburg.
Cherry, James.
Creekmore, Walter A., killed July 1st, 1862, Malvern Hill.
Culver, George D., died at Jefferson from wounds received August 28th, 1862, at Warrenton Springs.
Dillion, James A.
Dilsburg, John H.
Ewell, John, wounded August 30th, 1862, Second Manassas.
Fitz Simmons, Thomas.
Forbes, V.
Griffin, J. B.
Gaskins, James H., lost leg at Malvern Hill July 1st, 1862.
Goodson, Henry P., died from wounds September 16th, 1864, in hospital.

Hughes. William H. (sergeant), promoted to lieutenant in Lee's Battery.
Hopkins, Joshua H. L.
Hopkins, Hillery, died in Shenandoah Valley 1862.
Hansford, W. R., died on Rappahannock 1863.
Ironmonger, C. E.
Ironmonger, A. C.
Ives, Francis M.
Jones, William H., died in Charlottesville 1862.
Jones, George T., died in hospital June 1862.
Johnson, Ed. H.
King, George W.
Lewis, Robert.
Lewis, William A., wounded July 1st, 1862, Malvern Hill.
Lynch, Wilson B., wounded September 17th, 1862, Sharpsburg.
Lash, George W.
Linn, Charles B.
Liverman, H.
Morris, James E., died 1865.
Moore, W. A., wounded slightly at Spotsylvania C. H. May 12th, 1864.
Mahoney, William B.
Moreland, Edward.
Montgomery, Richard.
McHorney, Stephen.
Matthews, Alonzo.
Miller, P. H.
Morgan, A.
Miles, Henry, died in field hospital September 16th, 1864.
Matthews, Edward.
Matthews, John W., killed July 1st, 1862, Malvern Hill.
Murphy, John.
McDonell, Alex; H.
March, Edward G., discharged 1862, over age and disability.
Myers, William T.
Minter, A. M.
Murray, Dennis.
Miller, Thomas E.
Miller, John.
McDonell, George W. R., wounded Malvern Hill 1862, Brandy Station 1863, Wilderness 1864, Petersburg 1864.
Nicholson, F. J.
Newby, S. W.
Overman, Quinten, killed September 17th, 1862, Sharpsburg.
Parker, A. K.
Parker, Ephriam.
Peed, Robert.
Phillips, William, discharged 1862, over age.
Parker, Thomas.
Russ, Samuel P., captured April 2d, 1865, on Hatcher's Run, and died at Point Lookout 1865.
Reynolds, Joseph S., wounded on Petersburg lines 1864.
Rogers, F. D.
Reardon, Michael E., died in Richmond 1864.
Rieger, Joseph.
Rehm, Fred.
Swain, William, killed July 1st, 1862, Malvern Hill.
Stoakes, Joseph M., killed September 17th, 1862, Sharpsburg.
Stoakes, H. C.
Shephard, Edward J.
Stores, Richard.
Sprugg, Aaron.
Saunders, Robert, wounded at Brandy Station.

Sheppard, William E.
Snow, John W.
Stores, James.
Summers, E. T. W., died in hospital from wounds received July 1st, 1862, at Malvern Hill.
Straub, E. G., captured wounded in Pennsylvania in July, 1863, and died at Point Lookout.
Tyler, John B.
Virnelson, Thomas H.
Williams, Charles C., died from wounds received August 30th, 1862, at Second Manassas.
Williams, Charles L.
Warren, Cary R., discharged 1862, under age.
Whitehead, William.
Wing, Thos. P., promoted first sergeant, wounded near Petersburg 1864.
Wilson, Willis.
Webb, James, Jr.
Weymouth, John, died in hospital from wounds received July 1st, 1862, at Malvern Hill.
Widgeon, Jacob.
Whitehead, Severn.
Waller, James T.
Whitehead, Virginius.
White, Thomas J. D., wounded at Williamsport July 1863.
Wrench, John.
Warren, John J.
Wilson, John.
Webb, Thomas C., died at Churchland 1864.
 Killed and died,—26.

CHAPTER III.

DISMAL SWAMP RANGERS, COMPANY A, THIRD VIRGINIA REGIMENT.

This company was organized in 1856 at Deep Creek, in Norfolk county, on the edge of the Dismal Swamp. Deep Creek was a small village and the neighborhood thinly populated, the people, therefore, deserve commendation for their zeal and spirit in organizing and maintaining such a large and efficient company. At the breaking out of the war in 1861 the officers of the company were:

Captain—James C. Choat.
First Lieutenant—John R. White.
Second Lieutenant—John F. Stewart.
First Sergeant—Thomas M. Hodges.

And the company was attached to the 3d Virginia Volunteer Regiment.

In anticipation of trouble in Portsmouth with the Federal authorities in possession of the Gosport Navy Yard, and apprehending that orders would be issued by the Governor calling the regiment to arms, Captain Choat mustered his company on the 19th of April and marched with them to town. This was the day before the Navy Yard was burned. The next day the Governor's orders came and found the Dismal Swamp Rangers already under arms. The company was with the Portsmouth companies that night, and the next morning was sent to the Naval Hospital and assisted in building the batteries there.

In the shifting of the original companies composing the 3d Regiment the Rangers were retained on it and became Company A. Shortly after being mustered into service Sergeant Thomas M. Hodges was elected 3d Lieutenant. Captain Choat resigned in the fall of 1861. Lieutenant White became captain. The other Lieutenants were promoted one grade, and Sergeant Littleton H. White was elected 3d Lieutenant, and these officers continued on duty until the reorganization of the company in April, when several changes were made. Captain White was appointed Commissary of the regiment, and was, later in the war, sent to the Blackwater river as commissary in charge of the purchase of provisions. Lieutenant Stewart was appointed Adjutant of the regiment and the following were elected officers:

Captain—Thomas M. Hodges.
First Lieutenant—Fred Martin.
Second Lieutenant—Wm. James Williams.
Third Lieutenant—Littleton H. White.

The company left the Hospital battery on the 7th of June,

1861, with the regiment and went to Burwell's Bay, where it remained until the middle of March, 1862, when it was ferried over the James river to reinforce General Magruder on the lines at Yorktown. It took part in a skirmish at Dam No. 2, and assisted in repulsing McClellan's attempt to cross; was in the battle of Williamsburg and fell back with the army towards Richmond. It took part in the battle of Seven Pines May 31st and June 1st, and all of the battles of the seven days' fighting except Malvern Hill, where it was held in reserve. The company suffered very severely at Frazier's farm July 30th. It carried sixty-eight men into the battle and five of them, including Lieutenants Martin and Williams, were killed and seventeen others were wounded, of whom five subsequently died from their wounds.

Shortly after the seven days' battles Lieutenant L. H. White was retired on account of physical disability and John R. Edwards was elected 1st Lieutenant, S. W. Gary 2d, and Osceola White 3d. The company went through the campaign of 1862, beginning with Second Manassas, taking in Harper's Ferry and Sharpsburg, and terminating in the crushing defeat of Burnside's army at Fredericksburg December 13th. At the battle of Gettysburg Company A was deployed as skirmishers, and, under command of Captain Hodges, led the charge of Kemper's Brigade of Pickett's Division up Cemetery Hill. Captain Hodges and Lieutenant White were wounded and Lieutenant Gary was captured. They recovered from their wounds and rejoined the company. Lieutenant Osceola White was killed at the battle of Dinwiddie Courthouse on the 31st of March, 1865 (the day before the battle of Five Forks), in which a portion of Pickett's Division defeated Sheridan's Cavalry. Captain Hodges had command of the 3d Regiment at the battle of Five Forks, and surrendered it at Appomattox.

It is a singular fact that, though the company was in the line of skirmishers at Gettysburg and received the fire of the entrenched Federals before the main line of battle, none of its men were killed. A number were wounded.

The company had three Orderly Sergeants during the war—Thomas M. Hodges, who was promoted to Lieutenant and afterwards to Captain; Nathan Hodges, who was captured at Gettysburg and died in prison at Point Lookout, and Patrick Henry Miller, who was captured at Gettysburg and exchanged. He was appointed Orderly Sergeant upon his return and filled that position until the close of the war. He was wounded at the battle of Dinwiddie Courthouse March 31st, 1865, and conveyed to the hospital at Farmville, where he again fell into the hands of the enemy upon the retreat of the army to Appomattox.

Maurice Liverman, of Company A, was mortally wounded at the battle of Frazier's Farm June 30th, 1862, and turning to some of his comrades, he said: "Boys, I can't live much longer, so hold me up so that I can fire one more shot and kill one more Yankee before I die, to get even with them for my own death." His comrades complied with his request.

The following members of the company were in the charge of Pickett's Division at Gettysburg. The company was detailed as skirmishers for the 3d Regiment:

Captain Thomas M. Hodges, wounded.
Second Lieutenant S. W. Gary, captured.
Third Lieutenant Osceola White, wounded.
First Sergeant Nathan Hodges, captured.
Sergeant P. H. Miller, wounded and captured.
" John Nash.
" John H. Cherry.

PRIVATES.

Barnes, Edward.
Benton, Joseph J.,
Britton, James J.,
Cherry, James E.,
Duke, Gideon.
Fentress, Batson.
Friedlin, John.
Forward, John W.,
Gallop, John, Jr.,
Godfrey, Mark.

Hodges, James, captured;
Hodges, Patrick H., captured;
Hodges, Josiah.
Halstead, William.
Herbert, William, captured;
Ha n'bury, Samuel W.,
Jolliff, John W.,
Kilgore, Mallory.
Liverman, Hardy, captured;
Nash, William H.

Below will be found a roll of the company:

Captain, James C. Choat, resigned 1861.
First Lieutenant John R. White, promoted Captain, appointed A. C. S. 1862.
Second Lieutenant John F. Stewart, appointed Adjutant 3d Regiment, wounded Aug. 30th, 1862, 2d Manassas, and July 3d, 1863, Gettysburg, captured at Five Forks.
Third Lieutenant Thomas M. Hodges, promoted Captain, wounded July 3, 1863, Gettysburg, and Frazier's Farm June 30, 1862, surrendered at Appomattox.
First Sergeant Littleton H. White, promoted Lieutenant, discharged for disability 1862.
Second Sergeant S. W. Gary, promoted Lieutenant, captured at Gettysburg and not exchanged.
Third Sergeant Fred Martin, promoted 1st Lieutenant, killed June 30th, 1862, Frazier's Farm.
First Corporal John H. Cherry, wounded Gaines' Mill June 27th, 1862, and Dec. 13th, 1862, Fredericksburg.
Second Corporal Nathan Hodges, captured at Gettysburg and died at Point Lookout.
Third Corporal John C. Nash, wounded June 27th, 1862, Gaines' Mill.
Fourth Corporal Thomas B. Bartee, wounded slightly June 30th, 1862, Frazier's Farm, and captured at Five Forks April 1, 1865.
Musician Ralph Cherry (colored).
" George Blamire "

PRIVATES.

Brown, Bartlett, detailed to work in Charlotte, 1862.
Barnes, Edward.
Bateman, Raynor, discharged 1862, disability.
Benton, Joseph J., wounded September 17th, 1862, Sharpsburg.
Britton, James J., captured at Five Forks.
Bright, Thomas J., died in hospital 1863, Staunton.
Cherry, James C., killed June 30th, 1862, Frazier's Farm.
Cherry, James E., wounded September 17th, 1862, Sharpsburg.
Casey, Raynor, died in hospital March, 1862, Camp Pemberton.
Culpepper, Maurice, severely wounded June 30th, 1862, Frazier's Farm, and appointed Provost Marshal at Waverly,
Culpepper, Miles.
Culpepper, Marshall, wounded June 30th, 1862, Frazier's Farm, disabled and discharged.
Coffield, J. A., transferred to Maryland cavalry.
Creekmore, Malachi, wounded April 1st, 1865, Five Forks.
Duke, Gideon, died in hospital August, 1863, at Gordonsville.
Eason, George W., wounded slightly April 1st, 1865, Five Forks, captured and died from disease contracted at Point Lookout.
Edwards, LeRoy B.
Edwards, John R., promoted to Lieutenant, wounded September 17, 1862, Sharpsburg.
Etheredge, Evan D., died in hospital 1862.
Etheredge, James M., died in hospital 1862.
Fentress, Batson.
Fentress, Joshua, died in hospital December, 1862.
Friedlin, John.
Fisher, William C., killed January, 1865, Dutch Gap.
Forward, John W., captured Five Forks.
Gallop, Samuel, discharged 1862, over age.
Gallop, John, Sr.,   "   "
Gallop, John, Jr., wounded slightly at Cold Harbor, 1864.
Godfrey, Stephen, died in hospital 1862.
Godfrey, Mark, surrendered at Appomattox.
Gordon, Benjamin F., died in hospital December, 1862.
Hodges, James, captured at Gettysburg and not exchanged, supposed to have died in prison.
Hodges, Joshua, mortally wounded April 5th, 1862, at Williamsburg and died in hospital, Richmond.
Hodges, Patrick H., captured at Gettysburg.
Hodges, Josiah.
Herring, Gideon, captured at Five Forks.
Halstead, Wilson.
Herbert, William, captured at Gettysburg and not exchanged.
Hanbury, Samuel W., killed November, 1864, Dutch Gap.
Jolliff, John W., wounded June 30th, 1862, at Frazier's Farm, wounded June 3d, 1864, Cold Harbor.
Joynes, William P.
Joynes, Custis T., transferred to artillery.
Keeling, Robert N. W., detailed for hospital duty, transferred to Signal Corps.
Kilgore, Malory, captured at Five Forks.
Liverman, Hardy, wounded June 30th, 1862, Frazier's Farm and Gettysburg, captured at Gettysburg and not exchanged.
Liverman, Maurice, killed June 30th, 1862, Frazier's Farm.
Miller, Patrick H., promoted 1st Sergeant, wounded and captured at Gettysburg, exchanged and wounded at Dinwiddie Courthouse March 31st, 1865, and captured at Farmville on retreat.
Morse, Luke, discharged 1862, disability.

McGuire, Dudley P., transferred to Kentucky regiment and promoted to Assistant Surgeon.
McConnell, G. B., transferred to Kentucky regiment.
Nash, James E.
Nash, William H., detailed in hospital.
Peaks, John D., detailed in hospital, Richmond.
Reed, Thomas P., wounded 1865 on picket, Dutch Gap.
Simmons, W. A., discharged 1861, disability, and died.
Sawyer, Kader, killed June 30th, 1862, Frazier's Farm.
Tucker, James A., died in hospital in Richmond July, 1862.
Tucker, Willis, discharged 1861, disability.
Taylor, John.
White, Edward P., transferred to 14th Virginia Regiment.
Whitehead, John D., died in hospital January, 1863.
Williams, Wm. J., promoted 2d Lieutenant, killed June 30th, 1862, at Frazier's Farm.
White, Osceola T., promoted 3d Lieutenant, wounded July 3d, 1863, at Gettysburg, killed March 31st, 1865, at Dinwiddie Courthouse.
Weston, W. W., captured at Five Forks.
Killed and died,—20.

CHAPTER IV.

THE VIRGINIA RIFLEMEN, COMPANY B, THIRD VIRGINIA REGIMENT.

This company was originally the Marion Rifles, which was organized in Portsmouth about the year 1856, and was one of the original companies in the Third Virginia Regiment. At the breaking out of the war it responded to the call of Governor Letcher and turned out with about eighty men on the 20th of April, 1861. The officers were:
Captain—Johannis Watson.
First Lieutenant—William C. Taylor.
Second Lieutenant—George W. Hutchings.
Third Lieutenant—Alex. C. Mathieson.

The company was mustered into service with the rest of the Portsmouth companies, and, on the 21st of April, was sent to the Naval Hospital point, doing there its full share of duty and responding willingly to every call made upon it. On the 17th of April the Virginia Convention passed the Ordinance of Secession, but directed that it be submitted to a vote of the people on the 23d of May for ratification or rejection. On that day the Marion Rifles were still on duty at the Hospital batteries, and the first fifteen men, as their names came on the roll, were allowed to go to the Court House to vote. Those men were opposed to the State seceding from the Union, and fourteen of the fifteen voted against the ratification of the Ordinance of Secession. Before their return to camp the news had arrived there as to how they had voted, and Colonel Roger A. Pryor, who was then commander of the 3d Regiment and of the post, became furiously angry, refused to allow any more men from the company to go to town to vote, and, upon the return of those who had voted, had them put in confinement in the lower rooms in the hospital building. An election was being held, but Colonel Pryor did not seem willing that any one in the command should vote who entertained different views from his own. He telegraphed that night to Governor Letcher that he had put the men in confinement for voting against the Ordinance of Secession and asked what he should do with them. Governor Letcher telegraphed back to release them immediately; that the election was intended to be a free one, and every citizen had a right to vote as he chose. Colonel Pryor released the men and the next day disbanded the company upon the charge of "disloyal conduct," and turned its guns over to a Petersburg company which had been armed with boarding pikes.

Many conservative men disapproved of this proceeding, and regarded it as an attempt on the part of Colonel Pryor, at the very outset of the Southern Confederacy, to suppress the right of suffrage, and perhaps that officer himself subsequently regretted his ill considered action. It lost to the Confederacy and Virginia the services of more than fifty men, who would doubtless have proved themselves good soldiers. They had followed the lead of Governor Letcher, though opposed to leaving the Union, and in so doing had acknowledged that their allegiance was due first to the State. They voiced their sentiments by their votes, but would have yielded their support to the sovereign authority of the State, as thousands of others did, who felt that she was doing wrong in seceding.

On the 6th of June about thirty of the old members of the company, with a few additional recruits, reorganized the company under the name of the Virginia Riflemen, and elected the following officers:

Captain, Alonzo B. Jordan.

First Lieutenant, William C. Taylor; Second Lieutenant, George W. Hutchings; Third Lieutenant, Vernon C. Grant.

First Sergeant, Alex. C. Mathieson; Second Sergeant, Robert Guy; Third Sergeant, Thomas Gleason; Fourth Sergeant, Daniel T. Brownley.

First Corporal, Robert A. Hutchings; Second Corporal, William Outten; Third Corporal, Robert Walton; Fourth Corporal, William H. Lumber.

The next day, June 7th, 1861, the company left the Hospital point with the regiment for Burwell's Bay, in Isle of Wight county. The following September Lieutenant Taylor resigned on account of a difficulty with Colonel Pryor, and on the 13th of September Captain Jordan resigned to take a position in the corps of engineers. Lieutenant Grant's appointment as quartermaster of the regiment created another vacancy, and Captain John W. H. Wrenn was elected Captain. Second Lieutenant Hutchings was promoted to First Lieutenant, and Sergeants Mathieson and Guy were elected Second and Third Lieutenants. Captain Wrenn resigned early in 1862. Lieutenant Hutchings was promoted to Captain, Lieutenants Mathieson and Guy were advanced one grade each, Sergeant Thomas Gleason was elected Third Lieutenant and Sergeant Daniel T. Brownley became First Sergeant. The above were the officers of the company at the beginning of the campaign around Richmond in 1862.

Captain Hutchings was wounded at Frazier's Farm June 30th, 1862, but subsequently rejoined the company. He was with it at Gettysburg July 3d, 1863, while under the shelling from the Federal batteries on Cemetery and Round Top hills. The 3d Regiment was in Kemper's Brigade, Pickett's Division, and was kept lying down in line of battle from 10 A. M. to 3 P. M. under a scorching July sun, with scarcely a breath of air to temper the heat, and Captain Hutchings and Sergeant Brownley were sun struck. A number of the men, too, were overcome by the heat and were unable to advance when the charge was ordered. Lieutenant Guy was killed by a shell while the company was in the line before the advance was ordered. The shell cut off his arm and he died shortly afterwards from the wound. The same shell killed Private Joshua Murden and wounded Private Walter Leggett. Lieutenant Gleason was wounded at Gains' Mill June 27th, 1862, but recovered and rejoined the company in time to go on the Gettysburg campaign. He commanded the company in the charge and was captured at the stone wall. He was not exchanged. Lieutenant Mathieson was with the company whenever it was possible for him to do so, but his health was delicate and he finally died in a hospital in Petersburg early in 1865.

The company was a small one originally, numbering only fifty-seven, rank and file, as appeared from the muster roll for September, 1861, and it was still further reduced by details, &c. Some of the men were excellent mechanics, whose services were needed to work upon the vessels being built for the navy, and eleven of them were detailed for that purpose, three were discharged, three were promoted to positions out of the company, four were transferred to the navy and three (officers) resigned. This brought the effective strength down to thirty-three, and of these nine were killed or died, besides one of those transferred to the navy, eight are recorded with having received wounds, and five were captured at Gettysburg and not exchanged. Only thirteen of those who remained with the company escaped. At the battle of Gettysburg July 3d, 1863, the company had three commissioned officers and twelve non-commissioned officers and privates present for duty.

It will be remembered that Pickett's Division arrived on the battle field about 10 A. M. and was drawn up in line of battle until 3 P. M. before it was ordered to charge, and all that time the men in the 3d Virginia Regiment were exposed to the sun and to the enemy's artillery fire. The two together disabled nine of the fifteen men in Company B. Lieutenant Guy was killed, as was also Private Joshua Murden. Private Walter Leggett was wounded, six of the others were overcome by heat, so that only six were in condition to advance when the order was given. Those six were Lieutenant Gleason, Sergeant Robert A. Hutchings, Corporal William H. Lumber and Privates William A. Fiske, William E. Herbert and William Moran, all of whom, except Private Fiske, were captured. Providentially none were struck in the advance. Company B was next to the colors, and when nearing the stone wall the color sergeant was killed and the colors fell with him, but Sergeant Robert A. Hutchings picked them up and carried them to the stone wall from behind which the enemy were driven. A full account of this charge will be found in the history of the 9th Virginia Regiment, chapter XII, further on in this work. The Virginia Riflemen, Company B, participated in all the battles and skirmishes in which the 3d Regiment was engaged up to the winter of 1884-5, and in proportion to the number of men actively on its roll suffered as heavily as any company which left the city. Its death rate was about one out of every three.

The company had a second difficulty with Colonel Pryor at the reorganization near Yorktown. The men re-enlisted for the war, and when doing so re-enlisted with the understanding that the company would be assigned to a regiment which Colonel D. J. Godwin was raising. Colonel Pryor put Captain Hutchings and several of the men under arrest upon the charge of mutiny, but the matter blew over and the company remained in the 3d Regiment.

The company became very much disorganized and reduced on the lines in front of Bermuda Hundreds in the winter of 1864-5, and being left without a commissioned officer Lieutenant John Edwards of Company A, the Dismal Swamp Rangers, was assigned to the command. There were only five men present for duty at the battle of Five Forks. These were James Archer, W. A. Fiske, William Morrissett, Peter Morrissett and William Wilkins, all of whom, except Archer, fell into the hands of the enemy. Private Fiske was wounded. Archer surrendered at Appomattox.

Below will be found the names of the members of the company as per the muster roll for September, 1861:

Captain Alonzo B. Jordan, resigned September 13th, 1861, appointed in Engineer Corps.
Captain John W. H. Wrenn, elected Sept. 13th, 1861, resigned 1862.
First Lieutenant William C. Taylor, resigned 1861, September.
Second Lieutenant George W. Hutchings, elected Captain, wounded June 30th, 1862, Frazier's Farm.
Third Lieutenant Vernon C. Grant, appointed Quartermaster of regiment.
First Sergeant Alex. C. Mathieson, elected Lieutenant, died in hospital 1865, Petersburg.
Second Sergeant Robert Guy, elected Lieutenant, killed July 3d, 1863, Gettysburg.
Third Sergeant Thomas Gleason, elected Lieutenant, wounded July 27th, 1862, Gains' Mill, captured July 5th, 1863, Gettysburg and not exchanged.
Fourth Sergeant Daniel T. Brownley, promoted to First Sergeant.
First Corporal Robert A. Hutchings, promoted Second Sergeant, captured July 3d, 1863, at Gettysburg, with colors of the 3d Regiment.
Second Corporal William Outten, promoted Third Sergeant.
Third Corporal Robert Walton, detailed 1862 to work in Navy Yard.
Fourth Corporal Wm. H. Lumber, captured at Gettysburg July 3d, 1863.
Musician James Archer, captured April 1st, 1865, Five Forks.
Musician Abraham Choat, discharged 1861, being a slave.

PRIVATES.

Anderson, Charles.
Borum, Edward C., detailed 1862 to work in Navy Yard.

Borum, John, detailed 1863 to work in Navy Yard.
Bush, Joseph M., detailed 1862 to work in Navy Yard.
Bowen, Hine, wounded June 30th, 1862, Frazier's Farm.
Broughton, Joseph.
Butler, John.
Butters, Francis H., detailed 1861 to work in Navy Yard.
Bright, John T., captured in Maryland September, 1862, and not heard from.
Butler, Thomas, discharged 1862, under age.
Davis, John W., detailed 1863 to work in Navy Yard.
Dunn, Edward, appointed Regimental Drum Major June 22d, 1861.
Etheredge, Cornelius, transferred to Navy.
Fiske, William A., wounded April 1st, 1865, Five Forks, and captured.
Fitchett, George, detailed 1863 to work in Navy Yard.
Grimes, Bartlett, wounded September 17th, 1862, Sharpsburg, and enlisted in Navy.
Herbert, Wm. E., captured July 3d, 1863, Gettysburg, and not exchanged.
Host, George.
Hawkins, Wm., transferred to Navy and killed at Little Washington, N. C.
Hall, Henry C., died in hospital.
Heath, William, killed August 30th, 1862, Second Manassas.
Jarvis, Benjamin, detailed 1862 to work in Navy Yard.
King, Charles A., detailed 1861 to work in Navy Yard.
Jordan, James, killed June 30th, 1862, Frazier's Farm.
Leggett, Walter, wounded July 3d, 1863, Gettysburg.
Loudoun, James T., killed June 29th, 1862, Cold Harbor.
Moran, William, captured July 3d, 1863, Gettysburg, not exchanged.
Morrisett, William, captured at Five Forks April 1st, 1865.
Morrisett, Peter, captured at Five Forks April 1st, 1865.
Murden, Joshua, killed July 3d, 1863, Gettysburg.
Norsworthy, Francis.
Parker, William, wounded June 30th, 1862, Frazier's Farm, transferred to Signal Corps.
Parsons, William H., transferred to Navy.
Powell, Benjamin F., wounded slightly twice.
Read, Charles, wounded June 30th, 1862, Frazier's Farm, and died in hospital from wound.
Simmons, Thomas, died in hospital 1862.
Smith, George A., transferred to Navy.
Thomas, William, detailed 1861 to work in Navy Yard.
Wilkins, William, promoted to Commissary Sergeant, captured at Five Forks April 1st, 1865.
Wilkins, Andrew, discharged June 20th, 1861, disability.
White, Charles.
 Killed and died,—10.

CHAPTER V.

THE NATIONAL GRAYS, COMPANY H, THIRD VIRGINIA REGIMENT.

This company was organized in Portsmouth in May, 1856, and at once a friendly rivalry sprang up between it and the Old Dominion Guard as to which company should attain the largest number of members and the greatest proficiency in drilling. Captain P. H. Daugherty was the first captain of the company, and was succeeded by Captain John E. Deans, who continued in command until the reorganization in 1862, when he was not re-elected. It was handsomely uniformed in gray, and its soldierly appearance on parade was marked At the time of the John Brown war, in 1859, the Grays volunteered their services and were sent to Harper's Ferry, taking with them on the trip five commissioned officers, ten non-commissioned officers, forty-three privates, two non-commissioned staff, commissary and ordnance sergeants, and two musicians, a total of sixty-two men. They were on duty at Charlestown from November 27th until December 20th, and returned home after John Brown was hung.

When Governor Letcher issued his orders on the 20th of April, 1861, for the troops in this city to take up arms the National Grays were as ready to serve their State as they were in 1859, and the company turned out with full ranks under the following officers:

Captain John E. Deans.
First Lieutenant—James Dongan.
Second Lieutenant—William F. Whitehurst.
Third Lieutenant—George W. Mitchell.
Fourth Lieutenant—William F. White.

There was no authority in military law for the position of 4th Lieutenant, but as the company numbered about a hundred members before the war and wanted an officer to command the fourth section, Lieutenant White was given that honorary title, but with the beginning of actual war the fictitious had to give way to the real, and the honorary position of 4th Lieutenant passed out of existence. Lieutenant White joined Company E, 61st Virginia, and was subsequently promoted to Captain of one of the companies in the 6th Virginia Regiment. The company was ordered to the Gosport Navy Yard on the 21st of April, 1861, and remained there doing guard duty until August, when orders were received to rejoin the regiment, the 3d Virginia, at Burwell's Bay, in Isle of Wight county. The 3d Regiment left the Naval Hospital batteries on the 7th of June, but the Grays, Company H, were continued in the Navy Yard. While thus engaged on guard duty news arrived of the battle of Manassas on the 17th of July, and fancying that the war would end before they would have an opportunity to do any fighting, the Grays asked to be ordered to their regiment. Their first application was denied, but their second attempt was more successful, and General Huger ordered them to report to Colonel Pryor. They left the Navy Yard and marched to the ferry wharf under an escort of the 3d Georgia Regiment, crossed to Norfolk and took the Norfolk and Petersburg cars for Zuni, from which station they marched to Camp Cooke, near Burwell's Bay, and from there they moved to Camp Pemberton, near Smithfield. Death made its first appearance in the ranks of the company while at Camp Pemberton. Julian Peed, one of the youngest members of the company, died there in the hospital in 1861, and Corporal Robert A. Sherwood died in 1862.

Nothing of special note occurred there until the middle of March, when, upon the landing of General McClellan's army at Fortress Monroe, March 17th, 1862, the 3d Regiment was carried across James river in canal barges to reinforce General Magruder, who was holding the Confederate lines from Yorktown to Warwick river. While getting on the barges Captain Deans fell overboard from the wharf. He was dressed in full uniform and was weighed down by his sword and pistol, and had a narrow escape from drowning. The regiment remained on the north side of the river only one day, when it was taken back to Camp Cooke, but was ferried over again to General Magruder's assistance on the day following. This proves that the Confederate counsels at that time were attended with much doubt and uncertainty. However, upon the second trip the regiment was retained on the north side and was attached to General Colston's Brigade of Longstreet's Division.

The company was on duty at Dam No. 2 when General McClellan made his first attempt to advance upon General Magruder's lines, and assisted in repulsing his attempt to cross the stream, and upon the strength of this repulse General McClellan halted his troops and proceeded to dislodge General Magruder by regular approaches and a series of earthworks. The regiment was ordered into the battle of Williamsburg April 5th, 1862, late in the afternoon and held its position until the battle ended and General Johnston had made all of his arrangements to fall back towards Richmond, when it was ordered to retire.

While the Grays were in the lines at Yorktown an incident happened which, in the lapse of time that has intervened since then, becomes laughable and proves how unreasonable men can become when they are clothed with authority over other men. While the regiment was at Camp Pemberton Major Bradford, who was mustering officer for Huger's Division, visited the camp for the purpose of ascertaining how many of the men were willing to re-enlist, as they were nearing the expiration of the year for which they had been originally mustered into service, and informed them that they could re-enlist in any command they might desire. Colonel Pryor was very unpopular with the Grays and they were very anxious to be removed from under his command, consequently, though all of the them re-enlisted, most of them expressed a desire to re-enlist in some of the Portsmouth companies which were in other regiments. They thought Colonel Pryor was too overbearing.

On the 19th of April, 1862, the company was on picket duty and was relieved on the 20th, marched to their quarters and stacked arms. This was just one year after the original muster of the company into service, and, as has been observed before, most of the men had re-enlisted into other organizations. Colonel Pryor had the company mustered and said to them:

"I understand some of you men want to go home."

One of them answered: "No, sir, we do not want to go home, but we want to go to the companies in which we re-enlisted."

Colonel Pryor became very angry at this reply, told the company a battle was about to be fought and accused the men of wanting to get away to avoid that battle, and asked how many were willing to remain until after the battle.

This taunting speech aroused the anger of the men, and Lieutenant Lingo, speaking for the others, said:

"Colonel Pryor, we are not leaving on account of the enemy or the approaching battle, but we do not desire to serve any longer under *your* command, but if we are put under the immediate command of Major Scott (the Major of the 3d Regiment) every man will cheerfully remain here until the battle is over."

Colonel Pryor then said: "All who desire to be placed under the orders of Major Scott will step three paces to the front." The whole company, with the exception of four men, marched promptly the three steps, whereupon Colonel Pryor ordered Major Scott to march them to Yorktown and put them in jail upon the charge of mutiny. They remained in jail three hours, when they were marched to the headquarters of General D. H. Hill, placed in a pen with a rope stretched around it, and put under the guard of a company of North Carolina troops. Shortly afterwards the men were sent to work upon the breastworks as a punishment. Lieutenant Dongan ventured to protest against this treatment of his men, but was placed under arrest for it. The officers of the regiment took the matter in hand and brought about a settlement. A law was read to the men which the Confederate Congress had passed, and of which they had been ignorant, requiring men who re-enlisted to re-enlist in their original commands, so the Grays remained in the 3d Regiment and Colonel Pryor apologized to the company for the harsh language and treatment he had used towards the men.

At the reorganization of the company on the Yorktown Peninsula, the following officers were elected:
Captain—John D. Whitehead.
First Lieutenant—George W. Mitchell.
Second Lieutenant—William S. Cooke.
Third Lieutenant—John W. Lingo.

After the battle of Fredericksburg Lieutenant Cooke was discharged under a surgeon's certificate of disability and Lieutenant Mitchell was killed at Gettysburg under the shelling immediately before the charge of Pickett's Division July 3d, 1863. Orderly Sergeant John C. Fulford was elected Lieutenant, and Lieutenant Lingo also having been discharged upon a surgeon's certificate of disability, Lieutenant Fulford became First Lieutenant. Captain Whitehead was among those who reached the stone wall at Gettysburg alive, but was captured there. He was exchanged in March, 1865.

The company had six Orderly Sergeants during the war, viz.: William P. Sturtevant, who was discharged for over age the first year of the war; William S. Cooke, promoted to Lieutenant 1862; Richard Mahone, killed at Frazier's Farm June 30th, 1862; Benjamin Mitchell, died in hospital 1863; John C. Fulford, promoted to Lieutenant, and Frank T. Tyran, who held the position when the war ended.

Captain Whitehead lived through the war and escaped without a wound, notwithstanding the many battles in which he led his company. After the war he moved to Richmond, and when the 1st Virginia Regiment of that city was re-organized he was elected its Lieutenant Colonel. He was a gallant soldier and a good man, and was well worthy to lead the Grays.

M. D. Montserrate of the Grays was acting Sergeant Major of the regiment, and just before the battle of Five Forks was appointed color bearer. He carried the colors in that fight and was wounded twice, once in the shoulder and once in the forearm, but continued carrying the colors until he was surrounded and captured. John Yost carried the colors of the 3d Regiment at the battle of second Manassas, and was the first man in the regiment to reach a Federal battery which it was charging.

The following men were present with the company at Gettysburg and participated in the charge of Pickett's Division:
Captain John D. Whitehead, captured.
Lieutenant George W. Mitchell, killed under the shelling.

PRIVATES.

Ashton, Edgar.
Arrington, James E..
Barrett, Solomon H..
Barrett, George, captured.
Beeks, William H..
Barrom, Osceola, wounded,

Keeling, William, wounded and captured.
Lash, James.
Loomis, James W..
Mahone, Harrison, wounded and captured,

NATIONAL GRAYS, CO. H, THIRD VA. REGT. 61

Goodson, Calvin, wounded and captured.
Gay, Henry B.,
Hanrahan, George,
Howard, James T. B., captured,
Hickman, Joseph,
Jenkins, Miles,
Kirby, Johnson,
McHorney, William H.,
O'Donnell, Patrick,
Smith, James, wounded,
Stoakes, Edward, wounded,
Tee, John C., captured,
Weddon, John R.,
West, William,
Yost, John,

Below will be found a copy of the names of the members of the company as per the muster roll for July and August, 1861:

Captain John E. Deans, dropped at reorganization, 1862.
" John D. Whitehead, elected Captain at reorganization.
First Lieutenant James W. Dougan, dropped at reorganization, 1862.
" " George W. Mitchell, killed July 3d, 1863, at Gettysburg.
" " John C. Fulford, surrendered at Appomattox.
Second " William F. Whitehurst, dropped at reorganization, 1862.
" " William S. Cooke, discharged for disability, 1863.
Third " John W. Lingo, discharged for disability, 1864.
Fourth " William F. White, promoted Captain Co. B, 6th Virginia.
First Sergeant William P. Sturtevant, discharged for over age, 1862.
" " Richard Mahone, killed June 30th, 1862, at Frazier's Farm.
" " F. T. Tynan, promoted First Sergeant.
" " Benjamin Mitchell, died in hospital, 1862.
Sergeant William H. Bloxom, promoted to Ordnance Sergeant of Regiment.
Corporal William R. Hanrahan, transferred to Signal Corps, 1862.
" Robert A. Sherwood, died at Camp Pemberton, 1862.
Musician Henry Foils.
" Johnson Tubb.
" William Brown.

PRIVATES.

Ashton, Edgar, wounded at Gettysburg July 3d, 1863.
Ashton, J. V. B., detached April, 1861, in employment of railroad company.
Arrington, James E.
Atkinson, George W., discharged 1861, under age.
Barrett, George, captured July 3d, 1863, at Gettysburg.
Barrett, Solomon H., wounded August 30th, 1862, Second Manassas.
Beeks, William H.
Boswick, William, discharged 1861.
Barrom, Osceola, wounded July 3d, 1863, Gettysburg.
Bland, Thomas, detached 1861 to work in Navy Yard.
Culpepper, David, wounded September 17th, 1862, at Sharpsburg.
Culpepper, Joshua, died from wounds received at Gaines' Mill June 27th, 1862.
Culpepper, Joseph, wounded June 27th, 1862, Gaines' Mill.
Coston, Thomas.
Cutherel, Arthur, transferred to Company B.
Deans, Robert E., promoted Sergeant, wounded and disabled June 27th, 1862, Gaines' Mill.
Deans, Joseph, discharged 1861, disability.
Deans, Thomas H., discharged August 23, 1861, disability.
Dolly, William.
Etheredge, John E.
Edgar, George, detached 1862.
Franklin, Thomas, killed June, 1862, at Frazier's Farm.
Friedlin, Adolph, killed June, 1862, at Frazier's Farm.
Flemming, Thomas, discharged for disability 1861.
Flemming, Caleb, discharged for disability 1861.
Grimes, James E., killed June 30th, 1862, at Frazier's Farm.
Goodson, Calvin, wounded July 3d, 1863, at Gettysburg.

Gay, Henry B., wounded and disabled June, 1864, at Turkey Ridge.
Gleason, George W., severely wounded 1862 and detached.
Graham, Thomas.
Harley, Thomas D., discharged August 19th, 1861, disability.
Hanrahan, George.
Hunley, John, discharged 1862, over age.
Howard, James T. B., captured at Gettysburg.
Hawkins, William, transferred to Company B.
Hickman, Joseph, captured at Five Forks April 1st, 1865.
Hoops, John, detached 1862 to work on ordnance.
Host, George, transferred to Company B.
Hoffler, Elias.
Herbert, William E., transferred to Company B, 3d Virginia
Joyner, Cordy J., detached 1861 to work in Navy Yard.
Jenkins, Miles.
Kirby, Johnson, wounded July 3d, 1863, at Gettysburg, and wounded and disabled April, 1865, at Five Forks.
Keeling, William, wounded and disabled July 3d, 1863, at Gettysburg.
Lee, Charles P., detached 1861, engineer on Seaboard railroad.
Lash, Joseph.
Linscott, David, detached 1861 to work in Navy Yard.
Lash, James.
Loomis, James W.
London, J. T., transferred to Co. B, killed June 30, 1862, at Frazier's Farm.
Merkie, George.
Monserrate, M. D., promoted Color Bearer of Regiment, wounded April 1st, 1865, at Five Forks.
Mahoney, James H., discharged for disability.
Mahone, Harrison, wounded, disabled and captured July 3d at Gettysburg and died in 1865 from disease contracted at Point Lookout.
Mahone, Wilmer, died in hospital in Richmond 1862.
McHorney, William H., severely wounded June 30th, 1862, Frazier's Farm.
McElwee, Andrew, transferred to Maryland line 1863.
McFarland, William.
McIntyre, George, killed September 17th, 1862, at Sharpsburg.
Nichols, Thomas J., discharged 1861 for disability.
Nichols, Jerry, detached 1861 to work in Navy Yard.
Nottingham, Jacob, detached 1861 to work in Navy Yard.
O'Donnell, Patrick, wounded December 13th, 1862, at Fredericksburg, and wounded and disabled March 31st, 1865, at Dinwiddie Court House.
Peed, Julian, died at Camp Pemberton 1861.
Rowan, William H., severely wounded June, 1862, Seven Days battles.
Rond, Charles, detailed 1861 to work in Navy Yard.
Roberts, Thomas, detailed 1861 to work in Navy Yard.
Rowell, William, died in hospital in Richmond 1862.
Scott, Robert G., discharged 1861, over age.
Smith, James, Third Sergeant, wounded July 3d, 1863, at Gettysburg.
Stoakes, Isaiah, Second Sergeant, discharged 1861, over age.
Savage, Thomas.
Stoakes, Edwd., wounded July 3d, 1863, Gettysburg, died in hospital 1864.
Tee, John C., severely wounded June 27th, 1862, Gaines' Mill.
Tabb, Thomas, detached 1861 to work in Navy Yard.
Tabb, Henry A., detached 1861 to work in Navy Yard.
Thomas, Samuel, detached 1861 to work in Navy Yard.
Veal, James.
Volkman, C. W., detailed 1862.
White, John S., discharged 1862, over age.
Weddon, John R.
West, William E.
Welslager, George, discharged 1861, disability.
Yost, John, wounded and disabled March 31st, 1865, at Dinwiddie C. H.
  Killed and died—15

CHAPTER VI.

THIRD VIRGINIA REGIMENT — COLSTON'S, PRYOR'S, KEMPER'S BRIGADES. LONGSTREET'S, ANDERSON'S, PICKETT'S DIVISIONS.

The 3d Virginia Regiment, previous to the breaking out of the late war, was composed of seven companies, five from the city of Portsmouth and two from Norfolk county, but with the commencement of hostilities some of the companies were transferred to other regiments, and only three of the original companies were retained in it. These were the Dismal Swamp Rangers of Norfolk county, which became Company A; the Marion Rifles of Portsmouth, Company B, and the National Grays of Portsmouth, Company H. The remaining companies of the regiment were from neighboring counties. Company C was from Petersburg, Company D from Dinwiddie, Companies E and G from Southampton, Company F from Nansemond, Company I from Isle of Wight and Company K from Halifax.

The old field officers of the regiment were removed by Governor Letcher and assigned to other commands, and Colonel Roger A. Pryor was assigned to it as Colonel, with Lieutenant Colonel Joseph Mayo and Major J. V. Scott.

The regiment was stationed at various batteries in the vicinity of Portsmouth, with headquarters at the Naval Hospital, until the 7th of June, 1861, when it moved to Burwell's Bay, and shortly afterwards to Camp Pemberton, near Smithfield. Company H remained behind doing guard duty in the Navy Yard until August, when it joined the regiment at Camp Pemberton.

About the middle of March, 1862, the regiment was ferried across James River to reinforce General Magruder at Yorktown. General McClellan had transported his army from the vicinity of Washington to Fortress Monroe with a view to reaching Richmond by the way of the Peninsula between the James and York rivers. Shortly after reaching Yorktown the 3d Regiment was assigned to Colston's Brigade, Longstreet's Division. Its first engagement with the enemy was on the 5th of April, 1862. The regiment was on duty at Dam No. 2, and the advance of McClellan's army attempted to cross Warwick river at that point but was driven back. It was in consequence of this repulse that McClellan decided to assail the Confederate lines by regular approaches. He therefore halted his troops and began building earthworks.

General Johnston, who relieved General Magruder in command of the Confederate forces, decided to withdraw from Yorktown and fall back towards Richmond, and in consequence of his determination the troops moved out of their works on the 4th of May and began their retrograde movement. McClellan followed after, and pressing so closely upon the retiring Confederates as to endanger their wagon train, General Johnston halted a portion of his army under Longstreet to check the pursuit. Longstreet made his dispositions for battle near Williamsburg, and the Federal advance was so roughly handled that it was driven back upon the main army with the loss of twelve hundred prisoners, besides killed and wounded. The affair took place on the 5th, and was a complete victory for the Confederates. The 3d Regiment participated in the battle.

After the army reached the vicinity of Richmond Colonel Pryor was promoted to Brigadier General and given command of the Brigade, and Lieutenant Colonel Mayo became Colonel. The Brigade was composed of the 3rd Virginia, the 14th Alabama, the 14th Louisiana and 2d Florida Regiments and 1st Louisiana Battalion. It participated in the battle of Seven Pines May 31st, 1862, in which, had General Huger acted with more promptness in moving his troops and beginning the attack, Casey's Division of the Federal army might have been destroyed instead of simply defeated.

The regiment, as a part of Longstreet's Division, was engaged in the battles of Mechanicsville, Gaines' Mill, Cold Harbor and Frazier's Farm. In this last battle its losses were very heavy. At the battle of Malvern Hill Longstreet's Division was held in reserve on account of its active participation in the previous fighting.

The next encounter with the enemy was at Thoroughfare Gap August 29th, where Longstreet brushed aside a force of Federals who sought to hold the Gap and thereby prevent him from uniting with Jackson's Corps at Manassas. Lee was chasing General Pope towards Washington. Jackson had gotten in his rear at Manassas and was holding his ground, waiting for the arrival of General Lee with Longstreet's Corps to give Pope a decisive blow. The battle of Second Manassas was fought on the 30th. Pryor's Brigade was a part of the right wing under Longstreet, and was in the front line. The brigade advanced across an open field and through a piece of woods, beyond which was another field, and on the farther side of this field was a battery of Federal field artillery and a double line of infantry. In marching through the woods the brigade became very much broken and a halt was called to rectify the alignment. While this was being done the 3d Regiment became separated from the rest of the brigade. While the alignment was being perfected General Pryor rode up to Colonel Mayo, commanding the 3d Regiment, and requested him to take command of the brigade, as he was too much exhausted to go any further.

During the confusion the 3d Regiment became separated from the rest of the brigade, and Major Urquhart, upon whom the command devolved, seeing General Pender's Brigade coming up on his left, reported to that officer and asked permission to charge with him and be accounted for in his report. General Pender acceded to the request and the 3d Regiment, joining on to the right of Pender's Brigade, charged with it. As soon as it passed out of the woods it became exposed to a very heavy fire of musketry and artillery, which, however, did not stay its onward rush. John Yost, of the Portsmouth National Grays, Company H, carried the colors of the 3d Regiment, and was the first man to reach the Federal battery which had been playing upon them. The cannoneers were driven from their guns, and the infantry being pushed back at the same time, the battery was captured. A dispute arose between the 3d Regiment and Pender's Brigade as to which had captured it, but there can be little doubt that John Yost was the first man to reach it, and that he planted the colors of the 3d Virginia there, and the regiment was at his heels.

The regiment took part in the investment and capture of Harper's Ferry September 14th, 1862. Was at the battle of Sharpsburg on the 17th of September and Fredericksburg on the 13th of December. On the 10th of November the regiment was detached from Pryor's Brigade, by order of General Lee, and attached to Kemper's Brigade, Pickett's Division. At Fredericksburg while the Federal Corps of Generals Couch, Wilcox and Hooker were making their assaults upon the positions held by McLaws' and Ransom's Divisions, Kemper's and Jenkins' Brigades, of Pickett's Division, were sent to reinforce Ransom's Division, should he need their assistance, and just before the last charge of Hooker's Corps the 3d Regiment was sent by General Ransom to relieve the 24th North Carolina Regiment of Ransom's Brigade, which had been in the trenches for forty-eight hours, and, shortly after it had relieved the North Carolinians, it contributed to the repulse of the last effort of Burnside to carry General Lee's position. For fuller details of this battle see Chapter XXIV., 61st Virginia Regiment, post .

The 3rd Regiment remained in the trenches all night, in anticipation of a renewal of the attack the next day, and all through the night the Federals were busy removing their wounded from the front of the Confederate works, where they had fallen in their repeated charges during the day. The groans of the wounded and dying, and the appeals for assistance were dismal beyond description. The night was intensely cold, and the Confederates made no effort to interrupt the work of the Federal ambulance corps.

The 3d Regiment left the vicinity of Fredericksburg in February, 1863, with Pickett's Division, for the neighborhood of Suffolk. The detachment, composed of Pickett's and Hood's

Divisions, under Longstreet, and numbering some twelve or thirteen thousand men, were on a huge foraging expedition, but their presence at Suffolk greatly alarmed Major General John Peck, commander of the Federal forces in that locality. On the 12th of April at 3 o'clock P. M. he telegraphed General Hooker, near Fredericksburg, to send a corps to reinforce him, that Longstreet had thirty thousand men with him. At 9 P. M. he telegraphed that Longstreet had thirty-five thousand men, and at 11 P.·M. telegraphed that he had thirty-eight thousand men and one hundred and fifty guns. There was considerable skirmishing going on around Suffolk until the 4th of May, when, having accomplished the object for which he was sent there, Longstreet broke camp and returned to the Rappahannock and rejoined General Lee.

After the defeat of Hooker at the battle of Chancellorsville, which was fought while Hood's and Pickett's Divisions were detached at Suffolk, General Lee moved his army into Pennsylvania and Hooker's army was withdrawn from Virginia to protect Washington. As is told in history, the two armies met at Gettysburg. The 3d Regiment was in Pickett's Division, and reached the battle field about 10 o'clock on the morning of July 3d, and was placed in line of battle in an open field, where it remained under the broiling sun for five hours before it was ordered to charge. The sun proved a valuable ally for the enemy, for scarcely half of the men in the regiment were able to move when the advance was ordered. (This charge is fully described in Chapter XII., the 9th Virginia Regiment, post.)

Returning from Gettysburg the 3d Regiment participated in the cavalry fights at Williamsport, while the army was waiting there for the Potomac river to subside so as to become fordable, and, upon the return of the army to Virginia, was sent with Pickett's Division to North Carolina. It took part in the storming and capture of Plymouth and the capture of Little Washington, and was ordered back to Virginia to unite with the forces under Beauregard, which were being concentrated to check Butler's advance from Bermuda Hundreds towards Richmond. When the train carrying the brigade from Weldon to Petersburg reached Belfield, information had been received that a raiding party of Federal cavalry was approaching that locality. The 3d Regiment was left behind to protect the railroad bridge and the rest of the brigade kept on to Petersburg, arriving in time to assist in the defeat of Butler at Drury's Bluff on the 16th of May, 1864.

The regiment rejoined the brigade later in May and was present in line of battle at Cold Harbor and Turkey Ridge from the latter part of May to the 13th of June, when Grant again moved off to the left and crossed James river below City Point. It crossed James river on pontoons near Drury's Bluff on the 16th and participated in the battle of Chester Station between Pickett's Division and Butler's troops. Butler was driven back over three lines of field works, behind each of which he endeavored to make a stand, and finally retired behind his fortifications at Bermuda Hundreds.

On the 26th of March, 1865, Pickett's Division was moved out of the lines in front of Bermuda Hundreds and sent to the extreme right of the army, defeated Sherman's cavalry at Dinwiddie Court House on the 31st, and the next day was caught in the trap at Five Forks and almost annihilated. The 3d Regiment was commanded that day by Captain Thomas M. Hodges of Company A, and enough of them escaped to keep up their organization. It was at Saylor's Creek on the 6th of April and participated in the defeat of Humphrey's Division at Farmville on the 7th, the last triumph of the Army of Northern Virginia. And all that was left of it surrendered on the 9th at Appomattox Court House.

The 3d Regiment took part in the following battles:

Dam No. 2, April 5, 1862.
Williamsburg, May 5, 1862.
Seven Pines, May 31, 1862.
Mechanicsville, June 26, 1862.
Gaines' Mill, June 27, 1862.
Savage's Station, June 29, 1862.
Frazier's Farm, June 30, 1862.
Thoroughfare Gap, August 29, 1862.
Second Manassas, Aug. 30, 1862.
Harper's Ferry, Sept. 14, 1862.
Sharpsburg, Sept. 17, 1862.
Fredericksburg, Dec. 13, 1862.

Suffolk, April, 1863.
Gettysburg, July 3, 1863.
Williamsport, July, 1863.
Plymouth, 1864.
Little Washington, 1864.
2d Cold Harbor, June 1-3, 1864.
Turkey Ridge, June 3-13, 1864.
Chester Station, June 16, 1864.
Dinwiddie C. H., Mar. 31, 1865.
Five Forks, April 1, 1865.
Saylor's Creek, April 6, 1865.
Farmville, April 7, 1865.
Appomattox C. H., Apr. 9, 1865.

The battle of Gaines' Mill, fought on the 27th of June, 1862, in which the 3d Regiment took quite an active part, was one of the most brilliant victories achieved by the Confederates during the war. The day before McClellan had been dislodged from his advanced position at Mechanicsville, and, falling back to Gaines' Mill, withdrew troops from his left wing and heavily reinforced his position there. Strong works were built to protect his men, and during the larger portion of the battle the Confederates were engaged storming those entrenchments. There were in reality two battles that day. The first is designated the battle of Ellison's Mill, and General Pryor, in his official report of it, says:

"In this affair at Ellison's Mill my command sustained a considerable loss. The battalion of Lieutenant Colonel Coppins and the 3d Regiment Virginia Volunteers were especially distinguished."

The enemy fell back about a mile and a half and assumed a new position on the farm of Dr. Gaines, where, receiving heavy reinforcements, a new stand was made. Pryor's brigade arrived in front of this position at 11 o'clock A. M. and advanced to attack, but finding the enemy too strongly posted, retired. A second attempt was likewise unsuccessful, and General Pryor waited for reinforcements. Being joined later by the brigades of Wilcox, Featherstone and Pickett, another charge was ordered and the victory was won. The enemy was driven in confusion from their works and his artillery fell into the hands of the victorious Confederates. General Pryor's report says: "In this brilliant fight my brigade bore a not unworthy part. Although they had been engaged with the enemy from the earliest dawn, and had already suffered serious losses, they were not behind the foremost in the final victorious charge."

At Frazier's Farm, also, the 3d Regiment played an important part. Pryor's brigade was ordered into the fight about 4 o'clock P. M., and was actively engaged until the enemy retreated, leaving prisoners and cannon in the hands of the Confederates, and leaving his wounded behind. The losses of the brigade during these engagements were heavy. The 3d Regiment had nineteen killed and seventy-eight wounded.

The regiment surrendered at Appomattox Court House April 9th, 1865, with three commissioned officers and sixty-two enlisted men. The following is a copy of the official roll:

COMPANY A.
Captain Thos. M. Hodges,
Private John W. Forward,
" Mark Godfrey.

COMPANY B.
Private James H. Archer.

COMPANY C.
Private John R. Carr,
" Robert Lewis,
" H. A. Liverman,
" Wm. Crowder.

COMPANY D.
Corporal Leroy W. Beal,
" Benj. Cleary,
Private Waverly Barham,
" L. Barrett,
" Thos. L. Cleary,
" M. R. Edwards,
" James C. Lane,
" Robert A. Hood,
" George F. Rawles,
" Ben O. Simons,
" T. R. Wells.

COMPANY D.
Private Geo. W. Williams,
" H. K. Williams,
" R. N. Williams.

COMPANY E.
Sergeant T. Lifsy,
" T. Blankenship,
Private John G. Bristoe,
" Charles E. Wells.

COMPANY F.
Captain P. E. Wilson,
Sergeant James M. Emmerson,
Private Henry Humphlet.

COMPANY G.
Sergeant D. C. Reid,
Corporal Lewis Marks,
Private John A. Critchlow,
" Wm. T. Critchlow,
" Thomas H. Gray,
" Andrew J. Harrison,
" Jesse Johnson,
" E. G. Joiner,
" J. R. Niles,

COMPANY G.

Private Thomas E. Pate,
" George A. Powell,
" George W. Simons,
" Joseph Turner,
" John Turner,
" Joseph A. Worrell.

COMPANY H.

Lieutenant John C. Fulford,
Private H. P. Foils,
" W. R. Gaultney,
" M. Jenkins,
" W. H. Keeling,
" W. H. Rowan,
" J. M. Tabb.

COMPANY I.

Private W. A. Durham,
" P. D. Mitchell.

COMPANY K.

Sergeant John A. Allen,
Private Alex. Bray,
" Z. Dunnaway,
" R. T. Elliott,
" W. J. Fletcher,
" Charles F. Guthrie,
" John D. Peck,
" James A. Seamster,
" P. R. T. Tuck,
" John P. Wilburn,
" W. W. Wilson,
" Nat J. Williams,
" R. R. James.

CHAPTER VII.

CAPTAIN JOHN H. MYERS' COMPANY, CO. E, SIXTH VA. REGIMENT.

This company had a short life and was the victim of too strict discipline. It was organized in Portsmouth immediately after the burning of the Navy Yard by Captain Myers, who was an Orderly Sergeant in the battalion of marines stationed in the Navy Yard, but being a Virginian and unwilling to fight against his State, he managed to make his escape when Commodore McCauley moved off with the Pawnee and Cumberland, and remained behind. He was an excellent drill master and had no difficulty in raising a company of which he was elected Captain. It was regularly mustered into the Confederate service and was assigned to the 6th Virginia Regiment as Company E. The regiment was then under command of Colonel William Mahone. The officers were:

Captain – John H. Myers.

First Lieutenant, Virginius C. Cooke; Second Lieutenant, V. O. Cassell.

First Sergeant, B. J. Accinelly; Second Sergeantt, Enos Murphy; Third Sergeant, Richard D. Brown; Fourth Sergeant, Chas. Syer.

The company was on duty with the regiment in the entrenched camp between Norfolk and Seawell's Point, but Captain Myers undertook to carry out with the volunteers the same methods which he had been accustomed to put into operation in the marine corps in the Navy, and every infraction of the rules, however slight, or any inattention to dress or parade or drill was visited by the severest punishment in his power to inflict. If a man was absent from a roll call Captain Myers would report him as a deserter and wanted to offer a reward for his arrest and return to camp, said reward to be deducted from his pay. Matters in the company became so unbearable that nearly every man in it applied for transfers to other commands, and as the best solution of the dilemma the Colonel recommended that the company be disbanded. Both of the Lieutenants had resigned and the men were trying to get out. The last report of the company is a curiosity in its way. It was dated September 1st, 1861, and twenty-two men who were merely absent from roll call were reported as deserters, with a recommendation that all of their pay be taken from them. Others were reported for other offences, with the recommendation that one month's pay be deducted from them, and scarcely a man in the whole list had met the entire approval of the Captain. This report was made up after the receipt of the order disbanding the company, and the summary was as follows:

Transferred to Company D.................. 11 men.
"   "   "   C................... 1   "
Appointed hospital steward................ 1   "
Mustered out, 1 officer and 20 men........ 20 "
Resigned, 2 officers.
Mustered out, unwilling to remain in service.. 6 "
Died, 1; discharged for disability, 7......... 8 "
Deserted.................................. 22 "
                                           ___
Total 3 officers and...................... 69 men.

Nearly all of the men enlisted in other companies and made good soldiers. It was unfortunate that the Captain could not appreciate the difference between a company newly organized of men who had been used to the widest liberty in all of their movements and who needed to be brought under a state of discipline by patient and persistent efforts, and a company of regulars on shipboard. There was abundant material for a good company, but it was badly managed. Below will be found a complete roll of the company from the date of its organization, in April, 1861, to its disbandment, September 1st, 1861. One private, Elijah Creekmore, died.

Captain—John H. Myers.
First Lieutenant—Virginius S. Cooke.
Second Lieutenant—V. O. Cassell.
First Sergeant—B. J. Accinelly.
Second Sergeant—Enos Murphy.
Third Sergeant—Richard D. Brown.
Fourth Sergeant—Charles Syer.
First Corporal—William White.
Second Corporal—James Thornton.
Third Corporal—William Parsons.
Fourth Corporal—John W. Howard.

PRIVATES.

Allen, Wm. A.,
Bullock, Joseph,
Barrett, Joseph,
Britton, Wm.,
Ballance, John,
Badger, M.,
Backus, Wm. T., Jr.,
Barrett, Matthew,
Cherry, Germain,
Curtain, Michael,
Collins, Wm. B.,
Cotton, John,
Creekmore, Elijah,
Doyle, Nathaniel,
Dewberry, James,
Elliott, Charles,
Eason, Augustus,
Elliott, John W.,
Frestine, John,
Graham, James,
Godwin, A. D. B.,
Gwynn, Isaac,
Hall, Henry,
Harrison, Chas. H.,
Halstead, Richard,
Hozier, Joseph,
Hudgins, Edward,
Hopkins, Hillary,
Halstead, Alex.,
Jordan, James,
Jordan, Wm. E.,
Jordan, Joseph,
Johnston, Geo. W.,

Knight, John M.,
Kent, Michael,
Lewis, Thomas,
Lingston, George,
Lee, Lewis,
Murphy, Patrick,
Mathews, Jacob,
Miller, Phliip,
Newby, Samuel,

Parker, George,
Parker, Robert W.,
Parker, E. K.,
Peel, John,
Reynolds, H. C.,
Rourke, Bernard,
Scheill, Mitchell,
Spaulding, John E.,
Tennis, T. S.,

Tennis, Wm.,
Walker, George,
Wagner, Fred,
Whitehurt, Robt. B.,
White, Charles,
Wallace, James,
Walsh, Michael,
Walsh, James,
Wilger, Thomas.

CHAPTER VIII.

THE VIRGINIA ARTILLERY, COMPANY D, NINTH VIRGINIA INFANTRY.

This company was organized about the 12th of April, 1861, for the purpose of offering its services to South Carolina, and elected the following officers:
Captain—William J. Richardson.
First Lieutenant—Charles R. McAlpine.
Second Lieutenant—Samuel W. Weaver.
Third Lieutenant—George Linn.
First Sergeant—John D. Skellin.

Virginia had not then passed the Ordinance of Secession, nor was the company uniformed or commissioned. It was unarmed also, and had not applied to Virginia for arms when the State seceded. When Governor Letcher issued his call for troops on the 20th of April, 1861, the Virginia Artillery gave up the idea of going to South Carolina and responded to Governor Letcher's call. The company was organized as an artillery company, but was not furnished with a battery and became an infantry company and was attached to the 3d Virginia Regiment at the Naval Hospital Point.

When the Navy Yard fell into the hands of the Virginia troops this company got a brass howitzer from off the old frigate United States, took it to the Independent Fire Company's engine house, put it in order and carried it to the Naval Hospital, but under orders from General Huger it was subsequently turned over to Grimes' Battery by Colonel Pryor. It was not given up willingly. The company took with them to the Naval Hospital Point about one hundred and twenty-five men, but most of them were skilled mechanics, and as their services were needed to work on vessels in the Navy Yard, quite a number of them were detached by orders from headquarters. So many were thus detached that when the company was ordered to Craney Island about a month later there were only eighty in the ranks. Until the company was ordered to Craney Island the men were armed with long boarding pikes which were obtained in the Navy Yard. Shortly after their transfer to Craney Island the ladies of Portsmouth organized a sewing circle and made uniforms for them and their boarding pikes were exchanged for flint lock muskets. Some months later, when Lieutenant Colonel De Lagnel was in command of the post at Craney Island, these guns were sent to Norfolk and changed into percussion guns.

While the company was at the Naval Hospital battery the men, by a very slight accidental circumstance, obtained the name of

"Wild Cats," which stuck to them to the close of the war. Being near home and no enemy nearer than Old Point, the men were very desirous of spending as much time at home with their families as possible, while Colonel Pryor's whole energies seemed to be bent on contriving means to keep them in camp. He placed sentinels very close together around the grounds, but in rear of the Hospital there was a very high brick wall which Colonel Pryor thought could not be scaled without a ladder, and as there were no ladders available he neglected to guard that part of the camp. The men in Company D soon found means of getting over, and one day a party of young ladies who were walking through the grove in rear of the Hospital saw three or four of them climbing over, and one of the young ladies remarked that they could climb equally as well as wild cats. Even to this day, thirty-one years afterwards, the men of Company D are spoken of as "Richardson's wild cats."

On May 29th, 1861, the company was detached from the 3d Regiment and ordered to Craney Island, then under command of Colonel George Richardson, and was placed in charge of a water battery of six 32-pound guns, bearing upon the main channel of the river from Seawell's Point.

Lieutenant McAlpine resigned on the 4th of May, 1861, to take command of a new company which was being organized under the name of Bilisoly Blues. This caused a vacancy in the position of First Lieutenant, and Orderly Sergeant Skellin was elected to fill it. Second Sergeant Richard Vermillion was promoted to 1st Sergeant. These were the officers of the company until the reorganization on the 20th of April, 1862, when the following were elected:

Captain—William J. Richardson.
First Lieutenant—Samuel W. Weaver.
Second Lieutenant—George Linn.
Third Lieutenant—Richard Vermillion.
First Sergeant—William A. Culpepper.
Second Sergeant—Thomas H. Myers.

Captain Richardson was promoted to Major of the 9th Regiment in June, 1862, and Lieutenant Weaver became Captain. Lieutenant Linn died in a hospital in Winchester in 1862, and Lieutenant Vermillion became 1st Lieutenant. Sergeant William A. Culpepper was wounded at Gettysburg and disabled from further service, and 2d Sergeant Thomas H. Myers was promoted to Orderly Sergeant.

When the 9th Virginia Regiment was organized in June, 1861, this company was attached to it as Company D. The boys were very much amused at the requirements of the Adjutant of the post at Craney Island, Lieutenant Thomas Smith, son of Colonel F. H. Smith, President of the Virginia Military Institute, who insisted upon their coming upon parades and drills with their faces cleanly shaved and shoes highly polished. If Lieutenant Smith followed the army after it got into active warfare he possibly omitted the polished shoes from the "army regulations." His connection with the 9th Regiment as Adjutant ceased when Craney Island was evacuated by the Confederates. There were on Craney Island in May, 1862, eight companies, of which one was from Portsmouth, two from Norfolk city, two from Petersburg, one from Chesterfield, one from Salem, one from Baltimore and Norfolk county, and when orders were received to abandon the island the troops forded the narrow channel between the island and the main land and marched to Suffolk, where they took the cars for Petersburg.

On the 24th of May, 1862, Company D was detached temporarily from the regiment and ordered to Battery No. 5 in the fortifications around Richmond; rejoined the regiment on the 2d of June, and about the 7th of June was sent to a battery on the York River railroad and placed in charge of two long 24-pounder rifle guns. The 4th Georgia Regiment was with the company as a support. While here an incident occurred which came near wiping out of existence the whole company. The magazine was close in rear of the earthworks, and was heavily stocked with powder, &c., and a shell from one of the enemy's guns fell right into it, but, fortunately, did not explode. There was powder enough in the magazine to have blown every man in the company to atoms. The company opened the battle of Mechanicsville on the 26th of June by shelling at long range a piece of woods in which the enemy had obtained a lodgment, and from which the Confederate infantry afterwards drove them. On the 27th the company was moved to Tree Hill battery, in front of Richmond, between the York River railroad and the river, and was there until after the battle of Malvern Hill, when it was ordered back to the regiment. After that it was constantly with the regiment and participated in all of its battles. Sickness, wounds and transfers of its members to other commands reduced its ranks. Many of its men were transferred to Grimes' Battery in April, 1862.

The following men were in the charge of Pickett's Division at Gettysburg July 3d, 1863:

Captain Samuel W. Weaver, captured.
First Lieutenant Richard Virmillion.
First Sergeant William A. Culpepper, wounded and captured.
Second Sergeant Thomas H. Myers.

PRIVATES.

Bailey, Thomas.
Bland, George.
Byrd, Daniel, killed.

Cutherell, Leonard.
Cross, John, killed.
Cowper, Walter G.,

Darden, Joseph, captured.
Hansford, Jas., wounded slightly.
McCoy, Rufus K., wounded.
Miltier, Daniel, wounded.
Reed, Robert E., killed.
Skinner, Abraham, captured.
Urqulart, William, wounded.
Williams, Samuel, captured.
Walton, George W., captured,
Yates, Josiah W., wounded.

Thus, of the twenty men who went in the charge fourteen were either killed, wounded or captured.

Below will be found the roster of the company for June, 1861. Conscripts from other portions of the State who were added to the company in 1864 and 1865, are omitted because they were not Portsmouth men.

Captain William J. Richardson, promoted to Major 9th Virginia.
First Lieutenant Charles R. McAlpin, promoted Captain Co. 1, 61st Virginia.
" " John C. Skelling, dropped at reorganization.
Captain Samuel W. Weaver, captured at Gettysburg July 3d, 1863, and not exchanged.
Lieutenant Richard Vermillion.
" George Linn, died in hospital in Winchester 1862.
Orderly Sergeant Thomas H. Myers, wounded August 26th, 1862, at Warrenton Springs.

PRIVATES.

Anderson, John, detached 1861.
Bright, Johnathan, discharged July, 1862, over age.
Bright, W. Jordan, transferred to Grimes' Battery 1862.
Brent, John.
Bailey, Thomas A.
Bland, George.
Brown, James, drummer.
Boutwell, Richard, transferred to Grimes' Battery 1862.
Bateman, Robert, died in hospital 1863.
Byrd, Daniel, killed July 3d, 1863, at Gettysburg.
Brownley, A. M., transferred to Grimes' Battery.
Culpepper, William A., promoted First Sergeant, wounded, disabled and captured at Gettysburg.
Cutherell, Leonard, wounded Drury's Bluff May 16, 1864, died in hospital.
Cross, John, killed July 3d, 1863, at Gettysburg.
Cowper, Walter G., severely wounded at Suffolk 1863.
DeGraw, William, furnished substitute 1861.
Deakin, George.
Darden, Richard.
Day, William, transferred to Governor's Guard.
Darden, Samuel.
Darden, Joseph L., captured at Gettysburg.
Eastman, Lewis, transferred to Navy.
Futtett, George.
Grant, George W.
Goodson, Henry, transferred to Grimes' Battery.
Greenwood, James, transferred to the Navy.
Gray, William.
Hansford, James, wounded May 16th, 1864, Drury's Bluff.
Hansford, Richard, transferred to Grimes Battery.
Houston, John, detached 1861.
Hall, Samuel, killed 1862 by falling tree.
Hall, Cary J., transferred to Navy 1862.
Hampton, Augustus.
Happer, Richard W. B., discharged 1861, under age.

Howell, Fletcher, died in hospital 1863.
Hand, Samuel T., Jr., discharged 1864, disability.
Harvey, Walter, accidentally drowned 1861.
Ironmonger, C. E., transferred to Grimes' Battery 1862.
Jarvis, John E.
Jollett, W. H., surrendered at Appomattox.
Linn, Charles B., transferred to Grimes' Battery 1862.
Long, L. C., discharged August 28th, 1862, over age.
McDonell, George W. R., transferred to Grimes' Battery 1862.
McCoy, R. K., wounded and disabled at Gettysburg and appointed Commissary Sergeant, surrendered at Appomattox.
Moore, Fred E., died in hospital 1863.
Minter, Andrew, transferred to Grimes' Battery 1862.
Morris, William T., detached 1861.
Matthews, John W., transferred to Grimes' Battery 1862.
Nicholson, C. M., died in Chimborazo Hospital February 26th, 1862.
Newman, John B., discharged July, 1862, over age.
Peed, Leroy S., detailed 1863.
Pitt, L. D., transferred to Navy 1862.
Quillan, John.
Reed, Robert E., killed July 3d, 1863, at Gettysburg.
Sale, Henry G., discharged for disability 1863 and entered the Navy.
Sheppard, William E., transferred to Grimes' Battery 1862.
Skinner, Abraham, died at Point Lookout 1864.
Seacrist, Barclay, died at Point Lookout 1864.
Stublin, William C. (Sergeant), discharged 1862, over age.
Thompson, John W., killed May 16th, 1864, at Drury's Bluff.
Urquhart, William, wounded July 3d, 1863, at Gettysburg.
Webster, ———, discharged July, 1862, over age.
Williams, Samuel.
Walton, George W.
Walton, John W., transferred to Navy 1862.
Wilkerson, William.
Watson, Joseph W.
White, Joseph, discharged for disability 1861.
White, Richard W; B., Sergeant.
Walsh, Joseph, detached 1861.
Wrench, John, transferred to Grimes' Battery 1862.
Wrenn, Edward, killed May 16th, 1864, at Drury's Bluff.
Yates, Samuel, died 1865.
Yates, Josiah D., wounded severely July 3d, 1863, at Gettysburg, and slightly in three other battles.

Killed and died—16.

CHAPTER IX.

THE PORTSMOUTH RIFLE COMPANY, CO. G, NINTH VA. REGIMENT.

This company was organized in Portsmouth in 1792, consequently it had passed through an existence of sixty-nine years and witnessed two wars, when Governor Letcher issued his order on the 20th of April, 1861, calling its members to arms. The company was armed with old style Mississippi rifles, without bayonets, but subsequently the City Council of Portsmouth made an appropriation to fit them with sabre bayonets, which were manufactured in the city at the Union Car Works.

For much of the information concerning this company and also concerning the 9th Virginia Regiment, to which it was attached, the author is indebted to Orderly Sergeant John W. Wood, who kept a diary from the evacuation of Portsmouth by the Confederates on the 10th of May, 1862, until the close of the war.

On the 20th of April, 1861, when the company was ordered into service, the following were the officers:

Captain—John C. Owens.
First Lieutenant—Lemuel T. Cleaves.
Second Lieutenant—William F. Tonkin.

Shortly afterwards Orderly Sergeant William J. Wood was elected 3d Lieutenant. The Rifles, like the other Portsmouth companies, was in the 3d Regiment. It responded promptly to the Governor's order, mustered under arms on the afternoon of the 20th of April, and on the morning of the 21st was ordered, one-half to the Navy Yard and the other half to the Naval Hospital Point. The following week the whole company was ordered to Pig Point, at the mouth of the Nansemond river, to fortify that point. They built there a strong earthwork and manned it with guns from the Navy Yard. Captain Robert B. Pegram of the navy was assigned to the battery as commander of the post, and also for the purpose of instructing the men in the use of the heavy guns, for which service his previous experience in the United States Navy eminently qualified him. The earthwork had not been completed and only four guns had been mounted before the United States cutter Harriet Lane, mounting eight guns, made an attack upon it. The Lane took a position where only two of the guns of the battery could be brought to bear upon her and succeeded in disabling one of the guns by a well directed shot, which entered the embrasure and struck the gun on its muzzle. The fight, however, was kept up with the other gun, and after a spirited engagement of about twenty minutes the Lane hauled off, considerably damaged and having a number of men injured. She was sent to Washington for repairs. No one was hurt in the battery. The members of the company acted with the coolness of veterans, though it was the first time they were under fire. This battle was fought June 5th, 1861.

After the fall of Roanoke Island, which took place on the 8th of February, 1862, the Federals landed a force of troops at Elizabeth City, N. C., and in April passed over to the opposite side of the Pasquotank river and landed a brigade, under General Reno, in Camden county, and pushed on through that county towards South Mills. The 3d Georgia Regiment, under Colonel A. R. Wright, hearing of the approach of the enemy advanced by orders from headquarters to meet them, and in an engagement near South Mills compelled them to fall back to Elizabeth City. The Portsmouth Rifle Company had suffered considerably from malaria in their camp at Pig Point and had been removed to Portsmouth for the purpose of recuperating, and were doing provost duty in the city at the time of General Reno's advance, hence, as the company was immediately available, it was ordered by General Blanchard to march to South Mills to reinforce the Georgians. The 1st Louisiana Regiment and Grimes' Battery from Portsmouth were also sent there as reinforcements, but the fight was over and the enemy had retired before their arrival.

The Rifles kept on to the vicinity of Elizabeth City and did duty there as the advanced picket until it was determined by the Confederate authorities to evacuate Portsmouth, when they received orders to return to the city, which they did, arriving in time to take part in the closing scenes. The company was camped at Oak Grove, on the South street road about a quarter of a mile from the city, and was the last body of troops to leave. After all the other commands had moved off the Portsmouth Rifles received orders to march into the city and destroy all of the cotton and tobacco which was stored there, to prevent it from falling into the hands of the enemy, and were eye-witnesses to all of the dread and distress which was manifested and felt by the women of Portsmouth, who were thus being abandoned to the uncertain treatment of their foes, while the men were marching off to battle and possible death.

Having accomplished the object for which they had been sent back, they started at 6 o'clock P. M. May 10th and marched to Bower's Hill, where they arrived about 9 o'clock and were camped in the quarters which had been built there by the 3d Louisiana Battalion, and from which they had moved only a few hours before. The next day, the 11th, the march was resumed, but orders were received by Captain Owens to return a couple of miles back toward Portsmouth as a rear guard for the division, and they kept that distance behind the rest of the troops until they reached Suffolk. The Rifles were then ordered up, placed on the Seaboard and Roanoke railroad cars and taken to Weldon, from which point they were carried by rail to Petersburg, arriving there on the 12th, and were quartered on Dunn's Hill.

The 9th Virginia Regiment was here united and organized by the election of field officers, an account which will appear further on. The Portsmouth Rifles became known in the regiment as Company G, and, as in the reorganization of the regiment Captain Owens was elected Major, a new election of officers was held in the company. Lieutenant Cleaves was elected Captain, which position he held until the close of the war; Lieutenants Tonkin and Wood were each advanced one grade, and Orderly Sergeant Nathaniel C. Gayle was elected 3d Lieutenant. William H. White was elected Orderly Sergeant. He was subsequently killed at the battle of Malvern Hill July 1st, 1862. Lieutenant Wood resigned in the winter of 1862-3, and Orderly Sergeant John H. Lewis, who had succeeded to that position on the death of Sergeant White, was elected 3d Lieutenant. There were no other changes among the commissioned officers during the war except that toward the close of the war Lieutenant Gayle received an appointment as carpenter in the Navy and was transferred to that branch of the service. Lieutenants Tonkin and Gayle were wounded at Gettysburg July 3, 1863, and Lieutenant Lewis was captured at the stone fence.

The company lost two Orderly Sergeants during the war, Sergeant William H. White, who was killed at Malvern Hill, and Sergeant John K. Beaton, who was killed at Drury's Bluff May 16th, 1864. Upon the death of Sergeant Beaton, John W. Wood was promoted to the position and held it until the close of the war, which ended with the surrender at Appomattox.

In 1862, while the company was in the vicinity of Elizabeth City, N. C., a number of the men went bathing about sundown in the Pasquotank river, but soon had a hornet's nest about them in the form of hundreds of moccasin snakes which, having had undisputed possession of the stream for years, entered a vigorous protest against the intruders upon their vested rights. The boys lost no time in getting to the shore and left the snakes in possession of the river.

On one occasion while on picket duty about five miles from Elizabeth City near a farm house on the banks of the Pasquotank river the company formed the acquaintance of a very pretty young girl about thirteen or fourteen years old, daughter of the gentleman who owned the place. The young lady told them that a short time before then a United States gunboat came up the river and stopped in front of the house, that a party of men came ashore from it, and one of them, a soldier, pointed his gun at her with the intention of shooting her, and would have done so had not an officer knocked down the gun with his sword.

After the company had been on duty a short while at Pig Point Company H (Captain Niblett commanding), 59th Virginia Regiment, was sent to the battery as a reinforcement. This company was from Lunenburg county, Virginia, and afterwards became a part of Wise's Brigade. Camped near them as supports, were the 1st Louisiana and the 4th Georgia Regiments.

While at Pig Point Private James W. Morgan died. He died in August, 1861, and was buried in Portsmouth. This was the first death in the company. Private Ephraim Bailey was taken sick from exposure while the company was in the vicinity of Elizabeth City, N. C., and died in a hospital in Richmond shortly after the Confederates evacuated Portsmouth. Later on, when the company became exposed to the dangers of the battle-field and to exposure amid snow and rain, deaths became more common, and in the remaining three years of the war twenty-two of its members gave up their lives an unavailing sacrifice upon the altar of their country, while many more were prostrated by wounds which disabled them for life and brought them to untimely graves. The Portsmouth Rifles made for themselves a gallant record and were in the front of the battle on many a hard fought field. In the charge of Pickett's Division at Gettysburg, which stands prominently forward as one of the most noted events in the history of the Army of Northern Virginia, the Portsmouth Rifle Company had forty-eight men, of whom seven were killed and so many were wounded and fell into the hands of the enemy that only seven of them were able to report for duty the day after the battle. Of three commissioned officers who went with the company in the charge two were wounded and the other captured. One of the men, Corporal Lemuel H. Williams, planted the colors of the 9th Regiment at the stone wall and was killed almost at that very moment. Sergeant Joshua Grimes of Company I of Norfolk county, was the color bearer of the regiment, and carried the colors to within twenty yards of the wall and was shot down, severely wounded. The flag fell with him, but Corporal Williams immediately picked it up and bore it to the farthest point of advance made by the division, when he received his death wound.

On the 24th of August, 1862, while Longstreet's Corps was pushing on after General Pope towards the battle-ground of Second Manassas the 9th Regiment was in the advance, and Company G was the advance picket. That day the company captured three Federal cavalrymen, and on the 10th of May, 1864, when the bold front made by Armistead's Brigade and Gracie's Alabama Brigade near Drury's Bluff checked Butler's advance upon Richmond and saved the city from capture, Company G was detailed as skirmishers in front of the 38th Virginia Regiment. In this action Privates James W. Findley and James Land were wounded and Private William T. Edwards was cap tured. On the 17th of June, 1864, after General Butler had been bottled up at Bermuda Hundreds Company G was a part of the picket line and made a charge upon and captured the Federal picket line in their front, but as the left of the Confederate picket line had failed to advance Company G returned to the original position, bringing a large number of prisoners with them.

While the 9th Regiment was advancing with Armistead's Brigade up the Gettysburg heights and when near the stone wall behind which the enemy was sheltered, Private William G. Monte of the Portsmouth Rifle Company, Company G, casting his eye along the line of advancing Confederates, then at the long lines of the enemy, who were pouring into them a deadly fire of artillery and musketry, and then over the country behind him where stood seven of the nine divisions of the Confederate army, exclaimed, "What a glorious sight!" He then took his watch out of his pocket, noted the time of day and put it back again. In less than two minutes he was dead. A Federal bullet found a vital spot, and one of the bravest and coolest men in General Lee's army passed to "the great unknown."

In his official report of the battle of Pig Point, June 5th, 1861, Captain Robert B. Pegram of the Navy, who commanded the post, says:

"For men who had never been in action, the Portsmouth Rifles were remarkably cool and self possessed, and, after a few rounds, got the range of the enemy and fired admirably well. Every officer and man behaved in the most spirited and creditable manner, and were so regardless of danger that I had often to interpose my authority to prevent their exposing themselves unnecessarily to the enemy's fire."

The following members of the company were in the charge of Pickett's Division at Gettysburg. Some were wounded who are not so recorded, but their names cannot be recalled to memory. Their wounds were slight.

Lieutenant W. F. Tonkin, wounded.
" Nat G. Gayle, wounded.
" John H. Lewis, captured.
Sergeant John K. Beaton, wounded.
" John R. Dunn, killed.
" John W. Wood.
" L. C. Gayle, captured.
" David W. Ballentine, captured.
Corporal Lemuel H. Williams, killed.
" William H. Brittingham.

PRIVATES.

Anderton, Wm. T., captured.
Brownley, Wm. K., captured.
Boyd, Henry C.,
Buxton, John T., captured,
Bourke, Jos. B., captured,
Bennett, William B., killed,

Barton, Robert P., captured,
Creecy, George A., wounded,
Etheredge, Sam'l, litter bearer,
Emmerson, George,
Edwards, William T.,
Edwards, Oney H.,
Denson, Virginius S.,
Ferebee, George W., captured,
Fiendly, James W.,
Ferebee, Joseph K., captured,
Grant, Jordan W., captured,
Gaskins, Thomas S., captured,
Harvey, Arthur W., captured,
Hargroves, John R., wounded and captured,
Harding, Milton L., captured,
Kelsick, John R.,
Land, James W. T., wounded,
Lattimer, John W., killed,
Lewis, George W., wounded,
Monte, William G., killed,
Moreland, J. Baker, captured,
Myers, Stephen A.,
Nash, Richard J., killed,
Neville, William S., captured,
Owens, Thomas C., killed,
Phillips, Henry O., wounded and captured,
Phillips, Michael, captured,
Peed, Samuel S., captured,
Revill, George A., captured,
Revill, Randall, wounded,
Sale, John E., wounded and captured,
Stewart, James T.,
Williams, Millard C., wounded.

The following were present for duty but were detailed upon other service and did not go into the charge:

Brownley, Charles,
Bailey, James M.,
Berry, George T.,
Johnston, Theophilus,
Murphy, Enos,
Owens, A. B.,
Roane, Alonzo B.,
Thompkins, Thos. G.
White, George A.,
Whitehurst, M. P.,
Wilkerson, Geo. P.,

Below will be found the list of names on the roll of the company for August, 1861:

Captain John C. Owens, promoted Colonel 9th Virginia, killed at Gettysburg.
Captain Lemuel T. Cleaves.
Lieutenant William F. Tonkin, wounded July 3d, 1863, Gettysburg.
Lieutenant William J. Wood, resigned 1862-3.
Lieutenant Nathaniel G. Gayle, wounded at Gettysburg, transferred to Navy 1865.
Lieutenant John H. Lewis, captured at Gettysburg July 3d, 1863.
First Sergeant William H. White, killed July 1st, 1862, Malvern Hill.
" " John K. Beaton, killed May 16th, 1864, Drury's Bluff.
" " John R. Dunn, killed July 3d, 1863, Gettysburg.
" " John W. Wood.
Sergeant L. Christopher Gayle, captured at Gettysburg July 3d, 1863.
" David W. Ballentine, captured July 3d, 1863, at Gettysburg.
Corporal Thomas George, transferred to Navy 1863.
" Theophilus F. Ash.
" Lemuel H. Williams, killed July 3d, 1863, Gettysburg.
" William H. Brittingham.

PRIVATES.

Anderton, William T., captured July 3d, 1863, Gettysburg.
Brownley, William K., captured at Gettysburg, died at Fort Delaware.
Boyd, Henry C.
Buxton, John T., captured at Gettysburg, died at Point Lookout.
Berry, George T., transferred to Navy 1863.
Bourke, Joseph B., captured July 3d, 1863, Gettysburg.

Bennett, William B., killed July 3d, 1863, Gettysburg.
Barrett, W. H.
Burton, Robert P., captured July 3d, 1863, Gettysburg.
Brownley, Charles.
Bailey, James M., killed May 16th, 1864, Drury's Bluff.
Bailey, Ephriam, died in hospital at Richmond May 5th, 1862.
Bousbell, John, detached 1861 to work in Navy Yard and promoted Captain in Naval battalion, Richmond.
Culpepper, Roland H.
Cressy, George A., wounded July 3d, 1863, Gettysburg.
Collins, George W. F. D., detailed 1862 to work in Navy.
Culpepper, Reuben, detached September, 1862.
Denson, Virginius S.
Etheredge, Samuel R.
Emmerson, George W.
Edwards, William T., captured May 10th, 1864, Drury's Bluff.
Edwards, Oney H.
Edwards, Amos W., detached 1861 to work on machinery.
Ferebee, George W., captured at Gettysburg July 3d, 1863.
Ferebee, Joseph K., captured at Gettysburg, died at Point Lookout.
Fiendly, James W.
Gleason, James, promoted Lieutenant Company H, 61st Virginia Regiment.
Grant, Jordan W., captured at Gettysburg, died at Point Lookout.
Grant, Benjamin F., wounded and died.
Gaskins, Thomas S., captured July 3d, 1863, at Gettysburg.
Harding, Milton L., captured July 3d, 1863, at Gettysburg.
Hennicke, Henry O.
Harvey, Arthur W., captured July 3d, 1863, at Gettysburg.
Hargroves, John R., wounded July 3d, 1863, Gettysburg, and captured.
Holt, Edwin W.
Hundley, James H., discharged 1861, disability.
Herbert, John D.
Hotller, Samuel, promoted Ordnance Sergeant Mahone's Brigade.
Hennicke, Fred.
Johnston, Theophilus.
Johnson, Columbus, wounded at Warrenton Springs and died.
Johnson, Augustus, killed at Warrenton Springs August 28th, 1862.
Jobson, J. Tyler.
Kelsick, John R.
Land, James W. T., wounded July 3d, 1863, at Gettysburg.
Lattimer, John W., killed July 3d, 1863, at Gettysburg.
Lewis, George W., wounded July 3d, 1863, at Gettysburg.
Mathews, W. R., discharged 1861, disability.
Morris, Frank, transferred to Company I, 13th Virginia Cavalry, wounded at Williamsport 1863 and Five Forks April 1st, 1865.
Monte, William G., killed July 3d, 1863, at Gettysburg.
Murphy, Enos, died in hospital May 4th, 1865.
Moreland, J. B., captured July 3d, 1863, at Gettysburg.
Myers, Stephen H.
Morgan, James W., died August, 1861, at Pig Point.
Mathews, H., discharged 1862, over age.
Nash, Richard James, killed July 3d, 1863, at Gettysburg.
Neville, William S., captured July 3d, 1863, at Gettysburg.
Owens, Thomas C., killed July 3d, 1863, at Gettysburg.
Owens, A. B., detailed as courier at brigade headquarters.
Owens, Edward M., captured at Sayler's Creek April 6th, 1865.
Oliver, William J., detached at Longstreet's headquarters 1862, rejoined the company in 1864 and surrendered at Appomattox.
Phillips, Michael, captured July 3d, 1863, Gettysburg, and died of pneumonia at Point Lookout.
Phillips, William R.

Phillips, Henry O., wounded July 3d, 1863, Gettysburg, and captured.
Peed, Samuel S., captured July 5th, 1863, in Pennsylvania.
Pugh, Lindsay, detached 1861 to work in Navy Yard.
Phillips, Charles T., promoted Sergeant Major 9th Regiment.
Revell, George A., captured July 3d, 1863, at Gettysburg.
Revell, Randall, wounded July 3d, 1863, Gettysburg.
Robertson, William D., discharged 1861 for disability.
Roane, Alonzo B.
Savage, T. A.
Sherwood, O. B., discharged 1862, over age.
Sale, John E., wounded July 3d, 1863, at Gettysburg.
Stewart, James T.
Smith, William F., discharged 1861 for disability.
Tyson, Luther.
Tompkins, Thomas G.
Thomas, William James, killed June 1st, 1862, at Seven Pines.
White, George A.
Watts, George W. H.
Whitehurst, Marshall P.
Williams, Millard C., wounded July 3d, 1863, at Gettysburg.
Wilkerson, George P.
Woodhouse, Thomas C.
Weaver, Joseph F., appointed carpenter in Navy.
Williams, Thomas H., transferred to Company K, 9th Virginia.
Williams, J. Herbert.
Whitfield, Lewis, killed August 30th, 1862, Second Manassas.
Virnelson, William B., detached 1862 to work in arsenal.
Virnelson, Joseph H., detached 1862 to work in Navy Yard and appointed engineer in the Navy.
    Killed and died—24.

CHAPTER X.

THE CRANEY ISLAND ARTILLERY, CO. I, NINTH VIRGINIA INFANTRY.

This company was organized immediately after the Governor issued his call for volunteers in April, 1861, and the members came from Norfolk county, in the vicinity of Churchland, and from the upper portion of Nansemond county, the larger portion, however, being from Norfolk county. The officers of the company under whom it was originally mustered into service were:
Captain, John T. Kilby.
First Lieutenant, J. O. B. Crocker; Second Lieutenant, William S. Wright.
First Sergeant, John H. Wright; Second Sergeant, James C. Bidgood; Third Sergeant, Keely Harrison; Fourth Sergeant, Henry B. Lewer.

Upon being mustered into service the company was ordered to the battery at Pinner's Point and was attached to the 9th Va. Regiment as Company I, remaining on duty there until the evacuation by the Confederates on the 10th of May, 1862, when it marched to Suffolk. At Pinner's Point the company occupied comfortable quarters which the men built for themselves with lumber furnished by the Quartermaster's Department, but the health of the men was not good in camp, and four of them died in hospital during the year they were there. The battery at Pinner's Point contained twelve 32 and 68-pounder Dahlgren guns, and, nearer the end of the point, there was another battery of four 6-inch rifle guns. These were originally 32-pounder Dahlgren guns, and were rifled and banded in the Navy Yard. These two batteries were manned by Company I and Company K. In rear of the batteries there were erected two furnaces for heating shot red hot, and also a bomb-proof magazine, but no opportunity presented itself of testing their efficiency as the enemy never appeared before the battery.

In May, 1862, there was a reorganization of the company, and the men re-enlisted for the war. There was also a slight change in the officers. On account of a disagreement or misunderstanding Lieutenant Wright declined a re-election and enlisted as a private in Company K. First Sergeant John H. Wright was discharged, at his own request, for the purpose of organizing another company. In this he succeeded, and became its Captain. It was attached to the 61st Virginia Regiment as Company H. Lieutenant Wright was with Company K in the battle of Seven Pines, and was wounded through the fleshy portion of the arm. After recovering from his wound he was appointed Adjutant of the 61st Virginia Regiment and died in camp in the fall of 1863 of congestive chill.

At the reorganization of Company I Captain Kilby and First Lieutenant Crocker were re-elected and Cornelius M. Dozier was elected Second Lieutenant. John Arthur was elected Third Lieutenant, but failed to qualify or to connect himself with the company. Private McKemmey Lewis was elected First Sergeant. After the evacuation of Pinner's Point the company went to Petersburg and was in camp on Dunn's Hill with the rest of the regiment, but remained there only a few days when it was detached and sent to Battery No. 5 in the fortifications around Richmond. On the 1st of June it was ordered to rejoin the regiment at Seven Pines and marched to that place, but did not reach there until after the battle was over. It missed one other battle, that of Drury's Bluff, which was fought on the 16th of May, 1864, while the company was absent from the regiment on detached duty, but, with those two exceptions, it participated in all of the battles in which the regiment was engaged.

During the month of June the regiment took part in several skirmishes and picket fights, which accustomed the men to fire, and when the battle of Malvern Hill was fought, the first general engagement in which Company I took part, the men acted with the coolness and steadiness of old veterans and were conspicuous for their gallantry. Color Sergeant John T. Bain of Company I had the colors of the regiment, and when the regiment was charging up the hill was shot down, receiving a wound from which he subsequently died. Captain Kilby picked up the flag, stood with it in front of the line, waved it to the men and held them to their position. While thus waving the colors the staff was shot in two just above his hand, but he caught it up again, and handing it to Joshua Grimes of his company told him to hold on to it under all circumstances and contingencies. Lieutenant Colonel Gilliam in his official report of the battle [see Chapter XII., the 9th Virginia Regiment, post] alludes to this incident, but speaks of it as the flag of another regiment. The 9th Virginia and 4th Georgia were somewhat mixed together at the time, which was possibly the cause of Colonel Gilliam's mistake.

Company I lost very heavily in this battle. Four men were killed outright on the battle field and two others died from wounds received there, while eleven others were wounded more or less severely. The killed were Lieutenant Cornelius M. Dozier, Sergeant Joseph Prentis, Corporal Lucillicus W. Jones and Private Thomas Parker. Sergeant Henry B. Lewer and Color Sergeant John T. Bain were mortally wounded, were taken to Richmond and died shortly afterwards in the hospital. The day before the battle Corporal Jones had been elected by the company to the position of Third Lieutenant, but was killed before he obtained his commission. Sergeant Prentis was a gallant boy, scarcely eighteen years old, son of Mr. Robert Prentis, proctor of the University of Virginia. His dead body was found the day after the battle, nearer the enemy's lines than any other, showing that in his zeal to snatch victory from the seething volcano of shot and shell they were endeavoring to storm, his young and chivalrous spirit had carried him far in advance of his comrades.

Captain Kilby was with the company at Warrenton Springs, Second Manassas, Harper's Ferry and Sharpsburg, and on the 2d of October, 1862, was appointed a Surgeon in the army and assigned to the 3d Georgia Regiment. Lieutenant Crocker then became Captain. On the 13th of August Corporal John C. Niemeyer and Private John Vermillion of Company K were elected Second and Third Lieutenants in Company I, and upon the promotion of Lieutenant Crocker to Captain they were advanced to First and Second Lieutenants respectively.

Captain Crocker was a steady soldier, something on the order of the Roman sentinel at Herculaneum, who stood at his post while the burning ashes were falling all around him and finally entombed him. He was a Norfolk county farmer at the beginning of the war, without any experience in military tactics, but as kind hearted as a woman, as brave as a lion and as steady as a stone wall. His men loved him like a father, and were fond of getting off practical jokes at his expense. On one occasion, in the midst of a battle, one of his men, knowing his total unacquaintance with military matters, and to see what he would say, exclaimed, "Captain! I have blown the tube out of my gun." "Well, blow it back again," replied the Captain. A little later another of his men sang out, "Captain, they are cross firing at us." "Well, cross fire back at them," came back his reply.

At the battle of Gettysburg the company was in the charge of Pickett's Division, and paid a heavy toll for the gallantry it displayed and the fame it won on that occasion. It carried thirty-eight men in the charge, of whom three were killed, thirteen wounded and eleven captured. Some of those captured were wounded also. Lieutenant Neimeyer and Privates Mills Brinkley and Jesse Norfleet were killed. Captain Crocker was captured and Lieutenant Vermillion was wounded and captured. Color Sergeant Joshua Grimes was severely wounded while carrying the flag, but recovered, and on the 17th of August, 1864, was appointed Ensign of the regiment with the rank of Third Lieutenant. He was again wounded at Drury's Bluff May 16th, 1864, this making the third time the bullets from the enemy made a lodgement in his body. Frank M. Arthur, who was captured at Gettysburg, was elected Second Lieutenant while in prison, and was subsequently exchanged and commanded the company until the battle of Five Forks, on the 1st of April, 1865, when he again fell into the hands of the enemy. During the interval between the battle of Gettysburg and the following spring the company was without any commissioned officer, and Orderly Sergeant McKemmy Lewis was in command, but in the spring of 1864 Lieutenant W. T. R. Bell of Accomac county was sent from Camp Lee to take charge of it, and remained until the return of Lieutenant Arthur from prison.

Captain Crocker and Lieutenant Vermillion were not exchanged but were kept in prison until the close of the war. Captain Crocker was one of the Confederate officers who were sent to Morris Island in Charleston harbor by the United States authorities and placed under the fire of the Confederate batteries. The reason they assigned for this proceeding was that there were some Federal officers confined in the city of Charleston who were exposed to the fire of their guns which were aimed at that city.

Just before the battle of Gettysburg Private Mills Brinkley had one of those mysterious presentments or premonitions of approaching death. While the regiment was passing up Cemetery Hill, in the charge of Pickett's Division, he turned to Lieutenant Niemeyer, who, with Lieutenant Vermillion, was at his post in rear of the line, and told him he felt as if he were going to be killed, and asked permission to leave the ranks. Lieutenant Niemeyer refused his request and ordered him to take his place in the line. Lieutenant Vermillion joined in his request. He reminded Lieutenant Niemeyer that Brinkley had always proved himself a brave and good soldier, but Lieutenant Niemeyer again refused and Brinkley resumed his position in the ranks. He had hardly taken twenty steps further in advance when a piece of shell struck him in the forehead, killing him instantly. In a very few minutes afterwards Lieutenant Niemeyer was himself killed.

The following members of the company participated in the charge of Pickett's Division at Gettysburg. Several who received slight wounds did not report to the hospital and are not recorded as having been wounded.

Captain J. O. Crocker, captured.
First Lieutenant John C. Niemeyer, killed.
Second Lieutenant John Vermillion, wounded and captured.
Sergeant McKemmie Lewis, wounded.
Color Sergeant Joshua Grimes, wounded.

PRIVATES.

Arthur, Frank M., captured,
Barnes, Belson, wounded,
Bidgood, W. D., captured,
Brinkley, Mills, killed,
Brinkley, Granville, captured,
Brinkley, Daniel,
Carney, Richard, wounded,
Capps, Josiah, wounded and captured,
Gomer, John D.,
Gwynn, George W., wounded,
Harrell, Reuben, captured,
Herring, R. H.,
Humphlet, J. T., wounded,

Jones, Nathan E. K., wounded
and captured.
Jordan, John L., wounded.
Lassiter, Richard, .
Norfleet, Jesse, killed.
Parker, William J..
Richardson, George Clay.
Raby, Thomas, captured.
Riddick, Amos, captured.
Stringer, John E..
Skeeter, William J.,
Small, Benjamin, wounded,
Stallings, J. Van,
Taylor, Benjamin, captured,
Taylor, Williamson B.,
Vann, William H., wounded,
Wilkins, Henry,
Walton, Henry, wounded,
Wilkins, George.

Below will be found the roster of the company. Those marked with a star were from Nansemond county.

Captain John T. Kilby, appointed Surgeon C. S. Army October 2d, 1862.
Captain J. O. B. Crocker, promoted Captain October 2d, 1862, captured July 3d, 1863, at Gettysburg and not exchanged.
*Second Lieutenant William S. Wright, resigned 1862, enlisted in Company K, wounded June 1st, 1862, at Seven Pines, promoted Adjutant 61st Virginia, died in fall of 1863.
Second Lieutenant Cornelius M. Dozier, killed July 1st, 1862, at Malvern Hill.
First Lieutenant John C. Niemeyer, killed July 3d, 1863, at Gettysburg.
First Lieutenant John Vermillion, wounded and captured July 3d, 1863, Gettysburg, and not exchanged
*Second Lieutenant Frank M Arthur, captured at Gettysburg, exchanged and captured April 1st, 1865, at Five Forks.
*First Sergeant John H. Wright, promoted Captain Company H, 61st Virginia Regiment.
First Sergeant McKemmy Lewis, promoted First Sergeant April, 1862, wounded July 3d, 1863, Gettysburg, and captured April 1st, 1865, at Five Forks.
*Sergeant Charles Badger, died in hospital October 4th, 1862, Richmond.
Sergeant Keely Harrison, transferred March 27th, 1862, to Company C, 13th Virginia Cavalry.
Sergeant Henry B. Lewer, wounded July 1st, 1862, Malvern Hill, died July 22d, Richmond.
Sergeant Joseph Prentis, killed July 1st, 1862, Malvern Hill.
Sergeant Joshua M. Grimes, promoted Ensign, wounded July 1st, 1862, Malvern Hill, July 3d, 1863, Gettysburg, May 16th, 1864, Drury's Bluff.
*Sergeant William H. Vann, captured at Five Forks April 1st, 1865.
Sergeant T. J. Grimes, wounded.
Corporal Henry Walton, wounded July 1st, 1862, Malvern Hill, and July 3d, 1863, at Gettysburg, promoted Color Corporal.
Corporal Willis D. Bidgood, captured July 3d, 1863, Gettysburg, and April 1st, 1865, at Five Forks.
Corporal Lucillicus D. Jones, killed July 1st, 1862, at Malvern Hill.
Corporal Belson Barnes, wounded July 3d, 1863, at Gettysburg, and captured at Five Forks April 1st, 1865.

PRIVATES.

Barnes, George.
Barnes, J. E., detailed in Division Provost Guard.
Bidgood, Nathaniel, furnished substitute 1862 and discharged.
*Bidgood, J. C., furnished substitute 1862 and discharged.
Bidgood, J. H., discharged September 13th, 1862, for disability.
Bidgood, Tully W., absent, sick in hospital.
*Bain, John T., wounded July 1st, 1862, Malvern Hill, died August 6th in hospital Richmond.

*Brinkley, Mills, killed July 3d, 1863, at Gettysburg.
*Brinkley, Granville, captured July 3d, 1863, at Gettysburg.
*Brinkley, Daniel.
*Brinkley, Mallory, died in hospital April 1st, 1862, Pinner's Point.
Bunting, William H., transferred to Navy January 11th, 1862.
Bunting, Lloyd, transferred to Company C, 13th Virginia Cavalry.
Bunting, Francis H., died in hospital March 27th, 1862, Pinner's Point.
Burley, William, killed 1864, Howlett House.
Busby, William A., wounded April 13th, 1863, at Suffolk.
*Crocker, W. H., captured September, 1862, died in Fort Delaware.
Carney, Richard, wounded August 28th, 1862, Warrenton Springs, and July 3d, 1863, at Gettysburg.
*Cox, William, died in hospital July 5th, 1862, Richmond.
Capps, A. J., transferred to Company C, 13th Virginia Cavalry.
Capps, Josiah, captured July 3d, 1863, Gettysburg, died at Point Lookout.
Dennis, Samuel, transferred March 27th, 1862, to Company C, 13th Virginia Cavalry.
Duncan, Blanch, surrendered at Appomattox.
Duncan, John, captured at Five Forks.
Duncan, Richard, captured at Five Forks.
*Dean, Edward G., discharged 1863 for disability.
Daughtrey, William, died March 27th, 1862, in camp, Pinner's Point.
Duke, Henry, transferred March 27th, 1862, to Company C, 13th Virginia Cavalry.
*Duke, Nathaniel, wounded July 1st, 1862, at Malvern Hill, and disabled.
Duke, Lewis.
Evans, Charles, died in hospital 1864.
Field, Richard.
Gwynn, George W., wounded July 3d, 1863, at Gettysburg.
*Gomer, John D., died in hospital 1864, Richmond.
*Greene, Jesse, died in hospital November 28th, 1862, Richmond.
George, J. W., supposed to have been killed 1865.
Gurley, J., died in hospital 1864, Richmond.
*Harrell, Elkana.
*Harrell, Abram, discharged in 1863 for disability.
Harrell, Edward.
*Harrell, Josiah, died in hospital in 1862, Richmond.
*Harrell, Reuben, captured July 3d, 1863, at Gettysburg and died in prison.
*Harrell, Henry, died in hospital in camp June, 1862, York River railroad.
*Herring, R. H., captured April 1st, 1865, at Five Forks.
Henry, William C., transferred to Navy January 18th, 1862.
*Humphlet, Jno. T., promoted Color Sergeant, wounded July 3d, 1863, at Gettysburg.
Johnson, Thos., died in hospital in 1863, Richmond.
Jones, Nathan E. K., wounded and captured July 3d, 1863, at Gettysburg.
*Jones, Jas. G., died in hospital November 28th, 1862, Charlottesville.
Jordan, John L., wounded July 3d, 1863, at Gettysburg, and captured April 1st, 1865, at Five Forks.
Johnigan, Richard.
Keeter, W. W., died in hospital November 20th, 1862, Staunton.
King, James.
King, Thomas.
Lewis, William, detailed cook.
Litchfield, Jacob, detailed cook.
Lewis, Ambrose, died in hospital June 22d, 1862, Richmond.
Lassiter, John, wounded August 28th, 1862, at Warrenton Springs, and died November 25th at Richmond.
*Lassiter, Richard, wounded July 1st, 1862, Malvern Hill, wounded at Suffolk, April 13th, 1863, and captured at Five Forks.
*Norfleet, Jesse, killed July 3d, 1863, at Gettysburg.
Parker, Thomas, killed July 1st, 1863, at Malvern Hill.

Parker, W. J., captured April 1st, 1865, at Five Forks.
*Parker, Jesse, captured April 1st, 1865, at Five Forks.
Ruthledge, Anthony, died in hospital 1865, Richmond.
Richardson, Geo. Clay, captured April 1st, 1865, at Five Forks.
*Rudd, Augustus S., died in hospital June 18th, 1862.
*Riddick, Mills, wounded April 13th, 1863, at Suffolk, disabled and detailed in passport office, Petersburg.
*Riddick, Amos, captured July 3d, 1863, at Gettysburg.
*Ruby, Thos., captured July 3d, 1863; at Gettysburg.
*Stallings, J. Van, captured April 1st, 1865, at Five Forks.
Savage, William, captured April 1st, 1865, at Five Forks.
Spivey, Jethro, transferred March 27th, 1862, to Company C, 13th Virginia Cavalry.
Sawyer, Albert.
Skeeter, W. J., surrendered April 9th, 1865, at Appomattox.
Small, Benjamin.
Savage, Mike L., died in hospital 1862, Pinner's Point.
Spaulding, John A.,
*Stringer, John E.,
Taylor, Benj., captured July 3d, 1863, at Gettysburg.
Taylor, Williamson B., captured April 1st, 1865, at Five Forks.
*Vann, Alfred, wounded April 13th, 1863, at Suffolk, and died in hospital.
Wagner, James, detailed as Ordnance Sergeant.
*Wilkins, Henry.
*Wilkins, George.
Wilson, A. J., transferred February 1st, 1862, to Company C, 13th Virginia Cavalry.
*Wright, Jos. S., transferred April 30th, 1862, to Signal Corps.
*Wright, J. Edwin, transferred April 30th, 1862, to Signal Corps.
    Killed and died—34.

CHAPTER XI.

THE OLD DOMINION GUARD, COMPANY K, NINTH VIRGINIA INFANTRY.

This company was organized in Portsmouth June 26th, 1856, and soon became one of the largest and most popular companies in Virginia. Even before the war it was nothing unusual for it to parade with from eighty to ninety men, and at the celebration of the 250th anniversary of the settlement of Jamestown, which took place on that historic island in 1857, and which drew together the military companies of the entire State, the Old Dominion Guard was the largest company on the grounds. The first Captain of the company was Captain John W. Young, who was succeeded by Captain Edward Kearns.

At the beginning of the late war the Old Dominion Guard was one of the companies in the 3d Virginia Regiment, and on the 20th of April, 1861, it was ordered into active service by Governor Letcher, and remained in the field until the close of the war.

On the night of the 20th the men were quartered in the Court House, and at daybreak on the 21st part of them were marched to the Navy Yard, with other troops, to take possession and guard property there, and the remainder were marched to the Naval Hospital point to build an earthwork to prevent the return of the United States vessels Pawnee and Cumberland, which had left the Navy Yard about 1 o'clock that morning. Subsequently the whole company went on duty at the Hospital point and remained there about a week, when it was detached from the 3d Regiment and ordered to Pinner's Point, just below the Hospital point, where they were shortly afterwards joined by the Craney Island Artillery under Captain John T. Kilby, one of the companies organized in Norfolk county and subsequently attached to the 9th Virginia Regiment as Company I. Here a strong earthwork containing twelve guns, six and eight-inch Dahlgrens, was built under the supervision of Major F. W. Jett of the Engineer Corps, and later another earthwork, containing four six-inch rifle guns, was thrown up nearer the point. In June, 1861, the 9th Virginia Regiment was organized and the Old Dominion Guard was attached to it as Company K. The post at Pinner's Point was under command of Lieutenant George Harrison of the Navy, who held the brevet rank of Major, and who was assigned to that duty on account of his previous experience in the use of heavy guns. The younger members of the company soon learned Major Harrison's weak points, and he was the victim of many a practical joke.

When the company was mustered into service on the 20th of April the following were the officers:
Captain—Edward Kearns.
First Lieutenant—Dennis Vermillion.
Second Lieutenant—L. A. Bilisoly.
And shortly afterwards, while in camp at the Hospital point, Sergeant Henry A. Allen was elected Third Lieutenant.

Camp life at Pinner's Point was not very exciting, and the main drawbacks were extra guard duty or temporary confinement in the guard house for going to town without leave of absence, restrictions which the young soldiers regarded as extremely onerous and unnecessary. While there the company lost one of its members. Young Jacob W. Keeling died from pneumonia. He came from Suffolk, originally, and his remains were taken there for interment. A detachment from the company escorted the body to the Norfolk and Petersburg Railroad depot in Norfolk.

During the summer and fall the company occupied tents, but when cold weather set in, timber was sent to the camp and the company built very comfortable quarters. They were the best military quarters in the harbor, and, considering the fact that very few of the men had ever had any previous experience in that kind of work, they were marvels of comfort and convenience.

While there the company enjoyed excellent health, and, on one occasion of inspection, while occupying the tents, there were one hundred and five men in line for duty. During the fall of the year, the season of chills and fevers, it was noticed that, while very few of the members of the Old Dominion Guard, a company raised exclusively in the city, were affected, Company I, which was on duty with them, and which was composed of men who were raised in the country, and nearly all of whom were used to hard work, had so many men on the sick list that Company K had to perform a part of their guard duty. This fact seems to bear out the theory that men raised in the cities can stand exposure better than those raised in the country.

While at Pinner's Point the gallant Captain Kearns made his first great and only attempt at oratory. The ladies of Portsmouth made a very handsome silk flag for the Old Dominion Guard and selected Miss Virginia Handy, daughter of Rev. I. W. K. Handy, of the Presbyterian Church, to make the presentation. The company was drawn up in line in a shady grove near the camp and a large number of ladies and other friends of the company were present. Miss Handy, in very appropriate and touching language, placed the handsome banner in the hands of Captain Kearns, "whose modesty was only excelled by his bravery." Captain Kearns began his response, and it was his first effort. He said: "Miss Handy and Ladies of Portsmouth! On behalf of the Old Dominion Guard, I accept this magnificent flag, which will be our guide in the front of battle, and, if I falter!" Here he forgot the rest of his carefully prepared speech, but he repeated, "If I falter!!" but memory would not come to his aid, and, after a lengthened pause, drawing his sword hastily from its scabbard and flashing it in the air, he exclaimed: "If I falter! I hope Christ may kill me!!"

A roar of applause and laughter greeted this abrupt and unexpected termination of the oration.

When the company left Portsmouth with the regiment and the Confederate battle flags were substituted for the State flags, this flag was left in Petersburg for safe keeping and disappeared in some way or other. The company never knew what became of it.

Nearly half of the members of the Old Dominion Guard were young men under the age of twenty-one years and were full of life and enjoyment. On one occasion the Hospital steward, who was not averse to an occasional dip into "something strong," returned to camp from the city with a demijohn of sherry wine in his wagon, and stopping in front of the guard house, left it in the wagon and went into the building occupied by the officers as quarters and in which he kept his drugs. The sentry at the guard house reported the condition of affairs to the company's quarters, and in a very few minutes three of the boys appeared upon the scene with two buckets, one empty and the other full of water, and in less time than it would take to tell it the wine was transferred to the empty bucket and the demijohn was filled with water. Shortly after the embryo doctor came out for his "jug," carried it in the house and the officers were invited to partake. Their smiles were "childlike and bland" when they saw the proportions of the demijohn, but upon tasting its contents they classed the luckless apothecary as a "heathen Chinee." He protested, however, that it was wine when he left town. That night No. 6 and No. 9 messes, with their invited guests, enjoyed a wine supper with hardtack accompaniment.

One night in the winter of 1861-2, a little after dark, the sentinel on duty at the battery heard cries of distress and for help coming from down the river. A gale of wind was blowing from the north, which brought the sound directly to the battery. The officer of the guard was called and the camp was aroused, and notwithstanding the heavy gale which was blowing, two frail skiffs were speedily manned by strong and brave men from both Company I and Company K and pushed forth in the teeth of the storm to rescue the drowning men. It was a severe struggle, but the brave hearts and strong arms of the oarsmen prevailed and two men who were found clinging to the piles which had been driven across the river near Lambert's Point by the

Confederates to obstruct the channel, were brought back nearly dead from cold and exposure. They were members of Company D, 9th Virginia Infantry (the Jackson Artillery of Portsmouth), and were stationed on Craney Island. They were returning from Portsmouth in a sailboat to their camp, but the boat was upset by the storm, near the obstructions. They managed to catch hold of the piles, but a third man who was with them in the boat, Walter Harvey, of Portsmouth, of the same company, was drowned. The rescue of those drowning men was as daring an act as was performed during the war. A terrible storm was raging, the waves were high and the cold spray was frozen upon the oarsmen as it was dashed over them in their frail skiffs. Unfortunately no record was kept of the names of the brave rescuers, and they are therefore lost to history. The men who were saved were Leonard Cutherell and William Day.

In April, 1862, one year after the original enlistment of the men, they re-enlisted in a body for the war and held an election of officers, with the following result:

Captain—Dennis Vermillion.
First Lieutenant—Edward Kearns.
Second Lieutenant—Henry A. Allen.
Third Lieutenant—L. A. Bilisoly.

Captain Kearns declined to accept the 1st Lieutenantcy and resigned, at the same time severing his connection with the company of which he had been Captain almost from its organization in 1856.

On the 10th of May the company received orders to burn their quarters and march with the rest of Huger's Division to the defence of Richmond, and of the one hundred and sixteen men who had been with the company during its stay at Pinner's Point, though they were leaving behind them their homes, mothers, sisters and sweethearts, soon to fall into the hands of the enemy, not one remained behind. The refusal of Captain Kearns to accept the 1st Lieutenantcy occasioned the promotion of 2d Lieutenant Allen to 1st Lieutenant, 3d Lieutenant Bilisoly to 2d, and Orderly Sergeant Robert M. Butler was elected 3d Lieutenant. The company was united with the rest of the 9th Regiment at Dunn's Hill, near Petersburg, on the 12th of May, and its identity as a separate organization was lost in that of the regiment. Its history then became the history of the regiment. It participated in all the battles in which the regiment was engaged except the battle of Drury's Bluff, May 16th, 1864, which took place while Company K and also Company I were temporarily detached from the regiment on other duty, and while so detached was moved to the north side of Richmond to resist the advance of Sheridan's cavalry raiders.

Lieutenant Butler resigned after the battle of Seven Pines,

June 1st, 1862; Captain Vermillion was killed at the battle of Malvern Hill July 1st, 1862; Lieutenant Bilisoly was wounded at Seven Pines June 1st, 1862, and again wounded and disabled from further service at Second Manassas August 30th, 1862, and retired. Lieutenant Allen was promoted to Captain upon the death of Captain Vermillion, and was captured at the stone wall in the charge of Pickett's Division at Gettysburg July 3d, 1863, and was kept a prisoner until the close of the war. He was one of the Confederate officers who were taken to Morris' Island, South Carolina, by the United States authorities and placed under the fire of the Confederate batteries defending Charleston harbor. He was not wounded during the war.

While the regiment was on the march with Longstreet's Corps towards Suffolk in the spring of 1863 Henry C. Hudgins was elected 1st Lieutenant and James H. Robinson 2d Lieutenant. Lieutenant Hudgins was wounded early in the charge of Pickett's Division at Gettysburg, but recovered from his wound and commanded the company till the close of the war. Lieutenant Robinson was severely wounded and captured at Gettysburg, was subsequently exchanged, recovered from his wound, and was with the company in the closing scenes of the drama, which culminated at Appomattox Court House. The following members of the company were in the charge at Gettysburg:

Captain Henry A. Allen, captured.
First Lieutenant Henry C. Hudgins, wounded.
Second Lieutenant James H. Robinson, wounded and captured.
First Sergeant James H. Walker, captured.
Second Sergeant Adolph Bilisoly, wounded.
Third Sergeant Thomas J. Dashiell, captured.
Fourth Sergeant William Wallace Williams, captured.
Third Corporal R. B. James, wounded.

PRIVATES.

E. E. Bilisoly, wounded,
E. K. Brooks, captured,
Thos. R. Borland, wounded,
Geo. W. Barnes, wounded,
J. C. A. Davis, wounded,
John A. F. Dunderdale, killed,
Robt. T. Daughtrey, captured,
Wm. Walter Dyson,
Andrew C. Host, wounded,
Joseph W. Jordan, wounded and captured,
Edward B. Williams, wounded.

Thus of the nineteen men who went into the fight eighteen were either killed, wounded or captured. The company lost heavily in the battles of Seven Pines, Malvern Hill and Five Forks. In this last battle the 9th Regiment bore the brunt of the flank attack of Warren's corps of General Grant's army. George W. Barnes, of Company K, carried the colors of the regiment in that engagement.

Below will be found a roll of the company to May, 1862, embracing the Portsmouth men. Later in the war a number of conscripts were sent to it, but as they were from other portions of the State, their names are omitted.

Captain Edward Kearns, resigned 1862.
Captain Dennis Vermillion, killed Malvern Hill July 1st, 1862.
First Lieutenant L. Augustus Bilisoly, wounded at Seven Pines June 1st and Second Manassas August 30th, 1862, and retired.
Captain Henry A. Allen, captured at Gettysburg July 3d, 1863, and not exchanged.
Third Lieutenant Robert M. Butler, resigned 1862.
First Lieutenant Henry C. Hudgins, wounded July 3d, 1863, at Gettysburg.
Second Lieutenant James H. Robinson, wounded July 3d, 1863, at Gettysburg.
Bilisoly, A. L., promoted 1st Lieutenant P. A. C. S.
Brown, Samuel Y., Sergeant, appointed hospital steward.
Benson, F. R., transferred to Signal Corps April, 1862.
Benson, F. L., Commissary Sergeant, appointed hospital steward.
Bilisoly, Adolphus, promoted Sergeant, wounded July 3d, 1863, at Gettysburg.
Bilisoly, P. B., wounded April 1st, 1865, Five Forks.
Bilisoly, Joseph L., detailed as Sergeant Major July, 1863, appointed hospital steward February, 1864.
Bilisoly, J. J., promoted Lieutenant Company D, 61st Virginia.
Brown, James W., transferred to Norfolk Light Artillery Blues May, 1862.
Bilisoly, E. E., wounded July 3d, 1863, at Gettysburg.
Brown, Joe Sam, transferred to Norfolk Light Artillery Blues May, 1862.
Brooks, E. K.
Brooks, Tudor F., discharged physical disability 1862, and employed in Commissary Department.
Blamire, E. B.
Borland, Thomas R., wounded slightly July 3d, 1863, at Gettysburg.
Bennett, John C., killed at Malvern Hill July 1st, 1862.
Barnes, George W., wounded July 3d, 1863, at Gettysburg.
Becks, G. W., discharged 1862, under age.
Butler, George W.
Butt, Josiah, discharged 1861, physical disability.
Bennett, William M.
Cutherell, George A., wounded at Suffolk April 13th, 1863, and discharged.
Collins, A. E.
Crocker, James F., promoted Adjutant 9th Virginia Regiment, wounded July 1st, 1862, Malvern Hill.
Cocke, John N.
Cocke, William H., appointed Assistant Surgeon 14th Virginia and mortally wounded April, 1865.
Cassell, Charles E., promoted 1st Lieutenant Topographical Engineers.
Crismond, James P., detached for naval service 1861.
Collins, William B., promoted Ordnance Sergeant.
Crockmur, Charles J., appointed Paymaster's Clerk in Navy, 1862.
Cherry, Eugene.
Dyson, W. Walter.
Dent, William, detached 1861.
Dashiell, Thomas J., slightly wounded at Five Forks, promoted Sergeant.
Daughtrey, Robert T.
Davis, J. C. A., wounded July 3d, 1863, at Gettysburg.
Dunderdale, J. A. F., killed at Gettysburg July 3d, 1863.
Foreman, William N., wounded at Five Forks April 1st, 1865.
Foster, Frank S., transferred to Signal Corps April, 1862.
Foster, A. R., transferred to Signal Corps April, 1862, and died in hospital 1864.
Forbes, Thomas N., died 1862, wounded Seven Pines June 1st, 1862.

Fiske, Melzar G., killed at Malvern Hill July 1st, 1862.
Gray, J. N. (Sergeant), discharged June, 1861, physical disability.
Godwin, Leroy C., transferred to Signal Corps April, 1862.
Grant, L. H., drummer.
Guthrie, Benjamin W., appointed Master in Navy.
Griffin, Cornelius.
Hambleton, William H., killed at Warrenton Springs August 28th, 1862.
Handy, S. O., died June 10th, 1862, in hospital, Richmond.
Hargroves, W. W., transferred to a North Carolina regiment.
Host, Andrew C., wounded July 3d, 1863, at Gettysburg.
Hudgins, J. Madison, promoted to Captain and A. C. S.
Hume, R. G., transferred to Norfolk Light Artillery Blues May, 1862.
Hobday, A. T., transferred to Commissary Department.
James, R. B., wounded July 3d, 1863, at Gettysburg.
Jordan, O. D., discharged July 1st, 1861, disability.
Jack, E. A., appointed Engineer in Navy.
Jordan, Joseph W., died of wounds received at Gettysburg, 1863.
Kilby, W. T., transferred to Norfolk Light Artillery Blues May, 1862.
Keeling, Joseph W., died in hospital 1861.
King, Leslie R., appointed Engineer in Navy.
Lewis, Jacob, detailed for hospital duty, over age.
Langhorne, John C., appointed Captain's Clerk in Navy.
Langhorne, William S., discharged, under age, September, 1862, and enlisted in Signal Corps.
Moore, Joseph P., transferred to Norfolk Light Artillery Blues May, 1862.
Myers, Robert W., discharged, physical disability, and died.
Morris, Charles S., slight wound at Five Forks April 1st, 1865.
Neaville, William A., wounded and disabled at Seven Pines June 1st, 1862.
Niemeyer, John C., promoted 1st Lieutenant Company I, 9th Virginia, and killed at Gettysburg July 3d, 1863.
Niemeyer, Henry V., discharged, under age, September, 1862, and enlisted in Signal Corps.
Owens, Charles.
Parrish, James H., promoted Surgeon C. S. A., Chambliss' Brigade.
Parker, Willis M.
Pierce, Thomas W., appointed Major and Quartermaster.
Pierce, William H., killed on picket June, 1862, near Richmond.
Porter, John W. H., transferred to Signal Corps April, 1862.
Richardson, John H., transferred to Signal Corps April, 1862.
Rodman, Robert C.
Richardson, N. F., transferred to Signal Corps April, 1862.
Richardson, Charles E., transferred to North Carolina regiment.
Reid, Charles, transferred to Signal Corps April, 1862.
Riddick, James W., promoted Captain and Adjutant General Scales' North Carolina Brigade and severely wounded.
Rudd, Benjamin F., transferred to Signal Corps April, 1862.
Smith, William A., died 1862.
Smith, William Alfred, transferred to Signal Corps April, 1862.
Smith, John, discharged 1862, over age.
Smith, Herbert L., transferred to Company I, 15th Virginia Cavalry.
Smith, Arthur, transferred to Company I, 15th Virginia Cavalry.
Savage, T. J., transferred to Signal Corps April, 1862.
Turner, G. M., discharged June, 1861, disability.
Tabb, William H., promoted Sergeant Major 3d Regiment and detailed 1862 to work in Navy Yard.
Vermillion, John, promoted 2d Lieutenant Company I, 9th Virginia, wounded at Gettysburg.
Vermillion, Alex. P.
Vermillion, G. S., discharged September, 1862, under age, and enlisted in Signal Corps.
White, Thomas J., transferred to Signal Corps April, 1862.

White, Frank J., promoted Surgeon C. S. A.
Walker, James H., promoted to 1st Sergeant.
Wingfield, R. C. M., transferred to Norfolk Light Artillery Blues May, 1862.
Williams, David A., wounded and disabled at Seven Pines June 1st, 1862.
Williams, David E., captured at Five Forks April 1st, 1865.
Woodley, Joseph R., promoted Lieutenant in Signal Corps April, 1862.
Williams, Luther, wounded and disabled at Seven Pines June 1st, 1862.
Williams, W. Wallace, promoted to Sergeant.
Williams, Ed. B., wounded July 3d, 1863, Gettysburg.
Williams, A. J., appointed hospital steward.
Williams, Thomas H.
Wilson, William H.
Wright, William S., wounded at Seven Pines, promoted Adjutant 61st Virginia and died 1863.
Williamson, Lewis W., appointed hospital steward.
Young, M. P., appointed Engineer in Navy.
Young, C. W., transferred to Signal Corps April, 1862.
   Killed and died—16.

CHAPTER XII.

THE NINTH VIRGINIA REGIMENT ARMISTEAD'S, BARTON'S, STEWART'S BRIGADE—HUGER'S, ANDERSON'S, PICKETT'S DIVISIONS.

We have traced the histories of Companies D, G and K, of Portsmouth, and Company I, of Norfolk county, from the beginning of the war until they lost their identity in the organization of the 9th Virginia Regiment of Infantry, and as their subsequent record is embraced in that of the regiment, it can be told best by recording the movements and battles in which the regiment was engaged. The actual date of the formation of the regiment has been lost for the reason that the field officers were not originally elected by the company officers, but were assigned to it by Governor Letcher while the companies were stationed in different localities, but the companies were assigned to it some time in June, 1861, and were as follows:

Company A, the McRea Rifles, of Petersburg, Captain James Gilliam.

Company B, the Baltimore Artillery, of Baltimore, Capt. John D. Myrick.

Company C, the Chesterfield Yellow Jackets, of Chesterfield county, Capt. John Mason.

Company D, the Virginia Artillery, of Portsmouth, Captain Wm. J. Richardson.

Company E, the Isle of Wight Blues, of Isle of Wight county, Capt. John Shevers.

Company F, Chuckatuck Light Artillery, of Nansemond county, Capt. James J. Phillips.

Company G, the Portsmouth Rifles, of Portsmouth, Captain John C. Owens.

Company H, the Salem Artillery, of Salem, Captain Happ.

Company I, the Craney Island Artillery, of Norfolk county, Capt. J. T. Kilby.

Company K, the Old Dominion Guard, of Portsmouth, Capt. Edward Kearns.

At the time of the formation of the regiment in June, 1861, the companies composing it were distributed among the various fortifications around the harbor of Portsmouth and Norfolk, doing duty as heavy artillerists as well as infantry. Companies A, B, C, D and H were on Craney Island, where the regimental headquarters were located. Companies E and F were at Day's Point, Company G was at Pig Point and Companies I and K were at Pinner's Point. The officers of the regiment who were assigned to it by Governor Letcher, were Colonel Francis H.

Smith, Lieutenant-Colonel John T. L. Preston, Major Stapleton Crutchfield, Adjutant Thomas Smith. All of these officers were attached to the faculty of the Virginia Military Institute, and before the evacuation of Portsmouth by the Confederates, Colonel Smith and Lieutenant-Colonel Preston were returned to their duties at that institution, and Major Crutchfield was elected Major of the 58th Virginia Regiment. After their departure, Lieutenant-Colonel DeLagnel, of the regular army, commanded the post at Craney Island until the 10th of May, 1862, when it was evacuated, and Major Harden seems to have been in immediate command of the 9th Regiment until it assembled at Petersburg on the 12th.

Upon the receipt of orders to evacuate their batteries, the scattered companies of the regiment marched by different roads to Suffolk, and from there were carried by rail to Petersburg and quartered on Dunn's hill to the north of that city, across the Appomattox river, and, on the 21st, orders were received for the company officers to elect field officers. The election was held the following day, and the officers elected were: Colonel, Johnston DeLagnel; Lieutenant Colonel, D. J. Godwin; Major, James Gilliam.

Colonel DeLagnel having been appointed to a position which was more satisfactory to him, declined to accept the command of the 9th, and Lieutenant-Colonel Godwin was promoted to Colonel, Major Gilliam to Lieutenant Colonel, and Captain John C. Owens, of the Portsmouth Rifles, was elected Major; Private J. F. Crocker, of Company K, was appointed Adjutant, and Private C. T. Phillips, of Company G, Sergeant Major; hence all of the field and staff officers, except the Lieutenant Colonel, were from Portsmouth.

On the 24th of May, Companies A, D and H were detached from the regiment and sent to man batteries in the fortifications of Richmond. Company D was ordered back after the battle of Malvern Hill, Company A rejoined in the fall of 1864 on the lines in front of Bermuda Hundreds, but Company H was not with the regiment again. It was given a battery of field guns and thus was turned from an Infantry to a Light Artillery Company. Company I, also, was absent on other duty at the battle of Seven Pines. The other companies of the regiment remained in camp on Dunn's hill until the 29th, when, with three days' rations, the command was marched at 7 a. m. to the depot in Petersburg to take the cars for Richmond, but remained at the depot until 6 p. m. before the cars were ready for them; and after getting on the cars they were four hours making the twenty-two miles to that city. That night the men made their beds on the grass in the capitol square, and the next morning at 7 o'clock marched to Blakely's farm in Henrico county. The regiment was there assigned to Armistead's Brigade, Huger's Division, composed of the 9th, 14th and 53d Virginia Regiments, and the 5th Virginia Battalion, and began in reality the life of a soldier. Up to that time the men had been sheltered in tents or comfortable quarters, and their first night in the field was passed amid a terrible down-pour of rain, without shelter of any kind.

On the 31st of May the regiment received orders to march to Seven Pines with the brigade, and at night slept in a camp of the enemy from which they had been driven during the battle of that day. The Federal dead and wounded lay thick all around them, and the boys enjoyed the lemons, sugar and other delicacies which they found in the deserted camp.

The next day, June 1st, proved the unfitness of the commander of that part of the Confederate army for the position he occupied. At 7 a. m. the 9th Regiment moved forward, under orders, about three hundred yards in advance of their camp of the night before, without pickets or skirmishers in front, and were told not to fire, that Pryor's Brigade was in front of them. The line was halted in a thick, swampy woods and the order was given to stack arms. The men were in fancied security, their guns not loaded, and, while obeying the order to stack, a line of battle of the enemy, occupying a position in their front, poured a volley of musketry into them at close range. The surprise was complete, but the men fell down upon the ground and began to load and fire in return. The left of the line, however, did the most sensible thing they could do, namely, fell back out of range of the fire, and as this exposed the flank of the 9th Regiment, that fell back also. It was evident that the Confederate commander in that part of the field did not know either the positions of his own troops or of the enemy, though there had been fighting all the day before, and that the lives of the men would be sacrificed without any special object in view or plan to be carried out. General Armistead afterwards did what he could to repair the mishap. He seized a Virginia state flag, and, having rallied the men in his brigade, led them forward again to the position from which they had retired, better prepared to do battle. While they were thus engaging the enemy, the 3d Alabama Regiment passed through them and charged the enemy's works, but the position was too strong to be carried by a direct assault and the Alabamians were repulsed with heavy loss, among the killed being their commander, Colonel Lomax, who was left dead upon the field. The 9th Virginia then fell back about a hundred yards out of range of the fire, and the enemy made no attempt to follow. Later in the afternoon the 9th was ordered to rejoin the brigade, and thus ended its connection with this unfortunate affair in which many brave men lost their lives without accomplishing anything thereby, and from which great results might have followed, had the movements of the division been wisely directed; but as it was even the simplest ordinary means were neglected to ascertain the position and strength of the enemy. The men in the ranks could plainly see that the battle was being fought on that portion of the field without any special plan or purpose, and were not, therefore, buoyed up by that confidence which inspires a soldier when he feels that his movements are being directed by wisdom, even though his life is being risked for success.

Colonel Godwin's horse was wounded by a minie ball in the battle of Seven Pines and bruised the Colonel's leg quite painfully by running against a tree. Colonel Godwin left the field in consequence thereof and the command of the regiment devolved upon Lieutenant-Colonel Gilliam; and, as Colonel Godwin was afterwards assigned to other duties and never rejoined the regiment, Lieutenant-Colonel Gilliam became its permanent commander. General Armistead, however, was not friendly towards him and prevented his promotion, so that in 1863 he tendered his resignation and Major Owens became Colonel, Captain James Jasper Phillips was promoted to Lieutenant-Colonel and Captain Wm. J. Richardson was promoted to Major.

During the month of June a number of small engagements took place in front of that portion of the Confederate lines held by Huger's Division. On the 20th Sickles' Brigade advanced beyond their entrenchments, but was driven back by the 1st Louisiana Regiment. On the 21st Sickles' Brigade, reinforced by Meagher's Brigade, attempted to advance their positions but the 1st Louisiana, 4th Georgia and a regiment of North Carolina regulars attacked them and forced them to retire within their original lines. At the same time the 16th Massachusetts, which attempted an advance, was driven back by the 53d Virginia. The 9th Virginia had a severe picket fight with the enemy in its front and on the 25th had another skirmish, in which it captured a number of prisoners. The engagement of the 25th was an extensive affair but the 9th regiment was not heavily engaged in it. On the 21st Armistead's Brigade was reinforced by the addition of the 38th Regiment, which from that time became permanently attached to it, and on the 28th the 57th Virginia also was attached to it.

On the 26th was fought the battle of Mechanicsville, the first of the seven days battles. McClellan's advanced position, his extreme right, was attacked and carried, those of the enemy who escaped fell back upon Gaines' Mill, where General Lee made an attack on the 27th. McClellan had reinforced his troops in that locality. The battle was a complete victory for the Confederates and McClellan began his return to Harrison's landing on the James river, his sole object being to save as much of his army as possible. Being a part of the right wing of General Lee's army, and the battles of Mechanicsville and Gaines' Mill having been fought on the left. Armistead's Brigade was not engaged in either of them and remained in position until the 29th, when it was ordered forward, down the Charles City road, in the direction of the enemy. That day an advance of ten miles was made and the brigade lay all night in line of battle.

On the next day, June 30th, the brigade moved forward at 7 a. m. under orders from General Lee, to intercept McClellan's retreat. The whole division was up, but the march was so slow and the halts so frequent that by 4 o'clock in the afternoon only seven miles had been passed over in the nine hours the troops had been marching, and a halt was made at 4 p. m., when the brigade went into camp for the night, though it lacked three hours of sundown. The brigade had not fired a shot during the day, and during the night McClellan marched his whole army by in safety and fortified the heights of Malvern Hill.

The blundering which had marked his operations on the right wing of the army up to that time continued to mark the counsels of the leaders, and the bravery of the troops could not counteract the mistakes of the generals. The 9th Regiment was aroused about day break on the morning of the 1st of July, arrived on the field in front of Malvern Hill about 1 o'clock p. m., and was kept in line of battle, exposed to the fire of nearly a hundred guns, the heaviest artillery fire of the war, for three hours, and, having stood the storm of shell and other deadly missiles for that length of time without firing a musket in reply, was marched to a ravine on their immediate right and a little in rear of a piece of rising ground from which two rifle guns of Grimes' Battery, of Portsmouth, without any assistance, were trying to silence nearly the whole of the artillery in McClellan's army.

After a short interval of rest, from a half-hour to an hour, the regiment was ordered to charge the enemy's guns and their infantry supports, and the men moved forward on a run, cheering as they went. They rushed over a long flat piece of ground, down a valley, up the opposite hill, down into another depression and up the hill, upon the top of which were a hundred cannon and forty thousand men, firing at them showers of shell, grape, canister and minie balls. It was like sending a small terrier to charge an elephant, and the long list of killed and wounded testify to the bravery of the men and the incompetency of the commander who sent them upon their hopeless errand. The color sergeant of the 9th Regiment was wounded and the flag-staff was shot in two, but Captain Kilby, of Company I, of Norfolk county, picked the flag up and brought it off the field. After its repulse the regiment fell back to the depression in the ground nearest to the enemy's line and, partially sheltered by the rising ground in front, continued the engagement until long after dark, when the battle ended and the troops were re-called from the field. The regiment lost heavily in this battle. Captain Dennis Vermillion and Privates John C. Bennett and Melzar G. Fiske, of the Old Dominion Guard, of Portsmouth, were killed, as were also Sergeant Wm. H. White, of the Portsmouth Rifles, and Lieutenant Cornelius Dozier and Sergeant Joseph Prentis, of Company I, of Norfolk county. Sergeant Prentis was a gallant boy not more than eighteen years of age, and was the son of Mr. Robert Prentiss, who, for a number of years before the war, was Proctor at the University of Virginia. His body was recovered the day after the battle and was found to be nearer the works of the enemy than any other. Sergeant Henry B. Lewer, Corporal Lucillieus Jones and Private Thos. Parker also were killed. Adjutant James F. Crocker was seriously wounded and did not rejoin the regiment until October, 1862. Grimes' Battery distinguished itself at Malvern Hill and made a reputation for gallantry which was marked, even in that army where gallant deeds were common. Had a Jackson commanded the right wing of General Lee's army General McClellan's retreat would have been cut off before he reached Malvern Hill and his army possibly captured. The positions of the two lines would have been reversed and he would have been compelled to have carried Malvern Hill himself by assault in order to have effected his escape. The result would not have been in doubt. His attack would have been repulsed in front while Jackson's, Hill's and Longstreet's Divisions would have closed in on his rear. For official reports of this battle see further on.

After the battle of Malvern Hill General R. H. Anderson was appointed commander of Huger's Division. The 9th Regiment was moved back toward Richmond and on the 9th of July crossed the James river into Chesterfield county and went into camp at Falling creek, where the men were put to work drilling daily and building earthworks. On the 16th of August the regiment marched to Richmond and took the cars for Louisa courthouse, reaching there at midnight. This movement was in connection with the advance of the army against General Pope, which culminated in the second battle at Manassas and the invasion of Maryland. Marching through Louisa and Orange counties, the men forded the Rapidan at Summerville, marched through Culpeper county and crossed the Orange and Alexandria railroad at Brandy Station. On the 24th the regiment had a skirmish with Federal cavalry on the opposite side of the Rappahannock river and on the 25th pushed across the river into Fauquier county. On the 28th it had a very severe fight at Warrenton Springs with the enemy's infantry and artillery, in which private Wm. H. Hambleton, of the Old Dominion Guard, and Augustus Johnson, drummer of the Portsmouth Rifles, and Ordinance Sergeant Giot, of Norfolk county, were among the killed, and Lieutenant-Colonel

Gilliam and Major Owens were wounded. On the 29th the march was resumed at 3:30 p. m. The brigade passed through Thoroughfare Gap and halted until 11 p. m., when the march was again resumed and continued all night. Passing through Haymarket and Drainsville, the brigade arrived on the battle field at Manassas about daybreak on the morning of the 30th. By an unexplained mistake the brigade was marched inside the Federal lines but withdrew quiety without being discovered and, marching back about a mile, the men lay down to rest and sleep, while waiting for orders. Anderson's Division was the rear division of the army and Armistead's Brigade was the rear of the division, so that, with their arrival, General Lee had his whole army at hand.

History has described the second battle of Manassas. It has told how Jackson, by his grand flank march, placed himself in rear of General Pope's army and intercepted his retreat upon Washington; how Pope attacked him on the 29th of August but was repulsed with overwhelming loss; how Jackson maintained his position with his right resting on the Warrenton turnpike, along which General Lee was advancing with Longstreets corps to reinforce him ; how General Lee formed his army in the shape of a letter V, with Jackson's corps on the left and Longstreet's on the right, and when Pope, on the morning of 30th, advanced to renew the attack upon Jackson, Longstreet's corps struck his flank. It has recorded also the important part which Anderson's Division of Longstreet's corps played in that great battle. It held the enemy in check until the time had arrived for a general advance along the whole line, when it joined in the grand rush of infantry and artillery, and the Federal lines in its front were swept out of existence. Guns, flags, stores and innumerable prisoners fell into its possession. During the battle Armistead's Brigade had orders to support Mahone's Brigade of the same division, which was in the front line, but Mahone's Brigade never faltered. It made a grand charge that day and covered itself with glory, and therefore Armistead's Brigade had no opportunity to get into the front line but followed it in reserve. The brigade was not an actual participant in the battle to the extent of engaging the enemy, though it was continuously exposed to the fire of the Federal artillery and lost a number of men, among them Private Lewis Whitfield, of the Portsmouth Rifles, Co. G, 9th Va. He was from North Carolina, and was attending school at the Virginia Collegiate Institute in Portsmouth when the war broke out, and as several of his school friends joined the Rifles he joined that company also. He was killed by a shell, which tore away one of his hips.

Armistead's Brigade and the 9th Regiment with it, moved on with the army into Maryland, took part in the investment and capture of Harper's Ferry, which surrendered September 14th, with 12,000 prisoners and 73 guns, and at 4 p. m. on the 15th started to rejoin General Lee, who was concentrating his army at Sharpsburg. The regiment crossed the Potomac into Virginia, made a detour through Jefferson county, recrossed the Potomac at Shepherdtown and reached the battle field at Sharpsburg at 9 a. m. on the 17th, in time to take part in the repulse of Sumner's corps, which was pressing heavily upon the Confederate left and left centre. General Lee in this battle, with 35,000 men, held his ground all day and repulsed General McClellan's assaults, with 90,000 men, and held possession of the battle field. General McClellan made no attempt to renew the battle the next day and as General Lee had nearly exhausted his supply of ammunition and was far from his base of supplies, he decided to fall back into Virginia. The 9th Virginia remained on the field until 3 p. m. on the 18th, when it fell back to the Potomac, recrossed at Shepherdtown and was retained on picket duty on the banks of the river on the Virginia side. The army marched by easy stages to Fredericksburg, the 9th Virginia arriving there on the 26th of November and remained in the lines until the 13th of December in momentary expectation of an attack by the Federal army, then under General Burnside, who had succeeded General McClellan. On that day was fought the battle of Fredericksburg. Burnside crossed his army over the Rappahannock river on the 12th, and early on the morning of the 13th advanced to turn the Confederate right under Jackson, but was driven back. Later assaults by Couch's and Wilcox's corps and one division of Hooker's corps upon the Confederate centre under Longstreet, were easily repulsed with heavy slaughter among the attacking columns. The 9th Virginia was in the Confederate line of battle but as the battle was fought on the defensive by General Lee and the enemy did not assail that part of the lines, they were more spectators than actual participants in the battle. A little to the right of the position held by the 9th Virginia, a brigade of Federals had secured a position in a railroad cut or an excavation of a similar character, but the 57th North Carolina Regiment, commanded by Colonel Archibald C. Godwin, of Portsmouth, (afterward promoted to Brigadier-General and killed in Early's campaign in the Valley) made a gallant charge upon them and drove them out.

The Regiment remained in the vicinity of Fredericksburg until the 15th of February, 1863, when the movement of Pickett's and Hood's Divisions, under Longstreet, towards Suffolk was begun. Shortly before then Armistead's Brigade had been taken from Anderson's Division and put in the Division of Virginia troops, under General Pickett. The Regiment broke camp near Fredericksburg on the 15th and on the evening of the 16th reached Hanover Junction. That night snow fell to the depth of about ten inches and the men were marched ten miles through it. On the night of the 18th a deluge of rain came down, and the 19th witnessed them wading through slush and mud about knee deep, through Richmond and Manchester, into Chesterfield county. On the 20th they reached Chester Station and went into camp, remaining there until the 1st of March, as the ground was covered with snow all the time. On the 1st of March the regiment moved on through Petersburg, where it remained until the 26th, and then pushed ahead to the vicinity of Suffolk. Here an attack was made on the enemy, who were driven back to the town, and the Portsmouth and Norfolk county boys in Pickett's Division were in high spirits, hoping that the army would keep on to Portsmouth and they could once more meet their families and friends, but the object of General Longstreet's movement there was to collect provisions, and after accomplishing that object, he returned with his army, Hood's and Pickett's Divisions, to the main army of General Lee. He reached Manchester May 16th. Armistead's Brigade was in camp near Hanover Junction from May 18th to June 3d, when it was sent to King William county to meet a raiding party of Federal cavalry which was reported to be advancing in that direction, returning to Hanover Junction on the 7th. On the 8th the brigade started on the march for Pennsylvania. The 9th Regiment marched through the counties of Caroline, Spottsylvania, Orange, Culpepper, Fauquier, Loudoun, Clarke, Jefferson and Berkley, crossed the Potomac river at Williamsport on the 25th, and at 4 o'clock p. m. on the 2d of July, went into camp within five miles of Gettysburg, in Pennsylvania. There had been heavy fighting that day between the enemy and the corps of A. P. Hill and Ewell and part of Longstreet's and it was felt that the 3d would be decisive of great events.

The division (Pickett's) moved forward from camp at 3 a. m. on the 3d, and after being halted twice on the road, reached the battle field at 10 o'clock and remained drawn up in line, under the shelling of the Federal artillery until 3 p. m., when it was ordered to storm the entrenched position held by the enemy on the top of Cemetery Hill. This charge has become historic. Pickett's Division of three brigades Kemper's, Garnett's and Armistead's, and numbering 4,500 men, rank and file, after lying for five hours under a burning July sun, exposed to the shelling of the Federal batteries, marched at ordinary quick step more than three-quarters of a mile across an open field, up the hill to a stone wall, behind which lay more than ten thousand Federal troops and sixty pieces of artillery, which were playing upon them as they advanced, drove the gunners from their cannon and the infantry from the wall, captured the position and hundreds of prisoners at an immense sacrifice of life, and, looking back over nearly a mile of open field for Hood's and McLaws' Divisions which were expected to support them, found that neither had started. Somebody had blundered.

Colonel Walter H. Taylor, General Lee's Adjutant General, in his admirable work, "Four Years with General Lee," lays the blame on General Longstreet for keeping back those two divisions, as it was General Lee's order that they should support Pickett's charge. It is due to General Longstreet to say that he denies having received any order to that effect, and held the two divisions to repel an anticipated Federal attack on his right; but as General Meade was fighting a defensive battle entirely, there seems to have been no reasonable ground for such an apprehension. However, the fact remains that those of Pickett's men who escaped the showers of grape, canister and leaden hail, and reached the stone wall, found themselves nearly a mile from any reinforcements, while more than three-fourths of the army remained idle spectators of their devotion, with every general of brigade and nearly every field officer of lower grade killed or disabled from wounds and with no one left to assume direction of affairs, while the enemy was concentrating against them a force ten times their number. They held the captured works and a number of prisoners for about twenty minutes when, finding themselves about to be surrounded and knowing that to remain there meant death or captivity, for half of General Meade's army was moving against them, the men began to retire. Some got back safely to their own lines, but they were few.

Only three brigades were in the charge. Generals Armistead and Garnett were killed and General Kemper severely wounded. Colonel Jno. C. Owens, of Portsmouth, commanding the 9th Virginia, was mortally wounded and died in the field hospital about 2 o'clock that night. Colonel J. G. Hodges, of Portsmouth, commanding the 14th Virginia, was killed. Lieutenant-Colonel Phillips, of the 9th, and Lieutenant-Colonel White, of the 14th, of Norfolk county, were wounded, and Major Richardson, of Portsmouth, of the 9th Virginia, was captured. Adjutant John S. Jenkens, of Portsmouth, of the 14th, was killed, and, of the officers of the five Portsmouth and two Norfolk county companies in the charge, Lieutenants Guy, Company B, and Mitchell, Company H, 3d Virginia, and Niemeyer, Company I, 9th Virginia, were killed, and Captain Hodges and Lieutenant White, of Company A, 3d Virginia, Lieutenants Vermillion, Company I, Tonkin and Gale, Company G, and Hudgins and Robinson, Company K, 9th Virginia were wounded, and Captains Whitehead, Company H, 3d Virginia, Allen, Company K, Crocker, Company I, and Weaver, Company D, 9th Virginia, and Lieutenants Gary, Company A, Gleason, Company B, 3d Virginia, and Lewis, Company G, 9th Virginia, were captured. Of eighteen commissioned officers who were in the charge with the seven Portsmouth and Norfolk county companies, only one— Lieut. Richard Vermillion—escaped. Three were killed, seven were wounded and seven were captured. Adjutant Crocker, of the 9th, of Portsmouth, was captured; Lieutenants Guy and Mitchell were killed by the shelling, previous to the advance; Sergeant Robert A. Hutchings, of Company B, of Portsmouth, caught up the colors of the 3d Virginia, when Color Sergeant Gray, of Dinwiddie county was shot, and carried them to the stone wall, and Joshua Grimes, of Company I, of Norfolk county, was ensign of the 9th Virginia and carried the colors of that regiment to within twenty yards of the wall when he was severely wounded and fell, but Corporal Lemuel H. Williams, of the Portsmouth Rifles, Company G, picked them up and carried them to the stone wall where he was killed. General Armistead led the charge of his brigade on foot, with his hat on the point of his sword, and had scaled the stone wall and stood beside a captured cannon, with his hand resting on it, when he was killed by a musket ball. Colonel Owens of the 9th Virginia, was shot through the groin with a musket ball before the line reached the stone wall, and was carried off the field. Company A, the Dismal Swamp Rangers, under Captain Thomas M. Hodges, was in the skirmish line in front of the 3d Virginia, and though two of its commissioned officers were wounded, none were killed outright.

Swinton, who is the fairest of all the Northern historians of the war, gives a very graphic account of the charge of Pickett's Division at Gettysburg in his "Army of the Potomac," though he falls into the error of all of the Northern writers in greatly exaggerating the strength of the Confederates. He fixes the strength of the attacking force at 15,000, and yet says "its front was so narrow that it did not cover more than two of the incomplete divisions of the 2d corps, numbering some 6,000 men. This inconsistency should have been apparent to the author. Pickett's Division numbered 4,500 men and Heth's Division could not have been much larger, and 15,000 Confederates would have over-lapped 6,000 Federals. With this exception, his account of the charge is very fair for an opponent. He says:

"As Pickett's Division of Longstreet's corps had reached the ground during the morning, it was appointed to lead the van. Pickett formed his division in double line of battle, with Kemper's and Garnett's Brigades in front and Armistead's Brigade supporting, while on the right of Pickett was one brigade of Hill's corps, under General Wilcox, formed in column by battalions; and on his left, Heth's Division (also of Hill's corps), under General Pettigrew. The attacking force numbered about fifteen thousand men, and it advanced over the intervening space of near a mile in such compact and imposing order that, whether friend or foe, none who saw it could refrain from admiration of its magnificent array. The hostile line, as it advanced, covered a front of not more than two of the reduced and incomplete divisions of the second corps, numbering, it may be, some six thousand men. While crossing the plain it received a severe fire of artillery which, however, did not delay for a moment its determined advance, so that the column pressing on came within musketry range, the troops evincing a striking disposition to withhold their fire until it could be delivered with deadly effect. The first opposition it received was from two regiments of Stannard's Vermont Brigade of the first corps, which had been posted in a small grove to the left of the second corps in front of and at a considerable angle with the main line. These regiments opened upon the right flank of the enemy's advancing lines, which received also an oblique fire from eight batteries under Major McGilvray. This caused the Confederate troops on that flank to double in a little towards their left, but it did not stay their onward progress. As, during the tramp of the enemy across the intervening plain, the rifled guns had fired away all their canister, they were withdrawn or left on the ground inactive, to await the issue of the impending shock between the two masses of infantry—a shock momentarily expected—for the assailants approached steadily while the Union force held itself braced to receive the impact. When at length the hostile lines had approached to between two and three hundred yards, the divisions of Hays and Gibbon of the second corps opened a destructive fire, and repeated it in rapid succession.

"This sally had the effect to instantly reveal the unequal metal of the assaulting mass and proved what of it was iron and what clay. * * * Pettigrew's troops broke in disorder, leaving two thousand prisoners and fifteen colors in the hands of Hays' Division. Now, as Wilcox's Brigade had not advanced, Pickett's Division remained alone, a solid lance head of Virginia troops, temperd in the fire of battle. Solitary this division, buffeting the fierce volleys that met it, rushed up the crest of Cemetery Ridge and such was the momentum of its assault that it fairly thrust itself within Hancock's line.

"It happened that the full strength of this attack fell upon Webb's Brigade of three regiments. This brigade had been disposed in two lines; two of its regiments, the 69th and 71st Pennsylvania, posted behind a low stone wall and slight breastworks hastily constructed by them, while the remaining regiment, the 72d Pennsylvania, lay behind the crest, some sixty paces to the rear, and so placed as to fire over the heads of those in front. When the swift advancing and yelling array of Pickett's force had, notwithstanding the volleys it met, approached close up to the stone wall, many of those behind it, seeing their fire to be now vain, abandoned the position; and the Confederates, detecting this wavering, rushed over the breastworks, General Armistead leading, and crowned the stone wall with their standard.

The moment was as critical as can well be conceived; but happily the regiments that had been holding this front line did not, on falling back, do so in panic; so that, by the personal bravery of General Webb and his officers, they were immediately rallied and reformed on the rear of the brigade, which held the second line behind the crest, and Hancock instantly drew together troops to make a bulwark against any further advance of the now exultant enemy.

"As the hostile front of attack was quite narrow, it left Hancock's left wing unassailed. From there he drew over the brigades of Hall and Harrow. * * * The 19th Massachusetts Regiment. * * * Mallon's 42d New York Regiment. * * While Colonel Stannard moved two regiments of his Vermont Brigade to strike the enemy on the right flank. These movements were quickly executed. * * * The breach was covered, and in such force that in regular formation, the line would have stood four ranks deep.

"Whatever valor could do to wrest victory from the jaws of hell, that it must be conceded, the troops of Pickett had done, but now, seeing themselves in a desperate straight, they flung themselves on the ground to escape the hot fire and threw up their hands in token of surrender, while the remnant sought safety in flight. * * The Confederate loss in killed and wounded was severe. Of the three brigade commanders of Pickett's Division, Garnett was killed, Armistead fell fatally wounded within the Union lines, and Kemper was borne off, severely hurt. In addition it left behind fourteen of its field officers, and only a single one of that rank escaped unhurt, while of the rank and file, three-fourths were dead or captives. * * But this illustrious victory was not purchased without severe price paid, and this was sadly attested in the thousands of dead and wounded that lay on the plain. The loss of officers was again especially heavy, and among the wounded were Generals Gibbon and Hancock."

After their repulse, Pickett's Division retired to their camp of the night before and remained there until the army started on its return to Virginia. General Meade succeeded in resisting General Lee's efforts to dislodge him from his advantageous position, but General Lee's army was not beaten. He remained in front of Gettysburg all of the next day to give General Meade an opportunity to attack him, but that officer was content with having succeeded in repelling the assault upon himself, and had no idea of leaving his fortified position to attack the Confederates. General Lee, finding that General Meade would not attack him, and having nearly exhausted his supply of artillery ammunition, the army fell back to the Potomac river at Williamsport, Pickett's Division being assigned the duty of guarding the thousands of prisoners who were captured in the battle.

When the army reached Williamsport, the river was swollen so high from recent rains that it was not fordable, and the army remained there from the 8th to the 13th of July, by which time a bridge had been constructed, and the army crossed over on it. All of this time General Meade kept his army at a respectful distance, sending forward occasionally a force of cavalry to try to gather up a wagon train or a few stragglers. While in Williamsport, the 9th Regiment was doing provost duty, and the boys had excellent sleeping accommodations. On the 18th of August the brigade, then commanded by Colonel Aylett, of the 53d regiment, camped at Gordonsville, and on the 7th of September was ordered to Richmond, arriving there at night on the 12th and immediately took the cars for Petersburg. That day the brigade marched twenty-six miles and traveled twenty-two miles on the cars.

From that time to the following June, it was hurried from place to place to head off raiding parties of the enemy, which were making their appearance at different points from Richmond to Goldsboro. On the 6th of October the brigade was sent by rail to Kinston, N. C., and on the 14th placed in very comfortable winter quarters near that town, but on the 1st of November it was moved back to Petersburg. On the 7th it was sent back to Weldon, and from there to Garysburg, arriving at 8 a. m. on the 8th. It remained there until the 11th, when it was carried back to Petersburg. On the 28th it started to rejoin the army of General Lee, then confronting General Meade at Mine Run, reached Hanover Junction the next day at 8 a. m. and went into camp. On the 10th of December it was again sent by rail to North Carolina and on the 13th went again into the camp of October near Kinston.

On the 30th of January, 1864, the brigade moved on towards Newberne and on the 1st of February formed line of battle and had a small engagement with the enemy, driving in the pickets, &c., which was merely intended to employ the force there to prevent it from interfering with the movement of a portion of the army which was operating elsewhere. On the afternoon of the 2d the brigade broke camp for Kinston, and on the 13th took the cars for Petersburg, crossed James river on the 15th on a pontoon bridge above Drury's Bluff and camped in Henrico county two miles to the east of Richmond. In February two raiding parties of Federal cavalry started towards Richmond, one from the direction of Fortress Monroe, under General Wister, which got no further than Bottom's bridge, and the other under General Kilpatrick and Colonel Dahlgren, from General Meade's army on the Rapidan. On the 1st of March the 9th Regiment was marched to Bottom's bridge, thence to the Virginia Central railroad to head off Kilpatrick, who was operating there, but escaped, and at night to the Mechanicsville turnpike to try and head off Dahlgren, who had reached the vicinity of Richmond that afternoon about sundown and had been attacked and defeated by the 3d Battalion of Virginia Reserves, under command of Senior Captain John A. McAnerny, and attached to the brigade of General Custis Lee, on the Westham plank road about three miles from the city. In this battalion was a company of boys from Richmond, whose ages ranged from sixteen to eighteen, under command of Captain Edward Gay, and they displayed the courage of old veterans. The author saw one of them bringing in a Yankee prisoner, about twice his own size, whom he had captured, though himself suffering from a wound in the arm.

Though this affair has no direct connection with the history of the 9th Regiment, but as it was of considerable importance in its results, though comparatively insignificant in itself, and for this reason has been overlooked, or merely touched upon in the histories of the war, the author asks the indulgence of the reader in giving his recollection of it as it appeared to him. He was at the time, temporarily with Company A, commanded by Captain John Manico, a gallant fellow from New Orleans, who came to Virginia with the Washington Artillery and was wounded at Manassas, disabled and discharged.

On the 28th of February General Kilpatrick left General Meade's army on the Rapidan with between three and four thousand cavalrymen, for Richmond, to capture the city and release the Federal prisoners who were confined in Libby Prison and on Belle Isle.

At Spotsylvania Court House the force divided, and Colonel Dahlgren with five hundred picked men, pushed on towards the James river above Richmond, while the main body, under Kilpatrick, headed directly for the city, reaching the north side of it on the 1st of March. The interposition of Armistead's Brigade, of which the 9th Regiment formed a part, stopped his further progress in that direction, and he escaped down the peninsula to Fortress Monroe.

Dahlgren pursued his course towards James River, reached it near Goochland Court House, and then followed the course of the river towards Richmond, reaching the vicinity of the city, on the west, the same day, March 1st, that Kilpatrick had arrived, but later in the afternoon. A considerable force had by that time been collected around the city for its defence. News reached Richmond of the approach of Dahlgren's party and the 3d Battalion, Custis Lee's Brigade, was sent to meet it. The battalion left the city about 4 o'clock p. m. and marched rapidly out the Westham plank road. The battalion was composed of seven or eight companies and had about four hundred men present in its ranks. The rain was pouring down in torrents, but the men were in the best of spirits, as if they were going to a frolic instead of a fight. First Lieutenant Morris, a brave young North Carolinian, 2d Sergeant John F. Mayer, of Norfolk, and another, were together on the left of Company A. One of the trio remarked, " If our sweethearts were here now they might call us their *rain dears*." Sergeant Mayer said " Yes, and though it has scarcely been an hour since we left Richmond, we are already ' *veterans*.'" Lieutenant Morris did not want to get left on the play of words, and, remembering the day and month, and having his wits freshened by stepping into a mud puddle over his shoe tops said he thought " *This first march* this year is the *softest thing* the battalion ever got into." This incident is recalled merely to illustrate the fine spirits which animated the battalion, from Captain McAnerny down.

After marching about three miles the battalion met a cavalryman on his way to the city, with a report, and he informed Captain McAnerny that the enemy, in considerable force, had attacked our cavalry picket and it had fallen back to a position about a quarter of a mile in advance of where we then were. The captain halted the battalion, gave orders to close up and load ; after which it moved forward again, the men joking as they marched. It was then about sundown.

Reaching the picket, the battalion filed to the right, in a field, and fronted to the advancing enemy, with the left resting on the road and the cavalry picket occupying the road. Captain McAnerny threw out skirmishers and ordered a charge, telling the men to reserve their fire until he gave the order, and then to fire together. The enemy were advancing also, some mounted and some on foot, and in less than a minute the sharp cracking fire of the skirmishers began. These fell back gradually or rather paused for the main line to overtake them, when they took their places in the ranks. Captain McAnerny halted the line so that the fire of his men could be delivered with more accuracy, and when the enemy's line had reached within about twenty yards gave the order to fire. That one volley settled the affair. Those of the enemy who were not killed or wounded, stood not upon the order of their going, but left at once. A second volley added speed to their retreat. A mounted section endeavored to turn the right of the battalion which was exposed in open field, but the rear rank of the right company faced to the rear and gave them such a well-directed volley that only one of them escaped. The battalion was armed with Austrian rifles, which were perhaps the best guns in the Confederate army. Those of Dahlgren's men who escaped made their way around to the north of Richmond, closely followed by the Confederates, and were stopped by a party of Home Guards in King and Queen county. An engagement ensued and Dahlgren was killed and the men with him were captured. On his body was found an order to his men to release the Federal prisoners on Belle Island, kill President Davis and other citizens of Richmond, and burn the city. He came near liberating the thousands of prisoners on Belle Isle, for he had gotten within less than two miles of them and there was nothing between him and them but the 3d battalion. Had that failed in its duty, the ten or twelve thousand prisoners might have been released, though the subsequent arrival of other troops would have been in time to have kept him out of the city.

Captain A. E. Wilson, of Portsmouth, was on duty in King and Queen county at the time of this affair and recovered from the prisoners about two bushels of silver plate which they had stolen from Virginia farm houses while on their raid.

The 9th Regiment remained in the vicinity of Richmond all the month of March. On the 23d there was a terrible storm and "the beautiful snow" fell to the depth of eighteen inches, and in April the bottom seemed to have dropped out of the Confederate commissary department. The men in the 9th had nothing to eat on the 8th or 9th. The next day, however, brought relief and rations.

On the 3d of May the brigade started to join General Lee's army on the Rapidan, and on the 5th had reached Taylorsville, on the Richmond, Fredericksburg and Potomac Railroad, when it was recalled in haste to Richmond to meet Butler's advance from Bermuda Hundreds, where he had landed with the corps of Generals Gilmore and W. F. Smith, numbering some thirty thousand men. Arriving in Richmond by rail, the brigade was immediately transported by steamer to Drury's Bluff and marched to the outer line of defences. On the 8th the brigade was drawn up in line of battle, the men about five feet apart and covering a space of three miles.

May 10th Armistead's Brigade and Gracie's Alabama Brigade formed an attenuated line of battle reaching from the Petersburg railroad to the river and advanced against the enemy to develop his strength and position. Armistead's Brigade attacked two lines of battle of the enemy and pushed them back for nearly a mile, when Gracie's Brigade having obliqued to the left, a large interval was created on the left of Armistead's Brigade, and as it was about to be flanked there by the increasing masses of the enemy, General Barton, who commanded it, ordered it to retire. In this battle the 9th Regiment captured a gun on the turnpike, but when the brigade fell back it was left behind, as there were no horses to bring it off. This affair served to keep General Butler quiet for a few days, and as Sheridan was then in the vicinity of Richmond on his gigantic raid with three cavalry divisions, Armistead's Brigade was moved from Drury's Bluff by steamer at 1 o'clock on the morning of the 12th to Richmond. Sheridan had repulsed Stuart's attack at Yellow Tavern and killed that great cavalry leader on the 11th, and on the 12th reached the outer defences of the city. At 9 a. m., on the 12th, Armistead's Brigade formed line of battle on the Mechanicsville turnpike, and during the day was moved to the Meadow Bridge Road and back to the Mechanicsville turnpike and to the York River Railroad. Gracie's Alabama Brigade made an advance early in the afternoon to feel Sheridan's position and retired to wait for re-enforcements. These arrived later in the day and an advance was made by Gracie's, Armistead's and Hunton's Brigades, but Sheridan had moved off.

While Sheridan was on the Meadow Bridge Road an incident occurred which made a deep impression on the memory of the author. There was a farm house down the road about a quarter of a mile from the Confederate works and Sheridan had placed there a battery of field guns which was firing at the Confederate works, and a battery in the works across the road was replying. While this artillery duel was going on, a tall, elderly gentleman, carrying in his arms a two or three-year-old child and accompanied by two beautiful young ladies, one of whom was leading a little six or seven-year-old girl by the hand, came down the side of the road along a path inside the bordering fence, walking quietly to the Confederate lines. Upon reaching the works the men helped them over. They lived in the house where Sheridan had placed his battery, and in coming along the side of the road paid no more attention to the shells which were flying past them than if they had been snow balls.

Sheridan effected his retreat in safety to the Pamunky river, where he rejoined General Grant, and, in the meantime, Butler having been encouraged to make another attempt to reach Richmond, advanced from Bermuda Hundreds. The brigade was moved to Drury's Bluff on the 15th, and the next day took part in what is known in history as the Battle of Drury's Bluff. It resulted in a victory for the Confederates, and would have been more decisive still but for the failure of General Whiting to advance with his division to attack the left and rear of the enemy, as ordered by General Beauregard. This failure on his part to attack, left open the line of retreat for the enemy, of which he availed himself and fell back within the fortifications at Bermuda Hundreds. In this battle the brigade was commanded by Colonel B. D. Fry, of the 13th Alabama Regiment, who was assigned to it by General Robert Ransom, under whose orders it was acting. General Ransom preferred charges against General Barton for some fault he found with him in the action of the 10th and removed him from his command. A correspondence ensued in relation to the matter in which General Barton got the better of it, and every officer of the brigade signed a petition to the Secretary of War asking that he be re-instated. A court of inquiry was ordered, but its delays were so numerous that the war ended befor the matter was settled, and in the meantime General George H. Stewart was ordered to command it August 27th, 1864. General Barton had been assigned to the brigade in 1863, after the death of General Armistead at Gettysburg.

General Barton, in his official report of the 10th of May, pays a high compliment to the 9th Regiment for their steadiness and good conduct on that occasion. On the 16th the battle was begun while a heavy fog was on the ground and Barton's Brigade was ordered to support Hoke's North Carolina Brigade, but owing to the fog Hoke's Brigade obliqued to the right and Barton's obliqued to the left, which brought the 9th Regiment under a very heavy and destructive fire of the enemy, to which they did not reply, thinking Hoke's Brigade was in their front. They were ordered to lie down, which they did, until a flanking force from the brigades turned the enemy's right and captured those in front of the 9th. The fog lifting at this time disclosed the fact that Hoke's Brigade had moved off to the right. The 9th Regiment pressed on to Bermuda Hundreds after the retreating Federals, and on 19th the brigade was ordered to join the main army, then near Spotsylvania Court House. It took steamer at Drury's Bluff and reached Richmond at midnight, where the whole brigade slept on the streets on the pavement. The next day they took the cars for Milford Station, where they debarked, pushed on, and camped within five miles of Spotsylvania Court House.

On the night of the 20th Grant moved off from Spotsylvania Court House, and Armistead's Brigade, now Stewart's, and again united with Pickett's Division, was marched towards Hanover Junction. The whole of the division had gotten together again. On the 24th the brigade was in line of battle on the North Anna river, and fronted the enemy in his unsuccessful effort to force a passage there, and remained in position until the 27th, when the army moved off to Cold Harbor, in consequence of another movement of General Grant to the left. On the 30th it was again drawn up in line of battle and had a heavy engagement on the picket line, and on the 1st, 2d, 3d, 4th and 5th of June, was in line of battle at Cold Harbor waiting for an attack from the enemy which never came. He made heavy assaults on 1st and 3d, upon other portions of the line and was repulsed easily, losing about thirteen thousand men in less than fifteen minutes.

On the 6th, Company G, 9th Regiment, was sent forward to try to establish a new picket line, but finding the ground occupied by a superior force of the enemy, fell back to the old line, and on the 16th the division crossed over James river on pontoons at Drury's Bluff, and at 3 p. m., while on the Richmond and Petersburg turnpike near Chester Station, the head of the column, Stewart's Brigade, was fired upon by the enemy, who proved to be Butler's forces, who had again started out from Bermuda Hundreds. Line of battle was formed immediately and the enemy were attacked and driven from a line of earthworks, the division spending the night in the captured works. On the 17th the attack was renewed and Butler was again driven back behind his entrenchments at Bermuda Hundreds, from which he did not again emerge during the war. Pickett's Division remained on the lines in front of Bermuda Hundreds until March 26th, 1865, when it was moved off to the extreme right of the army to check the advance of Sheridan's Cavalry. Three brigades of the division, Stewart's, Terry's and Corse's (Hunton's was somewhere else) struck Sheridan's command at Dinwiddie Court House and drove it before them. This was the 31st of March, and the next morning while they were fighting Sheridan in front, Warren's and Humphrey's corps of Federal infantry, attacked them in flank and rear. The 9th Regiment was marched to the left and thrown in reverse to try to stop the flood and bore the brunt of Warren's charge. It stood its ground, however, until it was overwhelmed. The enemy came on faster than the men could load and fire, and most of the 9th Regiment being killed, wounded or surrounded, fell into the hands of the enemy. The colors of the 9th Regiment were bourne in this battle by George W. Barnes, of the Old Dominion Guard, Company K, and the regiment was in the form of a letter L, with one side fronting out from the left of the Confederate line of battle and the other fronting to the rear. Very few of the men escaped from Five Forks, and those who did, were caught in a similar trap at Saylor's Creek on the 6th.

While the 9th Regiment, which was taken from the centre of the brigade in line of battle, was hurrying to the left to try to stay the progress of Warren's and Humphrey's Corps, it passed the 56th North Carolina Regiment, of Ransom's Brigade, commanded by Lieutenant-Colonel G. G. Luke, an old Portsmouth boy, and the Portsmouth companies in the 9th recognizing him, gave him a cheer, and George Barnes, the color-bearer, knowing as every other man in the line did, that the regiment was being sent as a sacrifice to give time to the others to escape, sang out: "Here goes old Portsmouth, Colonel—good-bye!"

Swinton, in his Army of the Potomac, speaking of this effort to stop the movement of Warren's Corps upon Pickett's left and rear, says:

"Held as in a vice by the cavalry, which controlled their whole front and right, they now found a line of battle sweeping down on their rear. Thus placed, they did all that men may. Forming front both north and south, they met, with desperate valor, this double onset. * * * * Yet, vital in all of its parts, what remained still continued the combat with unyielding metal. Parrying the thrusts of the cavalry from the front, this poor scratch of a force threw back its left in a new and short crotchet, so as to meet the advance of Warren."

Pickett's force of six thousand contended with twelve thousand cavalrymen under Sheridan and twenty-two thousand infantry in the two corps of Warren and Humphreys.

Nearly all of the men in the 9th who escaped at Five Forks were killed or captured at Saylor's Creek, and very few were left to surrender at Appomattox, except those who were with the wagons, or in the commissary or hospital departments, these being necessarily in the rear and not usually participating in the battles, escaped in the general destruction. The regiment was engaged in the following battles, besides numerous skirmishes and picket fights:

Seven Pines, June 1st, 1862.
Malvern Hill, July 1st, 1862.
Warrenton Springs, Aug. 28th, 1862.
Second Manassas, Aug. 30th, 1862,
Harper's Ferry, Sept. 14th, 1862,
Sharpsburg, Sept. 17th, 1862,
Fredericksburg, Dec. 13th, '62.

Suffolk, April, 1863,
Gettysburg, July 3d, 1863,
Newberne, Feb. 4th, 1864,
Drury's Bluff, May 10th, 1864,
Drury's Bluff, May 16th, 1864,
Chester Station, June 16th, '64,
Dinwiddie Court House, March 31st, 1865,
Five Forks, April 1st, 1865,
Saylor's Creek, April 6th, 1865.

It was engaged also in the numerous skirmishes, which might almost be termed battles, at Hanover Court House, Cold Harbor and Turkey Ridge, from May 28th to June 13th, 1864, while General Lee was holding General Grant at bay, and had a number of minor engagements with the enemy while on the line at Bermuda Hundreds. An amusing incident occurred while at this latter place. By a mutual understanding between the men on both sides, there had been an intermission of picket firing for several weeks, when, one day, a Federal soldier called out from his side, "Johnnie, look out to-morrow, there will be negro troops on picket." The answer went back, "All right, we'll fix them." The next day, sure enough, the negroes were observed holding the advanced line, and with a yell, they were charged by the Confederates. They scattered and ran as if an avenging angel was after them. Later, white troops were sent to the front, and the friendly feeling between the opposing pickets was restored. That was the last attempt to put negro pickets on that line.

Lieutenant-Colonel Phillips recovered from his wound received at Gettysburg, was promoted to Colonel, and commanded the regiment until the closing scenes on the retreat from Petersburg. Major Richardson, who was captured at Gettysburg, was not exchanged. He was paroled just before the close of the war, but not having been exchanged, was not with the regiment in its closing struggles.

MALVERN HILL.

The following is the official report of Lieutenant-Colonel James Gilliam, who commanded the 9th Regiment at the battle of Malvern Hill. It will be remembered that only seven companies of the regiment were present in that affair. Companies A, D and H had been detached and placed in batteries in the fortifications around Richmond:

FRAZIER'S FARM, NEAR RICHMOND, VA.,
July 2d, 1862.

SIR—I beg leave to submit the following report of the action of the 9th Virginia Regiment during the battle of July 1st:

On the morning of July 1st we left the Charles City road in pursuit of the enemy and arrived about 10 a. m. at this farm. We were first left to guard the road to prevent a flank movement of the enemy, and for two hours were exposed to a most appalling and incessant artillery fire, and, notwithstanding the terror of its rage, my officers and men behaved with great coolness and gallantry.

About 5 o'clock we were ordered to change our position and take post in rear of and to support an artillery battery, and, in about thirty minutes afterwards, were ordered to charge the enemy's battery, supporting Cobb's Brigade, and it is but just to say that no regiment ever charged with more impetuosity. On they went with utmost speed amid the deadly fire of musketry and artillery. Having a force in our front interfering with our fire we, by an oblique to the right, came within good musket range of the opposing lines of the enemy and poured in upon them volley after volley until night closed the scene.

Where all behaved so well, the mention of individual acts might seem to be invidious, but justice demands that I should call your attention to the acts of Captain J. T. Kilby, Company I, who, amid the fire of the enemy, seized a flag of some regiment that had been broken and tried to rally its scattered remnants and bring them against the foe, and while thus acting the flag staff was shot from his hand. Of Captain James J. Phillips, who, after our color bearer was shot down and its guard scattered, preserved the colors of his regiment and saved it from the dishonor of leaving its colors on the field and restored them, still to wave in their proper place. Of Lieutenant James F. Crocker, Adjutant of the 9th Regiment, who received several severe if not mortal wounds in bravely leading the regiment in front of its colors, encouraging the men by his bold and gallant bravery. And I might, indeed, mention every officer in the field as having done their duty nobly, not only in this fight, but in all the hard duty that we have had to undergo in the last thirty days.

In closing my report, it is with feelings of the deepest regret that we have to number among our fallen brave the names of

Captain Dennis Vermillion, Company K, and Second Lieutenant C. M. Dozier of Company I. These brave and gallant officers fell bravely fighting for their homes and firesides, martyrs to vandal tyranny; but a grateful country will cherish their sacrifice and preserve their memory.

Below you will please find a duplicate report of the casualties in my regiment, which you will discover to be quite large, since it carried not exceeding one hundred and fifty effective fighting men on the field.

Killed—Two officers and 7 enlisted men, wounded 1 officer and 33 enlisted men, missing 23 enlisted men. Recapitulation—Killed 9, wounded 34, missing 23; total, 66.

Believing that my regiment did its duty faithfully, I cherish the hope that we shall meet your kind approval.

I have the honor to be your obedient servant,

JAS. S. GILLIAM,

Lieutenant Colonel Commanding 9th Va. Regiment.

BRIGADIER GENERAL ARMISTEAD,

Commanding Fourth Brigade.

During the night McClellan abandoned Malvern Hill and retreated to Harrison's Landing. General Wright, in his official report of the battle, says his brigade was ordered by General Armistead to follow his (Armistead's) brigade in a charge upon the enemy's works at Malvern Hill, and he went because General Armistead ordered him to do so, though he felt it was an improper move to charge one hundred guns and twenty-five thousand men with two brigades not exceeding in numbers twenty-five hundred men. General Magruder's management of affairs after his arrival upon the field does not seem to have been more judicious than that which preceeded. Charges were made by single brigades and sometimes by separate regiments. The Confederate artillery was badly managed. Instead of massing there seventy-five or eighty guns, Grimes' battery was sent in first and disabled, then Moorman's was put in with a like result, and then Pegram's. The official reports of the Brigadier Generals make no mention of General Huger being on the field, and that officer disclaimed any responsibility for the way the battle was fought. In his official report he said:

"As the different brigades of my division were sent forward into the battle of Malvern Hill, and I was directed to report them to another commander, though myself present, I was not in command during this battle. As I was treated in the same manner at Seven Pines, I can only hope this course was accidental and required by the necessities of the service."

The report of Brigadier Robert Ransom, who was attached to Huger's Division for that occasion, throws some light upon the condition of affairs which left that division without a head on the field and led to the disaster at Malvern Hill. General Ransom says:

"In this position we remained exposed to the bursting of an occasional shell until about 5 p. m., when a message reached me from General Magruder asking that I would go to his support. The summons was not obeyed, but I sent word to General Huger to get instructions. His reply sustained my action. In about half an hour another order from General Magruder arrived. General Huger was present, and under his dictation I informed General Magruder that orders to me must come through General Huger. The engagement was now very warm and extended along our whole front. At 7 p. m. I received word from General Magruder that he must have aid, if only one regiment. The message was so pressing that I at once directed Colonel Clarke to go with his regiment and report to General Magruder, and, at the same time sent my aide-de-camp, Lieutenant Broadnax, to General Huger for orders. Lieutenant Broadnax brought me somewhat discretionary orders, to go or not, but not to place myself under General Magruder."

Major-General D. H. Hill in his official report of the battle says:

"The battle of Malvern Hill might have been a complete and glorious success had not our artillery and infantry been fought in detail. * * * Notwithstanding the tremendous odds against us and the blundering management of the battle, we inflicted heavy loss upon the Yankees."

General Longstreet blames General Magruder for it. He says:

"It was soon ascertained that the enemy was in position and great force at Malvern Hill. A little after 3 p. m. I understood that we would not be able to attack the enemy that day, inasmuch as his position was too strong to admit of it. About 5 o'clock, however, I heard the noise of battle, and soon received a message from General Magruder calling for reinforcements."

The Confederates lost in this blundering affair, 685 killed, 3,444 wounded, and 498 missing; total, 4,627.

Captain John T. Kilby, of Company I, 9th Virginia Regiment, has furnished the author with the following personal recollection of this unfortunate affair. He says:

"When we were lying down under the hill, in the ravine, before going into that fatal charge, General Armistead ordered me to send two videttes to the brow of the hill to watch the progress of the battle. The position was an exposed one, and I selected for the duty Joseph Prentis, a distant relative, and Mills Riddick, my nephew. In a few minutes Mills Riddick reported to me that he thought the enemy was about to advance, and form a new line, which I reported to General Armistead, who reported to General Magruder, who was very near me when he heard the report, and ordered our regiment to charge across the field. I was within a few feet of him and heard every word he said. He was in a towering passion and used very profane language. His actions and his language on that occasion left a very decided impression on my mind that General Magruder was quite under the influence of liquor. General Armistead protested against his men being sent into the charge, saying it was downright murder to have men ordered cut up as our regiment must necessarily be. From the time we entered that ravine, about 3 p. m., until the charge, I was with General Armistead and heard his protest to General Magruder in reference to that charge across the field."

Only Forty members of the 9th Regiment remained to surrender at Appomattox Court House. These were:

Captain J. P. Wilson, Jr., Company A, commanding regiment.
Surgeon A. R. Barry.
Quarter Master Sergeant W. R. Butler.

COMPANY A.
Sergeant Reuben Ruffin,
" Jas. C. Brister,
Private Marcus A. Clarke,
" Marion W. Stern.

COMPANY B.
Private James W. Moore.

COMPANY C.
Sergeant Ralph H. Stewart,
" John T. Morrisett,
Private L. M. Lundie,
" S. M. Wilkerson.

COMPANY D.
Private Rufus K. McCoy,
" Wm. H. Jollett,
" G. W. Martin.

COMPANY F.
Private James Graham,
" James Ritchie.

COMPANY G.
Sergeant J. W. Fiendley,
Private Chas. D. Brownley,
" Albert B. Owens,

COMPANY G.
" John E. Sale,
" D. White,
" W. J. Oliver,
" A. Savage,
" M. P. Whitehurst.

COMPANY H.
Corporal E. Aiken,
" H. Chambers.
Private H. Clements,
" H. Spiers,
" Richard A. Hargrave.
" T. B. Wills.

COMPANY I.
Private Jas. E. Barnes,
" Blanch Duncan,
" Wash. L. Gwynn,
" Wm. J Skeeter.

COMPANY K.
Private E. E. Bilisoly,
" W. B. Collins,
" T. R. Borland,
" Jas. M. Williams,
" Ed. Watkins.

The original roll is followed in the above list, though there may be some errors in the initials. The names in this list which are not on the rolls of the separate companies were conscipts, or men who joined after the evacuation of Portsmouth.

CHAPTER XIII.

VIRGINIA DEFENDERS, COMPANY C, SIXTEENTH VIRGINIA REGIMENT.

This company was organized in Portsmouth on the night of the 20th of April, 1861, immediately upon the receipt of Governor Letcher's proclamation calling for volunteers. In anticipation of trouble a paper had been in circulation for several days prior to that time seeking signatures for the organization of the company, and it culminated that night. The following officers were elected:
Captain—Edward T. Blamire.
First Lieutenant, A. T. Culpepper; 2d Lieutenant, John H. Gayle; 3d Lieutenant, Thomas Barrand.
First Sergeant, Joseph Sanner; 2d Sergeant, A. S. Watts; 3d Sergeant, J. Thompson Baird; 4th Sergeant, William W. Davis.

The company was mustered into service at once, assigned to the 16th Virginia Regiment as Company C and ordered with the regiment on duty in the entrenched camp back of Norfolk, leading there rather a quiet life, varied only by an occasional alarm, upon a report that the enemy were endeavoring to effect a landing at Seawell's Point or Willoughby's Spit.

In April, 1862, one year after the original muster of the company into service, those of the men who were in camp and had not been detached on other duties, re-enlisted for the war and elected officers. Camp life had produced some dissatisfaction, and all of the old officers were not re-elected. Fourth Sergeant Joseph Sanner had in the meantime been transferred to a Maryland company, and was not with Company C. The following was the result of the new election. Sergeant A. S. Watts was also out of the company, having been elected Sheriff of Portsmouth:
Captain—Thomas Barrand.
First Lieutenant, John H. Gayle; 2d Lieutenant, A. T. Culpepper; 3d Lieutenant, J. Thompson Baird.
First Sergeant, James H. Toomer; 2d Sergeant, William Bayton; 3d Sergeant, James H. Richardson; 4th Sergeant, Leonard J. King.

Upon the evacuation of Portsmouth and Norfolk May 10th, 1862, by the Confederates, Company C moved off with the regiment to Petersburg and then to Richmond. While in front of Richmond just before the battle of Seven Pines, the regiment was ordered to the Shenandoah Valley to reinforce General Jackson, but before reaching there the orders were countermanded and it was ordered back to Richmond. Returning by rail by way of Lynchburg, it reached the vicinity of Richmond June 3d, 1862, two days after the battle of Seven Pines. It was then attached to Mahone's Brigade and participated in all the battles in which the brigade was engaged.

Captain Thomas Barraud was killed in the battle of Bristoe Station October 14th, 1863, and Lieutenant John H. Gayle was promoted to Captain. Lieutenant A. T. Culpepper resigned in the winter of 1862-3 on account of ill health. Lieutenant J. Thompson Baird was promoted to 1st Lieutenant and lost a leg at Davis' Farm, near Petersburg, August 19th, 1864, and was incapacitated for further service and retired. Sergeant Leonard J. King was elected 2d Lieutenant to fill the vacancy caused by the resignation of Lieutenant Culpepper and the promotion of Lieutenant Baird, and was severely wounded at the battle of the 22d of June, 1864, at Wilcox's Farm. First Sergeant, James H. Toomer was appointed Captain in the Corps of Engineers in 1863, and Second Sergeant William Bayton was promoted to 1st Sergeant and held the position until the close of the war and surrendered at Appomattox.

Three of the privates of the company were promoted to the position of Adjutants of regiments. These were:

John S. Jenkins, Adjutant 14th Virginia, killed in the charge of Pickett's Division at Gettysburg.

Edward B. Ward, appointed Sergeant Major of the 16th Virginia, promoted to Adjutant, and escaped without a wound.

Levin Gayle, appointed Adjutant of the 12th Alabama Regiment of Rodes' Brigade, and wounded May 12th, 1864, at Spotsylvania Court House.

At the second battle of Manassas Martin McCoy of Company G led the charge of the regiment and was from ten to twenty feet in advance of it.

It is not necessary to say anything further to establish the reputation of a company for gallantry and good conduct during the war than to say it was in Mahone's Brigade, for no brigade in the army, not even the famous organization which Stonewall Jackson inspired with his own indomitable determination ranked higher in the Confederate Army, and among the many conflicts in which it took a prominent part none ranked higher or deserved more credit than the battle at Crampton Gap, Maryland, September 14th, 1862, in which four regiments of this brigade, the 6th, 12th, 16th and 41st Virginia (the 61st Virginia had not then joined the brigade), with about eight hundred men, rank and file, held in check Franklin's Corps of 20,000 men and prevented them getting up in time to relieve the garrison at Harper's Ferry. The Virginia Defenders, Company C, 16th Virginia Regiment, took an active part in that battle. The following account of this battle was prepared for the author by Captain James H. Toomer, of Portsmouth, who was, at the time, 1st Sergeant of the company. It contains his recollections of the affair as a participant therein:

"THE 'VIRGINIA DEFENDERS' AT THE BATTLE OF CRAMPTON GAP—RECOLLECTIONS OF A PARTICIPANT.

"On Saturday afternoon, September 13th, 1862, the company was ordered on picket duty and took position on a spur of South Mountain, keeping watch all Saturday night and Sunday morning. About midday we received orders to leave, and after marching some miles were placed in position to defend Crampton Gap, Mahone's Brigade occupying a path at the foot of the mountain, running at right angles to the road from Burkettsville over the mountain. Our company fortunately was placed behind a low stone wall, the two Suffolk companies on our right and on the other side of the main road, and the other companies of the regiment on our left. The battle commenced by the enemy placing two Parrott guns on a little eminence just this side of Burkettsville, in order to feel our strength and position. Pretty soon they advanced their skirmishers and followed this up by a heavy attack of their infantry. Several attempts were made to reach our lines, but we succeeded each time in repulsing them, until, massing their forces, we, were "overwhelmed by superior numbers" and forced to retreat. It was a trying time for the Confederates engaged in that struggle. Our force was only about eight hundred men, while it was said the enemy had twenty thousand, and from our position we could see the immense disparity of numbers against us. One of the prettiest sights I ever saw was the charge of one of their regiments against the lines just on our left. It was a large regiment, with very full ranks, and was supposed by us to be the "Pennsylvania Bucktails." They came over the field grandly, the officers all in place and cheering the men onward, the men well aligned on the colors, with the Stars and Stripes floating proudly above them and borne aloft by a stalwart sergeant, who bore himself every inch a soldier. Half way across the field the fire upon them was so deadly they halted and threw themselves upon the ground to avoid, as much as possible, the destructive rain of Minie balls poured into their ranks. But reinforcements coming up behind them, they were pushed forward and finally carried the left of the line. Meanwhile, on our side, we had successfully beaten back every effort against us. In our front was an open field and distant about eighty or one hundred yards was a fence running parallel with the wall behind which we were placed. The enemy ranged themselves behind this fence and across the field each side hurled its deadly missiles at the other. Twice the enemy left the fence and essayed a charge, but each time were driven back before they had gained half the distance between us, leaving the ground blue with their dead and wounded. After three hours hard fighting we were flanked on both our right and left and the order was given for the regiment to fall back. Three of us in our company were cut off from the road and had to make our retreat up the steep side of the mountain, the whole field by this time filled with the charging enemy, roaring like bulls of Bashan and howling like devils let loose from the infernal regions. Pulling ourselves up by laying hold of branches of trees and climbing from ledge to ledge, with the music of Minie balls continually in our ears, we succeeded in getting safely over the mountain.

"When the brigade reformed in Pleasant Valley only four in our company and seventeen in the regiment answered to their names. Nearly the whole regiment was captured, but we had succeeded in holding the Gap against Franklin's Corps till it was too late for him to march through to the relief of Harper's Ferry, and the next morning the place was surrendered to our forces.

"We afterwards had the satisfaction of hearing from good authority that the Secretary of War had pronounced our defence of Crampton Gap to be one of the most gallant performances of the war. Certainly it was a glorious exploit for eight hundred men to hold at bay twenty thousand for three hours, and but for the rapid succession of important events occurring just at this time this achievement of Mahone's Brigade would occupy a larger space in men's memories than it has done heretofore."

A section of Grimes' Battery was engaged in this battle and was withdrawn by order of Colonel Munford after firing all of its ammunition. Colonel Parham was in command of Mahone's Brigade, General Mahone having been wounded in a previous battle. Colonel Munford in his report says: "Colonel Parham did everything in his power to hold his position, and his little command fought splendidly."

When the army was falling back into Virginia after the battle of Sharpsburg, rations became scarce and the men were given ten ears of corn for a day's feed. One day one of the men in the Virginia Defenders was noticed by the other men coming from the direction of General Mahone's headquarters with his ten ears of corn upon his arm, and upon being questioned said he had been to the General to complain of the shortness of his rations. He said General Mahone told him it was the best that could be done, that he had nothing else for himself, and that he had informed the General that he did not object to the ten ears of corn, that was all right as far as it went, but that five bundles of fodder should accompany it as "a feed." He did not repeat General Mahone's reply.

The company took part in the following battles, besides numerous other engagements, some of which were of enough importance to be termed battles:

Charles City Road, June 30th, 1862,

Malvern Hill, July 1st, 1862,

Second Manassas, August 30th, 1862,

Crampton Gap, Sept. 30th, '62,

Sharpsburg, Sept. 17th, 1862, Turkey Ridge, June 4th to 13, '64.
Fredericksburg, Dec. 13th, '62, Frazier's Farm, June 13th, '64,
Chancellorsville, May 1st, 2d Wilcox Farm, June 22d, 1864,
and 3d, 1863, Gurley House, June 23d, 1864,
Salem Church, May 3d, 1863, Crater, July 30th, 1864,
Gettysburg, July 2d & 3d, '63, Davis Farm, Aug. 19th, 1864,
Bristoe Station, Oct. 14th, '63, Reams' Station, Aug. 25th, '64,
Mine Run, Dec. 2d, 1863, Burgess Mill, Aug. 29th, 1864,
Wildnerness, May 6th, 1864, Hatcher's Run, Feb. 6th, 1865,
Spotsylvania C. H., May 12th, Amelia C. H., April 5th, '65,
Hanover C. H., May 28-9th, '64, Cumberland Church, April 7, '65.
Cold Harbor, June 2d & 3d, '64, Appomattox, April 9th, 1865,

The following is a list of the names on the muster roll of the company in August, 1861, with the grades they attained:

Captain E. T. Blamire, thrown out at reorganization, 1862.
Captain Thomas Barrand, killed October 14, 1863, Bristoe Station.
Captain John H. Gayle, promoted Captain, captured at Crampton Gap September 14th, 1862, exchanged and surrendered at Appomattox.
Lieutenant A. T. Culpepper, resigned winter 1862-3, ill health.
Lieutenant J. Thompson Baird, lost leg August 19th, 1862, Davis' Farm, and retired.
Lieutenant Leonard J. King, severely wounded June 22d, 1864, Wilcox's Farm.
First Sergeant Joseph Sanner, transferred to Maryland line 1862.
First Sergeant James H. Toomer, promoted Captain of Engineers.
First Sergeant William H. Bayton, wounded, surrendered at Appomattox.
Sergeant A. S. Watts, elected Sheriff of Portsmouth November, 1861, and discharged.
Sergeant W. W. Davis, died from wounds received July 1st, 1862, Malvern Hill.
Sergeant James H. Richardson.
Sergeant Charles A. Etheredge, transferred to Commissary Department, rejoined the company in July, 1864, surrendered at Appomattox.

PRIVATES.

Anderson, John W., drummer, discharged August, 1862, under age.
Bain, R. T. K., Corporal, furnished substitute June, 1862.
Brittingham, James E., wounded.
Brownley, Joseph F.
Brown, Eugene H., Corporal, appointed Engineer in Navy, wounded at Fort Fisher.
Butt, Wilson A., killed May 12th, 1864, Spotsylvania.
Buff, August, appointed hospital steward 1861.
Collins, William W., wounded August 30th, 1862, Second Manassas.
Cherry, I. Jerome, promoted Assistant Surgeon C. S. Army.
Cooper, John G., wounded July 3d, 1863, Gettysburg, surrendered at Appomattox.
Cooper, Clarence, wounded near Petersburg.
Cutherell, Samuel, furnished substitute 1861.
Dann, Silas S., promoted Sergeant, surrendered at Appomattox.
Darden, Edward.
Deal, William, wounded August 19th, 1864, Davis' Farm, surrendered at Appomattox.
Diggs, William W., wounded August 19th, 1864, Davis' Farm, surrendered at Appomattox.
Emmerson, William.

Gayle, Levin J., promoted Adjutant 12th Alabama Regiment, wounded at Spotsylvania Court House May 12th, 1864.
Gayle, John M., killed October 29th, 1864, Burgess' Mill.
Grant, Robert S., detailed 1862, for service in Navy Yard.
Grant, Edward.
Godwin, Charles W., detailed 1861.
Godwin, William, severely wounded August 30th, 1862, Second Manassas.
Godwin, Ellison, surrendered at Appomattox.
Goruto, William, severely wounded August 30th, 1862, Second Manassas.
Hennicke, Albert V., appointed hospital steward Howard Grove.
Haynes, James K., wounded August 30th, 1862, Second Manassas, died in hospital.
Herbert, John L., wounded July 1st, 1862, Malvern Hill, discharged and enlisted in Engineer Corps.
Hunter, Samuel W., severely wounded and detailed on hospital duty, re-joined company and surrendered at Appomattox.
Hubbard, Alonzo S., detailed 1861 to work in Navy Yard.
Ivy, I. O., transferred to 13th Virginia Cavalry.
James, George W., captured on retreat from Petersburg.
Jarvis, J. M., discharged 1861, disability.
Jack, John, detailed 1861 to work in Navy Yard.
Jenkins, John S., promoted Adjutant 14th Virginia, killed July 3d, 1863, Gettysburg.
Lash, John W., detached with sharpshooters of regiment.
Langhorne, James K., appointed Engineer in Navy.
Latimer, Charles W., transferred to Navy.
Linn, John, Corporal, discharged 1862, over age.
Lynch, Stephen, killed accidentally 1862.
Manning, James, discharged 1862, disability.
Mercer, James.
McCoy, Francis, discharged 1862, over age.
McCoy, Martin V. B., died in hospital 1863, U. S. Ford.
McPherson, Noah.
Moreland, Robert, captured and not exchanged.
Moreland, W. H., discharged August, 1862, over age.
Munden, Nathan, wounded July 30th, 1862, crater.
Peters, Jas. H., transferred to naval stores department.
Proctor, Jas. C., wounded and disabled July 1st, 1862, Malvern Hill.
Poulson, George, discharged for disability and appointed hospital steward.
Spady, Thos. V., detailed as courier and surrendered at Appomattox.
Smaw, Daniel G., captured at Crampton Gap September 14th, 1862.
Shelton, Wm. Naylor, Corporal, detailed 1861 to work in Navy Yard.
Sibley, Robert E.
Scott, Albert A., detailed as hospital steward.
Tart, John Quincy, discharged 1862, disability.
Tomlinson, Ed R., drummer, discharged August, 1862, under age.
Ward, Edward B., promoted Adjutant 16th Regiment.
Watters, Jas. P.,
Wellener, Joseph, detailed 1861 to work in Navy Yard.
Whitehurst, N. E., lost arm May 12th, 1864, Spotsylvania.
Whitehurst, John W.
Wills, John S., killed 1864, near Petersburg.
Wills, Joseph P., died in 1863 at U. S. Ford in hospital.
White, N. E., discharged 1862, over age, enlisted in the Norfolk Light Artillery Blues.
Wilson, Wm. S., discharged 1861, over age.
Wilkins, Jas. E.
Williams, W. W., killed July 1st, 1862, Malvern Hill.
Williams, Walter.
Williams, Joseph.
 Killed and died—10.

CHAPTER XIV.

THE ST. BRIDE'S LIGHT ARTILLERY, COMPANY I, THIRTY-EIGHTH VIRGINIA REGIMENT.

This company was raised in St. Bride's parish of Norfolk county, and contained among its membership quite a number of men from Norfolk city. As its name will indicate, it was originally intended for a light artillery company, but was never furnished with a field battery, and, having served for some time as heavy artillerists, the company was, finally, towards the close of the war, put into the 38th Virginia Infantry Regiment. It was mustered into the Confederate service by Major Bradford, mustering officer for Huger's Division, on the 26th of June, 1861. On that day officers were elected as follows:

Captain--George A. Martin.

First Lieutenant, Wm. M. Chaplain; 2d Lieutenant, John J. Whitehurst; 3d Lieutenant, Benj. F. Halstead.

First Sergeant--Alfred B. Williams.

The company left this vicinity early in 1862 and was ordered to take charge of a battery on the Nansemond river, remaining there until May 10th, when the troops from here were moved to Richmond for the defense of that city. The guns, which were in the battery, were removed and carried to Richmond, and it seems probable that they were carried to Drury's Bluff, though the evidence on this point is not conclusive. At any rate Captain Martin says they were saved to the Confederacy. Upon reaching Richmond, the company being without a field battery, was given some old muskets and attached temporarily to the 14th Virginia Regiment of Armistead's Brigade, and took part with that regiment in the battle of Seven Pines, June 1st, 1862, after which it was detached from the 14th Regiment and ordered to the fortifications around Richmond and attached to the 20th Battalion Heavy Artillery, commanded by Major Robertson.

Lieutenant Whitehurst was discharged for disability, though the exact date of his discharge is somewhat uncertain, but on the 25th of April, 1864, when the company was relieved from duty in the fortifications of Richmond and attached to the 38th Virginia Regiment of Company I, 3d Lieutenant Benj. F. Halstead had been promoted to 2d Lieutenant, and 1st Sergeant A. B. Williams had been promoted to 3d Lieutenant. The company participated in the two battles of May 10th and 16th, 1864, near Drury's Bluff, and in the battle of Chester Station on the 16th of June, following, between Pickett's Division and the forces of

ST. BRIDE'S LT. ARTILERY, CO. I, THIRTY-EIGHTH VA. REGT. 133

General Butler, who had made an advance from Bermuda Hundreds towards the Richmond and Petersburg Railroad. Butler was driven back into his entrenchments and remained there until the close of the war. The company participated in the battles of Dinwiddie Court House, March 31st, 1865, and Five Forks, April 1st.

On the 28th of March, 1865, Captain Martin was promoted to Lieutenant Colonel of the Regiment, his commission to date from December 2d, 1864. Lieutenant Chaplain was wounded and disabled at the battle of Drury's Bluff, May 16th, 1864, and was retired on the 14th of December. Lieutenant Williams was discharged for disability in 1864, and upon the retirement of Lieutenant Chaplain, 2d Lieutenant B. F. Halstead was promoted to 1st Sergeant, Thos. A. McClanen was elected 2d Lieutenant, and Josiah W. Leath, 1st Sergeant. In comparison with the other companies which went from Norfolk county to the Confederate army its list of casualties was small. No record or other information is obtainable of the losses, if any, at Five Forks.

Below will be found a list of the members of the company who left with it at the evacuation of Norfolk county by the Confederates on the 10th of May, 1862, and were accounted for on the roll for December, 1864. In 1863 the company was strengthened by the remaining men in a disbanded company from Lynchburg, one of whom was killed, two wounded and three died in hospital.

Captain Geo. A. Martin, promoted Lieutenant Colonel 38th Virginia Regiment March 28th, 1865.
First Lieutenant Wm. M. Chaplain, wounded May 16th, 1864, at Drury's Bluff, disabled and retired.
First Lieutenant Benj. F. Halstead.
Second Lieutenant Jno. J. Whitehurst, resigned 1863.
Second Lieutenant Thos. A. McClanen.
Third Lieutenant A. B. Williams, resigned 1864.
First Sergeant Josiah W. Leath, promoted 1st Sergeant December 1st, 1864, wounded May 16th, 1864.

SERGEANTS.

| Chas. H. Melson, | Jno. E. James, | Robert M. Saddler. |

PRIVATES, ETC.

Aydlott, John,	Boggs, Wm.,	Cofer, Robert E.,
Allen, John R.,	Bush, Wm.,	Cofer, Reuben F.,
Brown, Jno. W.,	Blunt, Thos.,	Davis, Elzy,
Bullock, Wm.,	Cooper, M. V. B.,	Dier, Edward F.,
Brummell, Richard,	Cooper, James,	Dozier, Jas. W., Jr.,
Barcroft, Edward,	Capps, A. J.,	Downing, Chas. W.,
Beal, John,	Callis, Henry,	Everett, Chas.,
Balls, Jno. R.,	Constable, Chas. W.,	Fitchett, Wm.,

Forrest, John,
Frost, W. W.,
Flora, Henry C.,
Ferguson, Henry,
Garrett, W. T.,
Graham, Joseph,
Graham, Tinsley,
Graham, Jno. B.,
Godfrey, Gervais K.,
Godfrey, Wm. T.,
Guy, George,
Hudgins, Wm. H.,
Hudgins, Samuel N.,
Holland, John,
Harvey, John,
Harvey, Henry,
Howe, Wm.,
Ironmonger, James,
Jordan, Miles H.,
James, Geo. T.,
James, Jno. (Sergt.)
Jones, Jno. W.,
Kuhn, Thos. C.,
Lambert, Thos.,
Lee, Thos. J.,

Lamonte, Joshua,
Lamonte, Henry,
Lambert, Jno. N.,
Lambert, Henry J.,
Land, Henry,
Morris, A. W.,
Martin, Wm.,
Mott, Lewis,
May, Joseph S.,
Morse, Henry,
Minor, Wm. B.,
Needom, Wilson,
Omler, Joseph,
Old, W. W.,
Powell, Jno.,
Peyton, Jas. A.,
Pugh, Abraham,
Peed, Chas. W.,
Reed, John,
Reed, David,
Ross, Edward,
Rogers, Roderick,
Robinson, Wm.,
Rainey, Malachi,
Revel, John,

Sawyer, C. T.,
Smith, Jas. E.,
Stringer, Thos. J.,
Smith, W. S. (Corp'l)
Shermadine, Wm.,
Sykes, Wm.,
Spence, Abner,
Sykes, Jesse,
Tucker, W. H.,
Tucker, Samuel,
Tebault, Daniel,
Tripple, Chas.,
Vandenberg, James,
Whitehurst, Jas. H.,
Whitehurst, C. P.,
Whitehurst, W. A.,
Whitehurst, George,
Wilder, Jas. M.,
Wilder, Benjamin,
West, Jno.
Wood, Lorenzo,
Waterfield, Benj.,
Waterman, Absolem,
Walker, W. W.,
Woodward, Samuel,

CASUALTIES.

Private, Balls, John R., wounded May 16th, 1864, died July 16th.
" Crews, Jos. B., (Lynchburg) died in hospital, Richmond, August 19th, 1864.
Private, McGraw, Wm., (Lynchburg) died in hospital, Richmond, July 29th, 1864.
Private, Phelps, Robert S., (Lynchburg) died in hospital, Richmond, July 6th, 1864.
Private, Tinsley, Geo. W., (Lynchburg) wounded May 16th, 1864, died August 15th.
Lieutenant, Chaplain, Wm. M., wounded May 16th, 1864, disabled and discharged.
Private, Driscol, Chas. E., (Lynchburg) wounded May 16th, 1864.
" Graham, John B., wounded May 16th, 1864.
" Leath, Josiah W., wounded May 16th, 1864.
" Lee, Thos. J., wounded August 25th, 1864, lost a leg.
" Old, W. W., wounded June 1st, 1862, Seven Pines.
" Phillips, Aldusten D., (Lynchburg) wounded May 10th, 1864, and disabled, discharged November 28th, 1864.
Private, Reed, David, wounded August 25th, 1864.
" West, John, wounded May 16th, 1864.

Col. Geo. A. Martin, formerly Captain of the company, thinks the following were killed or died, though their names seem to have been omitted from the official reports:

Corporal Wm. Harden, killed May 10th, 1864, at Drury's Bluff.
Private Mathias Wright, killed May 16th, 1864, at Drury's Bluff.
" Joshua Lamonte, killed May 16th, 1864, at Drury's Bluff.

Private Henry Lamonte, killed August 25th, 1864, at Bermuda Hundred.
" Thos. Klnn, killed August 25th, 1864, at Bermuda Hundred.
" Henry Flora, died in hospital, Richmond.
" Chas. Whitehurst, died in hospital, Richmond.
" Wm. Sykes, died in hospital, Richmond.
" Jos. S. May, died in hospital, Petersburg.

PROMOTIONS.

Private W. W. Old was promoted to Captain and A. A. G. on the staff of General Edward Johnson, and afterwards on the staff of General Ewell.
Private Charles W. Downing was promoted to Captain in Cohoon's Battalion.
Private John Aydlott was promoted to Commissary Sergeant 20th Battalion Heavy Artillery.

The following members of Company I surrendered at Appomattox:

  *Edward Barcroft,   John W. Gunter,
  Jacob Connor,   Wm. Lettrell,
  *J. W. Dozier,   P. D. Mitchell,
  W. A. Dunham,   *A. Pugh,
  C. Driskell,   *J. F. Sykes.

 *Original members of the company. The others were transferred to the company.

CHAPTER XV.

THE NORFOLK COUNTY RIFLE PATRIOTS, COMPANY F, FORTY-FIRST VIRGINIA REGIMENT.

This was one of the largest and best companies which entered the service of the Confederate States. It was organized in 1860, the men being from that section of Norfolk county lying between Washington Point, now Berkley, and Great Bridge, and was mustered into service on the 21st of April, 1861, at Norfolk. The following were the officers of the company at the breaking out of the war and under whom it was mustered into service:

Captain—William H. Etheredge.

First Lieutenant, Philip Biddle; 2d Lieutenant, Jetson Jett; 3d Lieutenant, Arthur Portlock; 4th Lieutenant, John N. Etheredge.

Lieutenant Etheredge was physically unable, on account of ill health, to do military duty, but was mustered in with the company and served for the original term of enlistment of twelve months, when he was retired.

On the 21st of April the company was ordered to take possession of the arsenal at St. Helena, opposite the Gosport Navy Yard, and remained there until the latter part of May, when it was transferred to the Navy Yard and did guard duty there while the iron clad Virginia (Merrimac) was being built. Captain Etheredge has related to the author the anxiety of Commodore Forrest, who had command of the Navy Yard and who seemed burdened with a fear that the Yankees would attempt to burn it up. On one occasion he informed Captain Etheredge that he had received a letter telling him that the Yankees had offered a million dollars to any one who would set fire to the ship, and urged redoubled vigilance on the part of the guard. Captain Etheredge assured him that no Federal emissary should get near enough to set her on fire. Captain Etheredge says scarcely a day passed without some such incident as that happening between the Commodore and himself.

In March, 1862, the company left the Navy Yard, went to Seawell's Point and joined its regiment, the 41st Virginia, it being Company F. The officers of the 41st were Colonel John R. Chambliss, Lieutenant Colonel William A. Parham and Major Joseph Minetree. The company left Seawell's Point May 10th, 1862, with the balance of Huger's Division for Richmond. In March Lieutenant Jett resigned and organized a company called the Border Rifles, of which he was elected Captain. As Company F had more than the regulation number of men for one company about twenty five or thirty of them at their own request were assigned to Captain Jett's new company, and their names will not appear on the roll of Company F.

The first battle in which the 41st Regiment was engaged was the battle of Seven Pines. The regiment was under command of Colonel Chambliss and had already been assigned to Mahone's Brigade. It was advancing in line of battle, not aware of the close proximity of the enemy. Company F was on the extreme right and next to it was a company from Petersburg. While the regiment was advancing the left marched faster than the right, and being in an oblique position, received a flanking fire from the enemy, which, being unexpected, threw the regiment into confusion and that portion of it nearest the enemy retired very hastily. Captain Etheredge sprang to the front of his company, spoke a few words of encouragement to them, reminded them of their promise to follow wherever he led, and they stood by him manfully. A portion of the Petersburg company, on his left, under their captain, also stood their ground, and these two companies formed a nucleus upon which the other companies rallied.

In the midst of the confusion Colonel Chambliss rode in front of Company F and his horse was killed under him. Just as he fell Dr. James Parrish of Portsmouth, Surgeon of the regiment, rode up and offered his horse to the Colonel, who declined it, saying, "I believe I will stay here on foot with the old man," meaning Captain Etheredge. He reminded Dr. Parrish that his post was in the rear and ordered him to it. Colonel Chambliss assembled the captains of the various companies of the regiment at his tent the next day, and after complimenting Captain Etheredge, told them that the stand made by Company F had saved the credit of the regiment.

After the battle of Seven Pines Colonel Chambliss was transferred to a cavalry regiment and Captain Etheredge was promoted to Major of the 41st. This also caused a change in the officers of Company F, and Lieutenant Biddle became captain. Captain Biddle died in a hospital September 16th, 1862, and 1st Lieutenant Arthur E. Portlock succeeded him. He was wounded at Chancellorsville May 3d, 1863, recovered from his wound and died from sickness in Richmond August 9th, 1864. Lieutenant W. Scott Sykes became captain at the death of Captain Portlock and commanded it until the close of the war. He was wounded July 30th, 1864, at the Crater, but recovered and surrendered with the company at Appomattox April 9th, 1865, with seventeen members of the company. The company participated in twenty-one pitched battles and numerous smaller affairs and lost thirty-one men by death from wounds or sickness. First Lieutenant John T. Widgeon was killed May 1st, 1863, at Chancellorsville.

Captain Wm. H. Etheredge, promoted Major 41st Regiment, surrendered at
 Appomattox.
Captain Phillip W. Biddle, died September 16th, 1862, Winchester.
Captain Arthur E. Portlock, died August 9th, 1864, Richmond, wounded
 May 1st, 1863, Chancellorsville.
Captain W. Scott Sykes, wounded July 30th, 1864, Crater, surrendered at
 Appomattox.
Lieutenant John T. Widgeon, killed May 1st, 1863, Chancellorsville.
Lieutenant Robert C. Jones, surrendered at Appomattox.
Lieutenant Wm. T. Gray, promoted 2d Lieutenant March 11th, 1864, re-
 signed.
Lieutenant John N. Etheredge, not re-elected at reorganization in 1862.
Sergeant John H. Kirby, sick in hospital at time of surrender.
Sergeant David W. Whitehurst, surrendered at Appomattox.
Sergeant John F. Murden, wounded July 30th, 1864, Crater, surrendered at
 Appomattox.
Sergeant James E. Armstrong, killed May 6th, 1864, Wilderness.
Sergeant Robert W. Carson, died February, 1865.
Sergeant George T. Tart, died in prison, captured August 19th, 1864.
Corporal John D. Hudgins, died January, 1863.
Corporal Josephus Godfrey, killed August 30th, 1863, 2d Manassas.
Corporal John Z. Lowe, captured August 19th, 1864, not exchanged.
Corporal H. T. Williamson, surrendered at Appomattox.
Corporal Arthur H. Tatem, captured October 27th, 1864, not exchanged.

PRIVATES.

Butt, Frederick, captured October 27th, 1864, on parole at surrender.
Butt, Henry, wounded July 2d, 1863, and disabled, Gettysburg.
Butt, Francis, wounded August 30th, 1862, and disabled, Manassas.
Barrett, Wm. S., appointed musician for regiment.
Banks, Edwin, mortally wounded July 1st, 1862, Malvern Hill.
Butler, James N., detailed in Q. M. Department.
Bailey, Wm. H., (1) killed July 1st, 1862, Malvern Hill.
Bailey, Wm. H., (2) captured on retreat from Petersburg.
Ballentine, Thos. R., wounded June 1st, 1862, Seven Pines and furnished
 substitute.
Buck, David.
Cuthriell, Enos, detailed March 1st, 1862, by Secretary of War.
Cuthriell, John W., detailed March 1st, 1862, by Secretary of War.
Cuthriell, Joseph E., detailed March 1st, 1862, by Secretary of War.
Carter, Wm. E., captured at evacuation of Petersburg.
Creekmore, Gregory, detailed 1861 to work in Navy Yard.
Detrick, John, wounded July 1st, 1862, Malvern Hill, and furloughed.
Dashiell, Leven H., wounded Seven Pines, Malvern Hill and Manassas, and
 was detailed in Q. M. Department at surrender.
Dey, Apollos O., wounded June 1st, 1862, Seven Pines, furnished substi-
 tute.
Dey, David, detailed by order of Secretary of War.
Dunn, J. Thos., captured August 19th, 1864, not exchanged.
Davis, Wm. H., captured on retreat from Petersburg.
Davis, Wm. T.
Deyser, Luke, killed on retreat from Petersburg.
Edmonds, John J., detailed in hospital department.
Edmonds, W. C., detailed in ordnance department.
Edmunds, Henry.
Edmunds, Abel, captured October 29th, 1864, and not exchanged.
Elliott, Kemp B., discharged 1862.
Etheredge, Charles O., wounded June 1st, 1862, Seven Pines.
Edmondson, Gabriel, wounded September 17th, 1862, Sharpsburg, and
 transferred to navy.
Etheredge, Samuel A., surrendered at Appomattox.

NORFOLK CO. PATRIOTS, CO. F, FORTY-FIRST VA. REGT. 139

Forbes, Elijah B., wounded May 1st, 1863, Chancellorsville, and transferred to navy.
Foreman, Josephus, killed August 30th, 1862, 2d Manassas.
Fisher, Caleb, surrendered at Appomattox.
Forrest, John R., detailed in Q. M. department.
Foreman, Washington, wounded June 30th, 1862, Charles City Road, surrendered at Appomattox.
Foreman, Thos., in hospital during the war.
Fitchett, Wm. E., wounded June 1st, 1862, Seven Pines.
Fentress, John, wounded June 1st, 1862, Seven Pines, disabled July 1st, 1862, at Malvern Hill and discharged.
Godfrey, Walton, died December, 1862, near Fredericksburg.
Gibson, Peter H., sick in hospital at time of surrender.
Gilbert, Robertson, detailed by order of General Mahone.
Gilbert, Richard B.
Hodges, Riley W., killed July 1st, 1862, Malvern Hill.
Hodges, Wm. W., killed June 1st, 1862, Seven Pines.
Hodges, Josiah, died in hospital.
Hodges, David, killed July 2d, 1863, Gettysburg.
Hanbury, Wm. T., discharged.
Howell, Jesse B.
Hughes, Isaac B., killed June 1st, 1862, Seven Pines.
Harrison, Benjamin F., detailed in hospital, Richmond.
Halstead, Henry, captured.
Hodges, John H., wounded July 1st, 1862, Malvern Hill, furnished substitute.
Hodges, John K., wounded May 6th, 1864, Wilderness.
Hall, Samuel, wounded June 1st, 1862, Seven Pines, and killed July 30th, 1864, crater.
Hodges, Samuel, killed July 1st, 1862, Malvern Hill.
Hall, Edward, wounded May 6th, 1864, Wilderness, surrendered at Appomattox.
Hodges, Geo. A., discharged April 16th, 1862.
Hudgins, Wm., died in hospital April 18th, 1862.
Hall, Geo. W., captured on retreat from Petersburg.
Herbert, Melnotte, promoted 1st Lieutenant Company D.
Jones, Walter C., killed May 6th, 1864, Wilderness.
Kirby, Wm. H., discharged March 25th, 1862, disability.
Knight, Wm. H.
Lowe, Wm. J., captured in Petersburg.
Lockhart, Benj. H., wounded August 30th, 1862, Manassas, and detailed in passport office, Gordonsville.
Lynch, Oresmus M., wounded June 1st, 1862, Seven Pines, and captured.
Merchant, Francis M., promoted Lieutenat Company K, 61st Virginia.
Miller, Wm. H., detailed to regimental drum corps.
McClanen, Wilson L., died in hospital.
Murphy, Wm. J.
Murphy, James T.
Murden, Samuel, wounded June 22d, 1864, Wilcox Farm, and detailed in commissary department.
Murden, Reuben, mortally wounded May 1st, 1863, Chancellorsville.
Murden, Henry, died in hospital, 1862.
Murden, Camillus, killed May 1st, 1863, Chancellorsville.
Manning, Canning, captured and not exchanged.
McPherson, Robert, discharged April 25th, 1862.
Miller, W. H.
Nash, James E., discharged for physical disability.
Nicholson, Allen F., discharged April, 1862, over age.
Portlock, Wm. F., wounded August 30th, 1862, Manassas, surrendered at Appomattox.
Portlock, Dempsy, surrendered at Appomattox.

Pherral, Isaac, killed August 30th, 1862, 2d Manassas.
Randolph, James A., wounded and disabled August 30, 1862, 2d Manassas.
Ritter, James A., wounded July 30th, 1864, Crater, surrendered at Appomattox.
Sykes, James W., wounded July 2d, 1863, Gettysburg, surrendered at Appomattox,
Sykes, Alex F., wounded June 30th, 1862, Charles City Road.
Speight, David, died in hospital.
Scaff, John D., surrendered at Appomattox.
Squires, Seth W., died in hospital, 1861.
Tatem, Nathaniel C., detached with Ransom's Brigade, surrendered at Appomattox.
Tatem, Elijah A., wounded and disabled July 1st, 1862, Malvern Hill, and discharged.
Tatem, John W.,
Taylor, James F., died in hospital.
Whitehurst, Christopher, discharged.
Williamson, Virginius, captured on retreat from Petersburg.
Williamson, Samuel, captured.
Williams, Samuel, killed June 2d, 1864, Cold Harbor.
Woodhouse, Moses C.
Wright, David L., discharged.
Woodward, Oden, captured in Pennsylvania and never heard from.
Williamson, Everett, appointed Ordinance Sergeant of regiment, surrendered at Appomattox.
Vellines, Watson B., discharged April 16th, 1862, by General Huger.
Killed and died—31.

This company participated in the battles of—

Seven Pines, June 1st, 1862.
Charles City Road, June 30th, 1862.
Malvern Hill, July 1st, 1862.
Manassas, Aug. 30th, 1862.
Crampton Gap, Sep. 14th, 1862.
Sharpsburg, Sep. 17th, 1862.
Fredericksburg, Dec. 13th, 1862.
Chancellorsville, May 1st, 2d, and 3d, 1863.
Salem Church, May 3d, 1863.
Gettysburg, July 1st and 2d, 1863.
Bristoe Station, Oct., 14th, 1863.
Mine Run, Dec. 2d, 1863.
Wilderness, May 6th, 1864.
Spotsylvania, C. H., May 12th, 1864.
Turkey Ridge, skirmishing June 4th to 13th, 1864.
Frazier's Farm June 13th, 1864.
Wilcox Farm, June 22d, 1864.
Cold Harbor, June 2d and 3d, 1864.
Crater, July 30th, 1864.
Davis Farm, Aug. 19th, 1864.
Ream's Station, Aug. 25th,1864.
Burgess Mill, Oct. 29th, 1864.
Hicksford, Dec. 9th, 1864.
Hatcher's Run, Feb. 6th, 1865.
Cumberland Church, April 7th, 1865.

Amelia C. H., April 5th, 1865.

In all of the above battles the Confederates were victorious except Malvern Hill, Crampton Gap and Bristoe Station. In the first and last of these three the Federals successfully resisted the Confederate attacks, but retreated after the battles.

CHAPTER XVI.

THE JACKSON GRAYS, COMPANY A, SIXTY-FIRST VIRGINIA REGIMENT.

This company was recruited in St. Bride's Parish of Norfolk county, in the section now known as Pleasant Grove Magisterial District, and was organized at Pleasant Grove Baptist Church, July 1st, 1861. The company left Pleasant Grove on the 10th of July, and reached the Court House at Portsmouth on the 12th, and was mustered into service there. It was then officered as follows:

Captain, Wm. H. Stewart.

First Lieutenant, Wm. C. Wallace; 2d Lieutenant, John T. West; 3d Lieutenant, Geo. T. Hodges.

First Sergeant, Camillus A. Nash; 2d Sergeant, William A. West; 3d Sergeant, William A. Dudley; 4th Sergeant, Henry S. Etheredge.

First Corporal, Peleg Pritchard; 2d Corporal, Geo. D. Old; 3d Corporal, Thos. H. Sykes; 4th Corporal, Laban Mansfield.

The company was named after Mr. James P. Jackson, the proprietor of the Marshall House in Alexandria, who was killed in that city on the 24th of May for defending the flag he had hoisted over his hotel. That day, a large force of Federals, numbering eight or nine thousand men, was pushed across the Potomac river early in the morning, and occupied the town. Seeing the Confederate flag flying at the top of the staff on the hotel, Colonel Ellsworth, of Chicago, commanding a regiment of Fire Zouaves of New York city, went up to the top of the building, with several men from his regiment, and took it down. As he was descending from the elevation, Mr. Jackson, who had been aroused by the noise, came out from his bed room with a double barrel gun, and upon his asking the cause of the commotion, Colonel Ellsworth pointed to the flag in his possession and said: "This is my trophy." Mr. Jackson replied, "And you are mine," and immediately fired, killing him dead. Colonel Ellsworth's companions returned the fire, shooting Mr. Jackson and afterwards running a bayonet in him.

After remaining at the Court House for a few days, the company was ordered to the batteries at the Naval Hospital and remained on duty there testing the heavy rifled cannon which were being re-modeled in the Gosport Navy Yard, until December, when, at its own request, it was sent to Sewell's Point and put in charge of a masked battery of six heavy rifled guns of six-inch caliber. This was the most advanced battery among the defences of the harbor of Norfolk and Portsmouth, and was within range of the Federal guns at the Rip Raps or Fort Calhoun.

When the Confederate iron-clad Virginia, better known, however, as the Merrimac, went down to Hampton Roads and had her battles with the United States fleet, on the 8th and 9th of March, 1862, this battery took part, with two rifle six-inch guns, in the engagement, as the naval vessels, passing to and from Fortress Monroe, passed within range of its guns. Two men belonging to the company were wounded in this engagement. They were Lieutenant Wm. C. Wallace, who was slightly hurt, and Private A. B. Cooper, whose skull was fractured, and whose wound was so serious that he was incapacitated from further service and was discharged. They were wounded by a shell from the Sawyer gun at the Rip Raps. One of the rifle guns burst one of its bands from too rapid firing and becoming overheated. On the morning of May 10th, 1862, the company abandoned the battery by order of General Huger and formed the rear guard of the troops as they fell back upon Norfolk, crossed the ferry to Portsmouth and was the last command which left that city by rail, being moved out on flat cars late in the afternoon. Only one company remained after the departure of the Jackson Grays, namely, the Portsmouth Rifle Company, and that marched out of the city to Suffolk.

Upon the arrival of the company at Petersburg, it was assigned to duty with the 61st Virginia Regiment as Company A. At that time the regiment was under command of Lieutenant-Colonel Wm. Fred. Niemeyer, and, in a few days, the company, with Company C, the Blanchard Grays, of Norfolk county, was detached from the regiment, and with a two gun battery of six-pounders, ordered to the neighborhood of Bermuda Hundreds, in Chesterfield county, to watch the movements of the Federal fleet in James river. While there, during the seven day's battles, the fleet made a demonstration up the Appomattox river towards Petersburg, and attempted to secure a large quantity of coal which was stored at Port Walthal, but this small force attacked them and so annoyed them as to force them to hug the opposite shore, where several of the vessels stuck in the mud, and after two days the enemy was forced to set fire to and abandon one gunboat. This action took place on the 26th of June, 1862. From Bermuda Hundreds, the company was ordered to guard the fords of the Rappahannock river, while General Lee, with his army, was engaged in the Maryland campaign. While there, upon one occasion, while scouting near Bristoe Station, it met a Federal brigage belonging to Seigles' corps, accompanied by a battery of artillery and a company of cavalry. Under cover of a forest, which concealed the smallness of the Confederate force, an attack was made upon the Federals who were repelled. The company captured several prisoners and withdrew without having suffered any loss. After the return of General Lee's army from Maryland in October, 1862, the Jackson Grays, with the 61st Virginia Regiment, was assigned to Mahone's Brigade, and became a part of the army of Northern Virginia. From that time it followed closely the fortunes of that army, took part in all of its battles and victories and marches, and when the final defeat attended its banners, surrendered fifteen muskets at Appomattox Court House on the 9th of April, 1865.

Of the commissioned officers of the company, not one escaped the shots of the enemy. Captain Wm. H. Stewart, its first captain, was promoted to major and then to lieutenant-colonel of the regiment, and was twice wounded. First Lieutenant William C. Wallace was promoted to captain in May, 1862, upon the promotion of Captain Stewart to major. He was wounded slightly at Sewell's Point in the engagement of the 8th of March, 1862, between the ironclad Virginia (Merrimac) and the Federal fleet, in which the shore battery at Sewell's Point took part, and was mortally wounded on the 19th of August, 1864, at the battle on the Petersburg and Weldon railroad, sometimes called the battle of Davis Farm. He fell into the hands of the enemy and died within their lines. He was a little more than twenty-two years old at the time of his death, having been born at Wallaceton, Norfolk county, on the 23d of March, 1842. He was brave, gentle and polished, and loved by all who knew him.

Upon the death of Captain Wallace, Lieutenant John T. West became captain of the company. From November, 1863, until August 19th, 1864, Lieutenant West was detailed from the company by order of General Mahone, and placed in command of a select company of sharp shooters, which with four other companies, one from each regiment in the brigade, constituted the corps of one hundred and fifty men known as Mahone's sharp shooters, more than three-fourths of whom were killed or wounded during the campaign of 1864, but from that date, until the close of the war, commanded his own company. He was wounded twice, once by a bayonet thrust at the Crater, July 30th, 1864, and once by a piece of shell on the Plank Road in February, 1865. Third Lieutenant George T. Hodges, on account of the promotion of Captain Stewart and Lieutenant West, and the death of Captain Wallace, became First Lieutenant of the company and escaped with a slight wound, which he received May 3d, 1863, at the battle of Salem Church, a part of the battle of Chancellorsville, which took place between Sedgwick's corps of General Hooker's army and a portion of General Lee's army, which had been sent to stop his advance from Fredericksburg. First Sergeant C. A. Nash was promoted to second lieutenant, and was slightly wounded at the Crater, July 30th, 1864, but remained with the company. On the

19th of August, 1864, he received a very severe wound and shortly afterwards resigned his commission and volunteered as a private in Mosby's command. Lieutenant Nash is at this writing, 1892, Colonel of the 4th Virginia Volunteers. The company lost by deaths from wounds and disease forty-three men, probably more than any other company which went into the service from Portsmouth and Norfolk county and the roll which follows gives the names of seventeen others who were wounded. Some of them were wounded more than once. There were certainly others, though they have escaped from memory in the lapse of twenty-seven years. At the battle of the Crater, July 30th, 1864, the company lost four men killed and six wounded, which was fully half of those present for duty. It lost men killed in the battles of Chancellorsville, Gettysburg, the Wilderness, Spotsylvania, Cold Harbor, Wilcox Farm, the Crater, Davis Farm, Burgess Mill and Hatcher's Run, while in the other battles in which it was engaged its casualties embraced the wounded only. Very few of its members fell into the hands of the enemy and some of those were wounded. Company A was a company of whose war record Norfolk county may well feel proud, in fact, she may of all of her companies. Below will be found a roster of the company, copied from the muster roll of May, 1862:

Captain Wm. H. Stewart, promoted to Lieutenant Colonel 61st Virginia, wounded.
Captain W. C. Wallace, wounded Sewell's Point, killed August 19th, 1864.
Captain John T. West, wounded by bayonet at Crater, wounded February 28th, 1865.
Lieutenant Geo. T. Hodges, wounded May 3d, 1863, Salem Church.
Lieutenant Camillus A. Nash, wounded July 30th, 1864, Crater, and August 19th, 1864, Davis Farm.
Sergeant Wm. A. West, appointed Commissary Sergeant in 1864.
Sergeant Wm. R. Dudley, captured at Burgess Mill in 1864.
Sergeant Henry S. Etheridge, appointed hospital steward.
Corporal Polig Pritchard, wounded October 20th, 1864, Burgess Mill.
Corporal Geo. D. Old, promoted Captain and Commissary 61st Virginia.
Corporal Thos. H. Sykes, captured at Gettysburg.
Corporal Laban Mansfield, killed October 20th, 1864, Burgess Mill.
Musician James Toy.
Musician Wm. Mahoney.

PRIVATES.

Butt, Henry Jas., killed July 30th, 1864, at Crater.
Bright, Geo. W., killed May 1st, 1863, Chancellorsville.
Curling, Ashwell, killed June 22d, 1864, at Wilcox Farm.
Castine, Jeremiah, killed July 30th, 1864, at Crater.
Creekmore, Josiah, discharged in 1862 for disability.
Castine, J. T.
Cooper, A. B., wounded March 8th, 1862, Sewell's Point, and discharged.
Cooper, J. A., wounded by bayonet July 30th, 1864, at Crater.
Cooper, C. C., wounded July 30th, 1864, at Crater.
Creekmore, Marshall O., killed by sharpshooter May 14th, 1864, Spotsylvania C. H.
Creekmore, John W., promoted to Sergeant, captured October 20th, 1864, Burgess Mill.

JACKSON GRAYS, CO. A, SIXTY-FIRST VA. REGT. 145

Creekmore, Willoughby W., died in hospital, 1864.
Culpepper, Daniel R., died in hospital, 1863.
Culpepper, John, died in hospital, 1863, U. S. Ford.
Deford, John W., promoted to corporal, died in hospital, May, 1863.
Diggs, Benj. F., captured at Gettysburg.
Duncan, Abner, wounded and disabled February 28th, 1864, Germanna Ford.
Ferrell, John, died in hospital, April, 1862.
Foreman, Acelins G., killed May 6th, 1864, Wilderness.
Foreman, Carey, wounded October 20th, 1864, Burgess Mill.
Foreman, W. A., detailed in hospital.
Fulford, James E., killed February 6th, 1865, Hatcher's Run.
Fulford, James, died in hospital, U. S. Ford, 1863.
Grimes, J. A.
Grimes, J. F. W.
Gninn, Franklin.
Harrison, Wm. H., wounded October 14th, 1863, Bristoe Station, placed on roll of honor, by order of General Lee, for gallantry at Crater.
Halstead, J. P., wounded July 30th, 1864, at Crater.
Halstead, T. E.
Halstead, J. E., died in hospital.
Hodges, Isaiah, killed by sharpshooter May 14th, 1864, Spotsylvania.
Hodges, Caleb.
Hodges, Thomas H., died in hospital March, 1863, U. S. Ford.
Jennings, Lemuel, killed May 1st, 1863, Chancellorsville.
Jennings, Wickers P., promoted to corporal.
Lewis, Abner.
Lynch, John, died in hospital March, 1863, U. S. Ford.
Lynch, Leroy, died in hospital March, 1863, U. S. Ford.
Lee, Alexander O.
Mathias, Simon.
Morgan, W. P., died in hospital from wound.
Morgan, A. C., wounded August 19th, 1864, and died.
Miller, J. J., wounded July 30th, 1864, at Crater.
Miller, J. H.
Miller, Lovett.
Mercer, Sam. M., died in hospital.
Murphy, T. O. C.
Nash, Cincinnatus, promoted Sergeant.
Nash, Henry.
Only, Nahariah.
Overton, C. N., wounded at Gettysburg.
Overton, Grandy.
Prichard, Wiley, died in hospital, 1862.
Pritchard, Joseph, died in hospital January, 1862.
Ried, William M., wounded May 12th, 1864, Spotsylvania.
Scott, Wm. T., wounded and died in prison September, 1863.
Scott, Joseph.
Sivells, D. T., killed May 2d, 1863, Chancellorsville.
Sivells, Alexander.
Speight, Benj. F., died in hospital January, 1862.
Sykes, W. O., promoted to Corporal, killed August 19th, 1864, Davis Farm.
Sykes, Joseph, killed July 2d, 1863, Gettysburg.
Sykes, Josephus.
Sykes, Henry, died in hospital, U. S. Ford, March, 1863.
Sykes, J. C. C., died in hospital, September, 1863.
Thompson, Wm., detailed in Ordnance Department.
Warden, James.
Warden, Richard H., died in hospital.
Waller, W. George, died in prison.
Wood, Joseph N., promoted to Corporal.
Wood, Keeling, died in hospital, March, 1864.

Woodward, Joseph T., died in hospital, January, 1862.
Woodward, Leander, wounded at Gettysburg.
Whitehurst, Robert.
Whitehurst, Willoughby, killed May 6th, 1864, Wilderness.
Williams, D. A., killed July 30th, 1864, Crater.
Williams, Marcellus W., killed July 30th, 1864, Crater.
Wright, Peter, wounded May 6th, 1864, Wilderness and at Crater.
West, Leroy McC., promoted Corporal, wounded May 6th, 1864, Wilderness, October 20th, 1864, Burgess Mill.
West, W. W., transferred to navy.
Whitehead, Martin V.
Williams, Joseph, died in hospital December, 1861.
Williams, M. D., died in hospital January, 1863.
Worden, Wm. H., died in hospital February, 1862.
    Killed and died—43.

CHAPTER XVII.

THE WILSON GUARDS, COMPANY B, SIXTY-FIRST VIRGINIA REGIMENT.

This company was organized in 1861 in that portion of Norfolk county now known as Butt's Road and Pleasant Grove townships or magisterial districts, and contained a number of North Carolinians from Currituck county, near the Norfolk county line. The company was named after Colonel Samuel M. Wilson, who was then engaged in organizing a regiment of heavy artillery, and it was the intention of the Wilson Guards to form a part of that regiment. After being mustered into service the company was, at its own request, assigned to Colonel Wilson's command as Company B. The officers of the company at its organization were:

Captain, J. W. M. Hopkins.

First Lieutenant, Thomas F. Baxter; 2d Lieutenant, A. H. Lindsay; 3d Lieutenant, James E. Fulford.

First Sergeant, James A. Stott.

Lieutenant Lindsay resigned January 20th, 1862, and Lieutenant Fulford was promoted to 2d Lieutenant, and Sergeant Stott was elected 3d Lieutenant. This caused the promotion of Benj. F. Baxter to 1st Sergeant, but on the 19th of May he was transferred to the Petersburg Cavalry and A. B. C. Fisher became 1st Sergeant. Captain Hopkins resigned on the 3d of January, 1863. Lieutenant Baxter became Captain, Lieutenant Fulford was advanced to 1st, and Lieutenant Stott to 2d Lieutenant, and, on the 13th of January, Sergeant Fisher was elected 3d Lieutenant. Captain Baxter was wounded at the battle of Davis' Farm on the 19th of August, 1864, and Lieutenant Fulford was captured at the battle of Burgess Mill on the 27th of October. Lieutenant Stott was wounded at the battle of Burgess' Mill, but recovered sufficiently to rejoin the company, and surrendered with it at Appomattox Court House. He was acting Adjutant of the regiment at the time of the surrender. Lieutenant Fisher died in a hospital at Charlottesville on the 12th of March, 1864.

Upon the evacuation of Portsmouth, the Wilson Guards joined the 61st Regiment in Petersburg and assisted in the election of regimental officers, after which it did provost duty for a while in that city and was subsequently sent with Company A on picket duty on the Appomattox river in the vicinity of City Point. In August it rejoined the regiment and moved to Richmond, thence to the upper Rappahannock or Rapidan river. While there the company had two skirmishes with the enemy—one at Warrenton Junction on the 4th of November, 1862, and the other at Rappahannock bridge on the 7th. It rejoined the regiment on the 24th and was with it when it began the march to Fredericksburg. The company had two other first Sergeants in addition to those mentioned above. John H. Tucker succeeded Sergeant A. B. C. Fisher when the latter was promoted to 3d Lieutenant on the 13th of January, 1863, and held the position until August 17th, 1864, when he died from wounds received at the battle of the Crater, July 30th. Willoughby D. Barnard then succeeded to the first sergeancy and held it until the close of the war.

The company lost by death fully one-third of the members who left Norfolk county with it, and surrendered at Appomattox with one commissioned officer, four non-commissioned officers and eight privates. At the time of the evacuation of Portsmouth by the Confederates, it was on duty at Barrett's Neck.

Below will be found the roll of the company embracing both the Norfolk county and Currituck county men :

Captain J. W. M. Hopkins, resigned January 3d, 1863.
First Lieutenant Thomas F. Baxter, promoted Captain January 3d, 1863, wounded August 19th, 1864, Davis' Farm.
Second Lieutenant James E. Fulford, promoted 1st Lieutenant, wounded July 30th, 1864, and captured October 27th, 1864, Burgess' Mill.
Third Lieutenant James A. Stott, promoted 2d Lieutenant, wounded Aug. 19th, 1864, October 17th, 1864, rejoined company, surrendered at Appomattox.
First Sergeant Benjamin F. Baxter, transferred to Petersburg cavalry May 19th, 1862.
Second Sergeant A. B. C. Fisher, promoted 3d Lieutenant January 13th, 1863, died in hospital March 12th, 1864, in Charlottesville.
Third Sergeant John H. Tucker, promoted to 1st Sergeant, wounded July 30th, 1864, at the Crater and died August 17th.
Fourth Sergeant, Willoughby B. Barnard, promoted 1st Sergeant April 17th, 1864.
Fifth Sergeant Francis H. Williams.
Corporal Thomas Williams, promoted Ordnance Sergeant 61st Regiment, captured December 17th, 1863, in Currituck county, North Carolina, and exchanged.
Corporal Ivy C. Brown, promoted Sergeant, killed June 30th, 1864, Cold Harbor.
Corporal John H. Halstead, transferred to Signal Corps April 30th, 1862.
Corporal James E. Tucker, wounded August 19th, 1864, Davis' Farm.

PRIVATES.

Ansel, Andrew J., captured October 27th, 1864, Burgess' Mill.
Asbold, Wm.
Aydelott, Jacob.
Ballance, Stephen R., wounded August 19th, 1864, Davis' Farm.
Ballance, Stephen R. Jr., wounded and captured August 19th, 1864, Davis' Farm.
Bowden, John A., killed August 19th, 1864, Davis' Farm.
Beasley, Joachin, promoted Corporal.
Bunnell, Kenneth, captured May 26th, 1864 sick in hospital Atlee Station.
Ballentine, James M., died in hospital April 11th, 1862.
Bray, Thomas A., died in hospital June 1st, 1864, Richmond.
Bourke, Thomas, died in hospital 1862, Richmond.
Cotton, Benjamin C., died in hospital December 3d, 1862.
Creekmore, Seth.

Curling, Joseph H. Sr., wounded and captured August 19th, 1864, Davis' Farm.
Curling, Joseph H. Jr., died in hospital February 26th, 1864, Orange Court House.
Curling, Z. T., captured October 27th, 1864, Burgess' Mill.
Cooper, William A., wounded June 22d, 1864, Wilcox Farm.
Davis, William G. B., discharged July 25th, 1863, disability.
Davis, James, died in hospital 1862.
Doxey, David W., killed August 19th, 1864, Davis' Farm.
Dudley, Willis W., died at Point Lookout April, 1865.
Eason, John T., captured October 27th, 1864, Burgess' Mill.
Ferrell, George.
Fanshaw, Alpheus, detailed Teamster, June 17th, 1862.
Fentress, Joseph, died in hospital January 24th, 1864, Petersburg.
Foreman, John W., transferred to Company G, April 30th, 1863.
Grandy, A. W., transferred from Company C November 23d, 1863.
Gregory, William H., wounded June 22d, 1864, at Wilcox Farm, died June 25th.
Grimstead, Jonathan, died in hospital December 11th, 1862.
Hall, Thomas F.
Hall, Samuel, wounded and captured August 19th, 1864, Davis' Farm.
Halstead, William M., promoted Corporal, died in hospital June 25th, 1863.
Harris, Samuel.
Harrison, John S., captured October 27th, 1864, Burgess' Mill.
Hodges, Celius, wounded July 30th, 1864, at Crater, died August 3d.
Hodges, Thomas W.
Hodges, John W., died in hospital June 18th, 1862.
Hanbury, John W.
Jones, Celius W., died in hospital March 29th, 1862.
Keaton, Samuel, discharged December 22d, 1862, over age.
Kinsey, James M., detailed in hospital.
Kinsey, William H., detailed as nurse in hospital March 8th, 1863.
Kinsey, Samuel, captured October 27th, 1864, at Burgess' Mill.
Lee, Madison, wounded June 22d, 1864, at Wilcox Farm.
Lee, John J., captured October 27th, 1864, at Burgess' Mill.
Martin, Charles, discharged August 14th, 1864, over age.
Mathias, Hilliard W., wounded October 27th, 1864, Burgess' Mill.
Maund, David W., transferred to Signal Corps April 30th, 1862.
McClanan, Henry B., promoted Corporal, wounded July 30th, 1864, at Crater, died August 6th.
McPherson, Jesse, wounded July 4th, 1863, at Gettysburg.
Miles, A. W., died in hospital.
Mercer, Jacob B., wounded May 12th, 1864, at Spotsylvania and died.
Miller, Jesse, captured October 27th, 1864, Burgess' Mill.
Mills, James, wounded December 12th, 1862, at Fredericksburg, died December 13th.
Nichols, Thomas J., discharged July 15th, 1863, disability.
Nichols, Willoughby, killed July 30th, 1864, at the Crater.
Nichols, James, died in hospital December 16th, 1863, Richmond.
Parsons, Johnson T., captured July 5th, 1863, Gettysburg.
Parker, Peter, died in hospital 1863, Richmond.
Powers, Wesley, transferred to Company C November 23d, 1863.
Rogers, Charles E., died in hospital April 12th, 1863, U. S. Ford.
Saunders, Daniel, died in hospital February 13th, 1863.
Scarff, Charles S., captured June 6th, 1864, Cold Harbor.
Smith, Richard.
Simmons, John R., transferred to Company H January 1st, 1863.
Steel, William W., captured October 27th, 1864, at Burgess' Mill.
Stewart, Ashwell.
Stewart, Tazwell, died in hospital 1863, Richmond.
Stewart, William, killed May 12th, 1864, Spotsylvania C. H.

Stanley, Samuel, died in hospital April 15th, 1864.
Stanley, Hillary, died in hospital June 18th, 1862, City Point.
Sykes, William, discharged May 13th, 1862, disability.
Sykes, George A., killed July 30th, 1864, at Crater.
Thompson, Christopher.
Waterfield, Cone.
Waterfield, William T., died in hospital May 14th, 1863.
Waterfield, Alex., died in hospital June 22d, 1862.
Waterfield, Malachi J., killed in battle.
Wicker, C. W., wounded August 19th, 1864, Davis' Farm.
Waterfield, John C., wounded and disabled near Petersburg, 1864.
White, William, captured October 27th, 1864. Burgess' Mill.
White, Ryland C., captured April, 1865, on retreat from Petersburg.
Whitehurst, Walter S., discharged March 18th, 1862, disability.
Williams, Wilson W. D., killed October 27th, 1864, at Burgess' Mill.
Williams, Quinton T., transferred June 27th, 1862, to Petersburg Cavalry.
Wicker, William T., died in hospital Februrry 18th, 1863.
  Killed and died—38.

CHAPTER XVIII.

THE BLANCHARD GRAYS, COMPANY C, SIXTY-FIRST VIRGINIA REGIMENT.

This company was organized in the Great Bridge section of Norfolk county in 1861, and was named in honor of Colonel A. G. Blanchard, commander of the 1st Louisiana Regiment. Upon being mustered into service it was assigned to the battalion which Colonel Samuel M. Wilson was organizing for duty in the batteries around the harbor of Norfolk and Portsmouth. This battalion afterwards became the 61st Virginia Regiment, and the Blanchard Grays became Company C. The following were the officers:
Captain, John G. Wallace.
First Lieutenant, Ashville Simmons; 2d Lieutenant, St. Julien Wilson; 3d Lieutenant, Benj. James.
First Sergeant, John H. Bogart.

The company remained on duty near Portsmouth until the evacuation of the city, May 10th, 1862, when it was carried by rail to Petersburg and participated in the organization and election of officers of the 61st Regiment. It did provost duty in Petersburg for a while and went from there to the Appomattox river on picket duty, and about the 28th of August reported back to the regiment on Dunn's Hill and accompanied it to Richmond. Early in September it was ordered to the Rapidan with the regiment and did picket duty along the river guarding fords, and scouted as far as Warrenton Junction. Upon the return of General Lee's army from the Maryland campaign, the various companies of the 61st Regiment which were scattered along the Rapidan, were concentrated, and the regiment moved down to Fredericksburg to observe the movements of Burnside's army, and delay him as long as possible in crossing the Rappahannock river. The company was present at the battles of Fredericksburg, Chancellorsville, Salem Church, Gettysburg, Bristoe Station, Mine Run, Wilderness, Spotsylvania Court House, and in fact in all of the battles in which Mahone's Brigade was engaged after October, 1862.

Lieutenant Simmons resigned his commission as 1st lieutenant on the 30th of March, 1864, and Lieutenants St. Julien Wilson and Benjamin James were promoted to 1st and 2d lieutenants respectively. At the battle of the Crater, fought on the 30th of July, 1864, Captain Wallace was severely wounded and disabled, and Lieutenant Wilson was mortally wounded. Lieutenant James was promoted to 1st lieutenant upon the death of Lieutenant Wilson and was captured on the 27th of October following, at the battle of Burgess' Mill. This left the company without any commissioned officers.

This company lost as many men during the war, in proportion to its numbers, as probably any other which entered the Confederate army from Eastern Virginia. Of eighty-four names on its muster rolls six were transferred to other commands, and three were discharged from the army upon surgeon's certificates of disability, thus leaving with the company only seventy-five men and of these, thirty-three never returned. Disease carried off more than were killed in battle.

After the battle of Burgess Mill the company was commanded by Lieutenant V. A. Haynes, of Company D, and surrendered at Appomattox with six privates.

Below will be found the roll of the company:

Captain John G. Wallace, wounded and disabled July 30th, 1864, Crater.
First Lieutenant Ashville Simmons, resigned March 30th, 1864.
Second Lieutenant St. Julien Wilson, promoted 1st Lieutenant April 1st, 1864, wounded July 30th, 1864, Crater, died July 31st.
Third Lieutenant Benjamin James, promoted 1st Lieutenant July 30th, 1864, captured October 27th, 1864, Burgess Mill.
First Sergeant Jhon H. Bogart, captured October 16th, 1863, at Warrenton.
Sergeant Jas. E. Garret, captured October 27th, 1864, at Burgess' Mill.
" Wm. H. James.
" John Shirley.
Corporal Josiah Etheredge.
" Wm. H. Calhoun, transferred to Maryland line February 1st, 1864.
" Ed. W. Forbes, wounded July 30th, 1864, at Crater.
" John Gallup.

PRIVATES.

Banks, Wm., died in hospital May 6th, 1862, Norfolk.
Banks, James M.
Beals, Benj. J., captured October 27th, 1864, at Burgess' Mill.
Bell, Enoch F., died in hospital March 30th, 1863, U. S. Ford.
Byrum, Wm. F.
Berry, Martin, discharged March 29th, 1862, for disability.
Boushell, M. A., died in hospital February 13th, 1864, Orange Court House.
Berryman, Ed. F., appointed Sergeant Major 61st Regiment July 1st, 1862.
Bradley, Reuben.
Butt, John.
Burford, Samuel.
Byrum, James C., wounded May 1st, 1863, Chancellorsville, died May 7th.
Byrum, Gideon F., died in hospital January 23d, 1863, Richmond.
Cartwright, James E.
Cox, Sharp K.
Creekmore, Theophilus, died in hospital April 14th, 1863, at U. S. Ford.
Cowell, Benj. B., promoted corporal, killed July 30th, 1864, at Crater.
Curtis, Thomas, discharged January 30th, 1863, disability.
Darnold, John W.
Deconier, John, discharged February 24th, 1864, disability.
Doxey, Grandy B., wounded August 19th, 1864, Davis' Farm.
Eason, Geo. W.
Forbes, Nathaniel, died in hospital April, 1863, U. S. Ford.
Fulford, Thos. H., captured July 14th, 1863, in Maryland.
Glenn, Samuel T., transferred to Maryland line March 26th, 1862.
Grandy, Abner N., transferred to Company B November 21st, 1862.
Gallop, John C., died in hospital March 20th, 1863, Richmond.
Guilford, James, died in hospital May 16th, 1863, Charlottesville.
Halstead, Miles W., wounded July 30th, 1863, at Crater, died August 1st.

Harris, Miles D., wounded July 30th, 1864, and captured October 27th, 1864, at Burgess' Mill.
Hill, Solomon A., died in hospital October 16th, 1862, Culpepper.
Hughes, Charles.
Kher, William, wounded May 1st, 1863, Chancellorsville, died May 7th.
Lupton, J. W.
Lee, Willis, died in hospital June 17th, 1862, Petersburg.
Marchant, Johnston, captured July 30th, 1864, at the Crater.
Mansfield, Mathias, died in hospital October 10th, 1862, Petersburg.
Mercer, Samuel, died in hospital June 8th, 1862, Richmond.
Miller, Frederick.
Mathews, Ephriam, wounded August 19th, 1864, Wilcox Farm.
Mercer, Jas. P. W., wounded May 1st,' 1863, Chancellorsville, died May 7th.
Miller, Peter F., transferred to Company I, 61st Virginia Regiment.
Miller, Peleg, died in hospital April 18th, 1862, St. Helena.
Melson, Henry, died in hospital September 20th, 1863, U. S. Ford.
McPherson, James M., killed July 30th, 1864, Crater.
Northern, James, died in hospital June 24th, 1862, Richmond.
Only, Wm. H., captured October 27th, 1864, at Burgess' Mill.
Overton, Samuel S.
Paul, William James, transferred to Maryland line April 24th, 1862.
Powers, Wesley, wounded July 30th, 1864, Crater.
Powers, John, died in hospital May, 1863.
Rolison, John, died in hospital February 7th, 1863, Richmond.
Rhoner, John, died in hospital July 15th, 1864, Richmond.
Stewart, Adrian D., wounded July 4th, 1863, at Gettysburg.
Sawyer, Nelson, died in hospital January 20th, 1863, Richmond.
Savills, Marcus A., captured October 27th, 1864, at Burgess' Mill.
Shirley, John, wounded accidently June 21st, 1863.
Sawyer, Joseph, died in hospital February 24th, 1863, near Fredericksburg.
Spaight, Raynor, captured October 27th, 1864, at Burgess' Mill.
Sawyer, Gideon L., died in hospital January 19th, 1863, Richmond.
Stewart, David H., died in hospital June 29th, 1862, on Appomattox river.
Sawyer, William J.
Suggs, George F., wounded August 19th, 1864, Davis' Farm.
Turner, Thomas, wounded July 30th, 1864, at Crater, died July 31st.
Waller, Josiah, died in hospital June 15th, 1862.
Warren, James E., wounded June 22d, 1864, Wilcox Farm.
Waterfield, Saunders, died in hospital December 31st, 1862, Lynchburg.
Warren, John.
Whateley, Leven, transferred to Maryland line February 1st, 1864.
Whitehurst, David, killed by falling tree in camp November 30th, 1862.
Wright, William, captured October 27th, 1864, at Burgess' Mill.
Woodward, Lituness.
Musician Charles Hughes, captured July 5th, 1863.
  Killed and died—33.

CHAPTER XIX.

JACKSON LIGHT INFANTRY, COMPANY D, SIXTY-FIRST VIRGINIA REGIMENT.

This company was organized in the City Hall, Portsmouth, on the 10th of March, 1862, and elected officers as follows:
Captain, V. O. Cassell.
First Lieutenant, John Powers; 2d Lieutenant, Virginius A Haynes; 3d Lieutenant, Alex B. Butt.
First Sergeant, J. J. Bilisoly.

The original idea when the company was organized was to make it a heavy artillery company for duty in a regiment which was being organized for special services in the fortifications around the harbor, but it was furnished with muskets, and the evacuation of Portsmouth by the Confederates before the organization of the regiment was completed did away with its usefulness as heavy artillerists. Owing to the short period of time which elapsed between the organization of the company and the evacuation of Portsmouth, it had a very uneventful history independent of the general history of the regiment of which it formed a part. It was on duty at the entrenched camp south of Portsmouth known as the Forrest entrenchments, after Commodore Forrest, commanding the Navy Yard, when the city was evacuated. It was then moved to Petersburg, quartered for two or three days in that city, and then moved into camp on Dunn's Hill. It was with the regiment (the 61st Virginia) as Company D when it was ordered to the Rapidan, in the summer of 1862, and participated in all of the battles in which the regiment was engaged, a full list of which we be seen in the sketch of the regiment itself—Chap. XXIV.

After the 61st regiment became a part of Mahone's Brigade, Lieutenant Alex B. Butt was appointed Adjutant of the 41st Virginia Regiment of the same brigade, and was mortally wounded at the battle of Chancellorsville and died in a hospital. Captain V. O. Cassell lost a leg in the same battle and was incapacitated for further service and retired. This promoted Lieutenant John Powers to Captain, and 2d Lieutenant Haynes to 1st Lieutenant. Orderly Sergeant Julius J. Bilisoly was promoted to 2d Lieutenant. Those officers served throughout the war with the command. The company was in several small engagements or skirmishes with the enemy in 1862, and was in line of battle at Fredericksburg December 13th, 1862, and under a heavy artillery fire, but was not actively engaged, as the enemy's attack was made upon another portion of the Confederate lines to the right of the position held by them. Chancellorsville was the first battle of any magnitude in which it was engaged. In this battle Private J. Wiley Howard lost a leg and Private Joseph Barrett was wounded. It had two men killed at the Crater fight John Sheppard and John Wood and surrendered at Appomattox April 9th, 1865, with one Lieutenant, one Ordnance Sergeant and six privates, all that was left for duty of upwards of sixty men who left Portsmouth with the company on the 10th of May, 1862. More than one fourth were killed or died, and of the remainder some were wounded and some fell into the hands of the enemy and were not exchanged. The following is a list of the members of the company who left Portsmouth with it. The list of casualties opposite the names of the men has been prepared from memory, and some may have been omitted who were recipients of wounds, but it is probable that all who were killed or died have been reported properly:

Captain V. O. Cassell, lost leg at Chancellorsville, May 3d, 1863, and retired.
Captain John Powers, promoted to Captain in 1863.
First Lieutenant V. A. Haynes.
Third Lieutenant A. B. Butt, promoted Adjutant 41st Regiment, killed at Chancellorsville.
Second Lieutenant J. J. Bilisoly, promoted from 1st Sergeant.
Sergeant Jesse Ives, wounded August 19th, 1864, Davis' Farm, and February 6th, 1865, Hatcher's Run.
Sergeant Charles Syer, promoted Color Sergeant 61st Regiment, captured August 19th, 1864.
Sergeant David S. Robertson, discharged 1864, over age.
Corporal Joshua Denby, wounded July 2d, 1863, Gettysburg, near Petersburg, 1864, and captured the day before the surrender at Appomattox.
Corporal W. H. Dunstan, died in hospital in 1862, Petersburg.

PRIVATES.

Accinelly, B. J., promoted Ordnance Sergeant 61st Virginia Regiment.
Ashton, Gerdon C.
Ashby, William.
Butt, Robert P., died in hospital, 1863.
Barrett, Joseph, wounded May 3d, 1863, at Chancellorsville.
Butt, Wesley G., killed February 6th, 1865, Hatcher's Run.
Barber, George W.
Chamberlaine, William, died in hospital, 1862, Petersburg.
Chamberlaine, Thomas, wounded May 12th, 1864, Spotsylvania, killed August 19th, 1864, Davis Farm.
Coston, William C.
Coston, Henry C.
Coston, Thos. J.
Cherry, Wm. Alex. promoted Corporal, wounded August 19th, 1864, and died from wound.
Cooke, Thos. J., wounded May 12th, 1864, and died.
Cotton, John, Orderly at Colonel's Headquarters.
Denby, James, wounded July 30th, 1864, at Crater.
Davis, John Harrison, with medical corps.
Flarity, Thomas.
Flanagan, Edward, died in hospital, 1862.
Flemming, Malon R., wounded August 19th, 1864, Davis' Farm.
Godwin, A. D. B., wounded May 1st, 1863, Chancellorsville.

Hughes, Edward, wounded August 19th, 1864, Davis' Farm.
Howard, J. Wiley, promoted corporal, lost leg May 12th, 1864, Spotsylvania.
Hogg, John.
Hodges, Josiah, discharged 1862, over age.
Humphries, John.
Jordan, Wm. Thomas, killed February 6th, 1865, at Hatcher's Run.
Jarvis, Thomas.
Keeling, Joseph, wounded May 3d, 1863, Chancellorsville.
Lester, A. E., drummer.
Moore, William, discharged 1862, disability.
Mathews, Elbert, died in hospital, Petersburg, June 21st,1862.
Miller, Philip.
Moore, Wm. J., not heard of after the battle of Chancellorsville.
Marsh, Ben.
Mayo, George Washington, died in prison, Fort Delaware.
Murray, John T.
Nelson, John, discharged 1862, disability.
Only, John, died in hospital.
Only, James, died in hospital.
Ontens, John.
Only, Thos. E., wounded.
Pate, Wm., wounded.
Perry, E. A., detailed as sharpshooter, captured on retreat from Petersburg.
Parker, George, wounded May 12th, 1864, Spotsylvania.
Richardson, Benjamin.
Rutter, Thomas, wounded May 6th, Wilderness, and August 25th, 1864, Reams' Station, captured the day before the surrender at Appomattox.
Reynolds, H. C., wounded Spotsylvania, 2d Cold Harbor, and August 19th, 1864, captured the day before the surrender at Appomattox.
Rawson, Charles.
Singleton, John, wounded Hanover Junction, May 29th, 1864.
Shepperd, John, killed July 30th, 1864, Crater.
White, John, died in hospital.
White, Tim, died in hospital at Gordonsville.
Ward, Baker.
Walker, Wm. M.
Wood, John H., killed July 30th, 1864, Crater.
Williams, Hillary G.
Walker, Lewis Wilson, wounded May 8th, 1864, Shady Grove.
Young, George W.
    Killed and died—16.

CHAPTER XX.

THE BORDER RIFLES, COMPANY E, SIXTY-FIRST VIRGINIA REGIMENT.

This company was organized early in 1862, and was composed of about twenty-five of the Norfolk County Rifle Patriots, Company F, 41st Virginia, who left that company on the reorganization in April, and together with new recruits, formed this company. The members were mostly from that portion of Norfolk county now known as Washington and Pleasant Grove Magisterial Districts, but there were two men from Deep Creek and eight from the city of Portsmouth. The officers of the company at its organization, were:

Captain, Jetson Jett.
First Lieutenant, L. W. Godfrey; 2d Lieutenant, William T. Drewry; 3d Lieutenant, Walter C. Ives.
First Sergeant, Augustus W. Portlock; 2d Sergeant, Dennis M. Etheredge; 3d Sergeant, Augustus R. Pitts; 4th Sergeant, Camillus E. Tatem.
First Corporal, Alonzo Ives; 2d Corporal, Thomas Williamson; 3d Corporal, James M. Wilkins; 4th Corporal, Curtis O. Ives.

The company was mustered into the Confederate States service at Washington Point, now Berkley, and was quartered for a week or two at the Marine Hospital building, when it was assigned to the 61st Virginia Regiment as Company E, and ordered to Oak Grove, near Portsmouth, and remained there, doing provost duty in the city, until the evacuation. On the 10th of May, 1862, it was taken by rail to Petersburg, where the whole of the 61st regiment was collected, and remained there for two or three weeks, when, with Companies B and G, it was ordered to City Point on picket duty and remained there until late in August, when the regiment was called together on Dunn's Hill, near Petersburg, and on the 28th of August started to the front to join the Army of Northern Virginia, under General Lee. Upon reaching the Rapidan river, Companies E and F were detached from the regiment for special duty and ordered to report to Staunton. Company E was divided into small squads and stationed in the small towns on the Valley turnpike from Staunton to Strausburg. Company F was retained in Staunton. In June, 1863, the two companies were ordered to rejoin the regiment, which was then stationed in the vicinity of Fredericksburg, and after that participated in all of the battles in which the regiment was engaged. They missed Chancellorsville, but got back in time to join the army on its march to Pennsylvania and to take part in the battle of Gettysburg, July 2d and 3d, when Company E had its first experience in a general engagement. In this battle Lieutenant Walter C. Ives was killed and Lieutenant L. W. Godfrey was wounded. On the 12th of May following, Lieutenant W. T. Drewry was killed at the battle of Spotsylvania Court House. After the death of Lieutenant Drewry, Sergeant Griffin F. Edwards was elected 2d lieutenant, but prefering the position of sergeant-major of the regiment, which he then held, he declined to accept the lieutenancy. He was subsequently promoted to adjutant of the regiment, and held that position from early in 1865 until the close of the war. Private Wm. F. White, of Portsmouth, who was a member of this company, was elected in 1864 captain of one of the Norfolk city companies in the 6th Virginia Regiment, in Mahone's Brigade. The company lost by death from wounds and from sickness, twenty-nine men, while thirteen others are reported below as having been severely wounded. The list of wounded was much larger than this, but as it was made up from memory, many were forgotten. While the roster is believed to be correct and full as to those who were killed or died, it does not profess to include all of those who were wounded. This company retained its organization intact until the closing scenes of the drama at Appomattox, where it surrendered one officer, Captain Jett, and seventeen men.

The wounding of Adjutant Griffin F. Edwards at Cumberland Church on the 7th of April, 1865, was a singular exhibition of what some would term hard luck. The brigade (Mahone's) was lying down in line of battle, behind a slight breastwork about two feet high, which the men had thrown up hastily to protect themselves from the fire of a force of Federal sharp shooters, who, from the top of a piece of rising ground about a half a mile off, had perfect range of the position. They were armed with globe sight rifles and were expert in their use. Lieutenant-Colonel Wm. H. Stewart had command of the division picket line and a portion of it had been attacked by a heavy force of Federals and pushed back. General Weisiger, who commanded Mahone's Brigade, and who was at the left of the line, sent for Col. Stewart for the purpose of placing a force at his disposal to re-establish the line. Colonel Stewart moved over the front of the division for nearly a half mile, exposed all the while to the sharp shooters who took frequent shots at him, all of which missed. When he reached General Weisiger's position that officer ordered Colonel V. D. Groner, commanding the 61st Regiment, to make a detail of men, and Colonel Groner called Adjutant Edwards to him and repeated the order. While standing up before Colonel Groner, and before he could execute the order, one of the sharp shooters lodged a ball in his shoulder, which disabled him, and when the brigade fell back that night he was left behind. Two days afterwards, namely, the 9th, the army surrendered at Appomattox.

Colonel Stewart was standing near Adjutant Edwards when he was shot, and though the more and longer exposed of the two, escaped unharmed.

Below will be found a roll of the company, which is as complete as it is possible to make it at this late day, but it is believed to contain the names of every man who left with the company at the evacuation of Portsmouth by the Confederates on the 10th of May, 1862.

The names here following were on the muster roll of the company May 31st, 1862:

Captain, Jetson Jett.
First Lieutenant, L. W. Godfrey, wounded July 3d, 1863, Gettysburg.
Second Lieutenant, Wm. Drewry, killed May 12th, 1864, Spotsylvania.
Third Lieutenant, Walter C. Ives, killed July 2d, 1863, Gettysburg.
First Sergeant, Gustavus W. Portlock, wounded August 19th, 1864, Weldon railroad, died in hands of enemy.
First Sergeant, James M. Wilkins.
Sergeant Dennis M. Etheredge, died in hospital, Staunton, October 17th, 1862.
Sergeant Augustus R. Pitt, appointed musician.
Sergeant Camillus E. Tatem, wounded July 30th, 1864, Crater.
Sergeant Alonzo Ives, wounded May 6th, 1864, Wilderness, and July 30th, 1864, Crater.
Corporal Thos. Williamson, wounded August 19th, 1864, Petersburg and Weldon railroad, Davis' Farm.
Corporal Curtis O. Ives, wounded August 19th, 1864, Petersburg and Weldon railroad, Davis' Farm.
Corporal Joshua Charlton, wounded July 30th, Crater.
Corporal L. W. Charlton.

PRIVATES.

Ballance, Martin, wounded August 19th, 1864, Davis' Farm.
Butt, Andrew, wounded July 3d, 1863, Gettysburg, died in hands of the enemy.
Butt, Thomas, died in hospital 1862.
Brinkley, Wm. D., died in hospital 1864.
Cartwright, Dempsey, killed May 12th, 1864, Spotsylvania.
Charlton, Samuel Q., died in hospital 1862, Staunton.
Cherry, Absolem.
Cherry, Richard.
Corbit, Richard, died in hospital October, 1863, Richmond.
Creekmore, John W.
Creekmore, Wesley P., died in hospital 1862, Petersburg.
Curling, Bartlett.
Curling, Edmond, wounded May 12th, 1864, at Spotsylvania, captured Aug. 19th, 1864, Davis' Farm.
Cutherell, George,
Cutherell, Milton, wounded July 30th, 1864, Crater.
Cutherell, Wm. E., killed May 12th, 1864, Spotsylvania.
Deford, Richard H.
Dewberry, Wm. T., captured October 27th, Burgess' Mill.
Edmonds, Luther, appointed musician.
Edwards, Griffin F., promoted Sergeant-Major November 1863, Adjutant February, 1865, wounded April 7th, 1865, Cumberland Church, and left on field.
Etheredge, Frederick, killed May 8th, 1864, Wilderness.
Etheredge, Isaiah, captured October 27th, 1864, Burgess' Mill.

Etheredge, John, captured October 27th, 1864. Burgess' Mill.
Etheredge, Martin.
Ferrebe, Grandy, wounded August 19th, 1864, and died in hospital.
Foreman, John E.
Foster, James S., captured July 3d, 1864, near Petersburg.
Gammon, Joshua B., killed August 19th, 1864, Davis' Farm.
Gifford, Samuel, killed August 19th, 1864, Davis' Farm.
Gammon, Alex., killed May 12th, 1864, Spotsylvania.
Gibson, Wm. M., discharged 1864.
Grimes, John F.
Gwynn, Asbury, captured August 19th, 1864, Davis' Farm.
Gwynn, Frederick, died in hospital 1864, Richmond.
Gilbert, Thos., died in hospital May, 1862, Petersburg.
Hall, Cary W.
Hall, James S.
Hewett, M. W., discharged October 27th, 1862, disability.
Hanbury, Fred.
Hanbury, Horatis B.
Hanbury, James C.
Hodges, Dan'l, died in hospital October, 1863, Staunton.
Hozier, Jeremiah E., wounded May 12th, 1864, at Spotsylvania and August 19th, 1864, Davis' Farm.
Ives, Felix G.
Jarvis, Alex. A., killed July 30th, 1864, Crater.
Lane, James E., killed June 2d, 1864, Cold Harbor.
McLean, John A., detailed for service in Labratory, Charlotte, N. C.
McPherson, Peter, killed August 19th, 1864, Davis' Farm.
Only, Absolom, discharged for disability.
Only, Alexander, killed May 12th, 1864, Spotsylvania.
Osborne, Raison, wounded May 12th, 1864, Spotsylvania.
Ottley, Wm. N., captured October 27th, 1864, Burgess' Mill.
Owens, Geo.
Portlock, Thos. E., died in hospital 1863, Staunton.
Rudd, Wm. D.
Saunders, Wm. D. B., killed May 12th, 1864, Spotsylvania.
Stewart, Thos., killed May 12th, 1864, Spotsylvania.
Stokes, James.
Stokes, Robert.
Stokes, Wilson F., killed June 22d, 1864, Wilcox's Farm.
Tatem, Benj. F., promoted Quartermaster Sergeant, 1862.
Wagner, Lewis.
Williamson, Chas. C.
Williamson, Elton, wounded August 19th, 1864, Davis' Farm.
Williamson, Henry, wounded May 12th, 1862, Spotsylvania.
Wilkins, W. L. S., promoted 2d Sergeant.
White, Wm. F., promoted Captain 6th Virginia Regiment.
Wilson, Joseph.
Wilson, Joshua T., captured August 19th, 1864, Davis' Farm.
Wright, Benj., killed May 12th, 1864, Spotsylvania.
Lindon, Mitchel.

    Killed and died—29.

CHAPTER XXI.

THE VIRGINIA RANGERS, COMPANY H, SIXTY-FIRST VIRGINIA REGIMENT.

In March, 1862, Captain James C. Choat, formerly captain of Company A, 3d Virginia Regiment, and Sergeant John H. Wright, formerly of Company I, 9th Virginia Regiment, both of Norfolk county, were engaged trying to raise separate companies, and finding that the field had been very thoroughly gleaned over and that there were few men in the city or county who were not already in the Confederate service, concluded to consolidate their work and make one company of it. The members of the company were part from the city and part from the county near the western suburbs and towards Deep Creek. The company organized and elected officers on the 26th of March. Those officers were:
Captain, James C. Choat.
First Lieutenant, John H. Wright; 2d Lieutenant, James F. Carr; 3d Lieutenant, Henry E. Orr.
Firs tSergeant, James H. Gleason; 2d Sergeant, W. W. Rew; 3d Sergeant, John Sory.

The company was immediately mustered into service and assigned to the 61st Virginia Regiment as Company H. A short time before the Confederates evacuated Portsmouth Captain Choat accidently shot himself in the arm and resigned the command of the company to Lieutenant Wright, who was promoted to captain. The company left Portsmouth on the 10th of May, 1862, marched to Suffolk and there took the cars for Petersburg, and camped a short time on the heights to the south of that city, after which it was moved to Dunn's Hill with the rest of the regiment. While there Lieutenant Carr was appointed commissary of the regiment, but shortly afterwards resigned, and was discharged upon a surgeon's certificate of disability, and Sergeant James H. Gleason was elected lieutenant. The company did provost duty in Petersburg until August 28th, when the regiment broke camp and marched to Richmond, and from there took the cars for Rapidan Station, and assisted in rebuilding the bridge over that river, which had been burned. From there the company was ordered to Warrenton, and did provost duty until the latter part of October, when it was ordered to rejoin the regiment and marched to Fredericksburg. After that time the regiment was attached to Mahone's Brigade.

While the company was at Warrenton, Captain Wright received an appointment assigning him to other duty and he resigned the captaincy of the company. He subsequently enlisted as a private in the signal corps. Lieutenant Orr then became captain. Lieutenant Gleason was promoted to 1st lieutenant and Sergeant W. W. Rew was elected 2d lieutenant. Captain Orr commanded the company until the close of the war. Lieutenant Gleason was severely wounded and disabled at the battle of Spotsylvania Court House, May 12th, 1864, and was retired. At the battle of the Crater, July 30th, 1864, the company lost very heavily. One man was killed, and Lieutenant Rew and five privates were wounded. Lieutenant Rew's wound was very severe, but he recovered in time to rejoin the company and surrendered with it at Appomattox Court House, when there were present two commissioned officers, one sergeant and six privates. The company lost very heavily in proportion to its numbers, and participated in all of the battles in which the regiment was engaged. Below will be found a roll of the company, together with the casualties as far as it has been possible for them to be obtained. At this date none of the officers who were in actual service with the company are living, and the source of information concerning the killed and wounded has been narrowed down to very close limits, but the roll embraces all who left the county with the company on the 10th of May, 1862, and the list of casualties is correct as far as it goes:

Captain James C. Choat, accidently wounded May, 1862, and resigned.
First Lieutenant John H. Wright, promoted Captain, resigned 1862, enlisted in Signal Corps.
Second Lieutenant James F. Carr, appointed Commissary, discharged 1862.
Third Lieutenant Henry E. Orr, appointed Captain 1862, surrendered at Appomattox.
First Sergeant James A. Gleason, elected 1st Lieutenant, wounded and disabled May 12th, 1864, Spotsylvania, and retired.
Third Sergeant John R. Simmons, promoted 1st Sergeant.
Fourth Sergeant Washington W. Rew, elected Lieutenant, wounded July 30th, 1864, Crater.
Corporal John C. Sorey.
Corporal Edward L. Mansfield.
Corporal George Ross.
Musician John W. Mitchell.

PRIVATES.

Aydelott, Henry C., died in hospital 1863, U. S. Ford.
Adkins, G. B., wounded July 30th, 1864, Crater.
Brittingham, Francis O.
Ballentine, John.
Berryman, Ed. F., promoted Sergeant, wounded August 19th, 1864, Davis' Farm.
Bowden, Wm.
Crumpler, Solomon B.
Cherry, Richard J., promoted Sergeant, detached 1864.
Cherry, Miles, died in hospital 1862, Petersburg.
Cherry, John.
Cherry, David.
Cherry, Paul W., died in hospital 1862, at Petersburg.
Cooke, Antonio M., wounded Crater, Wilderness and Hatcher's Run.
Chamberlaine, Willis.
Culpepper, Franklin J.

Duke, Francis, killed May 12th, 1864, Spotsylvania.
Eddie, R., wounded July 30th, 1864, Crater.
Foreman, Isaiah, transferred to Company G.
Foreman, James R., died in hospital.
Friedlin, Amile C.
Gallup, John, Sr.
Gilding, Geo. F.
Gallagher, Carney.
Gallagher, Edward, captured.
Hodges, Thos., promoted Corporal.
Hodges, William.
Hozier, John W., made Corporal, wounded July 30th, 1864, Crater.
Hodges, John T.
Halstead, Thos.
Haynes, John W., promoted Sergeant.
Harrel, Alexander.
Johnson, Alonzo.
Johnson, James H., made Corporal.
Johnson, John B., captured April 8th, 1865, on retreat.
Johnson, Lender, made Corporal, detached for service at Danville, 1863.
Jordan, Wm.
Lassiter, James, died in hospital, U. S. Ford.
Miller, Christopher, wounded May 6th, 1864, Wilderness.
Miller, J. F.
Mansfield, James, killed near Petersburg.
McNider, Wm. H., killed July 30th, 1864, Crater.
Mansfield, Willoughby, made Corporal, killed May 6th, 1864, Wilderness.
Mears, Thos., lost leg June 22d, 1864, Wilcox Farm.
McTyre, Robt. W., made Corporal.
McGilone, J.
Only, Hollowell, died in Chimborazo Hospital of Pneumonia May, 1863.
Only, Joseph.
Robinson, E.
Taylor, Thos. H.
Tranham, A. S., wounded July 30th, 1864, Crater.
Turner, Mills.
Wilkins, Richard.
White, Geo. T.
Wyatt, H. T., wounded July 30th, 1864, Crater.
    Killed and died—10.

CHAPTER XXII.

THE BILISOLY BLUES, COMPANY I, SIXTY-FIRST VIRGINIA REGIMENT.

This company was organized in Portsmouth June 16th, 1861, and contained in its membership quite a number of men from the vicinity of Bowers' Hill, in Norfolk county. The following were the officers under whom it was mustered into service:

Captain, Charles R. McAlpine

First Lieutenant, Frank W. Armistead; 2d Lieutenant, John Hobday; 3d Lieutenant, C. W. Murdaugh.

The company was ordered to Seawell's Point and was attached to the 41st Virginia Regiment as Company G. It was on duty there until the 29th of April, 1862, when it was detached from the 41st Regiment and ordered to report to Lieutenant-Colonel Archer at Fort Boykin, near Smithfield. On the 27th of May it was ordered to report to the major commanding Battery No. 3, in the fortifications around Richmond, and on the 10th of July was ordered on provost duty in Richmond city, but was continued on that service only four days, when, July 14th, it was assigned by order of the secretary of war, to the regiment of Colonel Samuel M. Wilson, afterwards the 61st Virginia. On the 20th of July orders were received from Lieutenant-Colonel Wm. F. Niemeyer, commanding the regiment, to report to him on Dunn's Hill, near Petersburg, and on the 21st Captain McAlpine reported with his company. The battles around Richmond in June, 1862, took place while the company was in the batteries there, but it was not ordered in any of them. Upon reaching Dunn's Hill the company was given the letter I, as it was the ninth company which had been assigned to the regiment. The tenth company was assigned later. The strength of the company then was about fifty-nine men.

At the reorganization of the company in June, 1862, all of the old officers except Lieutenant Armistead were re-elected. Lieutenant Armistead severed his connection with the company and enlisted in one of the Nansemond companies in the 13th Virginia Cavalry. Lieutenants Hobday and Murdaugh became respectively first and second lieutenants, and on the 29th of July, at a special election held by order of the Department Commander, General French, Frank M. Marchant was elected 3d lieutenant.

Captain McAlpine was promoted to the position of Major of the Regiment May 12th, 1864, and on the same day Lieutenant John Hobday was appointed captain. Lieutenants Murdaugh and Marchant were each advanced one grade. Lieutenant Murdaugh was seriously wounded in the hip at the battle of Chancellorsville or more properly speaking, Salem Church, on the afternoon of May 3d, 1863. General Lee had shaken General Hooker from his entrenched position near Chancellorsville, and was about to sweep down upon him with his whole army, when he received news that General Sedgwick, having crossed the Rappahannock river at Fredericksburg and captured Marye Heights, was advancing in his rear.

General Lee detached a number of brigades, among them Mahone's, to check Sedgwick's further advance, and the two forces met at Salem Church. Company I was deployed as skirmishers, and while engaging the enemy in front, was fired into from behind by Semmes' Georgia Brigade. Thus caught between two fires, one from the enemy and the other from friends, the position of the company was by no means an agreeable one. It was here that Lieutenant Murdaugh was wounded. He was complimented in General Order No. 283 from General Lee's headquarters, for gallantry on that occasion. The battle was a complete victory for the Confederates and only the darkness saved Sedgwick from destruction. He made his escape during the night across the river.

Captain Hobday was killed October the 27th, 1864, at the battle of Burgess' Mill, and Lieutenant Murdaugh was promoted to captain. Lieutenant Marchant became 1st lieutenant, and these two continued the officers of the company until the close of the war.

The company was quartered on Dunn's Hill, doing provost duty in the city of Petersburg from July 21st to August 29th, 1862, when the regiment moved to the Rapidan river, and was engaged in guarding the fords of that river against the scouting parties of the enemy. Major McAlpine left behind at his death, some notes and memoranda relating to his company, and among others, mentions private Albert Powell, who was conspicuous for gallantry at the battle of Spotsylvania Court House May 12th, 1864, and W. F. Butt, who was mortally wounded there. He speaks of Private Butt as "a good man and reliable soldier." In that battle Mahone's Brigade charged and captured three lines of field works.

Speaking of Captain John Hobday at the battle of Wilcox Farm, near Petersburg, he says: "The conspicuous gallantry of Captain John Hobday on the 22d of June, 1864, will ever be remembered. It was through his sagacity that the enemy were flanked and defeated. With his small command of twenty-one men, he passed down the enemy's lines, a distance of two hundred yards, and demanded their surrender." Private Charles W. Collins is thus mentioned by him: "It was through the courage and gallantry of Charles W. Collins that Major Charles R. McAlpine's life was saved on this occasion. He shot and killed a Federal officer who had a pistol levelled at Major McAlpine's breast, at a distance of not more than six feet, and was about to fire at him." Private Collins was reported to brigade headquarters for special mention for distinguished gallantry at the battle of Shady Grove May 8th, 1864, a continuation of the battle of the Wilderness, and was killed in the battle of August 19th, 1864, on the Petersburg and Weldon railroad, sometimes called the battle of Davis' Farm. He was a very gallant boy, was not more than fifteen or sixteen years old when he joined the company in Portsmouth in 1861, and was the son of Mr. William B. Collins, who lived at the southeast corner of Court and Glasgow streets. He was never known to shirk duty or to shrink from danger. He was always in the front when fighting was going on and passed unscathed through twenty-three battles before he received his death wound. Captain Hobday too, was as gallant a man as ever lived.

The company was in twenty-five heavy battles, seven smaller engagements, and numerous skirmishes, and lost by death sixteen men, one out of every four, while scarcely a man escaped without a wound. In an order issued from the headquarters of the regiment in December, 1863, Colonel Groner said: "Company I, though composed of material difficult to control, is under the best discipline of any company in the regiment."

Captain Murdaugh recovered from the wound he received at Chancellorsville and rejoined the company in the lines around Petersburg, but at the time of the retreat from Petersburg he was attending an extra session of the Legislature, of which he had been elected a member, and which had been called to try to provide means to meet the emergency which was then too apparent in the affairs of the South and the State, and could not get back to his command in time for the surrender at Appomattox.

Below will be found the roster of the company, made up from the best information at hand. The list of names is correct, and embraces all who went into service with the company at the evacuation of Portsmouth by the Confederates:

Captain Charles R. McAlpine, promoted Major, wounded.
First Lieutenant F. W. Armistead, dropped at reorganization, May, 1862, joined 13th Virginia Cavalry.
Second Lieutenant John Hobday, Jr., promoted Captain May 12th, 1864, wounded July 30th, 1864, Crater, and killed October 27th, 1864, at Burgess' Mill.
Third Lieutenant C. W. Murdaugh, promoted Captain October 27th, 1864, wounded May 3d, 1863, at Salem Church (Chancellorsville).
First Sergeant John M. Sherwood, surrendered at Appomattox.
Second Sergeant Edward C. Shepherd, disabled, detailed for hospital duty.
Third Sergeant David W. Thornton, detailed to work in government shops.
Corporal George Oglevi, discharged October, 1861, disability.
Corporal Calvin L. Peek, promoted Sergeant, captured October 27th, 1864, and not exchanged.
Corporal Charles Evans, wounded May 3d, 1863—Chancellorsville, captured August 19th, 1864, and not exchanged.

Musician Joseph J. Smith, drummer.

PRIVATES.

Benton, Joseph, surrendered at Appomattox.
Bateman, Jonathan.
Barcroft, George W., left in hospital in Norfolk sick, May 10th, 1862, and never heard from.
Butt, William T., mortally wounded May 12th, 1864, Spotsylvania Court House, and died May 24th in Camp Winder Hospital, Richmond.
Berkley, Lycurgus, furnished substitute May 6th, 1862, substitute deserted May 10th.
Cooper, Arthur, died in hospital.
Casey, Elvin K., lost an arm May 6th, 1864, Wilderness.
Casey, James A.
Cherry, Elias W., captured July 4th, 1863, Gettysburg, and died in prison.
Collins, Chas. W., killed August 19th, 1864, Davis' Farm.
Collins, Thomas, promoted Corporal.
Curtis, Revel W., killed July 3d, 1863, Gettysburg.
Dollett, Wm. W.
Duke, Robert.
Duke, Parker, wounded July 30th, 1864, Crater.
Eure, Hillary.
Eure, Henry.
Eure, Augustus, over age, furnished substitute October 23d, 1861.
Ferrill, John, died June, 1862, Battery No. 10, Richmond.
Fowler, A. J.
Godwin, Laban T., promoted Sergeant, captured August 19th, 1864, and not exchanged.
Hyslop, Denwood, captured August 19th, 1864, not exchanged.
Halloway, Joseph.
Hewlett, Joseph F., captured July 4th, 1863, not exchanged.
Heckrotte, Oliver.
Herbert, Joseph T., transferred to 15th Virginia Cavalry.
Horton, Daniel W., sent to hospital September 26th, 1862, and supposed to have died.
Jones, Walter J., promoted Lieutenant in 41st Virginia Regiment, and killed May 6, 1864, Wilderness.
Jackson, Wm. A., furnished substitute April 24th, 1862.
King, Joseph.
King, George, captured August 19th, 1864, and not exchanged.
King, Edward.
Kilgore, M. P., promoted Sergeant October 11th, 1862, killed July 30th, 1864, Crater.
Mason, Wm., killed Cumberland Church, April 7th, 1865.
Miller, John C.
Manning, S. D., died in hospital September, 1862, Petersburg.
Marchant, F. M., promoted 3d Lieutenant July 29th, 1862, promoted 1st Lieutenant October 27th, 1864.
Meares, James E., discharged for disability from wounds.
Mears, Thomas F., captured May 29th, 1864, not exchanged.
Nottingham, B. F., died in field hospital, October, 1863, Brandy Station.
Porter, Thomas.
Powell, Albert, name published for distinguished gallantry at Spotsylvania C. H., May 12th, 1864.
Peel, Thomas, captured August 19th, 1864, not exchanged.
Peek, Ammon, captured October 27th, 1864, not exchanged.
Ribble, Joseph, furnished substitute May 6th, 1862, substitute deserted May 10th.
Rodman, Pierce, discharged September, 1861, disability.
Sibley, Wm., captured July, 1863, in Pensylvania and never heard from.

St. George, Wm. E., captured July 2d, 1863, Gettysburg, not exchanged.
Smith, W. J., died in Richmond May 20th, 1863.
Tompkins, Joseph.
Toppin, Smith, promoted Sergeant, killed July 30th, 1864, Crater.
White, John D., wounded July 30th, 1864, at the Crater, and discharged December 23d, 1864, disabled.
White, Richard, wounded seriously July 30th, 1864, at the Crater, discharged January 9th, 1865, disabled.
Ward, Julius, killed July 2d, 1863, Gettysburg.
Whitson, William, discharged September, 1861, disability.
Wise, Stephen, died in hospital, 1863.
Youre, Stephen.
    Killed and died—20.

CHAPTER XXIII.

COMPANY K, SIXTY-FIRST VIRGINIA REGIMENT.

This company was organized in 1861 in that portion of Norfolk county known as Ferry Point, now Berkley, and was gotten up through the efforts of Captain Herbert. It contained in its ranks a number of old men and young boys, but these were soon sifted out as not being within the military age and were discharged. The officers of the company under whom it was mustered into the Confederate service were:

Captain, Maximillian Herbert.
First Lieutenant, Joseph T. Herbert; 2d Lieutenant, Revel I. Taylor; 3d Lieutenant, Maximillian Herbert, Jr.
First Sergeant; Frank M. Marchant.

The company was attached to a mixed battalion of four companies, some of whom were from Virginia and some from North Carolina, under the command of Lieutenant-Colonel John T. P. C. Cohoon, and known as Cohoon's battalion. The command does not appear to have been a very efficient one, however, for on the 14th of July, 1862, it was ordered to report at Camp Lee, near Richmond, for the purpose of being disbanded. The commander at Camp Lee was directed to discharge such men in the battalion as were above or below the legal military age and to retain the others. The men in Captain Herbert's company were, at their own request, assigned in a body to Captain Chas. R. McAlpine's Company, Company I, 61st Virginia Regiment. The four commissioned officers were retired and forty-seven men were turned over to Captain McAlpine, all of whom were subject to military duty.

Captain Herbert was not satisfied with the order disbanding his company, and having obtained from Captain George A. Martin, of the St. Bride's Artillery, of Norfolk county, whose company exceeded the regulation number, a promise to turn over to him enough men to recruit his command up to the standard required for a company, he sought an interview with the Secretary of War and obtained on order revoking the former order concerning Cohoon's battalion, so far as it affected his company, and directing Lieutenant-Colonel Niemeyer to turn the men over to him again. Lieutenant-Colonel Niemeyer hesitated in obeying the order, represented to the Secretary of War that he thought the men would be more efficient under Captain McAlpine, and recommended that they be permitted to remain with him. His recommendation was disapproved, however, and Captain Herbert got his men again. They were re-assigned to him on the 28th of August, 1862, and, having gotten about a dozen recruits from Captain Martin, the company was, that day, assigned to the 61st Regiment as Company K, thus completing the regiment. While the men were in Company I, two of them were discharged for physical disability, and one, Sergeant Frank M. Marchant, was elected 3d Lieutenant of Company I, so that only forty-four men were re-assigned to Captain Herbert, and of these, Albert Powell and Jonathan Bateman were subsequently transferred to Company I. Captain Herbert died in Petersburg the 30th of September, 1862. The three Lieutenants were each advanced one grade, and Sergeant John S. Cason was elected 3d Lieutenant. Captain Joseph T. Herbert resigned on the 13th of August, 1864, and the company remained under command of 1st Lieutenant Taylor until the battle of Burgess' Mill, October 27th, 1864, when he was captured. Lieutenants Max Herbert, Jr., and Cason were on the picket line in front of Bermuda Hundreds when the army fell back from Petersburg about the 1st of April, 1865, and fell into the hands of the enemy, and First Sergeant James Adams became commander of the company on the retreat. Adams was an excellent soldier and richly deserved a commission, which, however, he never received.

The company followed the fortunes of the regiment, participated in all of its battles, contributed its share of the regular toll of dead and wounded which was paid for victory, and at the surrender of the remnant of the army at Appomattox, had two privates left for duty. First Sergeant Adams was captured on the retreat the day before the surrender. He had been without anything to eat for two or three days, and managing to come across a little food, he and one of his men stopped to cook it, thinking they were far enough in advance of the enemy to do so with safety; but in the midst of the operation they were surprised by a body of pursuing cavalry and gathered in. The company was a small one and its losses were proportionately heavy. One man out of every three who left their homes on the 10th of May, 1862, at the evacuation of Norfolk and Portsmouth, paid with their lives the penalty of their devotion to their State.

The following roll is believed to be complete and embraces all who were killed or died in hospital, or were so badly wounded as to require them to report to a hospital. Some who received slight wounds which did not incapacitate them from duty, are not recorded as having been wounded. The roll embraces the men who were transferred to the company by Captain Martin, as well as Captain Herbert's original members.

Captain Max A. Herbert, died in hospital, September 30th, 1862, Petersburg.
First Lieutenant Joseph T. Herbert, promoted Captain September 30th, 1862, wounded May 3d, 1863, at Chancellorsville, resigned August 13th, 1864.

Second Lieutenant Revel I. Taylor, promoted First Lieutenant, captured October 27th, 1864. Burgess' Mill.
Third Lieutenant Max A. Herbert, Jr., promoted 2d Lieutenant.
First Sergeant John S. Cason, promoted 3d Lieutenant.
Second Sergeant, Littleton D. Reed, captured September 23d, 1863, never rejoined the company.
Third Sergeant Geo. W. Tatem, discharged August 30th, 1862, disability.
Fourth Sergeant James Adams, promoted 1st Sergeant, captured on retreat from Petersburg.
Corporal Thomas H. Edwards.
Corporal James Bradley, died in hospital, 1863, Richmond.

PRIVATES.

Absolem, Leonard, died in hospital, 1864, Richmond.
Burfoot, Jesse, captured April 5th, 1865, on retreat from Petersburg.
Burton, George, sick in hospital, Lynchburg, at the surrender at Appomattox.
Bateman, Martin, wounded August 19th, 1864, Davis' Farm, reported for duty August 31st and captured October 27th, 1864, at Burgess' Mill.
Bradley, Charles M., discharged for disability June 10th, 1863.
Bailey, Chas. L., captured April, 1865, on retreat from Petersburg.
Bean, Frederick, wounded and captured July 3d, 1863, and never rejoined the company.
Dillon, Lee W., captured September 22d, 1863, and never rejoined the company.
Franklin, Peter J., died in hospital March 20th, 1863.
Fields, John, died in hospital June 14th, 1862, Petersburg.
Forbes, Simeon, died in hospital 1864, Richmond.
Flannagan, Andrew, captured April, 1865, on retreat from Petersburg.
Hozier, David T., died in hospital June 11th, 1862, Petersburg.
Griggs, Chas. W., killed July 30th, 1864, Crater.
Garress, Isaiah, captured October 27th, 1864, Burgess' Mill.
Hozier, Jas. K. P., promoted Corporal, captured on retreat from Petersburg.
Hitchcock, Malachi, wounded July 30th, 1864.
Hunter, John B., died in hospital April 10th, 1863, U. S. Ford.
Halstead, Wm. R., discharged 1864.
Harrison, Thomas, captured April 19th, 1863, and never rejoined the company.
Halstead, Chris., promoted Sergeant, wounded June 22d, 1864, at Wilcox Farm, and captured.
Jackson, Abner, died in hospital June 20th, 1862, Petersburg.
Jennings, Edward, died in hospital 1864, Richmond.
Lewton, Wm., killed July 30th, 1864, Crater.
Morris, Wm. H., killed August 19th, 1864, Davis' Farm.
Melson. Levi.
Mitchel, John.
Roberts, Wingfield, wounded May 12th, 1864, at Spotsylvania C. H., captured April, 1865, on retreat from Petersburg.
Sawyer, John I., wounded May 8th, 1864, Shady Grove, captured October 27th, 1864.
Stafford, Richard, surrendered at Appomattox.
Sykes, Jos. J., died in hospital 1864.
Stephens, Jos. L., discharged June 22d, 1863.
Sorey, Evan, wounded June 15th, 1864, Turkey Ridge, surrendered at Appomattox.
Staylor, Thos., wounded May 2d, 1863, Chancellorsville, captured on retreat from Petersburg.
West, Delaware, died in hospital, Richmond, 1862-3.
Wilson, John, captured October 27th, 1864, at Burgess' Mill.

Wilson, Willis, captured October 27th, 1864, at Burgess' Mill.
Wilson, Benj. R.
Williams, William, captured July 5th, 1863, and never rejoined the company.
Williams, Jordan, died in hospital June 23d, 1864, Richmond.
Wickings, Jas. J., died in hospital April 10th, 1863, U. S. Ford.
    Killed and died—17.

CHAPTER XXIV.

THE SIXTY-FIRST VIRGINIA REGIMENT— MAHONE'S, WEISIGER'S BRIGADES—ANDERSON'S, MAHONE'S DIVISIONS.

The companies composing this regiment were organized and mustered into the Confederate service early in the war, as will be seen from the short sketches of each of them which precede this chapter, and were on duty in different localities in the vicinity of Portsmouth and Norfolk. In the winter of 1861-2, Colonel Samuel M. Wilson obtained authority from Governor Letcher to raise a regiment of heavy artillery for service in the fortifications around the harbor, and at his request, several companies applied to be assigned to it, and others were assigned without having made application, so that, when Portsmouth was evacuated, May 10th, 1862, the regiment lacked only two companies of having a full complement. Company I was afterwards assigned to it, July 14th, 1862, and Company K, August 28th, thus making ten companies. These were:

Company A, Jackson Grays, of Norfolk county, Captain Wm. H. Stewart.

Company B, Wilson Guards, of Norfolk county, Captain John W. M. Hopkins.

Company C, Blanchard Grays, of Norfolk county, Captain Jno. G. Wallace.

Company D, Jackson Light Infantry, of Portsmouth, Captain V. O. Cassell.

Company E, Border Rifles, of Norfolk county, Captain Jetson Jett.

Company F, ———— ————, of Isle of Wight county, Captain ———— Holland.

Company G, ———— ————, of Greenville county, Captain R. E. Moseley.

Company H, Virginia Rangers, of Portsmouth and Norfolk county, Captain John H. Wright.

Company I, Bilisoly Blues, of Portsmouth, Captain Chas. R. McAlpine.

Company K, ———— ————, of Norfolk county, Captain Max. Herbert.

Company F was partly from Southampton county, and Company G contained a few men from Sussex county and also some from Northampton county, North Carolina, near the Greenville line, and among these latter was Captain Moseley. Companies B and C had a number of North Carolinians also, from Currituck county, near the Norfolk county line.

The officers of the first eight companies held a meeting in Jarrett's Hotel, in Petersburg, about the middle of May, 1862, and elected field officers. They were:
Colonel, Samuel M. Wilson.
Lieutenant-Colonel Wm. F. Niemeyer.
Major, Wm. H. Stewart.

Owing to the evacuation of Portsmouth and Norfolk by the Confederates, there was no longer need for the services of the regiment as heavy artillery, and it was changed into an infantry regiment and numbered the 61st. Colonel Wilson failed to join the regiment after it was organized and the command devolved on Lieutenant-Colonel Niemeyer. It remained on Dunn's Hill, near Petersburg, doing provost duty in that city and picket duty on the Appomattox river as far down as Bermuda Hundreds and City Point, until August 28th, when it was ordered to Richmond and went into camp on the Brook turnpike. It remained there a very short time and early in September it was ordered to the Rapidan to guard the fords of that river, while the army of General Lee was in Maryland. Companies E and F were sent to Staunton to do provost duty and did not rejoin the regiment until after the battle of Fredericksburg. The other companies were distributed at Warrenton, Culpepper, Rappahannock and other places.

Wm. S. Wright, who was then serving as a private in the Old Dominion Guard, of Portsmouth, Company K, 9th Virginia Regiment, was, in the summer of 1862, appointed Adjutant of the 61st, and shortly afterwards, while the regiment was at Warrenton, Colonel Virginius D. Groner, of Norfolk city, was elected colonel and took command.

On the 17th of September, Major Stewart, with three companies of the regiment and a squadron of cavalry belonging to the 15th Virginia Cavalry Regiment, was at Bristoe Station on the Orange and Alexandria railroad, where he had been ordered for the purpose of getting up several locomotives, which had been thrown from the track there, during the operations previous to the battle of Second Manassas. That day General Birney, who commanded the Federal forces near Fairfax Court House, sent an officer with a flag of truce, ostensibly to obtain permission to bury or remove their dead, who had been killed in the battles of August 29th and 30th, but really to ascertain how much of a force was there. General Birney made report to the authorities at Washington that his "flag of truce met a party of Confederates at Bristoe Station, under command of Major Wm. H. Stewart, who stated that it would take three days to communicate with his general and declined to receive the flag." He further reported that "the force there was small and might be surprised and captured if he had authority to send a cavalry force against them."

The necessary authority was given him and he made the attempt, but Major Stewart had succeeded by that time in getting the locomotives on the track, and, steam having been gotten up, the whole train moved off to the Rapidan, carrying the three companies of the 61st Regiment with it.

In the fall of 1862 a Federal spy, acting under orders from General Seigel, went to Staunton, and in his report, dated November 13th, says: " Staunton, with its manufactories of boots, shoes and clothing for the enemy, its extensive hospital preparations for thousands of sick, the general supply depot, the place of safe keeping of all the captured Harper's Ferry plunder, is defended by one company of the 61st Virginia Infantry, twenty-four field pieces, and a mixture of cavalry and artillery, though small in numbers." This was Company F. Company E was doing provost duty on the Valley turnpike.

Early in November the Secretary of War seems to have become alarmed for the safety of Richmond, and on the 5th he sent orders to General Lee to send the 61st Virginia Regiment and the Norfolk Light Artillery Blues to that city. General Lee replied on the 10th that he had not obeyed the order because he had not been able to supply their places on the upper Rappahannock.

On the 10th of November the three Florida Regiments in General Roger A. Pryor's Brigade were organized into a separate brigade, and placed under command of General Perry, of that State, and General Pryor, by order of General Lee, was relieved from duty with the army of Northern Virginia and ordered to report to the Secretary of War, in Richmond, who, on the 12th, issued an order to General Lee to send the 1st and 61st Virginia Regiments to Richmond, to be forwarded to Petersburg, as the nucleus of a new brigade for General Pryor; but, having need for them on the Rappahannock, General Lee did not comply with the order. General Pryor became impatient at the delay in sending those two regiments to him and wrote to General Lee, November 23d, asking that they be sent at once to him, as he wished them to operate in the vicinity of the Blackwater river. General Lee sent him the following reply:

HEADQUARTERS ARMY OF NORTHERN VIRGINIA, }
November 25th, 1862. }

Brig. Gen. R. A. Pryor, Richmond, Va.:

GENERAL.—Your letter of the 23d inst. has been received. I regret my inability to detach from this army the two regiments you desire to constitute a brigade, to operate on the Blackwater, under your command. As far as I am able to judge, troops are more wanted here than there, and it might be better to bring the troops which it is contemplated to unite with those in question, to this army. I regretted, at the time, the breaking up of your former brigade, but you are aware that the circumstances which produced it were beyond my control. The 61st Virginia has, in accordance with the desire of the colonel of the regiment, been attached to Mahone's brigade, which was organized from the section of country from which it came. I hope it will not be long before you will be again in the field, that the country may derive the benefit of your zeal and activity. I thought, and still think, that your services would be more valuable to the country south of James river, after your brigade was dismembered, and that troops could be organized in that region sufficient to form your command.

I have the honor to be, very respectfully, your obedient servant.
R. E. LEE,
General.

On the 15th of November General Burnside started with his army from Warrenton towards Fredericksburg, and General Lee ordered the 61st Virginia and the Norfolk Light Artillery Blues to that town. The advance of Burnside's army, Sumner's corps, reached Falmouth on the afternoon of the 17th, and an attempt was made as if to cross the river. According to the official report of General Lee it was checked by the 15th Virginia Cavalry, four companies of Mississippi infantry and Lewis' battery of light artillery. General Sumner says he made no attempt to cross, that his batteries drove Lewis' men from their guns, and he was anxious to cross and take possession of them, but was prevented by positive orders from General Burnside. The 61st Regiment reached Fredericksburg on the morning of the 18th, and found a large force of the enemy on the opposite side of the river. Colonel Groner, in order to create the impression upon their minds that a large Confederate force was present, had large fires built all along the heights and burned up nearly every fence rail in the vicinity. The ruse was successful and the enemy waited for reinforcements and to establish his communications before attempting to cross. In the meantime General Lee's army began to arrive from Culpepper and Orange Court House, and continued coming in, until he had collected an effective force of 72,564 men for duty, including infantry, artillery and cavalry.

General Lee was apprehensive that Fredericksburg would be occupied by the enemy before the 61st Regiment could reach there, and gave Colonel Groner orders how to proceed in that event. The commander of that cavalry operating on the river was ordered to keep Colonel Groner advised as to the movements of the enemy so as to guard against surprise. Shortly after the army reached Fredericksburg, the 61st Regiment was attached to Mahone's Brigade, which was then composed of the 6th, 12th, 16th, 41st and 61st Virginia Regiments, and was a part of Anderson's Division.

The battle of Fredericksburg took place on the 13th of December, 1863, and its details are a part of the history of the war. On the 12th General Burnside crossed one hundred thousand men over the river, and on the 13th attacked the right of General Lee's army, which was drawn up on the range of hills overlooking Fredericksburg, and about a mile or a mile and a half back from the town. Jackson's corps of three divisions, A. P. Hill's, D. H. Hill's and Ewell's - the last under command of General Early held the right of the line, and Longstreet's corps held the left, arranged in the following order by divisions: Hood on the right and joining Jackson's left, next Pickett, next McLaws, next Ransom, and next Anderson, with his left resting on the river. The 61st Regiment was with Anderson and was exposed to the fire of the Federal artillery, but was not actively engaged in the battle. The attack on Jackson was repulsed after heavy fighting, with loss to the Federals. Then an assault was made upon the position held by Ransom's and McLaw's Divisions, but it was easily repulsed. The enemy advanced four times and were driven back with great slaughter. The attacking columns were composed of the 2d corps, General Couch, the 9th, General Wilcox, and three divisions of Hooker's corps. Burnside's loss in the battle was 12,321, and that of the Confederates was 4,201, according to General Lee's official report.

After the battle of Fredericksburg the 61st Regiment remained in camp near that town, enjoying rather a quiet time, until the latter part of April, 1863, when the Federal army again got into motion. General Hooker had been assigned to the command, relieving General Burnside. He had an army, according to United States official reports, present for duty of one hundred and twenty thousand infantry and artillery, twelve thousand cavalry, and more than four hundred guns. General Lee had previously detached Hood's and Pickett's Divisions under Longstreet to Suffolk, and Ransom's Division to North Carolina, in February, and had left to oppose Hooker's advance, only fifty-seven thousand effectives. General Hooker left about thirty thousand men under General Sedgwick in his lines opposite Fredericksburg. These consisted of Sedgwick's own corps, the 6th, of twenty-two thousand men, as per his official report, and Gibbon's Division, of Couch's corps, numbering between seven and eight thousand additional, and were designed to mask the real purpose, which was to cross the Rappahannock River higher up and turn General Lee's left. This movement was successfully accomplished, and General Hooker took up a position at Chancellorsville and began to fortify it. General Lee left Early's Division and Kershaw's Brigade, in all, about nine thousand men at Fredericksburg to oppose Sedgwick, and with the remainder of his army amounting to forty-eight thousand, including the artillery and the cavalry of Stewart, drew out of his works and marched to attack Hooker's main army. This was on the 1st of May, and the advance of the two armies met late in the afternoon near Chancellorsville. A considerable engagement followed, during which Hooker withdrew to the position which he had fortified. The next morning General Lee retained McLaw's and Anderson's Divisions to hold Hooker in check in front, and sent Jackson with his own corps, composed of the divisions of A. P. Hill, Trimble and Rodes, numbering twenty-two thousand men to make a detour and attack his right flank and rear. While Jackson was making his flanking march, Lee drew Hooker's attention from him by feints upon his front, with McLaw's and Anderson's Divisions. About 6 o'clock in the afternoon Jackson got into a position to strike, and sending forward Rodes' Division, overran the Eleventh corps which formed Hooker's right, capturing prisoners, guns and wagons. Night terminated the battle for that day, and Jackson, riding through the Confederate lines with his staff to ascertain the position of the enemy, was, in the darkness, mistaken by his own men on his way back, for Federal cavalry, and fired upon. He received three wounds, one of which necessitated the amputation of his arm, and he died about a week after the battle. The next day, May 3d, Stuart took command of Jackson's corps, and extending his right formed a connection with the left of Anderson's Division, near the Chancellor House, whereupon General Lee ordered a general advance of the whole army and Hooker was driven out of his works into a second line, which he had constructed across the angle formed by the junction of the Rappahannock and Rapidan Rivers. General Lee was about to assault this position when his movements were arrested by news from Fredericksburg. Sedgwick had crossed the river at Fredericksburg, captured Marye Heights from General Early, who fell back before him, and was advancing in General Lee's rear towards Chancellorsville, to assist Hooker. General Lee sent back Mahone's Brigade, Wilcox's Brigade, and three of the brigades of McLaws' Division, the whole under command of General McLaws, to check him. They met near Salem Church and Sedgwick was driven back with a loss of five thousand men, including his loss in his attack upon Early. The next day General Early joined McLaws and General Lee sent Anderson with his three remaining brigades to assist. With these forces the attack was renewed, and Sedgwick, overwhelmingly defeated, was saved from total destruction only by the approach of night, under cover of which he recrossed the river at Banks' Ford. This attack was made principally by Early's Division which assailed Sedgwick's left.

On the 5th General Lee got his army together again and made arrangements to renew the attack on Hooker on the morning of the 6th, but when his skirmishers advanced at day break, they found Hooker had decamped across the river, leaving behind his wounded, twenty thousand stand of arms and fourteen guns. His loss was seventeen thousand one hundred and ninety-seven. The Confederate loss was ten thousand two hundred and eighty-one.

The 61st Regiment, as a part of Anderson's Division, was actively engaged in every day's fighting and lost heavily. Major Stewart, Captain Cassell and Lieutenant Murdaugh were wounded, as was also Lieutenant Alex. Butt, of Portsmouth, adjutant of the 41st Regiment, who died from his wound. This was the first battle of importance in which the 61st was actively engaged. It was ready at Fredericksburg, but was not called upon. At Chancellorsville the men fought with the steadiness of veterans.

After Chancellorsville, General Lee began the invasion of Pennsylvania and on the 1st, 2d and 3d of July fought the battle of Gettysburg. The 61st Regiment took part in the battle of the 2d and was held in reserve on the 3d. It was, however, exposed to the fire of the enemy's artillery on that day and lost a number of men killed and wounded. It was heavily engaged on the 2d and its losses were proportionate. The Confederates were successful in their attacks on the 1st and 2d and the Federals were pushed back with heavy losses in killed, wounded and prisoners, but in falling back, General Meade secured an advantageous position on the night of the 2d, from which General Lee failed to dislodge him. General Lee's losses in the Gettysburg campaign amounted to nineteen thousand men, killed, wounded and missing. General Meade's were somewhat larger. An account of the third day's fighting will be found in the history of the 9th Virginia Regiment, earlier in this work—chapter XII. General Lee had present for duty at Gettysburg sixty-eight thousand three hundred and fifty-two men (of whom fifty-four thousand three hundred and fifty-six were infantry) including cavalry and artillery and official reports place the Federal army at one hundred and five thousand effectives.

Two days after the battle of Gettysburg, General Lee fell back to the Potomac river. His march was slow and deliberate. He was anxious for General Meade to attack him. He was not strong enough to drive Meade from his fortified position, but was very willing to be attacked. He remained on the north bank of the Potomac four or five days on account of the swollen condition of the river, hoping the enemy would attack him, but, finding he would not do so, and unable to remain any longer away from his base of supplies, he crossed over into Virginia, followed at a respectful distance by his antagonist.

During the fall of 1863 nothing of special importance was done on the Rapidan. In October General Lee endeavored to bring about an engagement, and chased Meade into Fairfax county. His advance overtook the rear of the retreating force at Bristoe Station October 14th, and an engagement ensued, in which the Confederates were badly handled by the officers in command on the field, and the Federals, Warren's corps, held their ground until night, when they retired into Fairfax county. The 61st Regiment was present in that affair. It had an opportunity at Mine Run the following month to repay the enemy two fold. General Lee had detached a portion of his army and General Meade thought himself strong enough to whip the remainder, but he was checked at Mine Run with the loss of upwards of two thousand men, while the Confederate loss was scarcely as many hundred.

After that the army remained in winter quarters near Culpepper Court House until the following May, 1864, when General Grant began his overland campaign towards Richmond. With an army of one hundred and forty thousand men, of all arms, and a wagon train consisting of upwards of four thousand wagons, he started out to overwhelm General Lee, who had with him an army composed of fifty-two thousand six hundred and twenty-six infantry, cavalry and artillery.

Grant crossed the Rapidan May 5th, 1864, and launched his army forward into the region called the Wilderness, a thick, woody section of country in the northern part of Spotsylvania county, well grown up with underbrush and short pines, with a view of turning the right flank of Lee's army and compelling his retreat towards Richmond. Lee, however, had no idea of retreating, but threw Ewell's and A. P. Hill's corps across his front and ordered Longstreet, with his two divisions, Hood's and McLaw's, to join the army at once. They were camped near Gordonsville. Pickett's Division of Longstreet's corps was near Richmond and Petersburg. Ewell and Hill attacked the oncoming masses of the enemy, drove in their advance brigades and took up positions for the battle which it was evident would be fought the next day. Anderson's Division, to which the 61st Regiment and Mahone's Brigade were attached, had not then come up, and did not reach the field until some time after the battle had been joined the next day. General Lee formed his line of battle with Hill's corps on the right and Ewell's on the left. Longstreet's corps, which was expected to arrive during the forenoon, was to form on Hill's right, but Grant began his attack on Hill's troops about daybreak, before either Anderson or Longstreet had gotten up, and by greatly superior numbers, forced Hill's line back. It gave ground stubbornly and slowly until about seven o'clock, when the arrival of Anderson's Division enabled Hill to successfully resist his assailants. Hancock commanded that wing of the Federal Army, and was reinforced to such an extent that he had under his command more than one half of Grant's forces, but he made no further headway. Hill held his ground, and soon Longstreet's men began to arrive and take position. About noon Longstreet ordered an advance of his own and Hill's corps and the Federals were beaten back in confusion and completely disorganized. Longstreet turned their left and doubled it back upon the center, and was preparing a grand movement by which he expected to destroy that entire wing of Grant's army. He had sent forward Mahone's Brigade as a flanking party and advanced, himself at the head of Jenkins' South Carolina Brigade, to renew the attack in front. His own and Jenkins' staff were mounted, and had with them several captured United States flags, and, coming near Mahone's Brigade, they were mistaken for Federal cavalrymen and fired upon. General Jenkins was killed and Longstreet was wounded and disabled, while a number of the members of their respective staffs were also killed or wounded. This put a stop to the flanking movement and the Federals fell back and began entrenching themselves, and, after some sharp fighting, the Confederates also began building works. On the left of the Confederate line, the enemy made several unsuccessful attacks upon Ewell's corps, and, after repulsing these, Ewell turned the right of the Federal army, broke completely two of its divisions, and captured a number of prisoners.

Grant made several attempts on the 7th to carry the Confederate lines by assault, but without success, and on the night of that day drew out of his works and moved off to the left for the purpose of turning General Lee's right, but upon arriving at Spotsylvania Court House the next morning, found a portion of General Lee's army again posted across his front. An attack on the Confederate lines was repulsed and during the day both armies were getting into position. Upon the wounding of General Longstreet, General Anderson was assigned to the command of his corps and General Mahone was promoted to the command of Anderson's Division, which, from that time, was known as Mahone's Division.

On the 12th of May was fought the battle of Spotsylvania Court House, in which General Lee successfully repulsed every effort of General Grant to carry his lines and inflicted on him a very heavy punishment. Grant's losses in the two battles of the Wilderness and Spotsylvania Court House, according to his official reports, exceeded forty thousand.

The 61st Virginia Regiment was in the thickest of the fight, and its loss was severe. Colonel Groner was wounded, as was also Major Stewart, and Lieutenant-Colonel Niemeyer was killed. The fighting was nearly over at the time he was killed. The regiment, with the brigade, had charged and carried a line of breastworks defended by a thin line of the enemy, and Captain Chas.

R. McAlpine, of Company I, had captured a very fine horse, fully accoutred. Calling Lieutenant-Colonel Niemeyer to him he presented the horse to him, and as that officer accepted it, and was extending his hand to take it, a minie ball from the enemy's skirmish line pierced a vital spot in his body and his young life passed out to the great unknown. He was just twenty-four years old and singularly, had a presentiment that morning that he would be killed during the day. He informed Major Stewart of his belief that morning and before night his presentiment had become verified. His remains were carried to Richmond and interred. The funeral ceremonies took place in the Broad Street Methodist Church.

The death of Lieutenant-Colonel Niemeyer occasioned the promotion of Major Wm. H. Stewart to that position and Captain Charles R. McAlpine was promoted to Major. In the fall of 1863 Adjutant Wm. S. Wright died with a congestive chill, and in March, 1864, W. A. S. Taylor, of Norfolk, was appointed by Colonel Groner to fill the vacancy.

Grant remained in position in front of Spotsylvania Court House until the night of the 20th, when, finding himself powerless to force Lee's position, he once more moved off to the left, but Lee interposed again between him and Richmond, at Hanover Court House and Cold Harbor, and each time took heavy toll. There was constant fighting from the 24th of May to the 13th of June, in all of which the 61st Regiment and Mahone's Brigade took part. The principle assault on the Confederate lines at Cold Harbor was made on the 3d of June, between daylight and sunrise. Grant ordered an attack all along the lines. The battle lasted scarcely ten minutes, and in those ten minutes more than thirteen thousand Federal soldiers were killed or wounded. The Confederate loss barely exceeded one hundred.

On the 13th General Grant again moved off to the left, but had already made his nearest approach to Richmond, and further movements in that direction were carrying him away from the city. He reached the James river and crossed over on the 15th and 16th, at Wilcox's landing, below City Point. Official reports from his corps commanders made his losses from the Wilderness until he reached James river, more than sixty thousand men, a number greater than General Lee's army.

General Lee reported from Taylorsville on the 24th of May, to the Secretary of War, that Mahone had driven three regiments of the enemy across the river and captured a stand of colors and a number of prisoners, among them an aide of General Ledlie.

Repeated assaults by the Federals upon the Confederate lines in front of Petersburg, from the 15th to the 20th of June, were defeated, and each time the assaulting columns suffered severely, their total losses amounted to about twelve thousand. On the

20th Grant began regular seige operations. On the 22d he undertook to extend his left, composed of the 2d and 6th corps, to envelop General Lee's right, but Hill's corps attacked them. Mahone's Brigade, with the 61st Regiment on the right, turned the flank of the Federal forces and captured two thousand prisoners, fifteen hundred stand of arms, four Blakely guns and eight stand of colors. The entire Federal losses that day exceeded four thousand, of whom twenty-five hundred were captured. It was in this battle that Major McAlpine complimented the skill and good judgment of Captain John Hobday, of Portsmouth. [See ante, Chapter XXII, Company I, 61st Virginia.]

On the 23d the brigade had another smart brush with the enemy, in which it carried off a number of prisoners. On the 28th Wilson's Division of cavalrymen, returning from a raid against the Southside Railroad was headed off at Reams' Station, on the Petersburg and Weldon Railroad, and scattered. The Confederates captured one thousand prisoners, thirteen guns and the wagon train of the enemy.

The 61st Regiment was at the battle of the Crater, July 30th. The Federals had excavated a culvert or mine from their lines to a point underneath the Confederate works, and placing therein two hundred barrels of gun powder, exploded it about day break. The works immediately at that point were blown into the air and the guns and many of the artillerymen were buried beneath the falling debris. An attack was made by three divisions of white troops, Ledlie's, Potter's and Wilcox's, and one division of colored troops, composing the whole of Burnside's corps. These troops rushed into the breech, but were held in check by the Confederate batteries on the right and left of the opening, which began playing upon them. Mahone's Division was the nearest available force which could be sent to repel the intruders, and three of its brigades—Mahone's Virginia, Wright's Georgia and Saunders' Alabama—were hurried there. Mahone's and Wright's arrived first, and, forming line of battle, with Mahone's on the left, advanced to the charge. Wright's men faltered in face of the withering volleys which met them and fell back. Later its place was taken by Saunders' Brigade, which made a charge and dislodged the enemy from that portion of the field. The following account of the charge of Mahone's Brigade, then under command of General Weisiger, was written by Lieutenant Colonel Wm. H. Stewart, who commanded the 61st Regiment, Colonel Groner being absent on account of his wound received at Spotsylvania Court House:

BATTLE OF THE CRATER—RECOLLECTIONS OF THE RECAPTURE OF THE LINES—SCENES AND INCIDENTS.

As the wild waves of time rush on, our thoughts now and then run back over the rough billows to buried hopes and unfulfilled anticipations, and oft we linger long and lovingly, as if standing beside the tomb of a cherished parent. Thus the faithful follower of the Southern Cross recalls the proud hopes that led him over long and weary marches and in bloody battles. These foot-sore journeys and hard contested fields are now bright jewels in his life around which the tenderest cords of his heart are closely entwined. They are moments of duty! They are sacred resting places for his baffled energies! They are rich mines from which the very humblest actor gathers the wealth of an approving conscience! He bears no pæans by a grateful country—no bounty rolls bear his name—yet these are sweet choristers ever chanting priceless praises to the zeal and manhood with which he faced his foe. The veteran of an hundred battles always points with greater pride to one as the crowning glory of the many achievements. So the soldiers of Mahone's Old Brigade look upon the great battle which I shall here attempt to describe.

My little fly tent, scarcely large enough for two persons to lie side by side, was stretched over a platform of rough boards, elevated about two feet above the ground, in that little grave yard on the Wilcox farm, near Petersburg. I was quietly sleeping within it, dreaming, perhaps, of home and all its dear associations (for only a soldier can properly appreciate these), when a deep rumbling sound, that seemed to rend the very earth in twain, startled me from my slumbers, and in an instant I beheld a mountain of curling smoke ascending towards the heavens. The whole camp had been aroused, and all were wondering from whence came this mysterious explosion. It was the morning of Saturday, the 30th day of July, 1864. The long-talked-of mine had been sprung, a battery blown up, and the enemy were already in possession of eight hundred yards of our entrenchments.

Two hundred cannon roared in one accord, as if every lanyard had been pulled by the same hand. The grey fog was floating over the fields and darkness covered the face of the earth, but the first bright streak of dawn was gently lifting the curtain of night.

The fiery crests of the battlements shone out for miles to our left, and the nitrous vapors rose in huge billows from each line of battle, and sweeping together formed one vast range of gloom.

The sun rose brilliantly, and the great artillery duel still raged in all its grandeur and fury. An occasional shell from a Blakely gun would swoop down in our camp and richochet down the line to our right, forcing us to hug closely the fortifications.

Soon after, Captain Tom. Bernard, General Mahone's courier, came sweeping up the lines on his white charger to the headquarters of Brigadier General D. Weisiger. Then the drums commenced rolling off the signals, which were followed by "fall in" and hurried roll calls. We were required to drive back the Federals, who were then holding, and within the very gates of the city of Petersburg. It was startling news; but our soldiers faltered not, and moved off at quick step for the seat of war.

Wright's Georgia Brigade, commanded by Lieutenant-Colonel Hall, and our Virginia Brigade, the latter numbering scarcely eight hundred muskets, constituted the force detailed to dislodge the enemy, who held the broken lines with more than fifteen thousand men, and these were closely supported by as many more. I remember that our regiment, the 61st, did not exceed two hundred men, including officers and privates, which I am quite sure was the strongest in the two brigades. I suppose we had marched the half of a mile when ordered to halt and strip off all baggage except ammunition and muskets. We then filed to the left a short distance to gain the banks of a small stream in order to be protected from the shells of the Federal batteries by placing a range of hills between. These the enemy were already viewing within four hundred yards with covetous eyes, and making dispositions to attempt their capture, for they were the very keys to the invested city. When nearly opposite the portion of our works held by the Federal troops, we met several soldiers who were in the works at the time of the explosion. Our men began ridiculing them for going to the rear, when one of them remarked: "Ah, boys, you have hot work ahead—they are negroes, and show no quarter." This was the first intimation that we had to fight negro troops, and it seemed to infuse the little band with impetuous daring, as they pressed onward to the fray. I never felt more like fighting in my life. Our comrades had been slaughtered in a most inhuman and brutal manner, and slaves were trampling over their mangled and bleeding corpses. Revenge must have fired every heart and strung every arm with nerves of steel for the herculean task of blood. We filed up a ditch, which had been dug for safe ingress and egress to and from the earthworks, until we reached the vale between the elevation on which the breastworks were located and the one on the banks of the little stream just mentioned—within two hundred yards of the enemy. The ill-fated battery of six-guns which had been demolished by the explosion of eight tons of gun-powder, projected from the line of earthworks for the infantry at an acute angle. It overlooked the enemy's line of works which were on the northeastern slope of the same elevation, distant about one hundred yards.

The "Crater," or excavation, caused by the explosion, was about twenty-five feet deep, one hundred and fifty feet long and fifty feet wide. About seventy-five feet in rear of the supporting earthworks there was a wide ditch with the bank thrown up on the side next the fortifications. This was constructed to protect parties carrying ammunitions and rations to the troops. Between this irregular and ungraded embankment and the main line the troops had constructed numerous caves, in which they slept at night to be protected from the mortar shells. The embankment from the bottom of the ditch was about ten feet high and commanded the outer or main line. The space from the outside of the fortifications to the inner edge of the ditch was more than one hundred feet wide.

The "Crater," and the space on both sides for some distance, were literally crammed with the enemy's troops. They were five lines deep, and must have numbered between fifteen and twenty-five thousand men. Their historians admit that their charge was made by the whole of the ninth corps, commanded by General A. E. Burnside, and that the fifth and a part of the second corps were massed in supporting distance.

Mahone's old Brigade, after being deployed, covered their front from the centre of the Crater to their right. Their silken banners proudly floating on the breezes, supported by countless bayonets glistening in the sunlight, might on an ordinary occasion have daunted our little band and made them forfeit a trial at arms; but they were desperate and determined, and reckoned not the host that confronted them. I recollect counting seven standards in front of our regiment alone. Our column was deployed in the valley before mentioned, in full view of these hostile thousands. As the soldiers filed into line, General Mahone walked from right to left, commanding the men to reserve their fire until they reached the brink of the ditch, and after delivering one volley to use the bayonet. Our line was hardly adjusted, and the Georgians had not commenced to deploy, when the division of negroes, the advance line of the enemy, made an attempt to rise from the ditch and charge. Just at that instant General Mahone ordered a counter charge. The men rushed forward, officers in front, with uncovered heads and waving hats, and grandly and beautifully swept onward over the intervening space with muskets at trail. The enemy sent in the ranks a storm of bullets, and here and there a gallant fellow would fall; but the files would close, still pressing onward, unwavering, into the jaws of death.

The orders of Major-General Mahone were obeyed to the very letter, the brink of the ditch was gained before a musket was discharged, the cry "No quarter!" greeted us, the one volley responded, and the bayonet plied with such irresistible vigor as insured success in the shortest space of time. Men fell dead in heaps, and human gore ran in streams that made the very earth mire beneath the tread of the victorious soldiers. The rear ditch being ours, the men mounted the rugged embankment and hurled their foes from the front line up to the very mouth of the Crater. In the meantime, the Georgia Brigade had charged, but were repulsed; and soon after it was re-formed in column of regiments and again charged, but was met by such a withering fire that it again recoiled with heavy slaughter.

Our bloody work was all done so quickly that I had scarcely an idea of the time it required to accomplish it, some say it was twenty minutes. It was over I am sure about noon, and then for the first time we realized the oppression of the scorching rays of that July sun, and many almost sank from exhaustion. The brigade captured fifteen battle flags, and our own regiment owned five of the seven that I had counted in its front. How many men rallied to each of these captured flags I have no means of ascertaining; but the Ninth Corps had been recently recruited, and its regiments must have been well up towards the thousands, and from these captured flags alone the reader may form an idea of the numbers we had overcome. In that supreme moment, when exulting over a great victory, how great I shall leave for others to judge, as our eyes fell upon the bleeding comrades around us, our hearts sickened within, for more than half our members lay dead, dying, wounded and writhing in agonies around us.

The wonderful triumph had been won at the price of the blood of the bravest and best and truest. Old Company F, of Norfolk, had carried in twelve men, all of whom were killed or wounded. The Sixth Regiment, to which it was attached, carried in ninety-eight men, and mustered ten for duty at this time. The Sharp-shooters carried in eighty men, and sixteen remained for duty. Nearly half of our own regiment had fallen, and the 12th, 41st and 16th Regiments suffered in like proportion. Up to this time only an inconsiderable number of prisoners had been captured.

Mention of special acts of bravery would, perhaps, be out of place here, for all who marched from that vale crowned themselves heroes, and need no encomiums from my feeble pen.

During the charge, about fifty yards from the ditch, Captain John G. Wallace, of Company C, 61st Virginia Regiment, was stricken down with a broken thigh. He lay upon his back, refusing to allow his men to take him from the field till the battle was over, waving his hat and urging his men to " go on ; go forward."

Lieutenant St. Julien Wilson, of the same company, was mortally wounded, and died the next day. He was a young officer, generally admired for his gallant conduct on the field and manly christian virtues in camp.

Captain John T. West, of Company A, encountered two burly negroes at the brink of the ditch, and while parrying their thrusts with his sword, was bayoneted in his shoulder by one of his own men, who was too eager to assist him. Privates Henry J. Butt, Jeremiah Casteen and D. A. Williams, three of the bravest of the brave, from the same company, were instantly killed.

Private John Shepherd, a noble soldier of Company D, was slain just before reaching the main line of breastworks.

Captain W. Scott Sykes, of Company F, Forty-first Virginia Regiment, was wounded in the shoulder while gallantly leading his men.

Colonel Harry Williamson, of the Sixth Virginia Regiment, lost an arm.

Captain David Wright, Company H, Sixth Virginia Regiment, was instantly killed while leading his men. He had been promoted from the ranks to captaincy on account of his gallant and meritorious conduct.

Our townsmen, Judge C. W. Hill and John T. Hill, members of the same regiment, the Sixth Virginia, were wounded almost at the same instant ; the former through the left arm, which was afterwards amputated, and the latter through the wrist.

Major W. H. Etheredge, of the Forty-first Regiment, displayed great gallantry, as was always his custom on the field. As he jumped in the ditch, a brave Federal in the front line fired through the traverse and killed a soldier at his side. He immediately dropped his empty musket and snatched another from a cowering comrade to kill Major Etheredge. At this juncture, the Major, with remarkable self-possession, caught up two Federals who were crouching in the ditch, and held their heads together between his determined opponent, swinging them to and fro to cover the sight of the musket, the Federal doing his best to uncover it so as to unharm his friends by his bullet. Peter Gibbs, of the Forty-first Virginia Regiment, Company E, of Petersburg, rushed to the assistance of the Major, and killed his foe. Gibbs was a gallant soldier, and fought with great desperation. It was said at the time that he slew fourteen men that day.

Captain W. W. Broadbent, the brave commander of the Sharpshooters, was mercilessly murdered, his skull was broken in and almost every square inch of his body was perforated with a bayonet stab.

Although our principal task was completed, yet more heavy work remained to be done to fully re-establish our lines. Brigadier-General Bartlet, with about five hundred men, were cooped up in the Crater, and their capture was the crowning event of the bloody drama. Our wounded was sent to the rear as fast as possible, and after piling the enemy's dead on each side of the trenches, to make a pass-way, our ranks were closed up in proper order. We were then ordered to keep up a sharp fire on the enemy's works in front to keep them close, and on the Crater to our right to prevent Bartlet's escape, as our position commanded his rear, while Saunders' Alabama Brigade formed in the valley and charged. The Alabamians made a grand charge under a terrible fire, reaching the crest of the Crater without faltering, and here a short struggle ensued. They tumbled muskets, clubs, clods of earth and cannon balls into the excavation on the heads of the enemy with telling effect. This novel warfare, as before stated, lasted only a few minutes, when Bartlet ordered up the white flag, and about five hundred prisoners marched to our rear. The negroes among them were very much alarmed, and vociferously implored for their lives. One old cornfield chap exclaimed: "My God, massa, I nebber pinted a gun at a white man in all my life; dem nasty, stinking Yankees fotch us here, and we didn't want to come fus!"

The appearance of this rough, irregular hole beggars description. It was estimated that it contained six hundred bodies. The importance of re-construcing this broken line of earthworks at once, prevented the removal of these bodies—therefore, they were buried as they had fallen, in one indiscriminate heap. Spades were brought in, and the earth thrown from the side of the Crater until they were covered a sufficient depth. By 3 o'clock in the afternoon all was over, and we were enjoying a welcome truce.

The extreme heat of the sun had already caused putrefaction to commence, and the bodies in our front and rear, and especially the blood-soaked earth under our feet in the trenches, exhaled such a nauseating smell that I was forced to abandon my supper, although I had not tasted a morsel of food since the previous night.

There were thousands of captured arms around us, and during the night some of our men would shoot ramrods at the enemy just for the fun of hearing them whiz. One that was sent over drew from a Federal the exclamation, "Great God! Johnnie, you are throwing turkey spits and stringing us together over here. Stop it!"

A correspondent of one of the New York dailies, writing a description of this battle from accounts obtained from wounded officers, who arrived at Washington on the 2d of August, 1864, uses the following language: "Often have the Confederates won encomiums for valor, but never before did they fight with such uncontrollable desperation. It appeared as if our troops were at their mercy, standing helpless or running in terror and shot down like dogs. No such scene has been witnessed in any battle of the war. The charge of the enemy against the negro troops was terrific. With fearful yells they rushed down against them. The negroes at once ran back, breaking through the line of white troops in the rear. Again and again their officers tried to rally them. Words and blows were useless. They were victims of an uncontrollable terror, and human agency could not stop them."

Next morning was a bright and beautiful Sabbath, and nothing of moment occurred. At least three thousand of the Federal dead were still on the field putrifying under the scorching rays of the sun. I remember a negro between the lines, who had both legs blown off, crawled up to the outside of our works, stuck three muskets in the ground, and threw a small piece of tent cloth over them to shelter his head from the hot sunshine. Some of our men managed to shove a cup of water to him, which he drank, and immediately commenced frothing at the mouth, and died in a very short time afterwards. He had lived in this condition for nearly twenty-four hours.

On Monday morning a truce was granted, and the Federals sent out details to bury their dead between the lines. They dug a long ditch, and placed the bodies crosswise, several layers up, and refilled the ditch.

After the Federals had finished burying their dead and were moving off, General Mahone noticed that they had left the dirt piled high enough for breastworks, midway between the two lines. He quickly discerned the danger of this, as it would have afforded shelter for another assaulting column. He stopped the burial detail and made them level the ground as they found it. General Pendleton, commander of the artillery of General Lee's army, was standing near and paid a high compliment to General Mahone's foresight.

The official reports of the various regiments give the losses in the brigade as follows, omitting a number of slightly wounded:

	Killed.	Wounded.	Missing.
Sixth Regiment, Col. Geo. T. Rogers, commanding	13	50	12
Twelfth Reg., Major R. H. Jones, commanding	12	26	
Sixteenth Reg., Maj. J. T. Woodhouse, commanding	21	18	
Forty-first Reg., Maj. W. H. Etheredge, commanding	13	31	
Sixty-first Reg., Lt. Col. W. H. Stewart, commanding	19	43	
	78	168	12

Total losses—258.

General Weisiger, commanding the brigade, was wounded. The next battle of importance in which the regiment took part, was fought on the 19th of August, on the Petersburg and Weldon Railroad. This battle is sometimes called Davis' Farm and sometimes Johnson's Farm, as it took place on both. Warren's corps had been advanced to the left to occupy a position on the railroad, but was attacked by parts of Mahone's and Heth's Divisions and his works handsomely carried. Twenty-five hundred prisoners belonging to Crawford's and Ayers' Divisions were captured, among them, Brigadier-General Hays. Mahone's Brigade suffered more severely in this battle than in any other in which it was engaged. While the main battle was being fought elsewhere, this brigade was detached to check the advance of reinforcements and was placed by General Weisiger in a very disadvantageous position in which it was unnecessarily exposed, and its losses were heavy. After it had been badly cut up, General Mahone, going to that part of the field, ordered it to fall back to a better position. It accomplished the object, however, of preventing the reinforcements getting up in time. The 61st Regi-

THE SIXTY-FIRST VIRGINIA REGIMENT.   191

ment carried nineteen officers, fifteen ambulance corps and one hundred and fifty enlisted men to the fight, of whom seven were killed, fifty-five wounded and fourteen missing. Total, seventy-six.

On the 25th the 61st Regiment took part in the defeat of Hancock's corps at Reams' Station, in which battle Hancock lost about three thousand men, of whom seventeen hundred were captured, with twelve guns and numerous standards.

On the 17th of December Grant sent a large force of infantry, cavalry and artillery to destroy the Petersburg and Weldon Railroad south of Reams' Station; but upon reaching Hicksford December 9th, it was driven back by a Confederate force, among whom was the 61st Regiment.

It participated in the battles of Burgess' Mill, October 27th, 1864; Hatcher's Run, February 6th, 1865; Amelia Court House, April 5th; Cumberland Church, April 7th, and surrendered at Appomattox April 9th. One Colonel, one Lieutenant-Colonel, three non-commissioned staff, three Captains, two 1st and four 2d Lieutenants, thirteen Sergeants, ten Corporals, seventy-eight privates, two musicians and one teamster. Total, one hundred and eighteen.

Below will be found their names.

Colonel—Virginius D. Groner.
Lieutenant-Colonel—Wm. H. Stewart.
Captain—Alex. E. Etheredge, Assistant Quarter Master.
Hospital Steward—Henry S. Etheredge.
Ordnance Sergeant—Bartholomew J. Accinelly.
Quarter Master Sergeant—Benjamin T. Tatem.

COMPANY A—SERGEANTS.

| W. R. Dudley, | Wm. A. West, | Thos. H. Sykes. |

CORPORALS.

| J. N. Wood, | W. H. Harrison, | Leroy M. West. |

PRIVATES.

Columbus C. Cooper,	Alex. O. Lee,	Simon Mathias,
J. H. Miller,	T. E. Halstead,	L. Miller,
J. J. Miller,	Josephus Scott,	E. Sivills.

COMPANY B.

Second Lieutenant—James A. Stott.

SERGEANTS.

| W. D. Barnard, | F. H. Williams, | T. Williams. |

First Corporal J. Beasley.

PRIVATES.

Jacob A. Aydlott,	W. A. Cooper,	A. Fanshaw,
F. F. Hall,	T. W. Hodges,	R. Smith,
A. Stewart,	C. W. Wicker.	

COMPANY C—PRIVATES.

J. M. Banks,	S. K. Cox,	R. Bradley,
G. W. Eason,	J. W. Lupton,	W. Powers.

COMPANY D.

Second Lieutenant, Julius J. Bilisoly.

PRIVATES.

J. H. Davis,	W. C. Costen,	A. D. B. Godwin,
Benj. March,	Thos. Only,	G. Parker.

Teamster, Alex. E. Lester.

COMPANY E.

Captain, Jetson Jett.

SERGEANTS.

J. M. Wilkins,	W. L. S. Wilkins,	A. Ives.

CORPORALS.

Joshua Charlton, Littleton Charlton.

Musician, L. R. Edmonds.

PRIVATES.

M. Ballance,	Milton Cutherell,	M. Etheredge,
J. E. Foreman,	J. F. Grimes,	C. W. Hall,
J. S. Hall,	F. G. Ives,	Geo. Owens,
W. D. Rudd,		Chas. C. Williamson.

COMPANY F.

First Lieutenant, R. R. Owens.
First Sergeant, J. J. Anderson.

CORPORALS.

W. H. Beale, W. B. Holland.

PRIVATES.

J. Beale,	S. Carr,	L. Carr,
W. W. Corbitt,	B. D. Council,	J. Eley,
J. M. Eley,	T. Hayes,	W. Joyner,
J. Johnson,		J. H. Moundfield.

COMPANY G.

Captain, R. E. Moseley.
First Lieut., W. F. Baugh. Second Lieut., J. M. Perkins.
First Sergeant, P. F. Howell.
Corporal, G. W. Collins.

PRIVATES.

K. Cobb,	R. H. Cobb,	A. Hawkins,
W. A. Harrison,	A. Ivey,	P. Lee,
J. Mulder,	J. S. Nicholson,	E. Reese,
	T. Tudor.	

COMPANY H.
Captain, Henry E. Orr.
Second Lieutenant, W. W. Rew.
First Sergeant, E. F. Berryman.

PRIVATES.

A. Harrell,	Thos. Hodges,	J. F. Miller,
J. M. McGlone,	E. Robinson,	Mills Turner.

COMPANY I.
First Sergeant, Jno. M. Sherwood.
Corporal, Thomas Collins.
Musician, Joseph J. Smith.

PRIVATES.

Jos. Beaton,	Wm. W. Dollett,	Robt. Duke,
A. J. Fowler,	Joseph Holloway,	Edward King,
Albert Powell,		Jos. Tompkins.

COMPANY K — PRIVATES.

Richard Stafford,	E. Sorey.

At the battle of Cumberland Church, Mahone's Division and General G. T. Anderson's Brigade of Georgians, surrounded a Federal brigade in a ravine and captured the whole brigade, with their colors, and marched them to Appomattox Court House, where, upon learning that the army was about to be surrendered, they asked General Mahone to give them their colors back again, as it was a matter of pride with the regiments to have them at the close of the war. General Mahone complied with their request, and after the surrender of General Lee they were released.

Major McAlpine, after being with the regiment in all of its toils and triumphs, resigned January 25th, 1865, to raise a battalion of Partizan Rangers. A misunderstanding with General Weisiger was the prime cause of his leaving the regiment. Adjutant W. A. S. Taylor resigned in February, 1865, and Sergeant-Major Griffin F. Edwards was promoted to that position. He was severely wounded at Cumberland Church, April 7th, and left behind on the retreat to Appomattox Court House.

The 61st Virginia was one of the best regiments in the army of Northern Virginia, and made a record second to none other that fought beneath its banners.

Lieutenant J. M. Perkins, of Company G, served faithfully with his company throughout the war without having received a wound, and surrendered at Appomattox. After the surrender he started for his home in Surry county, and in attempting to ford a stream near Hicksford, almost within sight of his home, was swept under by the current and drowned.

The regiment participated in the following battles, besides numerous skirmishes:

Catlett Station, Sept. 29th, '62,
Fredericksburg, Dec. 11th, 12th, and 13th, 1862,
Zoah's Church, April 30th, '63,
McCarthy's Farm, May 1st, 63,
Chancellorsville, May 2d and 3d, 1863,
Salem Church, May 3d, 1862,
Gettysburg, July 2d and 3d, 1863,
Bristoe Station, Oct. 14th, '63,
Mine Run, Dec. 2d, 1863,
Wilderness, May 6th, 1864,
Shady Grove, May 8th, 1864,
Spotsylvania C. H., May 12th, 1864,
North Anna River, May 21st to 23d, 1864,
Hanover C. H., May 28th and 29th, 1864,
Atlee Station, June 1st, 1864,
Cold Harbor, June 2d and 3d, 1864,
Turkey Ridge, (skirmishing) June 4th to 13th, 1864,
Frazier's Farm, June 13th, '64,
Wilcox Farm, June 22d, 1864,
Gurley House, June 23d, 1864,
Crater, July 30th, 1864,
Davis' Farm, Aug. 19th, 1864,
Reams Station, Aug. 25th, '64,
Burgess' Mill, Oct. 27th, 1864,
Hicksford, Dec. 9th, 1864,
Hatcher's Run, Feb. 6th, 1865,
Amelia C. H., April 5th, 1865,
Cumberland Church, April 7th, 1865,
Appomattox C. H., April 9th, 1865.

The regiment was also engaged in the following battles with the Federal Cavalry:

Rappahannock Bridge, Nov. 7th, 1862,
Hagerstown, July 6th to 11th, 1863,
Culpepper or Brandy Station, Aug. 1st, 1863,
Reams' Station, June 27th, 1864.

GENERAL MAHONE'S REPORT OF CHANCELLORSVILLE BATTLE.

HEADQUARTERS MAHONE'S BRIGADE, ANDERSON'S DIVISION, }
May 27th, 1863. }

MAJOR I beg leave to report the operations of this brigade in the late battles of the Rappahannock. It is proper to premise that this brigade, with that of General Posey, had been stationed near the United States ford for the purpose of defending that crossing of the Rappahannock.

On Wednesday, April 29th, it was reported to me that the enemy had made his appearance in force at the Germanna and Ely's crossings of the Rapidan. This appearance of the enemy on our flank and rear, rendered our position at the United States ford no longer tenable, and, with a view to checking his advance on the flank of our army, as was now clearly discovered to be his aim, the two brigades—General Posey's and mine—were immediately placed in position near Chancellorsville, so as to cover the roads from Germanna and Ely's crossings of the Rapidan and that of the United States ford, uniting at Chancellorsville. In the meantime our camps, stores, equipage, transportation and such, were sent to the rear and without any material loss of any of them.

The brigades occupied their positions at Chancellorsville as indicated, until next morning, (Thursday, the 30th inst.) when, under the direction of the Major-General commanding the division, (who had happily joined us during the night) they fell back to the United States Mine road, this brigade at and covering the crossing of that road by the old turnpike. Before leaving our position at Chancellorsville, however, the enemy's cavalry advance on the Ely's ford road had made its appearance, and after a precipitate advance upon our pickets (capturing several) he subsequently came upon our rear guard—the 12th Virginia Infantry, Lieutenant-Colonel E. M. Field commanding—was repulsed, and so effectually as to leave us free from any further annoyance during the change of position to which I have already referred, and then in process of execution. Shortly after we had taken up our new position at the intersection of the mine and turnpike roads, the enemy came down the turnpike in considerable force of cavalry and infantry, but nothing occurred at this point beyond a little skirmishing with the sharpshooters and reconnoitering parties.

The next day (Friday, May 1st,) this brigade led on the turnpike road in the general advance of our forces, and very shortly engaged the enemy under General Sykes, when we had quite a brisk little engagement, infantry and artillery, Major-General McLaws commanding. The enemy (United States regulars, many of whom we captured) was promptly repulsed, and our line of battle, now formed, was moved rapidly forward to a point on the turnpike south of Chancellorsville, about 1¼ miles, known as McGee's. This brigade continued here with Major-General McLaw's force, confronting the enemy's line of battle in that quarter until the next day, when it was transferred, and occupied our front line, immediately on the left of the plank road. In this position we continued up to the fall of Chancellorsville, engaging the enemy more or less warmly as the progress of General Jackson's operations on his flank and rear seemed to call for, and as the range of his (General Jackson's) enfilading fire would allow. It was during this service of the brigade that the advance line of skirmishers of the 6th Virginia Infantry (Colonel George T. Rogers) under the immediate command of Captain W. Carter Williams, charged over the enemy's abatis, near the plank road, fired upon him in his rifle pits, captured there prisoners from four different regiments, and the colors and color-bearer of the 107th Ohio, returning to his position with his handful of men, with the loss of an officer as prisoner. This gallant and successful sortie was made a little after dark Saturday, May 2d, when General Jackson's fire was heavy, and it was in fighting over the same ground the next morning that the valliant Williams fell, mortally wounded. The standard, a most elegantly finished work, was duly delivered.

Immediately following the fall of Chancellorsville, this brigade was sent, with a brigade of Major-General McLaw's Division, to look after the enemy, then reported to be advancing up the plank road from Fredericksburg, under General Sedgwick. Meeting General Wilcox with his brigade, about the divergence of the plank and turnpike roads, and finding that the enemy was really and rapidly advancing, it was at once determined to meet him at Salem Church. At this point, possessing the advantage of ground, our line was formed.

In the meantime, Major-General McLaws had joined us with the balance of his division. My brigade, in the spirited fight at this place, occupied the extreme left of the line, lying wholly in the woods, and participated in the successful resistance made to the enemy's very determined effort to break our line at that point. Upon the conclusion of this battle, (Tuesday, May 5th) the brigade joined its division. The conduct of the officers and men (in braving the hardships and privations attending eight consecutive days of exposure and excitement, as well as in battles,) deserve high commendation, and at least this acknowledgment at my hands.

The 12th Virginia, Lieutenant-Colonel E. M. Field commanding, for its rigid and efficient resistance of the superior force of enemy while covering the formation of our line of battle on the turnpike, Friday, May 1st; the 6th Virginia, Colonel George T. Rogers commanding, for its vigorous pressure and bold sorties upon the enemy and his works around Chancellorsville Saturday and Sunday, May 2d and 3d, for its veteran-like behavior at Salem Church, receiving without disorder, the enemy's sudden fire, while moving by the flank, and the 61st Virginia, Colonel V. D. Groner, for its gallant and successful skirmish with the enemy during the formation of our lines at Salem Church, deserve special mention, while the part borne by the 16th Virginia, Lieutenant-Colonel Richard O. Whitehead commanding, and the 41st Virginia, Colonel William Allen Parham commanding, was everywhere, though less arduous, well and bravely performed. In this connection it is but due that I should record here my high appreciation of the efficient and gallant conduct of the staff officers with me—Captain R. Taylor, Assistant Adjutant-General, and First Lieutenant Richard Walke, Ordnance Officer.

Among the gallant spirits who were seriously wounded, Captain Robert R. Banks, Company E, 12th Virginia Infantry, must be mentioned. He fell among the foremost in the skirmish fight of his regiment on the turnpike, May 1st, and was, at that time, commanding an advance guard. His conduct on this occasion was beautifully heroic. The number of prisoners taken by the brigade was large, but cannot be accurately stated, owing to the hurried and detached manner in which they had to be sent to the rear. The casualties of the brigade in all of these battles were as follows:

	Killed	Wounded	Missing	Total
Sixth Virginia Infantry	8	33	6	47
Twelfth Virginia Infantry	5	31	50	86
Sixteenth Virginia Infantry	1	17		18
Forty-first Virginia Infantry	6	23		29
Sixty-first Virginia Infantry	4	30	3	37
Detail bridge building, Germanna			38	38
Total	24	134	97	255

I am, major, very respectfully, your obedient servant,

WM. MAHONE,
Brigadier General.

Major Thos. S. Mills, A. A. A. G., Anderson's Division, 1st Corps, Army Northern Virginia.

General R. H. Anderson, commanding the division, in his report says: "It would be doing an injustice to Brigadier General Mahone, to omit to mention his bold, skillful and successful management, so well seconded by his brave Virginians." He also says: "Major William C. Wingfield, chief commissary of the division, rendered valuable service by careful and unremitting attention to his duties."

THE WOUNDING OF GENERAL LONGSTREET.

Colonel Virginius D. Groner, colonel of the 61st Virginia Regiment, Mahone's Brigade, has furnished the writer with an account of the wounding of General Longstreet in the battle of the Wilderness, which, as it differs somewhat from the usually accepted theory of that unfortunate occurrence, is here added. Colonel Groner says Mahone's Brigade was on the extreme right of Longstreet's line when it advanced and drove the enemy from its front in utter confusion. That the brigade was formed with the 6th Regiment on the left, then the 16th, then the 61st, then the 41st and the 12th on the right. That in order to turn the flank of the enemy the brigade was ordered to make a left turn, the regiments following each other in eschelon. After moving some distance in this manner through the woods, which were on fire and strewn thickly with dead and wounded men, the 12th Regiment became separated from the rest of the brigade, so that the 41st, which was next to it, became uncovered on its right. This was communicated to Colonel Groner, who halted that regiment and his own and reported to General Mahone that the 12th Regiment could not be found. General Mahone then approved of his halting the 41st and 61st Regiments, and ordered him to look for the 12th. When the 16th and 6th Regiments got up on the line with the two other regiments, they halted also. Colonel Groner says the line, thus formed, was about seventy-five yards from the road in which General Longstreet was wounded, and that the smoke from the burning woods and the underbrush was so dense that it would have been impossible to have seen that distance through them. He moved across the road and found the 12th Regiment coming back. That regiment had crossed the road, but finding that it had advanced too fast and was alone there, had started back to rejoin the brigade, and on its return it was mistaken by the 41st for the enemy and fired into. He says as soon as the 41st Regiment began firing, the regiments to the left of it took it up, and there was a general fusilade from the whole brigade, and that General Longstreet's party were in front of the position held by the 16th and 6th Regiments, and he was struck by the random firing of one of those regiments. He further says that when he crossed the road to rejoin his regiment, after finding the 12th Regiment, he noticed the party of horsemen coming up, but is satisfied that, on account of the thickness of the undergrowth in the woods and the dense smoke from the burning leaves, they were not visible from the position occupied by the brigade.

ANOTHER ACCOUNT.

Captain John T. West, of Company A, 61st Virginia Regiment, has furnished the author with his recollections of the affair, which differ quite materially from Colonel Groner's. Captain West says:

"On the morning of May 6th, 1864, I was in charge of a section of Mahone's Sharpshooters battalion, commanded by Lieutenant-Colonel Field, of the 12th Virginia. We were deployed in the dense forest of the Wilderness, considerably in advance of the brigade (Mahone's.)

By order of Colonel Field, I had just examined, with a scouting party, the woods in our immediate front, and reported that a brigade of our men had just marched to the left, leaving the front uncovered, with the enemy a short distance in advance. At this moment a shot from a single musket came crashing through the brain of the gallant and daring Acelius G. Foreman, of Company A, 61st Virginia. Immediately the order forward ran along the line, and in a few minutes, the brigade coming up at a double quick, the battle was joined, the Federal line broken and driven from its position, retreated in disorder. Then followed a running fight for a mile or more, when the Federals were driven into corral beyond the plank road. Just as the left of our brigade had reached, and in part crossed this road, it was ordered to halt and firing ceased. At this moment the left of the 61st Virginia rested on or near the road which cut through our line, passing to the right and front at an angle of 30 or 40 degrees, and thus so receding from our line of battle, that the regiments to the right of the 61st could not see, and in all probability did not know that a road was in their front.

In a very short time after the halt, General Longstreet and staff, with General Jenkins and brigade, passed to the front, along this road, obliquely to our right. The writer and all that portion of our brigade near the road, saw the movement and understood it, but the regiments on the right further in the forest and in rear of the road, did not see it or know that fresh troops were being marched to their front, hence, when some of the men of one of these regiments saw indistinctly through the forest the waving of the colors of Jenkins' Brigade, and the gleaming of muskets, they very naturally supposed that the Federals, who had just retreated in that direction, had rallied and were returning to renew the battle, and unfortunately, at once opened fire. The firing rapidly extended through several companies, and was only stopped by Lieutenant-Colonel W. H. Stewart and Captain W. C. Wallace, who ran rapidly forward, calling out, "Cease firing, you are shooting down your own men." Only one volley was fired, but alas, Longstreet was disabled, Jenkins and many officers and men killed and an end put to a pursuit which possibly would have proved a route to Grant's Army."

CHAPTER XXV.

IN OUTSIDE COMMANDS.

The following Portsmouth men were in companies from other localities. There were probably others but they have passed out of memory, and there are no muster rolls by which it can be refreshed. The list of wounded is correct as far as it goes, but probably many were wounded who are not so credited here:

Adams, Charles S., private, Signal Corps.
Ashton, R. N., private, Company K, 5th Virginia Cavalry.
Ashton, John C., private, Norfolk Light Artillery Blues.
Allen, Wm. A., private, Harbor Guard, transferred to artillery and lost a leg at Newberne, N. C.
Brown, John B., private, N. L. A. Blues, appointed engineer in Navy.
Brown, Henry C., private, N. L. A. Blues, detailed to work for navy.
Backus, Wm. T., private, Company I, 13th Virginia Cavalry.
Binford, James M., sergeant, Company C, 23d Virginia Cavalry.
Barrett, T. S., Ordnance Department.
Boutwell, L. Warrington, private, Huger Battery.
Brinkley, W. D., private, Company E, 61st Virginia Regiment, died in hospital.
Briggs, Wm., C. S. Navy.
Brockett, Wm., private, Company H, 12th Virginia Regiment, appointed engineer in navy.
Busby, W. A., private, Company I, 9th Virginia Regiment, wounded at Suffolk.
Bratt, Mark, private, 2d North Carolina Battalion, Lieutenant-Colonel Williams.
Butt, Channing M., private Signal Corps.
Bingley, Wm. H., private, Signal Corps, died in hospital 1864.
Ballance, John, private Company D, 6th Va. Regt., died in hospital Sept. 1st, 1862, at Salem.
Blamire, James A., hospital steward, 19th street, Richmond.
Belote, Smith, Company H, 16th Virginia Regiment.
Cooke, Wm. G., private, 4th Virginia Battalion.
Crow, Charles, lieutenant, Purcell Battery, Richmond.
Crow, Benj. M., sergeant, 1st Virginia Regiment, wounded August, 1862, at Cedar Mountain.
Clarke, W. H., pilot, C. S. Navy, killed in fight between the Merrimac and Monitor.
Curlin, Ashwell, private, Company A, 61st Virginia Regiment, killed Wilcox Farm.
Cherry, Virginius, seaman, C. S. Navy.
Cone, Edward, seaman, C. S. Navy.
Culpepper, Joseph S., private, Signal Corps.
Dilworth, John R., private, Signal Corps.
Denson, C. B., captain, Company E, 10th N. C. Regiment.
Dunn, Wm. H., private, Norfolk Light Artillery Blues.
Diggs, C. C., private, Company A, 3d Georgia Regiment, wounded July 1st, 1862, Malvern Hill.
Dockerty, Wm., private, Company I, 13th Virginia Cavalry.
Denson, Jos. E., private, Company E., 10th N. C. Regiment.

IN OUTSIDE COMMANDS.

Day, John H., private, N. L. A. Blues, wounded May 3d, 1863, Chancellorsville.
Deconian, John, private, Company C, 61st Va. Regiment.
Dunn, J. Thos., private, Company F, 41st Va. Regiment.
Diggs, Benj. H., private, Company A, 61st Va. Regiment.
Downing, Charles W., captain, Cohoon's Battalion.
Doyle, Nathan, private, Company C, 6th Virginia, captured at Gettysburg.
Elliott, Thos., private, Norfolk Light Artillery Blues.
Emmerson, John, corporal, Signal Corps, promoted to captain and A. C. S.
Elliott, John W., private Company D, 6th Virginia, captured at Gettysburg.
Frestine, J. E., private Ludlow's Company, Norfolk, Company D, 6th Virginia.
Ford, Wm., private, Upshur's Cavalry Company, 13th Virginia.
Godfrey, W. J., private, Company I, 38th Va. Regiment.
Grant, Frank H., private, Company B, 9th Va. Regiment.
Grimes, Geo. W., lieutenant, Company G, 17th, N. C. Regiment.
Gray, James, seaman, C. S. Navy.
Gallagher, Edward, private, Company H, 61st Va. Regiment.
Gaffney, Lawrence, private, Company C, 1st Va. Regiment.
Griffin, Randolph, private, Company C, 3d Georgia Regiment.
Godwin, E. C., private, Signal Corps.
Helt, Wm., private, Stuart's Cavalry, wounded in arm.
Hope, A. M., private, Company H, 5th Va. Cavalry.
Hudgins, R. K., captain, Ordnance Department.
Hudgins, R. D., private, Company A, 3d Va. Battalion.
Haynes, James, private, N. L. A. Blues.
Haynes, Mich., private, Stuart's Cavalry.
Harrell, Jos. H., private, 13th Va. Cavalry.
Halstead, W. W., private, Company A, 3d Va. Regiment.
Hester, Thos., private, W. H. Rogers' Company.
Hutchins, Edward, private, United Artillery, Norfolk.
Hodges, H. H., private, Captain Chalmouth's Company.
Halstead, Chris., private, Company K, 61st Virginia Regiment, wounded June 22d, 1864.
Hatton, Wm. L., private, Signal Corps.
Hull, Jacob B., private, Signal Corps.
Handy, F. A. G., private, Signal Corps.
Handy, Moses P., courier.
Hume, John H., private, Signal Corps, detailed in "Tax in kind" Department. Tuscaloosa, Ala., and appointed to command Company C, Wood's Battalion, Alabama Reserves.
Huestis, B. H., private, Company E, 32d Va. Regiment.
Jordan, Jos. P., private, Company D, 6th Va. Regiment.
Jones, B. G., private, Company A, 16th Va. Regiment.
Jarvis, Alex., private, Company E, 61st Va. Rsgiment, killed at the Crater.
Jenkins, Chas. E., private, Signal Corps.
James, Stephen, private, Artillery Company, Richmond.
Jarvis, W. R., carpenter's mate, C. S. Navy.
Knott, Elvington, private, Company C, 13th Va. Cavalry.
Kreiger, Geo. A., sergeant, Company M, 2d Va. Reserves.
King, Geo., private, Jackson's Division.
Keeter, W. W., private, Company I, 9th Va. Regiment, died in hospital.
Knight, Geo., private, United Artillery.
Lattimer, C. C., corporal, Huger Battery, eye shot out near Petersburg.
Lane, James, private, Company E, 61st Virginia Regiment, killed at Cold Harbor.
Lassiter, John, private, Company I, 9th Va. Regiment, mortally wounded, Warrenton Springs.

Lilliston, Robt. W., private, Company C, 6th Va. Regiment, Drum Major
  Mahone's Brigade.
Liverman, H. H., private, Company A, 3d Va. Regiment, wounded Frazier's
  Farm and Gettysburg.
Livesey, James E., private, Signal Corps.
Levy, Richard B., private, Signal Corps.
Lanier, Samuel, private, Graham's Battery, Petersburg.
Minter, Wm. R., private, Naval Brigade, surrendered at Appomattox.
Manpin, Geo. W. O, Jr., private, N. L. A. Blues.
Mahoney, E. N., private, Richmond Howitzers.
McMahon, Hugh, private, C. S. Navy.
Moore, George T., private, C. S. Navy.
McLane, J. A., private, Company E, 61st Va. Regiment.
Moore, F. M., private, Signal Corps.
Martin, John, private, Harbor Guard (Young's).
Nimmo, John, lieutenant, Richmond Howitzer's.
Niemeyer, H. Woodis, captain's clerk, C. S. Navy, killed at Island No. 10.
Nash, V. W., lieutenant, 32d Va. Regiment.
Nash, Wm. C., private, Signal Corps.
Owens, Joseph T., captain, Company D, 26th Va. Regiment, wounded June
  16th, 1864, near Petersburg.
Owens, B. H., private, Signal Corps.
Parker, Wm. H., private, Signal Corps.
Peters, Osmond, Captain of Artillery, C. S. Army, and assigned to ordnance
  duty.
Porter, Robert, private, N. L. A. Blues.
Peed, C. C., private, Company G, Naval Brigade.
Parker, Jos. A., private, McNeil's Independent Cavalry.
Palmer, Geo. O. N., private, Company I, 15th Va. Cavalry, discharged for
  disability.
Parker, Stafford H., lieutenant, ordnance, lost an arm.
Parker, Wm. S., private, commissary department, 61st Va. Regiment.
Pierce, Elisha, private, Company I, 6th Va. Regiment.
Peters, Wm. R., private, Signal Corps.
Peters, Osmond, Jr., private, Signal Corps.
Pedrick, C. W., hospital steward.
Parker, Geo. D., captain battery Whitworth guns, Fort Fisher.
Rainier, John T., corporal, N. L. A. Blues.
Roberts, John B., private, N. L. A. Blues.
Rogers, Chas. E., private, Company B., 61st Va., died in hospital April
  12th, 1863.
Riley, Otey, C. S. Navy.
Ross, Joseph, private, 4th Georgia Regiment.
Ricketts, Augustus, private, Letcher Rangers.
Reynolds, Robert E., private, N. L. A. Blues, died in prison, Point Lookout.
Reed, Washington, private, Signal Corps.
Sullivan, Robert, petty officer, C. S. Navy.
Smith, James, private, N. L. A. Blues.
Smith, R. W., private, Company I, 15th Va. Cavalry.
Smith, O. V., corporal, Richmond Howitzers.
Shannon, Thos., lieutenant, Company F, 8th N, C. Regiment.
Sale, Geo, L., hospital steward.
Smith, Williamson, private, Company A, 16th Va. Regiment.
Saunders, W. D. B., private, Company E, 61st Va. Regiment, killed Spotsyl-
  vania C. H.
Stokes, Lemuel, private, 13th Va. Cavalry.
Spaulding, John A., private, Company I, 9th Va. Regiment.
Spooner, Alfred B., private, Signal Corps.
Scott, Thos., private, Signal Corps.
Sullivan, Henry, sergeant, Company C, 1st Va. Regiment, wounded, 2d Ma-
  nassas.

Sullivan, Anthony, C. S. Navy, killed 1864, boarding the U. S. Str. Underwriter in North Carolina.
Thompson, E. Jr., private, N. L. A. Blues.
Tyler, Julius H., Company B, 16th Virginia Regiment, surrendered at Appomattox.
Tyler, Henry C., private, Company B, 16th Virginia Regiment, surrendered at Appomattox.
Thomas, L. W., lieutenant, Company D, 26th Va. Regiment.
Tatem, John F., private, Company F, 41st Va. Regiment.
Toomer, Chas. H., lieutenant, 41st Alabama, Gracie's Brigade, was in 30 battles, in which his company lost men killed, and 10 others in which it had men wounded.
Toomer, Shelton, private, 3d Alabama Regiment, lost leg at Malvern Hill July 1st, 1862, and name placed on roll of honor of the regiment for gallantry in battle.
Turner, D. J. Jr., private, Signal Corps.
Tabb, Chas., private, Signal Corps.
Veale, Amos E., was probably the youngest soldier in the Confederate army. He enlisted in Company H, 59th Va. Regiment as a drummer, at the age of eleven years, and Captain Noblett, of the company, in a communication to the Richmond Dispatch in the summer of 1891, said: Whenever the regiment went into a fight, Veale laid aside his drum, got a musket and did as good shooting as anyone in it. He lived through the war without having received a wound.
Vickers, J. E., private, Huger's Battery.
Williamson, Clarance H., private, N. L. A. Blues.
Wilkerson, Nathaniel, private, Company —, 13th Va. Cavalry.
Walker, C. W., courier, Gen. Blanchard, and in Naval Brigade.
Wiersdorf, Edward, 6th Va. Regiment, musician.
Webb, Richard, private, Company B, 13th Va. Cavalry.
Williams, J. Q. A., C. S. Navy.
Walton, D. S., engineer corps, C. S. Army.
White, Wm. F., captain, Company B, 6th Va. Regiment.
Wootten, Peck, private, Wythe Rifles.
Wagner, Lewis, private, Company E, 61st Va. Regiment.
Williamson, Chas. C., private, Company E, 61st Va. Regiment, surrendered at Appomattox.
Woodward, Jas. T., private, Company —, 13th Va. Cavalry.
Williams, Daniel A., sergeant, 17th N. C. Regiment.
Wright, Wm., private, Company C, 61st Va. Regiment.
Wallace, Solon, private, Company C, 61st Va. Regiment.
Wilkerson, Samuel, private, Company H, 12th Va. Regiment.
Widgeon, John T., lieutenant, Company F, 41st Va. Regiment, killed at Chancellorsville.
Whitehurst, D, W., sergeant, Company F, 41st Va. Regiment.
White, Wm., sergeant, Company D, 6th Va. Regiment, transferred to navy January 22d, 1864.
Wright, Benj., private, Company E, 61st Va. Regiment, killed, Spotsylvania Court House.
Welsh, Patrick, private, North Carolina Regiment.
Whitehurst, John, private, 2d N. C. Battalion, Lieutenant-Colonel Williams.
White, Wm. A., private, Signal Corps.
White, James C. Jr., private, Signal Corps.
Wilson, St. Julien, lieutenant, Company C, 61st Va. Regiment, killed at the Crater.
Young, John W., private, Signal Corps.
Killed and died—19.

FROM NORFOLK COUNTY.

The following Norfolk county men were in the Randolph Dragoons, Company C, 13th Virginia Cavalry, which was raised principally in Nansemond county:

Second Lieutenant, Wm. F. Wise, wounded October 11th, 1863, at Brandy Station, and April 6th, 1865, at Saylor's Creek.
First Sergeant, Keely Harrison.
Sergeant, I. O. Ivy.

PRIVATES.

Bunting, Lloyd, wounded at Slaughter's Mountain.
Capps, Andrew J., captured at Stoney Creek, 1864, and died in prison at Point Lookout.
Dennis, Samuel.
Dennis, M. W., discharged 1862, for sickness.
Driver, Elliott J., wounded 1863, at Middleburg, Loudoun county.
Duke, Hardy.
Duke, Henry.
Dunford, Emanuel.
Ford, Wm.
Knott, Elvington, wounded, 1865, at Five Forks and captured.
Parker, Robert.
Skeeter, Joseph.
Spivey, Jethro, wounded, 1863, at Dutch Gap.
Spivey, Henry, died 1862.
Stokes, Lemuel, wounded at Snicker's Gap.
Wilson, Andrew J., wounded May, 1864, at Yellow Tavern.
    Killed and died—2.

Lieutenant Wise had a varied experience during the war. He was elected a lieutenant in the Craney Island Artillery, Company I, 9th Virginia Infantry, but declined, and joined a company of students from the University of Virginia, Company G, 59th Virginia Regiment (3d Regiment Wise's Legion) and went through the West Virginia campaign with it. The company was disbanded by order of the Secretary of War on the ground that "so much valuable material should be distributed for the good of the service." He was then temporarily with General Randolph at Suffolk as civil engineer, and upon the organization of Company C, 13th Virginia Cavalry, was elected 2d Lieutenant. He was wounded October 11th, 1863, at Brandy Station, and while disabled from active service, was acting assistant commissary to Major W. A. Shepherd at Weldon. He rejoined the regiment May 1st, 1864, while still unable to dismount or walk without assistance, and was assigned to temporary duty as aid to General Chambliss, but his wound breaking out afresh, he was examined by a medical board and retired as unfit for service. He, however, again rejoined the company on the Petersburg lines, and was actively engaged on the retreat from that city. He was wounded at Saylor's Creek April 6th, 1865, taken prisoner in the hospital by the enemy a day or two subsequently, and taken to a hospital in Washington, from which he was released May 21st, 1865, and returned to his home in the Western Branch section of Norfolk county.

In addition to the foregoing the author can recall the following Norfolk county men who were in the Confederate service, but whose names do not appear elsewhere:

Armistead, B. A., sergeant, Company I, 13th Va. Cavalry.
Baxter, O. F., private, Company I, 15th Va. Cavalry.
Drummond, H. P. P., private, Company I, 15th Va. Cavalry.
Drummond, Thos. F., private, Company F, 46th Va. Regiment.
Griffin, John T., captain and civil engineer, Petersburg fortifications.
Fisher, Laben J., private, Company C, 15th Va. Cavalry.
Halstead, W. F., private, Company I, 15th Va. Cavalry.
Hodges, John M., private, N. L. A. Blues.
Happer, George D. W., private, Wise's Legion, cavalry.
Ives, Luther C., private, Company I, 15th Va. Cavalry.
Johnston, James, mustering and inspecting officer, Huger's Division.
James, Cornelius, private, Company F, 3d Va. Infantry.
Jones, John, seaman in the navy.
James, Edward, private, Company F, 3d Virginia Infantry.
King, James, private, Company F, 3d Virginia Infantry.
Kilby, John, private, Company F, 3d Virginia Infantry.
King, Goodman, seaman in the navy.
King, Moscoe, private, Company F, 3d Va. Infantry.
Lawrence, Albert, Company F, 3d Virginia Infantry.
Lynch, Samuel, private, 7th N. C. Regiment.
Mortin, Eugene S., private, Signal Corps, killed on Appomattox river.
Outten, E. A., private, Company I, 15th Va. Cavalry.
Maund, David W., private, Signal Corps.
Richardson, John W., drummer, Company F, 3d Va. Regiment.
Smith, Samuel, private, Company I, 15th Va. Cavalry.
Scott, Jas. E., private, Company I, 15th Va. Cavalry.
Spaight, Henry, private, 68th North Carolina Regiment.
Taylor, Jas. E., private, Company F, 3d Va. Infantry.
Wilson, Thos., private, Louisiana Guard Artillery.
Wallace, Geo. W., private, Signal Corps.
White, Wm. H., private, V. M. I. Cadets.
Woodhouse, W. W., private, Mosby's Rangers.
Waterfield, John, private, 7th N. C. Regiment.
Willey, John M., private, 68th N. C. Regiment.
White, Fred. A., private, Signal Corps.
Williamson, Wm. A., private, Signal Corps.

Killed and died—1.

CHAPTER XXVI.

THE ST. BRIDE'S CAVALRY, COMPANY F, FIFTEENTH VIRGINIA.

This was one of the largest and best equipped cavalry companies in the Confederate service. Its members belonged principally in St. Bride's Parish of Norfolk county, and from that it obtained its name. It was organized at the beginning of the war and was mustered into service under the following officers:
Captain—John C. Doyle.
First Lieutenant, Moses Myers; 2d Lieutenant, Wm. Johnson; 3d Lieutenant, Charles Johnson.

The company was attached to Burroughs' Cavalry Battalion and did picket duty on the beach from Seawell's Point to Ocean View from its organization until the evacuation of Norfolk by the Confederates, when it moved to Petersburg and from there to Richmond. Upon arriving at the latter city it was ordered to join Johnston's army, then in the vicinity of Seven Pines, and did picket duty there. Shortly after the battle of Seven Pines it was consolidated with Critcher's cavalry battalion into a regiment and Critcher was made Colonel. The regiment was numbered the 15th, and the St. Bride's company became Company F. It was well mounted, well equipped and composed of excellent material. Colonel Critcher did not remain long with the regiment but resigned in the summer of 1862. He was succeeded in command by Colonel William F. Ball, who was stationed with the regiment in the summer and fall of 1862 on the upper Rappahannock river guarding the fords and watching the movements of the enemy. In November the regiment was assigned to the brigade of General W. H. F. Lee, and when General Lee was promoted to Major General the brigade was placed under the command of Brigadier General Lomax.

It will be impossible in this short sketch to follow the company through the numerous battles and skirmishes in which it was engaged. It was in active service in front until the close of the war, doing picket and scouting duty while the army was stationary, marching in front when it was on the advance and guarding the rear when it was falling back. It participated in all of the battles in which the regiment was engaged. The officers who were elected at the reorganization remained with it until the close of the war and were fortunate in not being killed or disabled.

While General Lee's army was in Maryland in September, 1862, the line of the Rapidan river was held by the 15th Virginia Cavalry, the 61st Virginia, and the Norfolk Light Artillery Blues, and its duties there were very arduous and its skirmishes with the enemy were frequent. It had an engagement of considerable magnitude at Falmouth with the advance of General Burnside's army on its march to Fredericksburg in November, 1862, and General Lee in his official report gives it the credit of having prevented it from crossing the river. In March, 1862, at the reorganization of the company all of the old officers were thrown out and left the company. The officers enumerated in the following list of names were elected.

Below will be found the roll of the company:

Captain John F. Cooper, captured at Louisa, Va.
First Lieutenant James L. Northern.
Second Lieutenant William H Wilkins, captured Culpepper C. H.
Third Lieutenant Lemuel J. Pritchard, wounded at Louisa, Va.
First Sergeant Columbus W. Foreman, wounded near Culpepper C. H. June, 1864.
Second Sergeant William T. Smith.
Third Sergeant Roscoe H. Brown.
Fourth Sergeant John F. Old, wounded near Fredericksburg December 13th, 1862.
First Corporal Edgar N. Outten, captured at Yellow Tavern May. 1864.
Second Corporal John J. Wilson.
Third Corporal William F. Ashly, killed near Petersburg, 1865.
Fourth Corporal William Pritchard, died in hospital 1863, Richmond.

PRIVATES.

Ansel, John H., died in hospital.
Barnes, William H.
Bunting, George S.
Brown, William B.
Berry, John, died in prison Point Lookout.
Berry, Samuel, wounded Orange Court House.
Brice, George D.
Bullock, Joseph A.
Cooper, Arthur.
Cooper, Edward P., discharged 1862, over age.
Culpepper, Daniel M., killed near Fredericksburg 1863.
Cox, Thomas, transferred to a North Carolina regiment.
Coleburn, Wm.
Creamer, James.
Creekmore, John J., killed near Fredericksburg 1863.
Creekmore, Alex. O., killed near Fredericksburg 1863.
Davis, Charles T., discharged 1862, disability.
Davis, Gideon V., discharged 1862, over age.
Denby, Andrew J., discharged 1862, over age.
Denby, Edward.
Dixon, Ralph.
Etheredge, Dennis, captured at Louisa, Va.
Eason, Israel.
Fentress, Joshua.
Fentress, David, discharged 1863, disability.
Fentress, Wm. H., died in 1862 in hospital.
Fentress, James, wounded at Yellow Tavern May, 1864.
Foreman, Claudius T.
Foreman, Wm. H.
Foreman, Alex.
Frizzell, Joseph.
Frizzell, John.

Fulford, Arthur, captured at Culpepper C. H.
Forbes, Peter S.
Flora, John T., transferred to a North Carolina regiment.
Fiske, James W.
Fiske, Richard B., captured at Yellow Tavern May, 1864.
Gammon, John W.
Gilbert, Timothy, captured at Yellow Tavern May, 1864.
Grandy, Thomas G., transferred to a North Carolina regiment.
Gornto, David T., discharged 1862, disability.
Guy, Benjamin F.
Hancock, Wm. S., wounded at Yellow Tavern May, 1864.
Hawkins, Wallace W.
Hancock, Francis A., discharged 1863, disability.
Harrison, Joseph M.
Hardy, J. Henry Clay.
Hanbury, Miles A.
Hanbury, Wm. T.
Hearring, Edward L.
Hewlet, Ambrose.
Holmes, Wm. H., discharged 1862, over age.
Holmes, Henry, killed August 30th, 1862, Second Manassas.
Holland, Wm., killed.
Humphries, Samuel.
Ironmonger, Thomas W., discharged 1862, over age.
Jennings, Noah M., killed in Pasquotank county, North Carolina, by Buffaloes.
Jordan, Edward, discharged 1862, disability.
Joliff, Josiah.
Johnson, James V., transferred to Navy.
Lee, James W.
Larke, Robert W., discharged 1862, disability.
Lockheart, John.
Martin, James G., discharged 1862, disability.
Martin, James E.
McPherson, Thomas G.
Mears, Elvington R., discharged 1862, over age.
Miller, Augustus.
Miller, James.
Munden, David T.
Nicholas, Willoughby L., captured at Yellow Tavern May, 1864.
Old, James Y.
Parsons, Napoleon B.
Petty, Wm.
Pitts, Andrew J.
Peyton, Joseph A.
Robinson, Lemuel D.
Reid, Wm. C., transferred to Navy 1862.
Russell, Thomas R.
Simpson, Wm.
Stroud, Edward, discharged 1862, over age.
Sykes, Cornelius, furnished substitute 1862.
Sanderlin, John, transferred to a North Carolina regiment.
Sylvester, Keeling, killed in Camden county, North Carolina, by Buffaloes.
Steward, Solomon.
Sadler, Robert.
Slack, Edward.
Tabb, Robert B., wounded accidentally at Fredericksburg, disabled and discharged.
Tyson, Wm. G., died in hospital 1863, Richmond.
Warden, Kosciusco, captured at Yellow Tavern May, 1864.

Williams, David, wounded accidentally and disabled.
Wilson, Amsey W., killed Yellow Tavern May, 1864.
White, Thomas J.
Whitemore, Marchant, died from wounds.
Wilkins, Thomas B.
Williamson, Joshua J., died.
Wallace, Solomon, killed near Fredericksburg 1862.
Wilson, George A., furnished substitute 1862.
    Killed and died—17.

CHAPTER XXVII.

FIELD AND STAFF OFFICERS.

The following field and staff officers from Portsmouth and Norfolk county served in the Confederate army:

FROM PORTSMOUTH.

Brigadier General Archibald C. Godwin, killed August 18th, 1864, at the battle of Winchester, Early's Valley campaign.
Colonel James Gregory Hodges, 14th Virginia Regiment, killed July 3d, 1863, at Gettysburg.
Colonel John C. Owens, 9th Virginia Regiment, killed July 3d, 1863, at Gettysburg.
Colonel David J. Godwin, 9th Virginia Regiment, lived through the war.
Colonel Bristor B. Gayle, 12th Alabama Regiment, killed September 14th, 1862, at Boonsboro, or South Mountain.
Colonel James Giles, 29th Virginia Regiment, lived through the war.
Lieutenant Colonel James C. Council, 26th Virginia Regiment.
Lieutenant Colonel G. G. Luke, 56th North Carolina Regiment, lived through the war.
Lieutenant Colonel Wm. F. Niemeyer, 61st Virginia Regiment, killed May 12th, 1864, at Spotsylvania Court House.
Major Giles B. Cooke, Assistant Inspector General on the staff of General R. E. Lee, lived through the war.
Major John Q. Richardson, 52d North Carolina Regiment, killed July 3d, 1863, at Gettysburg.
Major Charles R. McAlpine, 61st Virginia Regiment, lived through the war.
Major William James Richardson, 9th Virginia Regiment, lived through the war.
Captain Stephen A. Cowley, Adjutant General Quarles Division, killed at Franklin, Tenn., 1864.
Captain James W. Riddick, Assistant Adjutant General Scales' North Carolina Brigade, severely wounded but lived through the war.
Adjutant John W. H. Wrenn, 3d Virginia Regiment, lived through the war.
Adjutant James F. Crocker, 9th Virginia Regiment, lived through the war.
Adjutant Levin Gayle, 12th Alabama Regiment, lived through the war.
Adjutant Edward B. Ward, 16th Virginia Regiment, lived through the war.
Adjutant John S. Jenkins, 14th Virginia Regiment, killed July 3d, 1863, at Gettysburg.
Adjutant Alexander E. Butt, 41st Virginia Regiment, killed May 3d, 1863, at Chancellorsville.

FROM NORFOLK COUNTY.

Colonel William White, Fourteenth Virginia Regiment, lived through the war.
Lieutenant Colonel William H. Stewart, Sixty-first Virginia Regiment, lived through the war.
Lieutenant Colonel George A. Martin, Thirty-eighth Virginia Regiment, lived through the war.
Major William H. Etheredge, Forty-first Virginia Regiment, lived through the war.
Adjutant John F. Stewart, Third Virginia Regiment, lived through the war.
Adjutant Griffin F. Edwards, Sixty-first Virginia Regiment, lived through the war.
Adjutant William S. Wright, Sixty-first Virginia Regiment, died in 1863 of congestive chill.

MEDICAL CORPS.

Below will be found the names of the Portsmouth men who were in the Medical Corps of the army:

Dr. H. F. Butt, Brigade Surgeon, Daniels' North Carolina Brigade.
Dr. V. B. Bilisoly, Surgeon of an Alabama regiment and at hospital, Selma.
Dr. W. M. Cocke, Assistant Surgeon Fourteenth Virginia Regiment, mortally wounded in April, 1865, near Petersburg and died in Old Capitol prison.
Dr. J. M. Covert, Surgeon Louisiana Regiment, Hayes' Brigade.
Dr. James Parrish, Brigade Surgeon Mahone's Brigade, and subsequently Brigade Surgeon of Chambliss' Cavalry Brigade.
Dr. R. H. Parker, Assistant Surgeon Thirty-second North Carolina Regiment and Surgeon Rhodes' Division hospital.
Dr. Jesse C. Shannon, Assistant Surgeon North Carolina regiment.
Dr. Franklin J. White, Surgeon in hospital, Richmond, and subsequently in Kirkland's North Carolina Brigade.
Dr. Edwin M. Watts, Surgeon Simms' Brigade, Georgia.
Dr. Thomas H. Wingfield, Assistant Surgeon on staff of General R. E. Lee.

FROM NORFOLK COUNTY.

Dr. William E. Kemble, Surgeon North Carolina Brigade.
Dr. I. J. Cherry, Assistant Surgeon Chimborazo Hospital.

QUARTERMASTERS AND COMMISSARIES.

The following Portsmouth men held commissions in the Quartermaster and Commissary Departments:

Robert M. Boykin, Captain and A. C. S. Young's Cavalry Brigade.
John K. Cooke, Major and Purchasing Agent.
A. E. Etheredge, Captain and A. Q. M. 61st Virginia Regiment.
John Emmerson, Captain and A. C. S. Southwest Virginia.
George W. Grice, Major and Purchasing Commissary at Augusta, Ga.
J. Madison Hudgins, Captain and A. C. S. Army of Northern Virginia.
Thomas W. Pierce, Major and C. S. Army of Northern Virginia.
Wm. H. Peters, Navy Agent Charlotte, N. C.
William Sherwood, Captain and A. Q. M. Mahone's Brigade.
Arthur E. Wilson, Captain and Commissary 14th Virginia Regiment.
Wm. C. Wingfield, Major and C. S. Mahone's Division.

FROM NORFOLK COUNTY.

John R. White, Captain and A. C. S. 3d Virginia Regiment and Purchasing Commissary on Blackwater river.
George D. Old, Captain and A. C. S. 61st Virginia Regiment.

GENERAL ARCHIBALD C. GODWIN was engaged in business in North Carolina at the beginning of the war and received a staff appointment. He was afterwards appointed Colonel of the 57th North Carolina Regiment of Law's Brigade, Hood's Division, and proved himself to be a gallant soldier. His regiment distinguished itself at the battle of Fredericksburg December 13th, 1862. That was its first engagement and its ranks had not been depleted by sickness and battle. A brigade of the enemy, under cover of the banks of a creek which empties into the Rappahannock about two miles below Fredericksburg, approached the Confederate lines and took up a position in the railroad cut. Colonel Godwin charged them with his regiment and drove them out. He was promoted to Brigadier General in 1864 and was killed on the

18th of August in the battle near Winchester in Early's Valley campaign.

COLONEL JAMES GREGORY HODGES was born in Portsmouth on the 28th of December, 1829, and embraced the medical profession. He located in Portsmouth, and at the breaking out of the war he had quite a lucrative practice. He was popular with the people of that city and they testified their appreciation of his worth by electing him to the position of Mayor. When Governor Letcher issued his call for volunteers in April, 1861, at the commencement of hostilities, Colonel Hodges was in command of the 3d Virginia Volunteers, composed of the military companies of Portsmouth and Norfolk county, but was transferred by Governor Letcher to the 14th Regiment, which was on duty with General Magruder on the Peninsula near Yorktown. He was actively engaged in the battles of Williamsburg, Seven Pines, Malvern Hill, Sharpsburg, Suffolk and Gettysburg, and was present with his regiment, though not actively engaged, at the battles of Second Manassas and Fredericksburg. At Malvern Hill he was stunned by the explosion of a shell near him and part of his hair was burned by it. He was complimented in the report of General Armistead, his brigade commander, for gallantry and good conduct on this occasion. At the battle of Sharpsburg, and for some time after, he had command of Armistead's Brigade in the absence of General Armistead, who was appointed to command the provost guard of the army, and was killed July 3d, 1863, while leading his regiment at the stone wall in the charge of Pickett's Division at Gettysburg. His remains were buried on the battle field by the enemy and his grave was not marked. His family have, therefore, not been able to find them.

COLONEL JOHN C. OWENS was born in Mathews county, Virginia, March 19th, 1830, and removed to Portsmouth with his parents when quite a small boy. When the war broke out he was Captain of the Portsmouth Rifle Company, one of the best equipped and most popular companies in the city. He responded promptly to Governor Letcher's call and was mustered into service with his company, which numbered more than a hundred men, and was assigned to the 9th Regiment as Company G. He commanded the company at the battle of Pig Point, in which it drove off the U. S. steamer Harriet Lane, June 5th, 1861, and in May, 1862, at the reorganization of the 9th Virginia Regiment was promoted to Major of the regiment. He was with the regiment at Seven Pines and, during the Seven Days' battles when Huger's Division was moving down the Charles City road with orders to cut off McClellan's retreat, Major Owens became impatient at the slowness with which the division was being moved, and, fearing that McClellan would slip by before the division reached the place at which it was expected to intercept him, urged upon General Huger the importance of moving faster and of making fewer and shorter halts. He offered to take the advance with the 9th Regiment or any other force General Huger might place under his command and proceed rapidly until he met a force of the enemy sufficient to stop him, but General Huger would not accede to his request. McClellan did slip by, escaped with his army, and the useless waste of life at Malvern Hill followed. Major Owens was wounded August 28th, 1862, at Warrenton Springs but remained with the regiment through the Maryland campaign, on its return to Fredericksburg, on its march to Suffolk in the spring of 1863, and in June, 1863 was promoted to the position of Colonel of the regiment. On the 3d of July, 1863, he led the regiment in the charge of Pickett's Division at Gettysburg and was shot through the body with a shrapnel when a little more than half way across the field. He was taken to the field hospital in rear of the lines and died about two o'clock that night and was buried there. He was a quiet, modest man, but determined in the discharge of his duty. He died as he fought, bravely and without a murmur. After the war his remains were brought back to Portsmouth and interred in Oakwood cemetery.

COLONEL DAVID J. GODWIN was born in Suffolk in 1829 and removed to Portsmouth in 1853 and began the practice of law. Before the war he was several times elected Commonwealth's Attorney of Portsmouth and at the breaking out of hostilities was Lieutenant Colonel of the old 3d Virginia Volunteer Regiment of Portsmouth and Norfolk county, but was relieved by Governor Letcher. At the time of the evacuation of Portsmouth by the Confederates he was engaged in raising a regiment of heavy artillery, and after Huger's Division was moved to Petersburg in May, 1862, he was elected Lieutenant Colonel of the 9th Virginia Regiment and was promoted to Colonel. He commanded the regiment at the battle of Seven Pines, June 1st, 1863, and the horse which he was riding was wounded by a minie ball. This caused him to rear and plunge and he struck Colonel Godwin's leg against a tree, bruising it quite painfully. This disabled him temporarily and he was assigned to other duty and did not rejoin the regiment. He commanded a cavalry detachment in 1863 which was operating in the neighborhood of Gloucester Point.

COLONEL BRISTOR B. GAYLE was born in Portsmouth April 19th, 1839, and was educated at the Virginia Military and Collegiate Institute in Portsmouth. At the breaking out of the war he was teaching school in Alabama and raised a company of infantry at Summerville, which was organized with the 12th Alabama Regiment. At the reorganization of the regiment in May, 1862 Captain Gayle was elected Lieutenant Colonel, and at the death of the Colonel, who was killed at Seven Pines, was promoted to Colonel. The regiment came to Virginia in 1861 and was attached to Rodes' Brigade. It followed the fortunes of that gallant organization through the campaigns of 1862 and marched with it into Maryland. Rodes' Brigade, with other commands, was stationed at Boonsboro, or South Mountain, to hold in check McClellan's army until Jackson could succeed in the capture of Harper's Ferry and the army could be concentrated at Sharpsburg. The enemy attacked Rodes' Brigade at Boonsboro on the 14th of September, and after a stubborn fight, in which the enemy was checked until it was too late for them to relieve Harper's Ferry, the brigade was withdrawn under the cover of night. Colonel Gayle was killed in the battle and his body was left on the field when the regiment fell back. He was just a little more than twenty-three years old. General D. H. Hill, to whose command he was attached, spoke of him as "a most gallant and accomplished officer." Captain R. E. Park, who commanded the skirmish line of the 12th Alabama, thus describes his death: "The enemy pushed forward and soon came upon Colonel Gayle and the rear support. He was ordered to surrender, but drawing his pistol and firing into their faces, he exclaimed: 'We are flanked, boys, but let's die in our tracks,' and continued to fire until he was literally riddled with bullets, and surrendered up his pure, brave young spirit to the God who gave it." [Southern Historical Society Papers, Vol. I, No. 6, page 437.]

LIEUTENANT-COLONEL G. G. LUKE was born in Portsmouth October 19th, 1833, and was a grandson of Isaac Luke, who more than a hundred years ago was one of the best known and most prominent citizens of Portsmouth, and whose remains are interred in the burying ground attached to Trinity Episcopal Church. He was educated at the public schools in Portsmouth and in Partridge's Military Academy, and at the beginning of the war was teaching school in Camden county, North Carolina, and preparing for the practice of law. He raised a company of twelve months troops in Camden county, the North Carolina Defenders, Company H, 32d North Carolina Regiment, but his company was ordered to Fort Hatteras and attached to the 17th North Carolina. It was captured with that fort. Upon being exchanged he raised another company for the war and was assigned to the 56th North Carolina Regiment, Ransom's Brigade, and promoted to Lieutenant-Colonel. He led the charge of the brigade at the capture of Plymouth, was in the fighting around Newberne, was severely wounded at the battle of Drury's Bluff May 16th, 1864, was with the brigade in its battles around Petersburg, and was captured at Five Forks.

LIEUTENANT-COLONEL WILLIAM F. NIEMEYER was born in Portsmouth May 12th, 1840, of a family which had long resided there, and was appointed a cadet in the Military Academy at

West Point in June, 1857, which position he resigned in May, 1861, and tendered his services to Governor Letcher. The first year of the war he was assigned to the duty of drilling and superintending the equipping of the new companies which were being organized in the counties adjacent to Norfolk and Portsmouth, and in May, 1862, was elected by the officers of the 61st Virginia Regiment to the position of Lieutenant-Colonel, and in that capacity commanded the regiment from that time until the fall of 1862, when Colonel V. D. Groner was assigned to it as Colonel. Lieutenant-Colonel Niemeyer was with the regiment at the battles of Fredericksburg, Zoah's Church, McCarthy's Farm, Chancellorsville, Salem Church, Gettysburg, Hagerstown, Bristoe Station, Mine Run, Wilderness, Shady Grove and Spotsylvania Courthouse, in which last battle he received his death wound. The battle was over for the day and the enemy had been driven back. It was late in the afternoon, and Captain McAlpine, of Company I, had captured a fine horse that belonged to a Federal officer, which he presented to Lieutenant-Colonel Niemeyer, who, while in the act of extending his hand to take the horse, was shot through the heart by a sharpshooter on the enemy's picket line and died instantly. The battle was fought on his birthday, and he was just twenty-four years old at the date of his death. He was one of the youngest field officers in the army. His remains were taken to Richmond and there interred.

Major Giles B. Cooke was born in Portsmouth and belonged to a family which had a fondness for military life, his father, Major John K. Cooke having been an officer in the Mexican war. He entered the Confederate service as Adjutant of a regiment commanded by Colonel Philip St. George Cocke, and when Colonel Cocke was promoted to the command of a brigade he became Adjutant General of the brigade, and in that capacity took part in the first battle of Manassas. In the winter of 1862-3 he was Adjutant and Inspector General on the staff of Major General Sam Jones, commanding the department of Western Virginia, and from there was transferred to the staff of General Beauregard. Following that officer into Virginia in the spring of 1864 he was, after the battle of Drury's Bluff, transferred to the staff of General Robert E. Lee as Major and Assistant Inspector General. He followed the fortunes of the Army of Northern Virginia from then until the close of the war and surrendered with the remnant of the army at Appomattox.

Major John Q. Richardson was born in Portsmouth about the year 1837 and received a collegiate education. Happening to be in North Carolina when the war began he enlisted in one of the regiments from that State. Subsequently he received a staff appointment and was afterwards appointed Major of the 52d North Carolina Regiment. He was killed in the charge of his brigade at the battle of Gettysburg July 3d, 1863, while gallantly cheering his men on. He was a courageous soldier and one of the handsomest men in the army.

MAJOR CHARLES R. MCALPINE was born in Princess Anne county, Virginia in April, 1827, and removed to Portsmouth in 1855 and began the practice of his profession, medicine. He was extremely popular in the community and had a very large practice at the breaking out of the war. He was an ardent Secessionest, and before Virginia seceded assisted in raising a company in Portsmouth to go to South Carolina to offer their services to the Governor of that State. He was elected First Lieutenant of this company, but before it could obtain uniforms Virginia followed the lead of South Carolina and left the Union, and the company was mustered into service in Virginia as Company D, 9th Virginia Regiment. Lieutenant McAlpine resigned his commission May 14th, 1861, in Company D to accept the captaincy of a new company then being organized and afterwards assigned to the 61st Virginia Regiment as Company I. He was commissioned Captain of this company June 16th, 1861, and was promoted to Major of the 61st Regiment May 12th, 1864, which position he resigned March 25th, 1865, for the purpose of organizing a battalion of partizan rangers to operate in the Blackwater section of Virginia, but the close of the war put an end to his plans. He was a fearless and dashing soldier, was always in the front of the battle, and though several times wounded did not miss a battle in which the regiment was engaged up to the date of his resignation.

MAJOR WILLIAM J. RICHARDSON was born in Portsmouth February 29th, 1828, and for a number of years before the war was Captain of the Portsmouth Rifle Company. When the troubles between the North and South were about to ripen into a crisis he organized a new company called the Virginia Artillery, afterwards assigned to the 9th Regiment as Company D, and was elected its Captain. The company was on duty on Craney Island the first year of the war, and at the reorganization in April, 1862, Captain Richardson was re-elected Captain of the company, which position he held until June, 1863, when he was promoted to Major of the regiment. He was in the charge of Pickett's Division at Gettysburg and was captured there and not exchanged. He was paroled just before the close of the war and sent through the lines to Richmond but, not having been exchanged, he did not rejoin his regiment.

COLONEL WILLIAM WHITE was a broad-shouldered old soldier and was as brave as he was big. He was born January 7th, 1820, near Great Bridge, in Norfolk county, studied medicine at the Medical College in Richmond and in New York, and at the breaking out of the war was practicing medicine and lived at the village of Deep Creek, in Norfolk county, about eight miles from Portsmouth. He was one of the Lieutenants of the Dismal Swamp Rangers at its organization in 1856, but resigned shortly afterwards. In 1861 he was elected from Norfolk county and Portsmouth as a Union delegate to the Virginia State Convention which passed the ordinance of secession, and voted against its passage in that body, but after the State had decided to secede he yielded to her sovereign authority and tendered her his services. He was appointed by Governor Letcher Major of the 14th Virginia Regiment, then under General Magruder at Yorktown, and while there was placed in command of the detachment which General Magruder sent to burn Hampton. At the battle of Malvern Hill Lieutenant-Colonel Evans of the 14th Regiment was disabled by a wound, and Major White was promoted to Lieutenant-Colonel, which position he held until the battle of Gettysburg, where Colonel Hodges was killed, and he was promoted to Colonel of the regiment. He was severely wounded in the neck in the charge of Pickett's Division at Gettysburg, but escaped without being captured, and from that time until the close of the war was in command of the regiment, and frequently in command of the brigade. The regiment was in Armistead's Brigade, and Colonel White was present at all of the battles in which it was engaged. At the battle of Drury's Bluff May 16th, 1864, he planned and executed a flanking movement on the enemy's right which contributed materially to the Confederate victory on that occasion.

LIEUTENANT-COLONEL WILLIAM H. STEWART was born in the village of Deep Creek, Norfolk county, September 25th, 1838. He inherited a military disposition, for his grandfather was a soldier in the war of 1812 and died in the service, and his great grandfather was a soldier in the Revolutionary war, having been appointed a Lieutenant in the 11th Virginia Regiment. He entered the schools in the neighborhood of his father's home near Wallaceton, Norfolk county, and finished his education in 1859 at the University of Virginia. At the breaking out of the war he was engaged with his father in the shingle and lumber business, which he gave up and entered the army as 2d Lieutenant in the Wise Light Dragoons. (See chapter XXVIII). Upon the disbanding of this company he was instrumental in organizing an infantry company at Pleasant Grove Church, and on July 1st, 1861, was elected its captain. It afterwards became Company A, 61st Virginia Regiment. At the organization of the regiment in Petersburg in 1862 Captain Stewart was elected Major, and on the 12th of May, 1864, was elected Lieutenant-Colonel, which position he held until the surrender of the army at Appomattox. He was wounded at the battle of Chancellorsville and again at Spotsylvania Court House. He commanded the regiment at the battles of North Anna River, Hanover Court House, Atlee's Station, Cold Harbor, Turkey Ridge, Second Frazier's Farm, Wilcox Farm, Gurley House, Crater, Reams' Station, June 27th and August 25th, 1864, Burgess' Mill and Hatcher's Run, the colonel of the regiment being absent on account of wounds. He was with the regiment in the following battles also: Fredericksburg, Rappahannock Bridge, Zoah's Church, McCarthy's Farm, Chancellorsville, Gettysburg, Hagerstown, commanding brigade picket line, Culpepper, Mine Run, Wilderness, Shady Grove, Spotsylvania Court House, Davis' Farm, Hicksford, Amelia Court House, Cumberland Church and Appomattox, and was present with his company in the engagements at Seawell's Point March 8th and May 8th, 1862, with the Federal fleet. He missed only two battles in which it was engaged, namely, Bristoe Station, which took place when he was absent on leave, and Salem Church, which was fought while he was in the field hospital suffering from a wound received that morning at Chancellorsville.

LIEUTENANT-COLONEL GEORGE A. MARTIN was born at Mount Pleasant, Norfolk county, September 3d, 1833, and studied law at the University of Virginia. At the breaking out of the war he enlisted in the St. Bride's Artillery, a company organized in Norfolk county, and was elected its Captain. In May, 1862, his company was attached temporarily to the 14th Virginia Regiment and participated in the second day's engagement at Seven Pines June 1st, after which it was retained in the fortifications around Richmond until April 25th, 1864, when it was assigned to the 38th Virginia Regiment as Company I. Captain Martin subsequently participated in the battles of May 10th and May 16th, 1864, near Drury's Bluff and June 16th near Chester Station. In the battle of May 10th Colonel Cabell, commander of the regiment, was killed, and Captain Griggs, senior captain, was promoted to Colonel, and on the 28th of March, 1865, Captain Martin, the next in rank, was promoted to Lieutenant-Colonel, his commission to date from December 2d, 1864. For some days previous to his promotion Lieutenant-Colonel Martin was sick in a hospital in Richmond, and upon the evacuation of that city went to Lynchburg by rail and was assigned by General Colston to the command of the Home Guard for the defence of the city, but when General Colston surrendered it he pushed on into Carolina, following the fortunes of President Davis, and surrendered at Augusta, Georgia, after the surrender of General Johnston's army.

MAJOR WILLIAM H. ETHEREDGE was born near Great Bridge in Norfolk county on the 27th of July, 1820, and was raised a farmer, at which occupation he was engaged at the beginning of the war. Shortly before the war the men in that portion of the county organized the Norfolk County Rifle Patriots, one of the largest and best companies which entered the Confederate service, and he was elected Captain of it. It was subsequently assigned to the 41st Virginia Regiment, as Company F. Captain Etheredge on the 21st of April, 1861, took possession of the naval ordnance stores at St. Helena, opposite the Navy Yard, and for nearly a year did guard duty in the Navy Yard. He was very highly complimented by Colonel Chambliss, Colonel of the 41st Regiment, for gallantry at the battle of Seven Pines, and shortly after that battle, Colonel Chambliss having been transferred to the command of a cavalry regiment, Captain Etheredge was promoted to the position of Major of the 41st, which position he held until the surrender at Appomattox, when he laid aside the sword which he had carried so worthily. He was present in every battle in which Mahone's Brigade took part, and though he always fought in front of his men, was never wounded. He had a narrow escape at the Crater, an account of which is told in Lieutenant-Colonel Wm. H. Stewart's account of that battle, ante, chapter XXIV. No soldier in the Army of Northern Virginia has a better war record than Major Etheredge. In probably more than half of the battles in which the regiment was engaged he was its commander, his superior officers being disabled either from sickness or wounds.

CAPTAIN STEPHEN A. COWLEY was about 16 years old at the beginning of the war and was attending a military school in North Carolina, and was employed by the Governor of that State as drill master for new troops at Raleigh. In December, 1861, he went to General Beauregard's army in Kentucky and was appointed a Lieutenant in the regular army. He was at Fort Henry when it fell, but escaped and went to Fort Donelson, where he was captured at the surrender of the fort, was exchanged in October, 1862, and was appointed by Colonel Quarles Adjutant of his regiment, the ——th Tennessee. Colonel Quarles was promoted to Major General and Captain Cowley became Inspector General on his staff. He was with General Quarles in the campaign between Sherman and Johnston, and when Hood superceded Johnston he was with the army in its advance into Tennessee, and was killed on the enemy's breastworks at Franklin.

CHAPTER XXVIII.

THE WISE LIGHT DRAGOONS.

During the John Brown rebellion in 1859, a cavalry company was organized in Norfolk county under the name of the Wise Light Dragoons, of which Captain Aldustin Wilson was commander. The company retained its organization, but Captain Wilson resigned as its commander, and at the breaking out of the war its officers were:
Captain, John W. Young.
First Lieutenant, Columbus W. Foreman.
Second Lieutenant, Wm. H. Stewart.

The company turned out on the 20th of April, and was sent to Seawell's Point by the commanding officer in Norfolk to do picket duty on the beach between that point and Ocean View. It remained there for nearly two months, but not having the requisite number of men to be mustered into the Confederate service, it was disbanded.

While it was engaged on picket duty there the United States steamer Monticello was in the habit of shelling the woods, and one of the shells exploded near Private —— Sykes, wounding him in the leg. This was the first casualty of war in the vicinity of Norfolk, and Private Sykes was quite a lion for a short while. It is to be regretted that a roll of the company cannot be obtained but as the men entered the Confederate service in other commands, their names are recorded with those organizations. The company was not mustered into the service of the Confederate States, but a history of the part Norfolk county took in the war would not be complete without a reference to it.

CHAPTER XXIX.

IN THE NAVY—PORTSMOUTH.

In addition to a large number of seamen, Portsmouth was represented in the Confederate States Navy by the following officers: Captain, James W. Cooke.

LIEUTENANTS.
John J. Guthrie, Dulaney A. Forrest, A. S. Worth,
John H. Parker, Walter R. Butt, Chas. J. Hasker,
Wm. H. Murdaugh, Wm. E. Hudgins, Jno. W. Murdaugh.

SURGEONS.
Chas. H. Williamson, Wm. E. Wysham.

MASTERS.
Benj. W. Guthrie, D. W. Nash.

CHIEF ENGINEERS.
Michael Quinn, James H. Warner, John W. Tynan,
Chas. Schroeder, Edward W. Manning.

ASSISTANT ENGINEERS.
Eugene H. Brown, E. Alex. Jack, Joseph E. Virnelson,
John B. Brown, Leslie G. King, Jos. S. West,
Wm. B. Brockett, Chas. H. Levy, Thos. J. White,
Geo. W. City, Jas. K. Langhorne, Moses P. Young.

NAVAL CONSTRUCTORS.
J. L. Porter, Chief, Joseph Pierce, Wm. M. Hope.

GUNNERS.
John A. Lovitt, John Owens, Thos. Baker.

CARPENTERS.
Robert M. Bain, Hugh Lindsay, Joseph F. Weaver,
John T. Rustic, R. J. Meads, Nathaniel C. Gayle,
Edward Williams.

SAILMAKERS.
Wm. Bennett, E. A. Mahoney.

Boatswain, L. J. Nelson.
Norfolk county was represented in the Navy by:
Lieutenant, C. B. Poindexter.
Assistant Surgeon, Geo. N. Halstead.

CAPTAIN JAMES W. COOKE, who heads this list, was born in North Carolina, and entered the United States Navy from that State, April 1st, 1828, and resigned May 1st, 1861, as lieutenant. He married Miss Mary Watts, of Portsmouth, which city from that time became his home, and upon resigning from the United States Navy, he tendered his services to Governor Letcher, and received an appointment on the 4th of May as lieutenant in the Virginia Navy. On the 11th of June he was transferred to the Confederate States Navy. His first duty in the Virginia Navy was in connection with the erection of a battery at Fort Powhatan on James river, and from there he was transferred to the Potomac and assisted in blockading that river in the summer of 1861. In the fall of 1861 he was ordered to the Gosport Navy Yard to take command of a small steam tug, the Ellis, formerly a canal boat, which was manned with one 32-pounder Dahlgren gun, and with this he was ordered to North Carolina as a part of Commodore Lynch's mosquito fleet. He took part in the engagement at Roanoke Island, February 7th, 1862, with the Federal fleet, and his was the last of the Confederate vessels to withdraw. He held his ground until he had fired away his last round of ammunition, when he followed Commodore Lynch to Elizabeth City. On the 10th, when the attack was renewed at that town, the Ellis was boarded by the crews of two Federal vessels, and though Lieutenant Cooke received a musket wound in the arm and a bayonet thrust in the leg, he refused to surrender. He and his crew were surrounded by overwhelming numbers and taken by main force. He was paroled on the 12th of February and returned to his home in Portsmouth. He was subsequently exchanged, and on the 17th of September was promoted to commander. In 1863 he was ordered to the Roanoke river to superintend the building of the ironclad gunboat Albemarle, which was being constructed at Edward's Ferry, by Captain Gilbert Elliott, under contract with the Navy Department, and was indefatigable in his efforts to procure material with which to complete her. No stone was left unturned in his zeal and when he started down the river with her to engage the enemy, workmen were still hammering on her. The Albemarle mounted two guns, and on the 19th of April, 1864, arrived in front of Plymouth, which was being invested on the land side by the troops of General Hoke. History has told how Captain Cooke fought and defeated the Federal vessels. How he ran his prow into the Southfield, sinking her in ten minutes, and then drove the Miami out of the river into the sound, and was only prevented from destroying her by the inferiority of the machinery in his vessel, which was not of sufficient power to give her speed to overtake her. The result of this victory on the water was the capture of Plymouth with fifteen hundred prisoners and twenty-eight pieces of artillery. Relieved from the presence of the gunboats, General Hoke's men stormed the enemy's works on the land side and carried the town by assault. Lieut. Col. G. G. Luke, of Portsmouth, at the head of the 56th North Carolina Regiment, led the assaulting column and was the first man to enter the town, thus Portsmouth was represented by the captain of the Albemarle, on the water, and by the leader of the storming party on the land.

As personal reminiscences are always interesting, and frequently contain minutiæ which are not found in the matter of fact "official reports," the following account of this engagement, which was written by Captain Gilbert Elliott, her builder, and published in the St. Louis Republican of April 16th, 1887, will not be out of place here. Captain Elliott was, at the time he commenced building the Albemarle, adjutant of the 17th North Carolina Regiment, stationed near Drury's Bluff, on James river, and was given leave of absence from his regiment, by order of the Secretary of War, for that purpose. The leave of absence was "for two years on full pay," probably the longest leave of absence granted during the war. Captain Elliott says:

"Much to my gratification Captain Cooke was the officer assigned by the Navy Department to supervise the construction of, and afterwards command the ironclad ram Albemarle, which I succeeded in building, under my contract with the government, at a point on the Roanoke river known as Edward's Ferry, about twenty miles below the town of Halifax. Of course I had the warm sympathy of the citizens of that neighborhood, who rendered me all possible assistance, together with the support and aid of the government, and yet the difficulties with which I had to contend were so great as to seem almost insurmountable. However, after twelve months' unceasing labor, with a force averaging two hundred men, but few of whom, however, were skilled mechanics, but all working with an eye single to the end in view, I had the pleasure of delivering the ship into Captain Cooke's hands, and she went into commission just in time to take a leading part in the expedition organized by command of General Lee for the recapture of the town of Plymouth and surrounding country.

"The Albemarle was 152 feet long, and 45 feet wide over all. She drew about eight feet of water. Her armament consisted of two rifled Brooke guns, mounted on pivot carriages, the shield or house, was octagonal in shape, with three port holes at each end. The shield was built of timber about fourteen inches in thickness and covered with two courses of flat iron, two inches thick and eight inches wide, making eighteen inches of wood and iron as a protection against shot and shell. She carried a crew of seventy-five or eighty men. The plans and specifications were drawn and prepared by Naval Constructor John L. Porter, who also planned the conversion of the man-of-war Merrimac into the ironclad Virginia, at the Gosport Navyyard, and, as the Virginia was the first vessel ever covered with an ironclad shield, it may truly be said that to John L. Porter largely belongs the credit for the revolution in the naval architecture of the world, exemplified in the construction of that ship. The Albemarle was built on the same general idea, but she was intended for an ironclad, and built, from her keel up, for that purpose, while the Virginia was a frigate, with her upper works cut down or razeed.

"On April 18th, 1864, the Albemarle dropped down the river stern foremost, with a long chain payed out at the bow, by means of which she was steered, it being impracticable to proceed down the stream with the bow to the front, owing to the rapidity of the current, the freshet at that time being the heaviest in the memory of the oldest inhabitants. Captain Cooke kindly allowed me to accompany him as a volunteer-aid. Indeed I took with me a force of men and some portable blacksmith forges and we put the finishing touches on her armor only a few hours before she went into action. There was a Federal battery at Warren's Neck, on a considerable elevation, some three miles above the town of Plymouth, commanding Thoroughfare Gap, where the river divides into two streams, and piles, sunken vessels, and other obstructions with a plentiful supply of torpedoes, had been placed here to prevent our further descent, or to accelerate our possible descent to the bottom of the river, but, thanks to the high water, we floated safely over the obstructions and passed on down the river, paying no attention to the Warren's Neck fort, although a well directed fire was kept up against us as long as we were in range. We were much comforted to find, however, that the shot and shell did us no harm, and this was the case in all the engagements with the ram. Her shield was built at an angle of forty-five degrees, and, in time of action, was well covered with a greasy substance we called slush, to facilitate the outward course of the shot and shell striking against the roof. As a rule, the shot would scoup out a little place in the iron roof about as large as a table spoon and then ricochet over the ship and go on its way harmless. The Albemarle was struck hundreds and hundreds of times, and yet no one was hurt on her except a young sailor who had the curiosity to put his head out of a port hole to see what was going on outside, and was at once shot with a pistol from the steamer Miami, lying along side and engaged with us at the time. Very early on the morning of the 19th of April, 1864, the Miami and Southfield, lashed together with spars and with chains festooned from their sides, hove in sight, and so approached us, coming up the stream. The design undoubtedly, was to run the Albemarle down, but the pilot was equal to the occasion, and at Cooke's command, signalled to the engineer to open the throttle-valves, and with all the steam the engines would bear, and the immense force of the current with which we were sailing, he put his helm hard down and dashed the prow (or ram) of the Albemarle into the side of the Southfield, sending her to the bottom of the Roanoke river with a suddenness that seems awful to contemplate. The

Miami was a fast side wheel steamer. There was a brief engagement with her, in which her commander, Lieutenant Flusser, lost his life. A shell fired by his own hand struck our ship, exploded and a fragment rebounding, killed that gallant officer. The Albemarle was then making ready to ram the Miami, if possible, but discretion was considered the better part of valor by the commanding officer of the Miami, and he backed his vessel down the stream for a mile or two, then turned, and kept on his way. The Albemarle followed in pursuit, but the race was to the swift that day and the chase was soon abandoned. Plymouth fell as the result of next day's battle, the Albemarle holding the river front and rendering invaluable assistance in the bombardment of the strongly fortified town.

"Later on, May 5th, 1864, a most memorable engagement took place in the waters of Albemarle Sound, where, for the greater part of a day, the Albemarle contended with eight heavily armed Federal war vessels, some of them carrying 100-pounder Parrott guns. Her assailants moved around her in a circle, discharging broadsides as they passed. Shot and shell rained down upon her like hail on the roof of a house. Her smoke stack was riddled with holes and almost shot away. In consequence, the flues would not draw, and no steam could be made, propellers could not turn over and she lay like a log on the water. The Sassacus, a large double ender, ran into her, and jumped on her forward deck, hoping to sink the ram by this additional weight, but our gunner put a shot through one of the boilers of the Sassacus and she was glad to haul off with the steam made by the other. Two of the ships endeavored, by towing a large seine, to entangle the propellers, "but in vain is the net spread in the sight of any bird," and Captain Cooke was able to raise a little steam, and so manoeuvred his ship as to escape this ingenious contrivance for her destruction. A bold effort was made to throw kegs of gunpowder down her smoke stack, but that scheme failed also. One of her two guns was disabled early in the action, the muzzle being shot away. Night put an end to the conflict, and, with the aid of a quantity of lard and bacon, which was used for fuel, enough steam was gotten up to take the ship back to her wharf in Plymouth, and comparatively uninjured, although each one of the other combatants was seriously damaged, and some of them sunk. Captain Cooke was as cool in action as he was brave and determined. He did not know what fear meant and it has often been said of him that he would fight a powder magazine with a coal of fire."

Captain Cooke was promoted to captain in the navy for his gallantry on this occasion, and given a wider field of duty. Another commander was assigned to the Albemarle, and a careless guard being kept on her, Lieutenant Cushing, of the United States Navy, sunk her with a torpedo attached to the bow of a small launch, while she was lying at the wharf in Plymouth. Captain Cooke lived through the war, after which he returned to his home in Portsmouth, and died in 1869.

Lieutenant Wm. H. Murdaugh was born in Portsmouth, entered the United States Navy September 9th, 1841, and was appointed in the Confederate States Navy June 26th, 1861. When the secession movement began at the South he was executive officer of the U. S. Frigate Sabine, then stationed in Pensacola harbor, and upon the secession of Virginia, resigned his commission and entered the service of that State, and afterwards the Confederate States. He was severely wounded at the attack upon Fort Hatteras by the Federal fleet on the 29th of August, 1861. He had command of a gun and was directing its fire when a piece of shell shattered his arm. He was taken from the fort to one of the Confederate gunboats, and thus escaped capture when the fort fell. After recovering from his wound he was placed in command of the steamer Beaufort, in James river, and in 1863, was sent to Europe on special service for the Navy Department, and was there when the war ended.

Lieutenant Walter R. Butt was born in Portsmouth, and served on the Virginia in her battle with the Federal fleet in Hampton Roads, March 8th and 9th, 1862, and subsequently commanded the Nansemond in James river. He entered the Naval Academy in 1855.

Lieutenant Wm. E. Hudgins was born in Portsmouth, and at the beginning of the war was a lieutenant in the U. S. Revenue Service, and entered the Confederate Navy as a lieutenant May 26th, 1863. He was with Captain John Taylor Wood in August, 1863, in his boat expedition against the Federal Gunboats Satellite and Reliance, off the mouth of the Rappahannock river and after their capture, was placed in command of the Reliance. Captain Wood subsequently carried them up the Rappahannock, took from them everything movable, and then burned them. Lieutenant Hudgins served on various vessels after that and was on duty with the navy in Battery Buchanan, near Fort Fisher, at the entrance to Wilmington harbor, on the 15th of January, 1865, when it was captured. He was slightly wounded on that occasion.

Lieutenant Charles J. Hasker was a boatswain in the United States Navy and received a similar appointment in the Confederate Navy. He served in that capacity on the Virginia (Merrimac) and was promoted to a lieutenancy for gallantry on that and subsequent occasions.

Lieutenant Forrest was in delicate health at the beginning of the war and went to Western North Carolina to try to recuperate but died there on the 10th of April, 1863.

Engineers John W. Tynan and E. A. Jack, and Carpenter

Hugh Lindsay were on the Virginia in her battle in Hampton Roads, and Gunner John A. Lovitt served on the Patrick Henry in the same engagement. He and Engineer Tynan were on the gunboat Chattahoochee in Florida, on the 1st of June, 1863, when her boiler exploded, killing fifteen of her officers and crew. The vessel was under command of Lieutenant John J. Guthrie at the time, and Midshipman Charles K. Mallory, of Norfolk, was among the number killed. The magazine was within about three feet of the boiler and the coolness of Gunner Lovitt in quelling the panic which ensued in consequence of this proximity and an apprehended explosion, was very highly commended. He was in Battery Buchanan during the two attacks on that fort and Fort Fisher.

Carpenter Joseph F. Weaver was on the Seabird, Commodore Lynch's flagship, at the battle near Roanoke Island, February 7th, 1862, and was captured when she was sunk at Elizabeth City, on the 10th, by a 9-inch Columbiad shell from one of the pursuing Federal gunboats. He was paroled with Captain Cooke and subsequently exchanged.

Engineers Schroeder, Warner and Manning, as well as all of the others mentioned in the foregoing list rendered efficient services to the Southern Confederacy, and lived to see the termination of the war.

Engineer Schroeder made a cruise on the Tallahassee with Captain Wilkerson, was one of the officers sent to Canada on the expedition to release the Confederate prisoners confined on Johnson's Island, and was afterwards sent to Europe to assist in procuring and fitting out cruisers for the navy.

On the 30th of April, 1863, Congress passed a special act "to authorize the appointment of one Chief Constructor in the Navy." It was passed as a recognition of the services of Naval Constructor John L. Porter, and he was appointed to it by President Davis. Constructor Porter designed several sea-going ironclads, which the Navy Department endeavored to have built in Europe. The principal one was a powerful vessel, with a center turret containing ten guns, and sheathed with iron ten inches thick. The Navy Department made a contract with G. N. Saunders, Esq., to build her in England, but the war ended before she was completed. Her bow projected forward under water, and was built solid for about fifteen or twenty feet back from the stem, so as to serve for a ram. He designed another, with hinged gunwales, which could be raised or lowered at pleasure.

CHAPTER XXX.

OPERATIONS AROUND NORFOLK CITY, APRIL, 1861, TO MAY 10, 1862.

When this work was commenced and it was thought by the author that he would be compelled to rely solely upon the memory of the survivors of the war for what he might write, he feared it would be impossible for him to obtain from that source a sufficient amount of data pertaining to the troops who entered the Confederate service from Norfolk city, to do them justice, hence, his original attention was to leave them out entirely, for the reason that faint praise would be worse than none at all, but since then he has had an opportunity to inspect the muster rolls and official records of the various companies from their original muster into service until the 1st of January, 1865, and has, therefore, found himself in a position to record as accurately as an official report tells it, the story of those who marched away with their commands on the 10th of May, 1862, at the evacuation of the city, and did service in the field. After January 1st, 1865, the official records cease, and what appears upon the rolls of the different companies after that time has been supplied from memory.

Before the war the sentiment of a majority of the people of Norfolk city was opposed to the secession of the State, and at the election to send a delegate to the State Convention, which had been called to consider the situation, held February 4th, 1861, General George Blow was elected as a union delegate, over Mr. James R. Hubard, secessionist, by a majority of 480, out of 1,434 votes cast. After President Lincoln's proclamation, calling for 75,000 troops to coerce the States which had seceded, General Blow voted with the majority in favor of the passage of the ordinance of secession, under instructions from a mass meeting held April 4th.

Before the State had seceded the war fever was gathering force in Norfolk, and the news of the attack upon Fort Sumpter, April 11th, augmented it to a still greater degree of fervor, so that on the 19th of April, when General Taliaferro arrived in the city to take command of the State troops and it was evident that there was going to be war, the citizens, with singular unanimity, acquiesced in the inevitable and girded themselves for the contest.

Before the beginning of hostilities there were in Norfolk city the following military companies, fully equipped with everything except ammunition:

The Norfolk Light Artillery Blues, Captain Jacob Vickery.
The Woodis Riflemen, Captain Wm. Lamb.

The Norfolk Juniors, Captain F. F. Ferguson.
The Independent Grays, Captain Richard C. Taylor.
Company F, Captain H. W. Williamson.

All of these companies had full ranks, and in order to accommodate the hundreds who were desirous of responding to the call of the Governor, new companies were organized rapidly, as follows:

The United Artillery Company, Captain Thomas Kevill.
The Norfolk Light Artillery, Captain Francis Huger.
The Atlantic Artillery, Captain J. Hardy Hendren.
The Norfolk Light Infantry, Captain John R. Ludlow.
Company A, 6th Regiment, Captain Wm. N. McKenny.
The Norfolk Harbor Guard, Captain John J. Young.

Among these companies were quite a number of Norfolk county men from the Tanner's Creek section, but as they enlisted in the city, they cannot, at this late day, be fully identified.

On the night of the 19th of April, 1861, the Norfolk military companies took possession of Fort Norfolk, which was then used as a powder magazine, and the powder therein stored, amounting to five hundred barrels, or fifty thousand pounds, was placed on board the revenue schooner James Buchanan, and sent to Richmond, under guard, for safe keeping.

On the afternoon of the 20th all was bustle and excitement in Norfolk, and the " Pawnee war " raged there that night as well as in Portsmouth. That afternoon some unauthorized persons began sinking obstructions in the river below Fort Norfolk for the purpose of shutting in the Federal authorities at the navy yard and thus preventing them from removing the vessels and the vast amount of valuable war material which was on hand. This fact, coming to the knowledge of Commodore McCauly, commanding the navy yard, hastened his departure and the destruction of the navy yard.

General Taliaferro, who was sent to Norfolk at the beginning of hostilities to command and organize the State troops, was transferred to Gloucester Point, and on the 25th of April, General Walter Gwynn, an old army officer, assumed command, and in turn was relieved by General Huger, May 23d. In the meantime troops from all portions of the South were pouring into the city, and batteries were erected at Seawell's Point, Boush's Bluff and Fort Norfolk, and a line of entrenchments, with embrasures for heavy artillery, was thrown up back of the city to resist an attack from the direction of Fortress Monroe, should one be made. The Norfolk companies were assigned to regiments as follows:

Captain W. N. McKenny's Company to the 6th Virginia Regiment as Company A.

The Woodis Rifles to the 6th Virginia Regiment as Company C.

The Norfolk Light Infantry to the 6th Virginia Regiment as Company D.

Company F to the 6th Virginia Regiment as Company G.

The Independent Grays to the 6th Virginia Regiment as Company H.

The Juniors to the 12th Virginia Regiment as Company H.

The Norfolk Light Artillery Blues, to the 16th Virginia Regiment as Company H.

The United Artillery to the 41st Virginia Regiment as Company E.

Norfolk Light Artillery—unattached.

The Norfolk Harbor Guard—unattached.

The Atlantic Artillery—unattached.

In this connection it would not be out of place to give a brief history of the military movements in the vicinity of Norfolk prior to and which led to its evacuation by the Confederates. On the 19th of May, while detachments from the Blues, Juniors and the Woodis Rifles, of Norfolk, and the Columbus Light Guard, of Georgia, were at work upon the battery at Seawell's Point, and before it was completed, only three guns having been mounted and the sand blocking up the embrasures, the United States Steamer Monticello opened fire upon it. The fire was briskly returned by the fort and after a short engagement the Monticello hauled off. No one in the fort was injured. Captain Colquit, of the Columbus Light Guard, commanded the Confederates, and for want of a Confederate States flag, the battle was fought under the Georgia State flag, belonging to the Light Guard. During the firing the men had to work in front of the embrasures shoveling away the sand so that the guns could have play. Captain Wm. Lamb commanded the Woodis Rifles and the detachments from the Blues and Juniors were under Lieutenants W. T. Peet and John Holmes respectively. The bombardment was resumed by the Monticello on the 21st, but with like result. This was the second engagement in Virginia between the shore batteries and the Federal vessels, and the Norfolk boys, as well as the Georgians, were not alarmed at the bursting of the big shells, but stood their ground manfully.

During the winter of 1861-2, the soldiers from the far South, who were quartered near Norfolk, would have suffered severely from the cold, but for the patriotism and benevolence of the ladies of the city, who organized themselves into sewing circles, and by these and other means, raised funds to provide them with shoes, overcoats and blankets, necessaries which the Confederate authorities had not the means of supplying.

Two companies were started in Norfolk but failed of organization for want of sufficient numbers. These were the Old Dominion State Guard, of which Captain Charles B. Langley was elected commander, and the Lee Artillery, Captain James Y. Leigh. The name of the first company was afterwards changed to the Harris Guards, but neither was mustered into service. The men whose names were enrolled enlisted in other commands.

It was the intention of the United States Government to fortify and retain possession of the navy yard, and on the 19th of April General Scott ordered Captain H. E. Wright, of the engineers, to call at Fortress Monroe, get from Colonel Dimick, its commander, a regiment of troops, reinforce Commodore McCauley, and prepare for the defence of the yard. Captain Wright arrived at Fortress Monroe on the Pawnee, on the 20th, and Colonel Dimick placed at his command a regiment of 370 men under Colonel Wardrop. With this force he embarked on the Pawnee and reached the navy yard about dark that evening. He found that most of the vessels had already been scuttled and that Commodore McCauley was disposed to defend the navy yard to the last extremity. Accordingly the troops were landed and some preparations made for defence, but Commodore Paulding, who came from Washington on the Pawnee, decided to finish the destruction of the yard and evacuate it. Captain Wright and Commander Jno. Rogers were sent to blow up the dry dock, taking with them forty soldiers and a boat's crew from the Pawnee. From Captain Wright's report, which is somewhat confused and conflicting, he seems to have been considerably demoralized by the situation. His description of the arrangements for blowing up the dock does not tally with what the Virginia troops found there the next morning, but this may be accounted for by the supposition that he ordered such arrangements to be made and supposed his subordinates had carried out his orders. He said, when everything was ready, he sent away all of the men except one seaman from the Pawnee, and then they lighted four slow matches, the dock having been mined with 2,000 pounds of powder. Captain Wright and Commander Rogers, from Captain Wright's report, seem to have been left behind, among the burning buildings, after everybody else had gone, and made their way out of the main gateway, through the fire, seized a boat, imagined themselves fired upon from Portsmouth, saw in the darkness a large military force collecting against them "at a point below, where the river was narrow," and therefore concluded to land in Norfolk and surrender to General Taliaferro. They were kindly treated, forwarded to Richmond the next day and from there sent to Washington. To quiet their fears that they would be assailed by the people of Richmond, Governer Letcher escorted them to the cars and sent a couple of officers with them to Washington. Evidently "the man from the Pawnee" did not light the fuses, for the mine was not exploded, nor were the fuses found. Captain Wright's report omits to state what became of this man. A very well authenticated account of the dry-dock affair will be found in chapter I, ante.

The last mail from Baltimore was received in Norfolk on the 9th of May, though the port had been declared in a state of blockade earlier. The steamer arrived at Fortress Monroe from Baltimore that morning, and the Norfolk mail was sent up on the William Selden, which was sent to Fortress Monroe for it, but the Confederates did not send her down again. They detained her in Norfolk and would not permit her to return, for fear that she would be seized by the United States authorities. The army and navy officers in the department of Norfolk did not get on harmoniously together at first, and there was a warm dispute between General Gwynn and Commodore Forrest as to the possession and control of the property in the navy yard. General Gwynn complained to the Governor that he had been unable to obtain an inventory of the stores, &c., in the navy yard. General Lee, commanding the State forces, advised mutual concessions, and the breech was smoothed over. General Gwynn was relieved by General Benjamin Huger on the 23d of May.

Shortly after the breaking out of the war, the Confederates began fortifying the Nansemond river, but it was difficult to reach the batteries there from Norfolk, for the reason that the United States vessels controlled Hampton Roads, but on the night of the 5th of June Captain A. Sinclair, of the navy, commanding the small steamer Roanoke, eluded them and ran his boat into the river and established communications between the batteries and the railroad at Suffolk.

On the 15th of June, Saturday, the Federals opened fire upon the batteries at Seawell's Point with a Sawyer gun, which they had mounted at the Rip-Raps, and General Huger sent down to that point a lot of railroad iron to shield the magazine and the face of the batteries. The distance from the Point to the Rip-Raps, as measured by the engineers, was 3 5-8 miles.

On the 23d of April Governor Letcher appointed General R. E. Lee to command the State troops, and on the 10th of May the Secretary of War, Mr. L. P. Walker, placed all of the Confederate troops in Virginia temporarily under his orders. Colonel Talcott, of the engineers, reported to General Lee on the 26th of April that "seven guns had been mounted on the battery at the Naval Hospital; that at 10:30 a. m. on the 22d he commenced, with one hundred and twenty laborers, to build a work on Craney Island to mount twenty guns. A battery to mount twelve guns has been laid out on Pinner's Point. The work on this is under control of officers of the navy. [It was built under the supervision of Major F. W. Jett, of the Confederate Engineers.] The works in progress will mount sixty-one guns when completed. Of these, fourteen will be at the Naval Hospital, fifteen at Fort

Norfolk, twelve at Pinner's Point, and twenty at Craney Island."
On the 27th two eight inch shell guns and eight 32-pounders were ready for action at the Naval Hospital, with furnaces and fuel for heating shot. The work on the Pinner's Point battery was commenced that day. On the 26th four 9-inch Columbiads, with fifty rounds of ammunition for each gun, were sent to Craney Island and mounted. Colonel Talcott did not think very highly of Seawell's Point as a place for the erection of batteries. In his report he calls it Soller's Point.

General Lee recommended to General Gwynn the advisability of employing the naval officers in the construction and service of water batteries, or such as were intended to act against shipping, and in consequence thereof naval officers were stationed at all of the batteries around the harbor to instruct the men in the use of heavy guns. General Gwynn was constantly under apprehension of an attack upon Norfolk by the Federal forces at Fortress Monroe, and in reply to urgent letters from him for reinforcements, General Lee authorized him to recruit from the counties of Princess Anne, Norfolk, Nansemond, Southampton and Greensville, and the cities of Norfolk and Portsmouth, six regiments of infantry and artillery and four companies of cavalry, and on the 4th of May, at the request of Governor Letcher, all of the Georgia troops in and around Richmond were ordered to Norfolk. These were the 4th and 22d Regiments. The 3d Regiment and 2d Battalion had previously arrived direct from Georgia. General Gwynn wrote to Adjutant General Garnett in Richmond for 100,000 rounds of ammunition. General Garnett sent him 25,000, and suggested, as there was an abundance of powder and lead in Norfolk, that General Gwynn had better make arrangements to manufacture his own cartridges, as they were doing in Richmond.

On the 8th of May General Lee ordered the 1st Louisiana Regiment, Colonel A. G. Blanchard, from Richmond to Norfolk, and on the 14th General Gwynn reported that he had 6,000 troops and wanted 4,000 more, and on the 21st he reported that the enemy was reinforcing Fortress Monroe and asked for 4,000 more troops. Singularly, while General Gwynn was apprehending an attack from the garrison at Fortress Monroe the commander of that fort was writing to Washington for reinforcements to repel an apprehended attack by the Confederates.

On the 27th of May General Huger, who had relieved General Gwynn in the command of Norfolk, reported to General Lee that seven transports had that day landed troops at Newport News, and the same day General Magruder reported a force variously estimated at from 3,500 to 5,000 men had marched to that point from Fortress Monroe. General Lee became apprehensive that the accumulation of such a large force there was for the purpose of operating against Suffolk, either by way of the Nanse-

16

mond river or by crossing at Burwell's Bay, thus cutting off communication between Norfolk and Richmond, hence he directed General Huger to look particularly to the defence of the battery at Pig Point, to guard it against surprise or from an attack in the rear, and at the same time endeavored to collect a force at Suffolk. On the 27th General Huger divided the department into two military districts. The Norfolk division, or east of the Elizabeth river, was placed under command of Colonel Withers of the 3d Alabama Regiment, and the Portsmouth division, or west of the river, under Colonel Blanchard of the 1st Louisiana Regiment. Colonel Withers had under him the 3d Alabama Regiment, 2d Georgia Battalion, and the 6th, 12th, 16th and 41st Virginia Regiments. Colonel Blanchard's command embraced the 1st Louisiana, 3d, 4th and 22d Georgia, 3d and 9th Virginia Regiments, 2d North Carolina Battalion and 3d Louisiana Battalion.

General Huger was a man of high character, of undaunted courage, and an excellent ordnance officer, but lacked those peculiar qualifications which fit an officer to defend a post and command troops in the field, and from this sprang an Iliad of woes to the Confederacy which brought down upon himself the censure of the Confederate Congress.

On the 8th of June the Virginia troops which up to that time had been serving under orders from Governor Letcher, were turned over to the Confederate States Army. General Huger's district extended over the eastern counties of North Carolina from Weldon to the ocean, but being unacquainted with the topography of his district, and on account of his age not possessing the necessary activity to familiarize himself with it from a personal inspection, the Confederates suffered disaster after disaster, which possibly might have been avoided had proper precautions been taken. A perusal of the correspondence which passed between the subordinate commanders in North Carolina and the headquarters in Norfolk and Richmond indicates that there was a lamentable lack of judgment on the part of those in authority, if we may judge by results.

A powerful fleet was being fitted out in the North in August, 1861, and was gathering at Fortress Monroe. It destination was known to be Hatteras Inlet, yet no material effort was made to strengthen the little fort there, nor to reinforce it, but it was left to a small force of undisciplined North Carolina troops, badly drilled, with no experience in the use of heavy guns and with only guns of short range and light caliber to resist almost the whole navy of the United States government and a heavy land force. There could be but one result, the fort surrendered after a two days' bombardment by the fleet, which, anchored beyond the range of the guns of the fort, was unhurt. The fort was so badly constructed that the men had no shelter from the shells, which penetrated its walls or fell inside. This disaster occurred on the 29th of August, 1861, and opened to the Federal navy the waters of Pamlico Sound.

The next move of importance in that section was not made until the following February, so that the Confederates had from August to that date, nearly six months, to guard against further disaster. Had there been machinery or armor plate in the Confederacy with which to have equipped two iron-clad boats like the Albemarle, which was subsequently built, Hatteras could have been retaken and Norfolk held. The disasters at Roanoke Island, Newberne and Fort Macon would have been avoided, and the troops which were sent to oppose Burnside in Carolina could have been retained in Virginia against McClellan.

After the fort at Hatteras had been captured General Huger sent the 3d Georgia Regiment to reinforce it. There was a lamentable scarcity of transportation in that locality. Commodore Lynch of the navy being impatient at the want of suitable vessels for gunboats, got possession of nearly all of the tugs and small steamers in the sound and mounted guns upon them. They were valueless as gunboats, but might have been serviceable as army transports, but transposing them into so-called men-of-war deprived the army of their use, without adding anything to the strength of the navy, as subsequent events fully developed.

Colonel Wright of the Third Georgia Regiment, finding Fort Hatteras in possession of the enemy, stopped his regiment at Roanoke Island and began fortifying it to prevent the enemy from getting into Albemarle Sound, a movement which they were prevented from making at the time on account of the shallowness of the water in Pamlico Sound and the depth of the vessels in their fleet.

The importance of defending Roanoke Island, as the key to the defence of Norfolk, was urged upon General Huger and Secretary of War Benjamin in the summer and fall of 1861 by General Gatlin and Governor Clarke of North Carolina, but their recommendations were almost wholly disregarded. In December, 1861, by an order from the War Department the island was placed under the orders of General Huger and General Wise was sent there to command it. General Wise, time and time again urged upon General Huger and Secretary Benjamin the necessity of putting it in a proper state of defence and of reinforcing it with additional troops, but nothing seems to have been done by either of them towards carrying out the recommendation. General Huger had 15,000 well drilled and well armed troops around Norfolk, but it does not seem to have occurred to him that they could best protect Norfolk by being sent where the enemy was about to attack. In December he ordered the 3d Georgia back to Portsmouth, leaving on the island about 400 men of Wise's

Legion and 1,800 raw levies of North Carolina troops, badly drilled, undisciplined and badly armed. In reply to General Wise's urgent call for reinforcements he wrote: "You want supplies, hard work and coolness and not men," and on the 13th of January, 1862, he wrote: "I do not consider large forces necessary for the defence of the island. If the batteries can keep off the gunboats and transports the infantry will have little opportunity to act." And in a letter of the 18th to the Secretary of War he wrote that he "had no personal knowledge of the positions on the island."

In reply to a letter from General Wise to the Secretary of War for a supply of ammunition that officer wrote on the 12th of January: "At the first indication of an attack upon Roanoke Island a supply will be sent you." General Wise replied if they were to wait to be attacked before receiving powder from Richmond, the attack would be their capture, and defeat would precede the arrival of ammunition. This prediction was verified as to the navy.

A supply of ammunition for Commodore Lynch's fleet, sent to him from the Navy Yard, did not start until after the battle was over. Colonel Talcott of the Engineers reported to General Huger that the island was in an indefensible condition and needed guns, ammunition and men, but no action was taken upon his report. Early in December Commodore Forrest was applied to for pile drivers to drive piles across the channel to obstruct the passage of the Federal gunboats, and promised to send them, but Colonel Shaw, commanding the island, reported to General Wise that they had not arrived by the 30th and that Commodore Forrest's reason for the delay was that the men wanted to spend their Christmas holidays at home. One pile driver arrived on the 6th of January, and on the 7th of February, when the attack was made, there were still 1,700 yards of the sound open. All of the tugboats in the vicinity but one had been converted into gunboats, and that one, with two large barges, which General Wise held for transportation, was ordered away from him by General Huger just as the battle was about to commence, which left him no means of retreating from the island in case of defeat. Thus the garrison was shut up on the island and ordered to defend it, while they were denied the means with which to make the defence or of escape in case of defeat. The batteries were built on the west or Croatan side of the island, near the north end of it. The Governor of North Carolina applied to Secretary Mallory of the Navy for four rifled cannon for the defence of the island, but failed to get them, and, to add to the blunders which led to the disaster, General Huger's countermanding General Wise's order, lost the garrison the use of the six field pieces belonging to the Wise Legion. They were in Norfolk under command of Colonel

Henningsen, and General Wise ordered him to charter a steamer in Norfolk to bring the guns and ammunition to the island, and to march the horses down the Currituck beach directly to Nag's Head, but General Huger countermanded General Wise's order, ordered Colonel Henningsen to hitch up his horses to his guns, march the battery to Powell's Point and transport them from there to the island, but upon reaching Powell's Point Colonel Henningsen found himself fifteen or twenty miles from Roanoke Island, with Albemarle Sound between them and no means of getting across. The result of this blunder was that the battle was fought, the island lost, and this important force was powerless to render any assistance to their comrades.

The enemy made their appearance before Roanoke Island on the 7th of February, 1862, with about thirty gunboats and a force of transports, and opened fire on the shore batteries, taking up a position upon which the batteries could bring only three guns to bear, one rifle and two smooth bore 32-pounders. They also landed 10,000 men on the island, below the batteries. The fire upon the batteries was kept up all day, but no damage was done to them. During the engagement Commodore Lynch's fleet of tugboats, from a position near the main land, made a gallant fight with a portion of the enemy's fleet, and after firing away all of their ammunition, and having two boats sunk, fell back to Elizabeth City. The next morning the bombardment of the battery was resumed, and the land forces, marching up from the south end of the island, met the troops which were there to defend it, and, as might have been expected, defeated them, and, getting in rear of the batteries, compelled their evacuation, as they had no rear protection. Colonel Shaw fell back to the north end of the island, and finding there was no boat by which his garrison could be taken off, and knowing that his small, undisciplined force, badly armed and without artillery, could not successfully contend against the overwhelming force which was following them, decided to surrender, and thus was opened the gateway to the rear of Norfolk, which should have been kept closed, and would have been had the island been properly garrisoned and fortified. Lieutenant William Selden of Norfolk was in the engagement of the 8th and was very favorably mentioned in the official report. He was in charge of a six-pounder boat howitzer and was shot in the forehead by a minie ball just as he was firing his last round of ammunition at the enemy. The Confederate loss in the battle was 23 killed, 58 wounded and about 2,500 captured. The Federals lost 37 killed, 214 wounded and 13 missing.

The Confederate Congress appointed a committee to investigate the disaster, and their report says the cause of the disaster and defeat was "the want of necessary defences on the island, the want of necessary field artillery, armament and ammunition, and the great and unpardonable deficiency of men, together with the entire want of transportation by which the whole command might have been conveyed from the island after the defeat at the battery." After exonerating General Wise from blame the report goes on to say: "But the committee cannot say the same in reference to the efforts of the Secretary of War and the commanding officer at Norfolk, General Huger. It is apparent that the island of Roanoke is necessary for the defence of Norfolk, and that General Huger had under his command at that point upwards of 15,000 men, a large supply of armament and ammunition, and could have thrown in a few hours a large reinforcement upon Roanoke Island, and that himself and the Secretary of War had timely notice of the entire inadequacy of the defences, the want of men and munitions of war, and the threatening attitude of the enemy. But General Huger and the Secretary of War paid no practical attention to those urgent appeals of General Wise, sent forward none of his important requisitions, and permitted General Wise and his inconsiderable force to remain and meet at least 15,000 men well armed and equipped. If the Secretary of War and the commanding General at Norfolk had not the means to reinforce General Wise why was he not ordered to abandon his position and save his command? But, on the contrary, he was required to remain and sacrifice his command, with no means in his insulated position to make his escape in case of defeat. The committee, from the testimony, are therefore constrained to report that whatever of blame and responsibility is justly attributable to any one for the defeat of our troops at Roanoke Island on February 8th, 1862, should attach to Major General B. Huger and the late Secretary of War, J. P. Benjamin."

The fall of Roanoke Island has been treated of so extensively in this connection for the reason that to it was due the evacuation of Norfolk and Portsmouth by the Confederates the May following. It opened up to the incursions of the enemy the whole of Eastern North Carolina and compelled the Confederates to maintain a large army there to protect the Weldon and Wilmington railroad. This large detachment of troops from the army in Virginia weakened it so that it was impossible, in the opinion of the Confederate authorities in Richmond to spare troops enough to protect Norfolk both in front from Fortress Monroe and in rear from the direction of Elizabeth City, Edenton and the Blackwater river, hence it was abandoned.

It will be remembered that the 3d Georgia Regiment was sent by General Huger to Hatteras too late to be of service there, and that Colonel Wright stopped at Roanoke Island. On the 14th of October Colonel Wright, with 150 men from his regiment, embarked on three vessels from Commodore Lynch's fleet, the Raleigh, Curlew and Junaluska, under the Commodore, and started towards Chicamicomico. The expedition captured the tug Fanny and forty-seven prisoners. The Fanny was armed with two rifle guns, and Commodore Lynch added her to his fleet. On the 4th Colonel Wright started again with his regiment to capture the 20th Indiana Regiment, which had advanced from Hatteras to Chicamicomico, and effected a landing, but the Indianians ran so swiftly that by the utmost efforts of the Georgians they could not overtake them. A number of stragglers were picked up in the chase, and the Georgians lost one man, who died from exhaustion in his effort to overtake the fleeing foe. General Wool reported to General Scott that the Indiana Regiment "completely defeated" the Georgians. So much for official reports.

About the 1st of December the 3d Georgia Regiment was ordered back to Portsmouth and its place on Roanoke Island was taken by a newly organized regiment of North Carolina troops.

During the summer and fall of 1861 no effort was made by the Confederates to recapture Fort Hatteras, though it was weakly garrisoned, and though Governor Clarke of North Carolina was constantly urging it. On the 19th of September the Federal garrison consisted of only 946 men. General Wool, too, was expecting them to recapture it, and was constantly urging upon the Federal government the importance of strengthening the garrison if it was intended to hold the place. But General Huger had his eye fixed upon Fortress Monroe, and could see nothing but an expected landing of Federals at Ocean View. On the 5th of September Adjutant General Cooper telegraphed to know if he could not spare the sailors at the Navy Yard to be sent to the North Carolina Sounds, and he replied that he could not spare a single man, that he needed two more regiments. On the 30th of November his muster rolls showed an aggregate present of 13,451, and on the rolls, absent and present, 15,143. January, 1862, he had present 15,352. Present and absent, 16,761. He had also 24 field pieces and 192 heavy guns, of which 46 were in the vicinity of Suffolk.

On the 6th of December orders were received from Richmond to make all of the batteries around the harbor bomb proof, and on the 7th of January, 1862, General Huger reported to the Secretary of War the following naval officers on duty in the batteries, with their respective ranks under the act of Congress allowing army rank to naval officers on duty with the army.

Commander R. F. Pinkney, commanding Fort Norfolk and inspector of batteries, with the rank of Lieutenant-Colonel.

Commander Charles F. McIntosh, commanding Fort Nelson, Lieutenant-Colonel.

Commander W. L. Maury, commanding Seawell's Point battery, Lieutenant-Colonel.

Lieutenant G. W. Harrison, commanding Pinner's Point Battery, Major.

Lieutenant R. R. Carter, commanding Pig Point battery, Major.

Lieutenant B. P. Loyall, assigned to Roanoke Island, Captain.

Lieutenant J. S. Taylor, assigned to Roanoke Island, to rank as Major.

The Monitor, iron clad, was expected to arrive at Fortress Monroe the latter part of February, and General McClellan desired General Wool to make use of her to capture Norfolk. General Wool informed the Secretary that with 20,000 men and four batteries in addition to the force he then had at Fortress Monroe, of 11,000 men and two batteries, with the co-operation of the navy and of General Burnside's forces from North Carolina operating on its rear, he thought he could capture it. McClellan urged upon him specially to capture the batteries at Seawell's Point and spike the guns.

On the 16th of February, 1862, General Burnside sent an expedition up the Chowan river for the purpose of burning the Seaboard and Roanoke railroad bridges across the Blackwater and Nottoway rivers. It reached Winton on the 17th and had an engagement with the 1st North Carolina Battalion, under Lieutenant-Colonel Williams, and a battery of artillery, and fell back. During the night Lieutenant-Colonel Williams also fell back, and the next day the gunboats returned and burned Winton. The Richmond authorities then became very apprehensive for the safety of Norfolk and Portsmouth, and on the 27th General Huger was ordered to put the two cities under martial law, to enroll all the militia capable of doing military duty, and to make arrangements to remove the women and children and all other persons who would embarrass their defence in case of a siege.

General Burnside continued active in his demonstrations in North Carolina, and General Lee continued apprehensive of a joint movement from Edenton and Newport News upon Suffolk, and about the 1st of March the 14th and 53d Virginia, 2d Louisiana, 15th North Carolina, and 16th Georgia Regiments and Cobb's Georgia Legion, with Moseley's battery of artillery, were conveyed to that town from General Magruder's army on the Peninsula. They took steamers from King's Mill for City Point, and were conveyed thence by rail to Suffolk, reaching there on the 4th. The detachment numbered about 5,000 men, and on the 8th General Huger crossed the 3d Alabama from Norfolk to Portsmouth, near the Seaboard railroad, to be accessible in case there should be need at Suffolk.

On the 8th and 9th of March the iron-clad Virginia (Merrimac) had her battles in Hampton Roads, and the result of the second day's battle, the battle between the Virginia and Monitor, alarmed both General Huger and the Federal authorities. General Huger recommended that the narrow passage left in the channel below

Lambert's Point be closed with obstructions, so as to prevent the Monitor from coming up to Norfolk, and Secretary Wells of the United States Navy, wanted General Wool to tow some vessels loaded with stone to Seawell's Point and sink them in the channel there to prevent the Virginia from coming out again. General Huger's recommendation was disapproved by the Secretary of War at Richmond, who told him that the Federals were so alarmed about the Virginia that they would not venture to enter the harbor. The Secretary of War was correct, and the Federals abandoned the idea of attacking the harbor from that side. Assistant Secretary of the Navy G. V. Fox wrote to General McClellan on the 13th as follows:

" The Monitor is more than a match for the Merrimac, but she might be disabled in the next encounter. I cannot advise so great dependence on her. Burnside and Goldsboro are very strong for the Chowan river route to Norfolk, and I brought up maps, &c., to show you. It turns everything, and is only twenty-seven miles to Norfolk by two good roads. The Monitor may, and I think will, destroy the Merrimac in the next fight, but this is hope, not certainty."

See what a train of events followed the failure of Secretary Mallory to take the advice of Naval Constructor John L. Porter in June, 1861, to import armor iron and steam engines for iron-clad gunboats. Two of them in Albemarle and Pamlico Sounds would have been worth more than 30,000 men.

On the 10th of February, two days after the fall of Roanoke Island, the 6th Virginia Regiment, under Colonel Thos. J. Corprew, was sent to Currituck Bridge, the eastern entrance to the Albemarle and Chesapeake Canal, and the 3d Georgia Regiment was sent back to South Mills, the Carolina end of the Dismal Swamp Canal. A day or two afterwards, General Wise, falling back from Nag's Head with the remnant of his brigade, met the 6th Virginia Regiment at Currituck Bridge, took command and fell back to Great Bridge, taking the 6th Regiment with him. General Huger found him there, and requested the Secretary of War to detach him and his brigade from the division. Accordingly, on the 18th, General Wise was ordered to report with his infantry to General Joseph E. Johnston, at Manassas, and on the 20th turned over the post at Great Bridge and his artillery to General Mahone.

Colonel Wright pushed on towards Elizabeth City, and formed a junction with McComas' Battery of the Wise Legion, the Southampton Cavalry, Captain Gillett, and two companies of North Carolina militia, and on the 19th of April fought the battle of South Mills, or Sawyer's Lane, or Camden. General Reno, with five regiments, the 21st Massachusetts, 51st Pennsylvania, 6th New Hampshire, and 9th and 89th New York, and a detachment of the 1st New York Marine Artillery, with six boat howitzers, the whole numbering about 4,000 men, landed at Elizabeth City and started towards South Mills to destroy the canal locks to prevent the passage of iron clads, which, it was reported to them, were nearly ready at the navy yard at Portsmouth, for service in the North Carolina sounds. Colonel Wright formed six companies of his regiment in an advantageous position across the main road, with his flanks protected by a thick wood and swamp, placed two of McComas' guns in the road, and awaited the approach of the enemy. There was a large open field in front, and in this the battle was fought. Colonel Wright sent the rest of his command to the rear as a reserve and to guard a bridge across the Pasquotank river, in case there should be any attempt to cross from that direction to his rear. The enemy began the attack about 12 o'clock, and continued it, with occasional intermissions, as their assaults were repulsed, for about four hours. Several attempts to turn the flanks, as well as to attack in front, were defeated by the firing of artillery and infantry, and after the final repulse of the enemy, Colonel Wright fell back to his entrenchments, about two miles in the rear, and the enemy retreated to Elizabeth City and embarked immediately. Three of their regiments reached Roanoke Island the next morning, and the two others were conveyed to Newberne. The next day Colonel Wright was reinforced by the 1st Louisiana and the 32d North Carolina Regiments, and later by the Portsmouth Rifle Company and Grimes' Battery, under command of General Blanchard, who assumed command of the brigade. Colonel Wright's loss in the engagement was six killed, nineteen wounded and three missing. Among the killed was Captain McComas, of the artillery. The Federal loss, as per their official report, was thirteen killed, 101 wounded, and thirteen captured.

The uncertainty of the point of attack in North Carolina and the many exposed points required the withdrawal from Virginia of a large portion of General Johnston's army, and so great was this drain that in April, 1862, the muster rolls of General Holmes' command in North Carolina showed a force of nearly 25,000 effective men, and the only troops who could be taken to fill their places were those under command of General Huger, in the vicinity of Norfolk and Portsmouth. General Johnston announced his decision on the 28th of April to fall back from Yorktown and recommended the evacuation of Norfolk and Portsmouth, and General Lee, who had for some time apprehended a movement of the Federals upon Suffolk, and doubted the ability of the Confederates to detach troops enough to resist it, concurred in the movement, and orders were issued to General Huger to remove everything moveable, preparatory to marching away the troops, whom he was ordered to concentrate on Petersburg. The evacuation of

Norfolk was hastened by a much earlier retreat on the part of General Johnston than was anticipated.

There were no military movements of interest in the vicinity of Norfolk, after the battle of South Mills, until the 8th of May, when the Federal fleet from Fortress Monroe, includihg the Monitor, moved up towards Seawell's Point, and about noon opened fire upon the batteries. The Virginia moved down from the navy yard to take part in the engagement, but as she was turning Lambert's Point the Federal vessels saw her and retired towards Fortress Monroe. That morning the Galena and two other gun boats started up James river, shelling the Confederate batteries as they moved along. The Confederate steamers Patrick Henry and Thomas Jefferson retired before them as they advanced. Early in April, before it was anticipated that the evacuation of Norfolk and Portsmouth would be necessary, the Secretary of War directed that additional obstructions be put in the harbor, and after consulting with Secretary Mallory, of the navy, Captain S. S. Lee, who had relieved Commodore Forrest as commandant of the navy yard, was directed to have the old 74-gun ships Delaware and Columbus raised and taken to the narrow part of the channel near Seawell's Point and there scuttled. The sloop of war Germantown and the old frigate United States, which had been re-christened "the Confederate States," were to be used for the same purpose, while the Plymouth was directed to be fitted up as a receiving ship. A space was to be left open for the Virginia to pass in and out, but was to be closed with an arrangement of booms when not used for the passage of vessels. This was decided upon because the old obstructions near Lambert's Point were so close to the city that it could be reached from there by the enemy's shells, should they succeed in passing the batteries at Seawell's Point and Craney Island. Before anything could be done towards carrying out the proposed plan, the Confederates evacuated the place. In the meantime the wholesome fear the enemy had of the Virginia kept them from making any attempt to enter the harbor.

The Confederates left on the 10th of May, and knowing that they were moving off, General Wool landed a force of 6,000 troops on Willoughby's Spit, and about 9 a. m. started for the city. He marched very slowly, so as to give the Confederates time to get off without any hindrance on his part, and arrived within about a mile of the Norfolk at 5 o'clock p. m., having moved at the rate of about one mile an hour. Here he was met by Mayor W. W. Lamb, who surrendered the city, in the absence of military authority, and, though the city was in possession of the United States army and the guns which frowned from the numerous batteries were silent, with no soldiers near them to wake them into action, the Virginia still held a position inside of Craney Island,

and the Federal fleet held back from entering the harbor. That night the old ironclad was set on fire by order of her own commander, and just before daylight on the morning of the 11th, the fire reached her magazine and she was blown up. Then her late antagonists came boldly up to the city.

General Wool, in his official report of the landing of the Federal troops, and their occupation of the city, forwarded to the Secretary of War on the 12th of May, says:

HEADQUARTERS DEPARTMENT OF VIRGINIA,
FORTRESS MONROE, VA., May 12th, 1862.

SIR— On the 9th of May (Friday afternoon) I organized a force to march against Norfolk. On Saturday morning, May 10th, the troops were landed, under the direction of Colonel Cram, at Ocean View, and commenced the march towards Norfolk, under the direction of Brigadier Generals Mansfield and Weber, who proceeded on the direct route by the way of Tanner's Creek bridge, but finding it on fire, they returned to the cross-roads, where I joined them and took the direction of the column. I arrived by the old road and entered the entrenchments in front of the city at twenty minutes before 5 p. m. I immediately proceeded towards Norfolk, accompanied by Hon. Secretary Chase, and met the mayor and a select committee of the Common Council of Norfolk at the limits of the city, when they surrendered the city, agreeably to the terms set forth in the resolutions of the Common Council, presented by the Mayor, W. W. Lamb, which were accepted by me so far as related to the civil rights of the citizens.

I immediately took possession of the city and appointed Brigadier General Egbert L. Viele Military Governor of Norfolk, with directions to see that the citizens were protected in all their civil rights. Soon after I took possession of Gosport and Portsmouth. The taking of Norfolk caused the destruction of the ironclad Merrimac, which was blown up by the rebels about 5 o'clock on the morning of the 11th of May, which was soon after communicated to you and the President of the United States. On the 11th I visited the navy yard and found all the work shops, store houses, and other buildings in ruins, having been set on fire by the rebels who at the same time partially blew up the dry-dock.

I also visited Craney Island, where I found thirty-nine guns of large caliber, most of which were spiked ; also a large number of shot and shells, with about 5,000 pounds of powder, all of which with the buildings, were in good order. So far as I have been able to ascertain, we have taken about two hundred cannon, including those at Seawell's Point batteries, with a large number of shot and shells, as well as many other articles of value to the government.

Troops have been stationed at the navy yard, Craney Island, Seawell's Point and other places.

Secretary of War Stanton issued a congratulatory order to General Wool, claiming that his movement of 6,000 troops caused the evacuation of Norfolk. The secretary knew that the evacuation was due to orders received from Richmond two weeks previous thereto, and that the stores which could be moved had previously been sent to Richmond and Charlotte. What chance would General Wool's 6,000 men have had of capturing Norfolk or even escaping, in a contest with the 15,000 well drilled troops who were under General Huger's command.

General Wool knew before he landed at Ocean View that the Confederates had evacuated their batteries, and he took particular care not to approach Norfolk until he was certain that the last Confederate troops had left the city. Is any better evidence wanted than the fact that it took him from 9 o'clock a. m. to 5 p. m. to march from Ocean View to the intrenchments back of Norfolk, a distance of about seven miles.

The Confederate troops under General Huger were added to the army of General Johnston for the defence of Richmond. General Huger commanded the division until after the battle of Malvern Hill, when he was relieved from his command in the field and appointed inspector of artillery and ordnance, with instructions to report to the War Department for orders. His management of the division at the battle of Seven Pines and during the Seven Day's battles, terminating at Malvern Hill, did not meet the approbation of the Confederate war authorities. His troops were assigned to other commanders, and made records for themselves, as soldiers, second to none in the army of Northern Virginia.

The council of war which decided that Norfolk was untenable, was held before General Johnston went to the Peninsula. There were present Generals Longstreet, Smith and Lee, President Davis and Secretary of War Randolph. It was agreed then that if the Peninsula was evacuated, McClellan could cross a force over James river, take post at Suffolk, that Burnside could reinforce him from Elizabeth City, and starve out General Huger's forces and force a surrender. Persons not so high in authority as those who held the council, have always doubted the necessity of evacuating the city. They have taken the ground that if McClellan crossed over his army and located at Suffolk or advanced towards Portsmouth, General Johnston's army could have crossed over also and hemmed McClellan in between the two forces, while the Virginia, in Hampton Roads, could have prevented his receiving supplies from Fortress Monroe, and, if Burnside left North Carolina to unite with him, General Holmes' 25,000 Confederate troops in that State would have been released and could have joined General Johnston in Virginia. McClellan had his eye on Richmond, not Norfolk.

On the 3d of May an officer of General Johnston's staff arrived in Norfolk with an order to General Huger to evacuate the city immediately. The order was issued May 1st, but the Secretary of War, who was in Norfolk to see about the removal of stores, &c., ordered General Huger to delay the evacuation until he could remove such stores and munitions as could be carried off.

CHAPTER XXXI.

THE NORFOLK LIGHT ARTILLERY BLUES.

When the war ended, this was probably the largest company in the Confederate army, for though it had been through three years of active service after the evacuation of Norfolk, and had lost sixteen men by death, besides many wounded, it had more than a hundred and fifty men present for duty when the lines were broken at Petersburg on the 1st of April, 1865, and the final crash came, which involved the Southern Confederacy in its ruins. Twenty-two of its members were from Portsmouth, ten or twelve were from Princess Anne, six were from Maryland, while Norfolk county, Southampton, Nansemond, Prince George, Petersburg, Hampton and other places had representatives in its ranks, but a large majority of its members were from the city of Norfolk, and no company in the Confederate service was composed of better material.

The Blues were organized February 22d, 1828, with Captain Miles King as their first commander. Captain King passed away long before the war, but his work remained. At the breaking out of the late war "the Blues" turned out with full ranks, and were on duty April 19th, 1861, when the powder was removed from Fort Norfolk, and on the morning of the 20th, with two field pieces, they were sent down the harbor towards Craney Island, to intercept the Baltimore boat, which was supposed to have on board a detachment of marines for the navy yard. Their orders were to capture the marines and bring them to Norfolk. They stopped the steamer but the marines were not on board. The company was armed with four brass howitzers but these were turned over to the Huger Battery, and the Blues were attached to the 16th Virginia Infantry as Company H, until March 26th, 1862, when the company was detached from the 16th Regiment and reorganized as light artillery.

The officers of the company when the war began were Captain Jacob Vickery; 1st Lieutenant, W. J. Nimmo; 2d Lieutenant, John Branham; 3d Lieutenant, S. P. Moore, but Lieutenants Branham and Moore did not go into service with it, and the officers for the first year were Captain Vickery; 1st Lieutenant Nimmo; 2d Lieutenant, W. T. Peet; 3d Lieutenant, R. B. Banks; 1st Sergeant, Thos. Nash, Jr. On the 22d of April the Blues were ordered to Craney Island and remained there about three weeks, when they were sent to Boush's Bluff, near the mouth of Tanner's Creek. There were on duty at that locality, the Blues, the Juniors, of Norfolk, and a company organized by

Captain John J. Young, and doing duty as heavy artillery. On the 18th of May, 1861, the tug Kahnkee landed a force of laborers at Seawell's Point for the purpose of building a battery in that locality, and was shortly afterwards chased and fired upon by the United States steamer Monticello. The Kahnkee steamed for Norfolk, with the Monticello in pursuit, and when the latter vessel had gotten within range of the guns in the battery at Bonsh's Bluff, Captain Young fired a shot at her which turned her back. During that day and the following morning the Confederates were busy at work upon the battery at Seawell's Point, and by the afternoon of the 19th, had three guns mounted, when the Monticello took up a position to attack it. A detachment of the Blues, under Lieutenant Peet, was sent from Bonsh's Bluff to reinforce a company of Georgians, the Columbus Light Guard, which was stationed there, and assisted in the engagement which followed. After a brisk interchange of shots, the Monticello retired but returned again on the 21st. The Blues were present on this occasion also and did good service. Later that summer, the whole company was ordered to Seawell's Point, and remained on duty there until the evacuation by the Confederates in May, 1862.

On the 8th of March, 1862, several of the Federal vessels which were moving from Fortress Monroe towards Newport News, to engage the Virginia (Merrimac) passed within gun shot of the batteries at Seawell's Point, and among others, the battery which was manned by the Blues, opened fire on them. They were in the battery on the 8th of May when the Federal fleet from Fortress Monroe bombarded Seawell's Point, until the appearance of the Virginia, coming down from the navy yard, caused them to retire.

While at Seawell's Point several changes took place in the officers of the company. Sergeant Nash was elected 1st Lieutenant of the Huger Battery in April, 1861, Lieutenant Nimmo died on the 25th of September, 1861, Captain Vickery resigned on the 4th of December, and on the 21st Captain Charles R. Grandy was elected Captain. Other changes were made at the reorganization of the company, so that when it left Norfolk the following were its officers:

Captain—Charles R. Grandy.

First Lieutenant, Wm. T. Peet; 2d Lieutenant, R. B. Banks; 3d Lieutenant, James W. Gilmer.

After leaving Norfolk the company moved to Petersburg and was there furnished with two rifle guns, two brass howitzers and two Napoleons. It had then between ninety and a hundred men. In the summer of 1862 Sergeant Henry V. Moore was elected 4th Lieutenant and 2d Sergeant R. F. Vaughan became Orderly Sergeant. These officers continued with the company until the close of the war. Lieutenant Peet was wounded twice. The first wound was received at the battle of Chancellorsville on the 1st of May, 1863, and the other on the 1st of April 1865, when the Confederate lines in front of Petersburg were broken. Lieutenant Gilmer received a slight wound in the forehead in front of Petersburg in 1864, from a piece of shell which struck the ground and spent nearly all of its force before it struck him. The other officers escaped without a wound.

The company remained on duty around Richmond and Petersburg until the fall of 1862, when it was ordered to the upper Rappahannock to assist the 61st Virginia Regiment in guarding the fords of that river and the Rapidan, and on the 16th of November was ordered, with the 61st Regiment, to Petersburg, arriving there on the 18th. On the 13th of December was fought the battle of Fredericksburg. The Blues occupied a piece of high ground on the left of the Confederate line, with Anderson's Division, and rendered material assistance in repulsing the assaults of the enemy, but was fortunate in not losing any men. This was the first battle with infantry in which the company was engaged.

The winter of 1862-3 was spent on the Rappahannock river in the presence of the enemy, and when General Hooker commenced his turning movement in April, 1863, the Blues were on guard at United States Ford. This position was turned by Hooker's passage of the river higher up, and on the night of the 29th the Blues retired towards Chancellorsville, where, on the 1st day of May, they opened the three days' battle which is known by that name. One gun of the Blues' battery, together with another gun belonging to Jordan's battery, engaged Weed's battery of regulars, supported by two brigades of Sykes' Division, at a distance of three hundred yards, until the enemy retired. During this engagement a can of shrapnel from one of the guns of the enemy burst just in front of the Blues' gun, killed Private W. C. Land and wounded Lieutenant Peet slightly, Corporals J. H. Watters and M. C. Keeling and Privates J. W. Floyd, C. K. McKown, John H. Day, T. J. Wilkins and W. D. Montague. This left only two men to work the gun, and these two, with the assistance of Captain Grandy and Lieutenant Peet, who was not disabled by his wound, continued to serve it. Private Floyd lost his arm. This was the heaviest loss the company met with in any engagement during the war.

In June, 1863, the company was attached to Garnett's battalion of artillery and followed General Lee into Pennsylvania, took part in the battle of Gettysburg, and on the 14th of July recrossed the Potomac river into Virginia without having lost any men except one or two who were captured near Falling Waters.

The winter of 1863-4 was passed in comfortable quarters near Gordonsville, and in May, 1864, camp was broken to meet the

17

advance of General Grant in the Wilderness. The Blues were constantly in front until the army settled down in front of Petersburg, when the company was assigned a position in the lines near the Boydton Plank Road. While there three men were killed, Privates Wm. Booth, J. Theodore Taylor, and A. M. Watters. Taylor performed a very daring feat on the 30th of July, 1864, during the battle of the Crater. The company was then stationed near that locality and had not been moved to the Plank Road. A large shell from one of the enemy's guns made a lodgment in the roof of the magazine, and, exploding, set the magazine on fire. Seeing this, and apprehending an explosion, an infantry regiment which was near by supporting the battery scattered, and considerable demoralization was felt all around, but Taylor took a couple of buckets of water, went down into the magazine and put the fire out. In this battle the company had one man killed, Corporal R. M. Butler, and several wounded.

Towards the close of the scenes around Petersburg the Blues were divided into two sections, one of whom had charge of a mortar battery near the scene of the Crater fight and the other was farther to the right, near the Boydton Plank Road, and it was there that Grant made his assault upon the Confederate lines. All of the infantry had been withdrawn, and the Blues fought without supports. The enemy charged in front and to the right of them. The assault in front was checked, but the works were carried on their right and the exultant foe charged down the trenches upon the battery. A portion of the guns changed front to meet this attack, and they were fought until the enemy reached their muzzles, when the battery, with about sixty men, was captured. The enemy's loss was very heavy and the price paid for the battery was a dear one. The portion of the company stationed at the mortar battery escaped from the lines, joined the army on the retreat, and surrendered at Appomattox. The company took part in the following battles:

Seawell's Point, May 19th-21st, 1861.
Seawell's Point, March 8th, '62.
Seawell's Point, May 8th, '62.
Rappahannock Bridge.
Fredericksburg, December 13th, 1862.
Cold Harbor,
Chancellorsville, May 1st, 1863.
Gettysburg, July 2d-3d, 1863.
Bristoe Station, October 14th, 1863.
Wilderness, May 6th, 1864.
Spotsylvania C. H., May 12th, 1864.
Turkey Ridge.

Petersburg lines from June 16th, 1864, to April 1st, 1865.

The Norfolk Light Artillery Blues was one of the companies sent to Coggins' Point, on the James river, in July, 1862, to bombard McClellan's camp at Harrison's Landing, on which occasion the enemy were considerably surprised and alarmed, even if not greatly damaged.

The following rolls show, first, those who were discharged from the company or assigned to other fields of duty, and second, those who left Norfolk in its ranks at the evacuation or joined the company subsequently. Those marked with a star were from Portsmouth, and, of all these names, every man remained faithful to the Confederacy until the close of the war:

TRANSFERRED AND DISCHARGED.

Allyn, Joseph T., appointed 2d Lieutenant Ordnance C. S. Army, May 25th, 1863.
Bagnall, Richard D., appointed Assistant Surgeon C. S. Army October 18th, 1861.
Blow, W. W., transferred to Ordnance Department.
Borum, Charles, appointed Lieutenant in the Navy.
Branham, John B., detailed as Department Clerk, Richmond.
*Brown, John B., appointed Engineer in the Navy March 20th, 1863.
Bradford, O., appointed Lieutenant in the Navy.
Cornick, Henry, appointed Master in the Navy April 1st, 1863.
Freeman, J. M., Jr., appointed Engineer in the Navy May 12th, 1863.
Gatch, J. A., appointed Lieutenant Company H, 6th Virginia Regiment, April 7th, 1863.
Johnson, Ames C., appointed Engineer in the Navy.
*Kilby, W. T., transferred to Provost Marshal's office, Richmond.
Toy, Crawford H., appointed Chaplain 53 Virginia Regiment.
Whiting, John S., appointed Hospital Steward October 8th, 1861.
Walker, R. P., discharged on account of disability.
Wright, Minton A., appointed Lieutenant 57th North Carolina Regiment and killed.
*West, Joseph S., appointed Engineer in the Navy.
Webb, Wm. T., discharged July 3d, 1863.

Captain, Chas. R. Grandy.
First Lieutenant, Wm. T. Peet.
Second Lieutenant, R. B. Banks.
Third Lieutenant, Jas. W. Gilmer.
Fourth Lieutenant, Henry V. Moore.

SERGEANTS.

1st, R. F. Vaughan, 3d, Wm. E. Taylor, 5th, J. H. Watters,
2d, Geo. C. Hudgins, 4th, J. R. Wright, 6th, W. T. Clarke.

CORPORALS.

C. H. Busky, J. E. Keeling, W. D. Montague,
*J. T. Rainier, C. S. Rogers, S. N. Brickhouse,
R. M. Butler, M. C. Keeling, E. L. Wright,
R. S. Broughton, T. J. Wilkins, J. M. Zills.
Wm. Boothe, J. W. Elliott,

Quartermaster Sergeant, B. D. Thomas.
Commissary Sergeant, John L. Keeling.
Ordnance Sergeant, John H. Nash.

PRIVATES.

*Ashton, John C. Benson, O. S. Brock, L.
Beale, H. Bishop, W. I. E. Brickhouse, B. D.
Bell, A. S. Bell, N. Brooks, E. W.

Brown, V. H.
*Browne, Joe S.
*Brown, J. W.
Brown, E. P.
Cooke, John S.
Cooke, M. T.
Collins, W. W.
Capps, L. O.
Cornick, H.
Carroll, Wm. S.
Chamberlaine, A. E.
Cocke, W. R. C.
Cox, Wm. R.
Cutherell, Wm. S.
Cocke, P. St. Geo.
*Day, John H.
Denson, A. J.
Donghtie, H. S.
Doyle, W. H.
Drummond, R. J.
Drummond, C. H.
*Dunn, Wm. H.
Dunn, J. R.
Evans, R.
*Elliott, Thos. H.
Elliott, T. E.
Elliott, J. A.
Fitzgerald, W.
Fitzgerald, D.
Fitzgerald, E.
Fletcher, F.
Floyd, John W.
Gamage, J. O.
Gaskins, G. O.
Ghiselin, H.
Ghiselin, R.
Goodrich, A. J.
Gordon, J. P.
Gordon, Geo. W.
Graves, C. M.
Gwathney, R. H.
Gordon, M.
Hodges, John M.
*Haines, J. M. D.
Hill, A.
Halstead, R. L.
Hallett, Wm. R.

Hatton, John F.
Haughton, A. Jr.
Higgins, I.
Higgins, A.
Hodges, Samuel.
*Hume, R. G.
Hunter, J. F.
Holmes, W. H.
James, H.
Johnson, J. W.
Jones, George.
Jones, R. H.
Joynes, S. H.
Joynes, W. C.
Joynes, C. T.
Johnson, A. W.
King, W. C.
Lee, L. M. Jr.
Land, W. A.
LeCompte, J. W.
Lee, F. D.
Lovitt, R. C.
Lovitt, H. C.
McKown, C. K.
*Moore, Jos. P.
McGuire, J. B.
Morris, J. J.
Morse, B. N.
*Maupin, G.W.O.Jr.
Malborn, O. L.
Morris, D. P.
Masi, F. J.
Moore, J. E.
McCarrick, D.
Nash, W.
Newton, C. A.
Nimmo, P. E.
Norvell, C. R.
Petty, J. C.
Peet, J. D.
*Porter, Robt. T.
Reid, John S.
*Reynolds, Robt. E.
*Roberts, John B.
Rogers, John C.
Rogers, W. H. R.
Rogers, T. F.

Rogers, C. S.
Saunders, S. S.
Sebrell, N. C. H.
Smiley, C. D.
Sterrett, J. S.
Segar, T. F.
Smith, E. C.
*Smith, Jas. W.
Smythe, Wm.
Stewer, Edwin.
Swank, W. A.
Smith, C. A. Jr.
Smith, J. E.
Simmons, J.
*Thompson, E. Jr.
Taylor, W. J.
Taylor, J. Theodore.
Thomas, J. D.
Vaughan, E. S.
Veale, Samuel.
Walters, John.
Watters, A. M.
West, Wm. M.
Whiting, T. B.
Whiting, J. R.
Wilkins, C. L.
Wilkins, John F.
Wilkinson, James.
*Wingfield, R. C. M.
Whitehurst, L. H.
Whitehurst, S. T.
Woodhouse, P. D.
Worrell, J. R.
Wright, W. S.
Wilkins, W. A.
Ward, J. T.
Wilson, D. C. B.
Woodhouse, John
Woodward, W. W.
*White, N. E.
Wilkins, G. W.
White, C. E.
*Williamson, C. H.
Whitmore, C.
Zills, J. A.
Zills, A. C.

CASUALTIES—KILLED AND DIED.

Booth, Wm., killed 1865, Petersburg lines.
Butler, R. M., killed July 30th, 1864, Crater.
Dunn, J. R., died in hospital September 4th, 1863, Petersburg.
Gaskins, G. O., died in hospital, 1864, Petersburg.
Hatton, J. F., died in hospital, 1863, Petersburg.
Higgins, L., killed June, 1864, Turkey Ridge.
Land, W. C., killed May 1st, 1863, Chancellorsville.
McCarrick, D., died in hospital, 1864, Petersburg.
Nimmo, W. T., died in hospital September 21, 1861, Norfolk.
Reynolds, R. E., captured July 14th, 1863, Maryland, died at Point Lookout.
Rogers, W. H. R., died in hospital September 24th, 1862, Richmond.
Sterrett, J. S., died in hospital, 1862, Petersburg.
Taylor, J. Theodore, killed Plank Road, 1865, Petersburg.
Watters, A. M., killed Plank Road, 1865, Petersburg.
Wilkins, W. A., died in hospital, 1862, Petersburg.
Wright, Minton A., appointed Lieutenant 57th North Carolina Regiment and killed in battle.
Killed and died—16.

CASUALTIES—WOUNDED.

Broughton, Robert S., April 1st, 1865, Petersburg lines.
Cooke, M. T., on the lines near Petersburg.
Cutherell, Wm. S., Chancellorsville May 1st, 1863.
Drummond, R. J., Chancellorsville May 1st, 1863.
Day, John H., Chancellorsville May 1st, 1863, and Petersburg July 30th, 1864.
Floyd, John W., Chancellorsville May 1st, 1863, lost an arm.
Gilmer, James W. (Lieutenant), on the lines near Petersburg.
Gamage, John O., July 30th, 1865, at the Crater.
Johnson, John, April 1st, 1865, Petersburg.
Johnson, Augustus W., April 1st, 1865, Petersburg.
Keeling, M. C., May 1st, 1863, Chancellorsville, sent to Richmond wounded, captured by Stoneman's Raiders, paroled, and wounded July 30th, 1864, Crater.
Lee, F. D., Petersburg lines, 1864, wounded, again 1865, and disabled.
Lovitt, H. C., Petersburg lines, 1865.
McKown, C. K., May 1st, 1863, Chancellorsville.
Montague, W. D., May 1st, 1863, Chancellorsville.
Moore, Joseph P., July 30th, 1864, at the Crater.
Newton, C. E., Plank Road near Petersburg, 1864, lost a leg.
Peet, W. T. (Lieutenant), May 1st, 1863, Chancellorsville, and April 1st, 1st, 1865, Petersburg.
Rogers, T. F., May 12th, 1864, Spotsylvania C. H.
Reid, J. S., Petersburg lines, 1864.
Taylor, Wm. E., 1864, near Fredericksburg, on R., F. & P. R. R.
Taylor, Wm. J., near the Plank Road, Petersburg, 1864, lost a foot.
Wilkins, T. J., May 1st, 1863, at Chancellorsville.
Watters, J. H., May 1st, 1863, at Chancellorsville.
Walters, John, April 1st, 1865, Petersburg.
Worrell, J. R., May 1st, 1863, Chancellorsville.
Wilson, D. C. B., 1865, Petersburg lines.

The following names of members of the Blues were on the official muster roll as having been paroled at Appomattox:

Sergeant W. T. Clarke,
Sergeant W. H. Doyle,
Ordnance Sergt. Jno. J. Morris,
Hospital Steward Jesse J. Morris.
Q. M. Sergeant J. C. Petty,

Private C. H. Busky, special
   duty,
Private W. W. Collins, special
   duty,
Private Norman Bell, special
   duty,
Private W. Fitzgerald,
Private Ed. Fitzgeraid,
Private M. Gordon,

Private John Hodges,
Private J. H. Nash, special duty,
Private Robert Porter,
Private C. D. Smiley,
Private John B. Roberts,
Private W. W. Woodward,
Private N. E. White,
Private R. Whiting,
Private John Walters,

      Private R. C. M. Wingfield.

CHAPTER XXXII.

THE NORFOLK LIGHT ARTILLERY—THE HUGER BATTERY.

In May, 1861, there were on the rolls of the Norfolk Light Artillery Blues more members than were permitted to one company and on the 21st, by mutual consent, the company was divided and a portion, splitting off from the others, organized a new company under the name of the Norfolk Light Artillery, and requested Frank Huger, Esq., son of General Benj. Huger, then commanding the department of Norfolk, to become its captain. The invitation was accepted and the company was mustered into service about the 8th of June under the following officers:

Captain, Frank Huger.
First Lieutenant, Thos. Nash, Jr.; 2d Lieutenant, Joseph D. Moore; 3d Lieutenant, Wm. J. Parrish.
First Sergeant, W. J. Butt; 2d Sergeant, Jas. D. Gale; 3d Sergeant, Wm. K. Ferguson; 4th Sergeant, W. H. Caldwell.
First Corporal, John W. Stephens; 2d Corporal, Benj. F. Balsom; 4th Corporal, Richard D. Christian.

The company was given the guns belonging to the Blues, consisting of two brass six-pounder howitzers, one rifle gun and one boat howitzer. Later in the war it was armed with two rifle guns and two Napoleans.

Upon being mustered into service the company was sent into camp in the entrenchments back of Norfolk and placed in a battalion with Moorman's Battery, of Lynchburg, and Nicholson's Battery, of Petersburg, and remained there until the evacuation of Norfolk in May, 1862, when it was ordered to Petersburg and thence to the army in front of Richmond.

At the reorganization of the company in May, 1862, Captain Huger and Second Lieutenant Moore were re-elected, but Lieutenants Nash and Parrish were dropped. Lieutenant Nash received an appointment as Lieutenant in the Provisional army and was assigned to duty at various posts. For a long time he was on duty in the Provost Marshal's office in Staunton, and Lieutenant Parrish obtained a position in the navy. Private J. L. Tilghman was elected 1st Lieutenant and Sergeant Jas. D. Gale, 3d Lieutenant. Lieutenant Tilghman died in hospital in Richmond in October, 1862. This caused the promotion of Lieutenants Moore and Gale, and Sergeant F. M. Peed was elected 3d Lieutenant. In 1863 Captain Huger was promoted to Major of Artillery, Lieutenant Moore became Captain, Lieutenants Gale and Peed were advanced to 1st and 2d Lieutenants respectively, and 1st Sergeant Wm. J. Butt was elected 3d Lieutenant, and John W.

Stephens was promoted to 1st Sergeant. Sergeant Stephens became disabled in 1863, from the loss of a leg and John W. Ash, who was transferred to the company from Grimes' Battery, of Portsmouth, became 1st Sergeant. There were no other changes among the officers during the war.

In October, 1862, Grimes' Battery, of Portsmouth, was disbanded and about eighty men of that company were transferred to the Huger Battery. The names of these men do not appear on the roll which follows, for the reason that they already appear on the roll of their original company.

The Huger Battery was slightly engaged in the battle of Seven Pines, but suffered no loss, and during the Seven Days' battles had an artillery duel with a Federal battery at the battle of Oak Grove on the 25th of June, in which Captain Huger reported no casualties, except the loss of one horse, which was killed. The Federal battery was forced to retire. On the 28th of August the battery engaged a Federal battery at Warrenton Springs, and had one man wounded. It was present at Second Manassas, August 30th, 1862, but was again fortunate in not meeting with any losses. At Sharpsburg, September 17th, the battery was under command of Lieutenant Gale, and was quite heavily engaged. Here it lost one man killed and two wounded. Its next engagement was at Fredericksburg, December 13th, 1862, when it occupied a position with Anderson's Division on the left of the Confederate line of battle, but suffered no loss. It was again fortunate at Chancellorsville. It was posted with Wilcox's Brigade at Banks' Ford, and thus escaped the heavy fighting around Chancellorsville on the 1st, 2d and 3d of May. On the 3d the battery was moved from Banks' Ford to the breastworks on Taylor's Hill, opposite Falmouth,and with two rifled guns opened on the enemy's batteries across the river, and also upon a force of infantry, which was in sight, then, upon Sedgwick's advance from Fredericksburg, the battery fell back, following Wilcox's Brigade in the direction of the Plank Road. The battery retired beyond the brick church (Salem Church), when, meeting Mahone's brigade, it returned with that command to the church, but, not finding an eligible position, General Wilcox ordered it to retire down the road. In this affair only one man was hurt. Private David Boyce, who was assigned to the company from Grimes' Battery, was slightly wounded in the shoulder.

The battery was with the army in its advance into Pennsylvania, and at the battle of Gettysburg had one man wounded, and one wounded in a cavalry attack while falling back from Gettysburg. During this campaign Lieutenant Gale had command of Penick's Battery from Halifax county.

After the Gettysburg campaign the company enjoyed a season of rest until the beginning of Grant's overland campaign in May,

1864, when it was engaged almost constantly from the battle of the Wilderness until the enemy settled around Petersburg. Here, too, there was a constant round of firing, and the company did duty at various positions between the Jerusalem Plank Road and Rieves' Salient, and here it suffered its heaviest losses. When Grant broke through the Confederate lines at Petersburg on the 1st of April, 1865, the Huger Battery was in position on Hatcher's Run, and the whole company was surrounded and captured. It held its ground until further fighting became both useless and impossible, and then, yielding to the inevitable, became prisoners of war. First Sergeant John W. Ash managed to escape capture at Hatcher's Run and surrendered with the remnant of the army at Appomattox with Private Nathaniel G. Reid, the sole representatives of the battery. The company had three men killed at Hatcher's Run when the lines were broken, namely, Richard Boutwell and Edward Beaton, who were assigned to it from Grimes' Battery, and James O. Whitehurst, one of its original members.

The following is the roll of the company after the reorganization in May, 1862, and embraces only the original members. The men who were transferred to it from Grimes' Battery are not on it, as has been previously stated:

Captain, Frank Huger, promoted to Lieutenant-Colonel of Artillery.
First Lieutenant, John L. Tilghman, died in hospital October, 1862.
Second Lieutenant, Joseph D. Moore, promoted to Captain.
Third Lieutenant, James D. Gale, promoted 1st Lieutenant.
First Sergeant, W. J. Butt, promoted 3d Lieutenant.
Second Sergeant, Fred. L. Bedout, in charge of stables.
Third Sergeant, Fred. M. Peed, promoted 2d Lieutenant.
Fourth Sergeant, Benj. F. Balsom, appointed Commissary Sergeant.
First Corporal, Chas. Rogers.
Second Corporal, Jos. A. Jordan.
Third Corporal, John W. Stephens, promoted 1st Sergeant, wounded Sept. 17th, 1862, at Sharpsburg, disabled in 1863, and discharged.
Fourth Corporal, Carlton C. Lattimer, lost an eye at Spotsylvania Court House.

PRIVATES.

Abdell, James.
Addison, James, wounded near Gettysburg, July 6th, 1863.
Anderson, Chas. W., wounded September 17th, 1862, at Sharpsburg.
Barnes, Jno. C., died in hospital, Richmond.
Barnes, Samuel A.
Billups, Andrew J., killed by sharpshooters, 1864, Petersburg lines.
Bobce, Louis, in charge of Ambulance Corps.
Boole, John J.
Burford, Martin.
Boutwell, L. W.
Butt, Geo. W.
Butt, C. N: G., detailed clerk in Treasury Department.
Brown, Richard.
Browning, Henry C.
Carter, Richard W., assistant to Commissary Sergeant.
Conner, Christopher O., wounded on Petersburg lines.
Curran, Albert G.

Currier, Robt. A., died in hospital, 1863, Charlottesville.
Davis, Alex.
Douglas, Thos. H.
Edwards, John A.
Ewell, Jesse.
Ferguson, Wm. K.
Ferguson, Geo. S., transferred to cavalry.
Ferrat, John B., detailed in hospital, 1863, Richmond.
Forden, Wm. B.
Forrest, Wm. S., Jr.
Fugitt, Wm.
Gale, Jos. A., detailed December, 1862, Hospital Steward.
George, Jos. D.
Gale, A. C.
Gibbs, Wm.
Guyot, Thos., died in prison, 1865, Point Lookout.
Gormley, J. J., detailed 1862 in hospital, Charlottesville.
Hall, John P., wounded July 3d, 1863, at Gettysburg.
Hammett, Israel J., killed by sharpshooters on Petersburg lines.
Herbert, Henry W.
James, Robert T.
Lipscomb, Chas. R.
Legett, Robert.
Merwin, W. F.
Mitchell, T. G.
Moreland, Richard R.
Morris, G. W., died in hospital June 7th, 1862, Petersburg.
Morris, Joseph.
O'Niel, Chas.
Parrott, Augustus.
Peed, Geo. W., killed at Spotsylvania Court House.
Phillips, Thos. B., wounded at Spotsylvania Court House and died in hospital, Charlottesville.
Ransome, Alex.
Reed, Nathaniel G.
Robbins, Jas. W.
Robinson, Edward C., absent sick.
Rose, Louis.
Rye, Richard, wounded on Hatcher's Run, lost an eye.
Smiley, Walter F.
Smiley, Thomas S.
Stephens, Richard H. Jr.
Summers, Wm. R.
Sullivan, John T., transferred to company from a Georgia Regiment and killed September 17th, 1862, at Sharpsburg.
Taylor, John.
White, Wm. O., wounded on Hatcher's Run, 1865.
Whitehurst, Jas. O., killed on Hatcher's Run, April 1st, 1865.
Whitfield, Richard W.
Wickers, John.
Wright, Junius.
   Killed and died—11.

CHAPTER XXXIII.

COMPANY A, SIXTH VIRGINIA REGIMENT.

This company was organized in Norfolk immediately upon the beginning of hostilities, and numbered in its ranks a few Norfolk county men from the Tanner's Creek section. It was mustered into service on the 22d of April, 1861, under the following officers:

Captain—Wm. N. McKenney.

First Lieutenant, Robert B. Taylor; 2d Lieutenant, Chas. W. Perkinson; 3d Lieutenant, Chas. W. Wilson.

First Sergeant, Thos. D. Wallace; 2d Sergeant, Wm. E. Brotherton; 3d Sergeant, John Lee Hopper; 4th Sergeant, Arthur Jakeman.

First Corporal, Wm. T. Bailey; 2d Corporal, Wm. H. Hall; 3d Corporal, John Forsythe; 4th Corporal, Thomas Stringer.

On the 22d of August, 1861, Lieutenant Robert B. Taylor was elected Captain of the Woodis Rifles, Company H, 6th Virginia Regiment, and resigned his commission in Company A. First Sergeant Thomas D. Wallace was elected 3d Lieutenant October 3d, 1861. The other Lieutenants, Perkinson and Wilson, were each promoted one grade. The company was assigned to the 6th Virginia Regiment, Colonel Wm. Mahone commanding, as Company A, and ordered to report at what was afterwards known as the Entrenched Camp.

In April, 1862, the company re-enlisted and re-elected officers, with the following result:

Captain—Charles W. Perkinson.

First Lieutenant, Charles W. Wilson; 2d Lieutenant, George H. Steward; 3d Lieutenant, John Lee Hopper.

Lieutenant Steward was killed July 1st, 1862, at Malvern Hill and Captain Perkinson resigned on the 17th of November, 1862. First Lieutenant Wilson was promoted to Captain on the 18th and continued in command until the battle of Turkey Ridge, on the 8th of June, 1864, when he fell into the hands of the enemy. Lieutenant Hopper became 1st Lieutenant and was wounded at the battle of the Crater, July 30th, 1864. Sergeant Arthur Jakeman was promoted to 2d Lieutenant. In 1863 Captain Wilson was assigned to the command of the company of sharpshooters belonging to the 6th Regiment, and was on that duty when he was captured. Just before the evacuation of Norfolk this company was joined by a number of recruits from the counties of Patrick, Franklin and Henry, who were in the camp of instruction near Norfolk. Their names are designated by an * in the following roll. This roll embraces all of those members of the company who marched away with it at the evacuation of Norfolk by the Confederates, or who died or were honorably discharged before that date:

Captain, Wm. N. McKenney, not re-elected, discharged May 1st, 1862.
First Lieutenant, Robert B. Taylor, promoted Captain Company H, 6th Va. Regiment, 1861.
Second Lieutenant, Chas. W. Perkinson, elected Captain May 1st, 1862, resigned Nov. 17th.
Third Lieutenant, Chas. W. Wilson, elected 1st Lieutenant May 1st, 1862, promoted Captain Nov. 18th, 1862, captured June 8th, 1864, at Turkey Ridge.
First Sergeant, Thos. D. Wallace, promoted Lieutenant, not re-elected, discharged May 1st, 1862.
Second Sergeant, Wm. E. Brotherton, discharged Nov. 29th, 1861, for disability.
Third Sergeant, John Lee Hopper, promoted 1st Lieutenant, wounded July 30th, 1864, at the Crater.
Fourth Sergeant, Arther Jakeman, promoted 2d Lieutenant.
First Corporal, Wm. T. Bailey, promoted Sergeant.
Second Corporal, Wm. H. Hall, promoted Sergeant, wounded June 22d, 1864, at Wilcox's Farm.
Third Corporal, John Forsyth, promoted Color Sergeant, wounded July 1st, 1862, at Malvern Hill, transferred to Navy Nov. 11th, 1862.
Fourth Corporal, Thos. D. Stringer, committed suicide Oct. 18th, 1861, in Norfolk.
Musician, Geo. D. Cain, discharged January 17th, 1863, under conscript act.

PRIVATES.

Anderson, John R.
Anderson, Edward P., captured October 27th, 1864, at Burgess' Mill.
*Ackers, Wm. N.
*Arthur, Wm. G.
*Angel, Marshall J., wounded August 30th, 1862, Second Manassas.
*Altice, Samuel H., captured September 14th, 1862, Crampton Gap, and not heard from.
Buchanan, James, wounded, lost arm, June 21st, 1862, Charles City Road.
Baker, Isaiah G., captured May 22d, 1864.
*Byrd, Benj. E., died in hospital, Lexington, March 10th, 1863.
Banks, Wm. T., promoted Sergeant, wounded July 3d, 1863, at Gettysburg, killed July 30th, 1864, at Crater.
*Boone, Daniel, sick in hospital after August, 1862.
Beasley, James W., wounded May 3d, 1863, Chancellorsville, and June 22d, 1864, at Wilcox's Farm.
Bowman, Abraham.
*Boone, Jacob R., captured September 14th, 1862, and never rejoined the company.
Butt, John J., detailed hospital cook August 10th, 1861.
Bell, Jos. S., discharged Nov. 29th, 1861, disability.
Collin, Thos. W., appointed Hospital Steward Sept. 8th, 1861.
Cooper, Flemming, died in hospital, 1862.
Cooke, Ezekiel, captured Sept. 14th, 1862, at Crampton Gap, exchanged and captured Oct. 27th, 1864, at Burgess' Mill.
Coston, James, promoted Corporal, lost arm August 30th, 1862, Second Manassas.
Carter, Henry C., wounded June 22d, 1864, Wilcox's Farm, lost leg.
*Coleman, Skelton.
*Dyer, Stokeley, promoted Corporal April 27th, 1863.
Deal, Willis, discharged August 1st, 1862, over age.

COMPANY A, SIXTH VIRGINIA REGIMENT. 261

*Easter, George W.
*Easter, Edward W.
Flora, Joel, furnished substitute and discharged June 24th, 1862, and substitute deserted June 26th.
*Frith, Thomas D.
Field, Robert, died in hospital from wounds received June 21st, 1862.
*Guerrant, Stephen, furnished substitute.
Gregory, Quinton T., wounded and captured July 3d, 1863, at Gettysburg.
Gregory, John W., left behind in Norfolk, sick.
Hudgins, George McK., promoted Sergeant, killed July 30th, 1864, at Crater.
Hozier, Wm. J., discharged October 15th, 1861, disability.
Hudson, Philip, killed July 1st, 1862, Malvern Hill.
Hill, Severn J., discharged 1862, over age.
Hodges, Solomon, wounded July 1st, 1862, Malvern Hill.
*Haile, Creed, captured September 14th, 1862, at Crampton Gap and October 27th, 1864, at Burgess' Mill.
*Howell, Elkanah, wounded August 29th, 1862, at Thoroughfare Gap.
*Howell, Addison M., wounded August 29th, 1862, captured October 27th, 1864, at Burgess' Mill.
*Ingram, Isaac, detailed as teamster, 1862.
Jones, Robert C., died in hospital, 1862.
Judkins, Samuel, wounded July 1st, 1862, at Malvern Hill.
*Jones, Robert P.
*Jones, Aaron F., killed July 30th, 1864, Crater.
Karn, Joseph H.
Lee, Ivy, wounded May 6th, 1864, at Wilderness.
Lovitt, David, discharged February 6th, 1863, disability.
*Marsh, Smith, killed August 30th, 1862, at Second Manassas.
Moore, Henry L.
*Mason, Wm.
*Moore, Owen L.
Messick, Wm. J., wounded June 21st, 1862, and transferred to navy 1863.
Nottingham, Thomas J., detailed in Commissary Department on account of ill health.
Pitts, Marcellus, died in hospital from wounds received June 21st, 1862.
Steward, George H., promoted Lieutenant, killed July 1st, 1862, at Malvern Hill.
Stott, Samuel, discharged 1862, under conscript act and subsequently re-enlisted.
Sheppard, James, H., discharged 1862, being an alien.
*Shiveley, Jehu, wounded May 25th, 1864, on picket line.
Tulane, Alonzo J., killed September 14th, 1862, Crampton Gap.
Whitehurst, Wm. H., promoted 1st Sergeant, wounded September 14th, 1862, at Crampton Gap, and October 27th, 1864, at Burgess' Mill, and July 30th, 1864, at the Crater.
Wilkins, Wm. P., captured February 6th, 1865, at Hatcher's Run.
Warren, John M., captured April 29th, 1863, at Germanna Ford.
Williams, Newton J., discharged November 29th, 1862, disability.
  Killed and died—13.

CHAPTER XXXIV.

THE WOODIS RIFLEMEN, COMPANY C, SIXTH VIRGINIA REGIMENT.

This company was one of Norfolk's crack organizations at the beginning of the late war. It was organized on the 3d of March, 1858, at a meeting held for that purpose, and thirty-four names were enrolled. The meeting was presided over by Wm. C. Tarrant, Esq., and Thos. W. Colly acted secretary. It was held in the carpenter shop of Mr. Wm. F. Pumphrey, and a committee of five was appointed to select a name. The committee reported at an adjourned meeting, held on the 5th, and recommended that the company be named "the Woodis Riflemen," after Mayor Hunter Woodis, who died during the prevalence of the yellow fever in Norfolk in 1855. The name was unanimously adopted. On the 18th of March the company elected the following officers:
Captain, Wm. Lamb.
First Lieutenant, John Hayman; 2d Lieutenant, Peter Dilworth; 3d Lieutenant, A. A. Gwaltney.

On account of some informality in the election, as not conforming strictly to the law, these were re-elected on the 15th of April, and again on the 20th of May, before thay could obtain their commissions and the company its arms.

The uniform adopted by the company consisted of a dark green cloth single breasted frock coat, with black velvet trimmings, three rows of gold ball buttons on the coat and black velvet breast front. Dark green pantaloons and black velvet stripe, the whole trimmed with gold cord, and with a shamrock, in gold, at each end of the collar.

On the 11th of May the following non-commissioned officers were elected:
Sergeants—D. C. Waters, John W. Elliott, W. F. Pumphrey, J. M. S. Wiatt, Wm. C. Wickings.
Corporals—Chas. S. Dashiel, Geo. W. Peed, S. W. Spratt, Thos. J. Henderson, John W. White, Wm. R. James.

On the 5th of July, the 4th being Sunday, the company borrowed a flag from the Juniors and muskets from the Blues, and made its first parade, turning out with 59 men. A handsome flag was presented to the company in the Odd Fellows building, on the 19th of August. On one side was a bust of ex-Mayor Hunter Woodis and on the other the coat of arms of Virginia and the inscription "*Pace Cives, Bello Milites,*" which, being interpreted, meant, "In peace, citizens; in war, soldiers."

On the 22d of February, 1859, the company made its first anniversary parade, with sixty-seven men in line. The following winter it went to Harper's Ferry, on the occasion of the John Brown war, and remained in Charlestown until the last of the gang was hung. Its first duty in connection with the war between the North and South was on the 7th of March, 1861, when it did guard duty all night in the city of Norfolk. It was again ordered out on the 18th of April, and remained in service from that time continuously until the close of the war. On the night of the 19th of April, it was present at the removal of the powder from Fort Norfolk, and after that was accomplished was marched to the old Custom House at the foot of Church street. On the 21st the company was sent to Ocean View and a detachment of it, under command of Captain Lamb, participated in the defence of Seawell's Point battery against the attacks of the Monticello on the 19th and 21st of May. Upon the formation of the 6th Virginia Regiment, Colonel Wm. Mahone was assigned to it as commander, and the Woodis Riflemen were attached to it as Company C. Captain Lamb resigned the captaincy of the company in August, and on the 22d of the same month Lieutenant Robert B. Taylor, of Company A, was elected to succeed him. The officers of the company, when it was mustered into service on the 19th of April, 1861, were:

Captain, Wm. Lamb.

First Lieutenant, John Hayman; 2d Lieutenant, Wm. Sherwood; 3d Lieutenant, Ahmaine A. Gwaltney.

First Sergeant, David C. Watters; 2d Sergeant, James M. F. Wiatt; 3d Sergeant, Alex. J. Denson; 4th Sergeant, Thos. J. Henderson.

Lieutenant Sherwood was appointed commissary of the regiment, and, in May, 1862, at the reorganization of the field officers of the 6th Regiment, Captain Taylor was elected major, and at a meeting of the Woodis Riflemen, held during that month for the purpose of reorganization and re-enlistment, 1st Lieutenant John Hayman was elected Captain, David C. Waters 1st Lieutenant, Alexander J. Denson 2d and James W. Dashiel 3d. Thos. J. Henderson was elected 1st Sergeant. Lieutenant Waters was killed in the battle of Malvern Hill, July 1st, 1862. Captain Hayman resigned on the 11th of March, 1863, and Lieutenants Denson and Dashiel resigned on the 17th, thus leaving the company without commissioned officers. On the 4th of April, 1863, 2d Lieutenant George F. Crawley, of Company D, was elected Captain, 3d Sergeant Stewart Spratt was elected 1st Lieutenant, and on the 9th, Private Thomas W. Phillips was elected 2d Lieutenant.

Lieutenant Spratt was killed at the battle of the Crater, July 30th, 1864, and 1st Sergeant Henderson was severely wounded there. Sergeant James M. F. Wiatt was elected 3d Lieutenant in Company D. Captain Crawley lived through the war and escaped without a wound. He was captured at Chancellorsville and exchanged. At the breaking out of the war the Woodis Riflemen had a very fine drum corps attached to the company, which was subsequently transferred to the regiment. The men composing it were John B. Bohlein, John Flalack, John Foelman, Henry Haggedhorn, Henry Hastings, Robert Lilliston, Anson Palmer, Geo. W. Skinner and Edward Wiersdorf.

After his resignation in March, 1863, Lieutenant Denson enlisted in the Norfolk Light Artillery Blues as a private.

Below will be found the names of the members of the company who served with it after the evacuation of Norfolk by the Confederates:

Captain Wm. Lamb, promoted to Colonel 36th North Carolina Regiment August, 1861.
Captain Robert B. Taylor, elected Captain August 18th, 1861, promoted Major 6th Virginia Regiment, April, 1862.
Captain John Hayman, elected May 3d, 1862, resigned March 11th, 1863, on account of defective eyesight.
Captain George F. Crawley, promoted April 4th, 1863, from 2d Lieutenant Company D.
First Lieutenant David C. Waters, elected May 3d, 1862, killed July 1st, 1862, Malvern Hill.
Second Lieutenant Alex. J. Denson, promoted 1st Lieutenant July 1st, 1862, resigned March 17th, 1863.
Third Lieutenant James W. Dashiell, promoted 2d Lieutenant July 1st, 1862, resigned March 17th, 1863.
First Sergeant Thomas J. Henderson, wounded July 30th, 1864, Crater.
Second Sergeant James M. F. Wiatt, elected Lieutenant in Company D.
Third Sergeant Stewart M. Spratt, promoted 1st Lieutenant April 1st, 1863, killed July 30th, 1864, Crater.
Third Sergeant Samuel Crane, wounded May 2d, 1863, at Chancellorsville, and May 6th, 1864, at the Wilderness.
Fourth Sergeant Timothy D. Padgett, captured July 30th, 1864, at Crater.
Fifth Sergeant Henry A. Tarrall, promoted Commissary Sergeant, captured on retreat from Petersburg, 1865.
First Corporal Alex. Mason, captured on retreat from Petersburg, 1865.
Second Corporal Wm. H. Frost, captured October 27th, 1864, at Burgess' Mill.
Third Corporal John J. Williams, promoted Sergeant, killed May 6th, 1864, at Wilderness.
Fourth Corporal Arthur J. Balsom.

PRIVATES.

Angel, John R., discharged on account of disability.
Ashbury, John, wounded May 2d, 1863, at Chancellorsville.
Bell, Washington.
Bateman, Arthur, captured July 2d, 1863, at Gettysburg.
Brown, Edward.
Buchanan, Robert, wounded July 30th, 1864, at the Crater.
Balsom, Arthur J., captured July 2d, 1863, at Gettysburg.
Bland, Samuel.
Bourk, John, wounded July 1st, 1862, at Malvern Hill.
Belote, John W.
Clarke, John J., promoted Corporal, captured May 12th, 1861, at Spotsylvania C. H.
Corprew, Samuel S., died in hospital July 27th, 1862.
Coleman, John M.

Doyle, Nathan C., captured July 2d, 1863, at Gettysburg.
Edmonds, John T., captured October 27th, 1864, at Burgess' Mill.
Fredericks, Lewis, wounded and captured August 19th, 1864, at Davis' Farm.
Face, James P., discharged July 28th, 1862, over age.
Flannagan, John T., wounded Sept. 17th, 1862, at Sharpsburg, and June 22d, 1864, at Wilcox Farm.
Fentress, Hillary, wounded August 30th, 1862, Second Manassas, lost a leg.
Gauley, John R.
Garrett, Edward, captured October 27th, 1864, at Burgess' Mill.
Gale, Peter M., detailed as brigade butcher.
Hopkins, John, discharged July 28th, 1862, over age.
Ishon, George, captured July 2d, 1863, at Gettysburg.
Joyce, John M.
Land, Thomas F., captured April, 1865, on retreat from Petersburg.
Nellums, Wm.
Owens, Ammon H., killed May 2d, 1863, at Chancellorsville.
Peters, John, died in hospital October 22d, 1862.
Powell, Henry.
Peed, John W., discharged December 3d, 1862, disability.
Phillips, Thomas W., elected 2d Lieutenant April 9th, 1863, promoted to 1st Lieutenant October 20th, 1864, captured October 27th, 1864, at Burgess' Mill.
Pitt, Wm. J., killed May 2d, 1863, at Chancellorsville.
Pumphrey, Lemuel, promoted Corporal July 1st, 1863.
Ramsay, T., died in hospital, 1863.
Roberts, John R., captured July 2d, 1863, at Gettysburg.
Shipp, Wm. T.
Small, Caleb, killed June 21st, 1862, Charles City Road.
Shedd, Joseph, wounded May 6th, 1864, at Wilderness.
Sigman, John, Sr., conscript from Franklin county, wounded May 6th, 1864, at Wilderness, and died June 24th.
Sigman, John, Jr., captured May 12th, 1864, at Spotsylvania.
Sigman, Peter, wounded May 6th, 1864, at Wilderness, wounded and captured April 7th, 1865, on retreat from Petersburg.
Sigman, Joseph M., wounded June 25th, 1864, Petersburg.
Stanley, Robert J., captured June 6th, 1864, Cold Harbor.
Sheppard, John H.
Taylor, Richard, captured October 27th, 1864, Burgess' Mill.
Tarrant, Eleazer, wounded July 1st, 1862, at Malvern Hill.
Talbot, John B., wounded May 6th, 1864, at Wilderness, and died May 15th.
Turner, George W.
Wright, Joseph, Sr., discharged July 28th, 1862, over age.
Wright, Joseph A., wounded July 30th, 1864, at Crater.
Woodhouse, John J., promoted Corporal, died in hospital May 28th, 1863.
Wynn, Benjamin F., wounded August 30th, 1862, at Second Manassas, July 2d, 1863, at Gettysburg, and October 27th, 1864, at Burgess' Mill.
White, Thomas R., killed May 1st, 1863, at Chancellorsville.
Walters, Alfred, wounded August 30th, 1862, at Second Manassas.
Wray, John W., detailed as wagon driver June 24th, 1862.
Wallace, Wm., transferred to Maryland line July 12th, 1862.
Webster, W. D., died in hospital, 1862.
Young, Martial, died in hospital, 1862.
Young, J. B., died in hospital, 1862.

    Killed and died—16.

CHAPTER XXXV.

THE NORFOLK LIGHT INFANTRY, COMPANY D, SIXTH VA. REGIMENT.

This company was raised in Norfolk immediately upon the beginning of trouble between the sections, and was mustered into service before it was uniformed. The officers of the company at its organization and who were mustered in with it, were:
Captain, John R. Ludlow.
First Lieutenant, Montford N. Stokes; 2d Lieutenant, James Malbon; 3d Lieutenant, Geo. F. Crawley.
First Sergeant, Robert J. Carty; 3d Sergeant, Geo. F. Clarke; 4th Sergeant, Wm. F. Carty.

The company was attached to the 6th Virginia Regiment as Company D, and, uniting with the regiment at once, lost its identity as a separate organization. During the first year of the war the following members were honorably discharged for various reasons, which, however, were not specified in the muster rolls:

Davis Ballentine, Edwin Craig, Geo. F. Clark, Dennis Harding, Wm. Harrison, Henry Messfield, Geo. Sturgeon, Franklin A. Sibley, Geo. Walther, Wm. Young.

At the reorganization of the company, Captain John R. Ludlow was re-elected captain, 1st Sergeant Robt. J. Carty was re-elected, and Lieutenants Stokes and Crawley were elected 1st and 2d Lieutenants respectively, and James M. F. Wiatt 3d Lieutenant. Sergeant Carty was killed at the battle of Sharpsburg September 17th, 1862, and Robert Banks became 1st Sergeant of the company, and Wm. F. Carty was advanced to 2d Sergeant.

On the 4th of April, 1863, Lieutenant Crawley was elected Captain of Company C, 6th Virginia Regiment, and resigned his commission in Company D. Lieutenant Wiatt resigned on the 14th of May, 1863, and Lieutenant Stokes was mortally wounded at the battle of Bristoe Station October 14th, 1863, and died on the 14th of November. Corporal C. C. Benson was elected 2d Lieutenant April 7th, 1863, and Private E. H. Flournoy was elected 1st Lieutenant on the 17th of May, 1864. Captain Ludlow's health broke down during the war, and upon the recommendation of the regimental surgeon, he was detailed by special order, on account of disability, December 30th, 1862, and assigned to duty enrolling conscripts. He rejoined the company in 1863. The relative mortality of the company was, with one exception, greater than that of any other Norfolk company, for of the seventy-six men who left the city with it on the 10th of May, 1862, twenty-three were killed or died from disease contracted in the service.

Among the list of those who died or were wounded are three

men who joined Company D, from Captain John H. Myers' Company, of Portsmouth, (formerly Company E, 6th Regiment) when that company was disbanded on the 1st September, 1861. They are John Ballance, died in hospital September 1st, 1862; Jos. P. Jordan, died April 20th, 1863, and John Frestine, wounded August 30th, 1862, and June 1st, 1864. Wm. White and John W. Elliott, also joined Company D, from Captain Myers' Company.

The following is the roster of the company as per muster roll of May and June, 1862:

Captain, John R. Ludlow.
First Lieutenant, Montford N. Stokes, wounded Oct. 14th, 1863, at Bristoe Station, and died Nov. 14th.
Second Lieutenant, Geo. F. Crawley, promoted Captain Company C, April 4th, 1863.
Third Lieutenant, Jas. M. F. Wiatt, resigned May 14th, 1863.
First Sergeant, Robert J. Carty, killed September 17th, 1862, at Sharpsburg.
First Sergeant, Robt. Banks, wounded August 30th, 1862, 2d Manassas, and July 30th, 1864, at Crater.
Second Sergeant, Wm. F. Carty, wounded August 30th, 1862, 2d Manassas, and disabled.
Third Sergeant, Wm. White, transferred to navy January 22d, 1864.
Fourth Sergeant, Wm. Moore.
Fifth Sergeant, Wilson Coates, wounded July 30th, 1864, at Crater, and died August 6th.
First Corporal, James E. Brady, captured October 27th, 1864, at Burgess' Mill.
Second Corporal, Chris. C. Benson, promoted 2d Lieutenant April 7th, 1863, captured Oct. 27th, 1864.
Third Corporal, Wm. Stine.
Fourth Corporal, Stephen Blunt, wounded June 21st, 1862, on Charles City Road, and died July 3d.
Musician, Thos. Lowery.

PRIVATES.

Abdell, Thos. F.
Austin, Martin.
Absolem, Thos., died in hospital, April, 1863.
Adams, Thos. S.
Bradley, Edward H.
Ballentine, Thos., wounded May 3d, 1863.
Balance, John, died in hospital, September 1st, 1862, at Salem.
Burgess, Miles, died in hospital, Aug. 28th, 1863, Staunton.
Corprew, Geo., killed Aug. 30th, 1862, 2d Manassas.
Clarke, Wm. H.
Donald, Caleb J., died in hospital, Sept. 27th, 1862.
Dixon, Geo. W., wounded July 30th, 1864, at Crater.
Evans, Peter, wounded July 1st, 1862, at Malvern Hill.
Etheredge, Geo. W., wounded May 6th, 1864, at Wilderness.
Elliott, John W., captured July 5th, 1863, in Pennsylvania.
Frestine, John W., wounded Aug. 30th, 1862, at 2d Manassas, and June, 1864, at Hanover Junction.
Fulcher, Gabriel F., died in hospital, Oct., 1864, Richmond.
Fisher, Jas. E., died in hospital, April 7th, 1863.
Fowler, Robt., captured September 14th, 1862, Crampton Gap, and exchanged.

Flournoy, E. H., promoted 1st Lieutenant, May 17th, 1861.
Gills, Jos. P., killed Sept. 14th, 1862, at Crampton Gap.
Hollingsworth, John J.
Hogwood, John.
Hopkins, Andrew.
Harrell, John W., wounded Sept. 14th, 1862, Crampton Gap, and died December 26th, in Charlestown.
James, Jos. P., wounded July 30th, 1864, at Crater, and died Aug. 6th.
James, Richard Y., captured Oct. 27th, 1864, at Burgess' Mill.
Johnson, Wm. W.
Jordan, Jos. P., died in hospital, April 20th, 1863.
Jollie, Geo. F., conscript from Isle of Wight, killed Oct. 27th, 1864, at Burgess' Mill.
Kelly, Wm.
Lawrence, Geo. W., wounded, 1863.
Minnis, Clinton C.
Morris, Frank.
McCoy, Joseph.
Moreland, Robt., promoted Sergeant.
Martin, Samuel J.
Martin, Joshua, wounded June 29th, 1862, Charles City Road, and died July 1st, conscript from Patrick county.
Nottingham, Obed.
Oakley, Thos.
Owens, John.
Parr, Wm.
Purdy, John J., died in hospital, Oct. 31st, 1862, Richmond.
Ruthledge, Absolem F., captured Oct. 27th, 1864, at Burgess' Mill.
Robinson, Benj.
Ralph, John, captured Oct. 27th, 1864, at Burgess' Mill.
Swift, Wm. H., promoted Sergeant March, 1863.
Scarff, Wm., died in hospital, July 5th, 1863.
Spencer, Levi.
Trifford, Wm., wounded May 12th, 1864, at Spotsylvania C. H.
Thoroughgood, Geo., wounded Aug. 30th, 1862, at 2d Manassas, and died Oct. 1st, at Warrenton.
Taylor, James, wounded Sept. 17th, 1862, at Sharpsburg, and disabled.
Taylor, David R., wounded Sept. 14th, 1862, at Crampton Gap.
Voss, James.
Wills, Geo. T., wounded May 6th, 1864, at Wilderness.
Williams, Robt. S.
Wilkins, Wm. F., died in hospital, Feb. 10th, 1863, Richmond.
Wood, James M.
Wood, Alexander, died in hospital, Aug. 1st, 1862, at Liberty.
Woodhouse, Chas., captured sick in hospital, July 14th, 1863, at Hagerstown, Maryland.
Warren, W. J., died in hospital, July 15th, 1862, Richmond.
    Killed and died—23.

CHAPTER XXXVI.

COMPANY F, COMPANY G, SIXTH VIRGINIA REGIMENT.

This company was organized in 1859, and when it entered the service of the Confederate States, or rather the State of Virginia, it was the largest infantry company in Norfolk, numbering on its roll about one hundred and twenty-five or thirty members. Quite a large number of them were promoted to positions in other commands or given staff appointments. The officers of the company when it was first mustered into service were:

Captain –Henry W. Williamson.
First Lieutenant, W. W. Chamberlaine; 2d Lieutenant, Edward M. Hardy; 3d Lieutenant, Duncan Robertson, Jr.
First Sergeant, John T. Lester; 2d Sergeant, Adolph H. Jacqueman; 3d Sergeant, Edward A. Dodd; 4th Sergeant, James B. Marsden.
First Corporal, Robert G. Portlock; 2d Corporal, George K. Goodridge; 3d Corporal, Jonathan R. Smith; 4th Corporal, F. E. Goodrich.

The company, from its organization, was named "Company F," and by that name it was known. It was attached to the 6th Virginia Regiment as Company G. It mustered under arms on the 19th of April, 1861, and took part in the removal of the powder from the United States magazine at Fort Norfolk that night, and was ordered to Craney Island as a part of the garrison at that post. There it had charge of a battery of heavy guns. At the reorganization of the company in April, 1862, Captain Williamson was re-elected, Lieutenant Chamberlaine declined a re-election and retired from the company to another field of duty, and Edward M. Hardy, Duncan Robertson, Jr., and John T. Lester were elected 1st, 2d and 3d Lieutenants respectively. Captain Williamson was elected Lieutenant-Colonel of the regiment, Lieutenant Hardy was promoted to Captain, and the other two Lieutenants were advanced one grade each, leaving the 3d Lieutenantcy vacant, and when the company was near Drury's Bluff, in May, 1862, this was tendered to the former Lieutenant, W. W. Chamberlaine, and accepted by him, thus renewing his connection with the company. The officers, therefore, when it entered upon the stage of actual warfare were:

Captain –Edward M. Hardy.
First Lieutenant, Duncan Robertson, Jr.; 2d Lieutenant, John T. Lester; 3d Lieutenant, Wm. W. Chamberlaine.
First Sergeant, John R. Catlett.
Lieutenant Chamberlaine was wounded at Sharpsburg Septem

ber 17th, 1862, was detached from the company in December, 1862, and was promoted to Captain and A. A. G. on the staff of General Walker, Chief of Artillery of the 3d Corps, Army of Northern Virginia. Lieutenant Lester was captured at Crampton Gap September 14th, 1862, was exchanged, rejoined the company and was killed on the 12th of May, 1864, at the battle of Spotsylvania Court House. Lieutenant Robertson was severely wounded at Sharpsburg, but recovered, rejoined the company, and was captured October 27th, 1864, at the battle of Burgess' Mill. Captain Hardy was wounded on the 22d of June, 1864, at Wilcox's Farm, but recovered and rejoined the company.

The company remained on duty at Craney Island until the 10th of May, 1862, when the island was evacuated by the Confederates. It then marched to Suffolk with the rest of the troops and there took the cars for Petersburg, where it joined its regiment. During the battle at Drury's Bluff between the shore batteries and the Federal fleet composed of the Monitor, Galena and Naugatuck, Company G was stationed on the bluffs below the battery as sharpshooters and did considerable injury among such of the crews of the three vessels as exposed themselves upon the decks. After that, the company returned to the regiment and did duty with it to the end of the war. The company lost very heavily at the battles of Malvern Hill and Second Manassas. In the first, five of its members were killed or mortally wounded, and at the last, four sacrificed their lives upon the altar of their country's liberty. Among these last were Wm. G. Ridley, of Southampton county, a gallant youth scarcely more than twenty years of age, who was attending school at the University of Virginia when the war broke out, and joined Company G in order to be with his friends. Another, about the same age, John B. Merritt, of Brunswick county, a student at Randolph-Macon College, and a stranger in Norfolk, left college and joined this company on account of the friends he had in it. He was mortally wounded in the same battle in which Buck Ridley was killed.

Mahone's Brigade suffered quite severely at Second Manassas and about half of the remainder were lost at Crampton Gap, where it was sacrificed to hold Franklin's Corps in check until the fall of Harper's Ferry. Those who escaped fell back into Pleasant Valley and made the forced march to join General Lee at Sharpsburg. The brigade had been reduced so much by the casualties of battle and the fatigue of that extraordinary march that when it arrived upon the field of Sharpsburg it was scarcely larger than a full company, and Company G consisted of Lieutenants Robertson and Chamberlaine and Private Chandler W. Hill. Private George M. Todd came up during the progress of the battle. In this battle Lieutenant Robertson received a severe wound, which disabled him. At the battle of the Crater every man in the company who was present in the fight was either killed or wounded. Chandler W. Hill, then a Corporal, lost his arm there. The few men in the company who reached the battle field at Sharpsburg did good service while there. The remnant of the brigade, about eighty men, halted in rear of the town of Sharpsburg and was conducted by General Pryor, to whose brigade it was temporarily attached, to a piece of ground near the Piper House, in rear of the main line of battle. The Hagerstown road runs due north from Sharpsburg, and Dr. Piper's house is located to the right of the road, with a lane leading to it at right angles from the road, and on the side of this lane was a stone fence. General D. H. Hill's line of battle extended across the angle formed by the lines of the road and lane, about a quarter of a mile from the point of junction. As soon as the men reached that point the Federal artillery opened a terrific fire upon them. Some ran forward and reached the line of battle, but the larger portion sought shelter. It was here that Lieutenant Robertson was wounded, and Lieutenant Colonel Parham, of the 41st Virginia, commanding the brigade, ordered Lieutenant Chamberlaine to go to the rear and report to General Anderson the condition of affairs. Lieutenant Chamberlaine had not gone far in the execution of the order when he learned that General Anderson had been wounded. He was then near the head of Piper's lane, and noticed a six-pounder brass field piece and limber chest on the Hagerstown road which had been left there by the company to which it belonged. Just then the line of battle began falling back, and, getting a few men to help him, Lieutenant Chamberlaine dragged the gun into a commanding position, and, with the assistance of several other officers, rallied a number of the retreating infantry behind the stone fence. This force was continually increasing as stragglers would come up, and pretty soon the enemy made his appearance in front, preceded by a line of skirmishers. Lieutenant Chamberlaine obtained permission from Major Fairfax, of General Longstreet's staff, to open fire with the gun, and after a few rounds the enemy retired, but their artillery opened on this solitary piece such a heavy fire that it was moved to another position near the head of Piper's lane, where it could command the ground in its front and yet be somewhat sheltered from the enemy's batteries. Subsequently the enemy made three attempts to advance, but the well directed fire of that gun repelled them each time before they came within range of the fire of the infantry behind the stone fence. Lieutenant Chamberlaine sighted the gun and served the vent, and his gun's crew was composed of Georgia infantrymen of Colonel G. T. Anderson's Brigade, (General Jones, its commander, was wounded) with Privates Chandler W. Hill and George M. Todd, of Company G, as infantry supports.

After this third repulse there was a lull for about two hours, and as it became desirable to ascertain what the enemy were engaged in, Colonel Wm. Gibson, of the 48th Georgia Regiment, threw forward a strong line of skirmishers and met a full line of battle beginning to advance. The determined stand made by these skirmishers induced the enemy to believe they were backed up by a heavy force and caused them to suspend their contemplated attack. Thus ended the fighting on that part of the field, except by the enemy's artillery, which disabled Lieutenant Chamberlaine. The gun is said to have belonged to the Huger Battery of Norfolk, and was one of the guns which the Norfolk Blues had before the war, and which was turned over to Captain Huger. The battery had been engaged at that point earlier in the day, but, being ordered to another part of the field, had to leave that gun behind, as the horses belonging to it had been killed. The company sent a detachment for it that night and carried it off.

At the commencement of hostilities Colonel Walter H. Taylor, who was so well known throughout the Army of Northern Virginia as General Lee's Adjutant General, was a Lieutenant in Company G, but served only a few days with it before receiving an appointment in the Provisional Army, with the subsequent assignment to the staff of General Robert E. Lee.

Colonel Anderson, in his report of the action of his brigade at Sharpsburg, mentions the incident of the gun and says: "At this point I found a 6 pounder gun, and getting a few men to assist in placing it in position, a Lieutenant of infantry, whose name or regiment I do not know, served it most beautifully until the ammunition was exhausted."

Colonel Anderson is mistaken about the ammunition being exhausted. The gun ceased firing only when the enemy retired beyond its range. The fire of this gun is referred to also in the Federal reports, of the battle, by Brigadier General J. C. Caldwell, commanding the brigade which made the attack, and by Major General W. S. Hancock, both of whom thought there were two guns instead of one. They report that Colonel F. C. Barlow, commanding the 64th and 61st New York Regiments (consolidated), was wounded in the groin by a shrapnel from it.

Below will be found the muster roll of the company for May, 1862, with one recruit added in 1864:

Captain Edward M. Hardy, wounded June 22d, 1864, Wilcox's Farm.
First Lieutenant Duncan Robertson, Jr., wounded September 17th, 1862, Sharpsburg, captured October 27th, 1864, at Burgess' Mill.
Second Lieutenant John T. Lester, captured September 14th, 1862, at Crampton Gap, killed May 12th, 1864, at Spotsylvania C. H.
Third Lieutenant Wm. W. Chamberlaine, promoted Captain and A. A. G. on staff of General Walker, Chief of Artillery 3d Corps, December, 1863, wounded September 17th, 1862, at Sharpsburg.
First Sergeant John R. Catlett.

Second Sergeant Charles A. McCourt, wounded July 1st, 1862, at Malvern Hill and disabled, discharged November 12th, 1862.
Third Sergeant Albert B. Simmons, wounded October 14th, 1863, at Bristoe Station, and died October 15th.
Fourth Sergeant Howard S. Wright, wounded Aug. 30th, 1862, Second Manassas, promoted Ensign 6th Regiment, killed July 30th, 1864, Crater.
First Corporal Wm. H. Langley, detailed in Commissary Department April 27th, 1863, rejoined company and captured October 27th, 1864, Burgess' Mill.
Second Corporal Oscar M. Styron, wounded August 30th, 1862, at Second Manassas and disabled, discharged March 1st, 1863.
Third Corporal John T. Hill, promoted Sergeant April 25th, 1863, wounded July 30th, 1864, at Crater.
Fourth Corporal James L. D. Butt, appointed Hospital Steward November 22d, 1862.
Fifth Sergeant Wm. McLean, wounded July 1st, 1862, Malvern Hill, and died in hospital.

PRIVATES.

Archer, Robert L., detailed in Division Provost Guard, Sept. 25th, 1862.
Arrington, Peter, promoted Corporal March 24th, 1863, Sergeant Major 30th North Carolina Regiment.
Biggs, Wm. G., wounded August 30th, 1862, at Second Manassas and died August 31st.
Baylor, Robert B., captured October 27th, 1864, at Burgess' Mill.
Bell, Douglas, wounded August 30th, 1862, Second Manassas, transferred to 18th Battalion Va. Heavy Artillery January 26th, 1864.
Biggs, James H., died in hospital October, 1862.
Bell, Robt. S., detailed in Commissary Department, 1862, and transferred to 18th Virginia Battalion Heavy Artillery November 13th, 1862.
Bell, James N., wounded June 21st, 1862, disabled and discharged, appointed Sergeant Major 6th Virginia Regiment November 16th, 1863.
Chisman, John R., discharged 1864.
Clark, Fred W., discharged for disability, November, 1862.
Cole, Cornelius M., killed October 14th, 1863, Bristoe Station.
Core, John H., discharged for disability November, 1862.
Deiches, W., detailed in hospital, 1862, discharged for disability, 1864.
Dey, James B.
Etheredge, ——, captured September 14th, 1862, at Crampton Gap.
Fentress, Thomas, appointed Hospital Steward October 12th, 1862.
Fitchett, Julius M., transferred to Griffin's Battery, October 22d, 1862.
Fletcher, Oliver N., wounded June 21st, 1862, and never rejoined company.
Freeman, Robert, captured July 13th, 1863, in Maryland, exchanged and appointed Master's Mate in the Navy, June, 1864.
Gordon, John D., captured October 27th, 1864, Burgess' Mill.
Gordon, Wm., R. appointed Hospital Steward, August 16th, 1862.
Goodridge, F. E. detached May 1st, 1864.
Goodridge, Geo. K., detached October 27th, 1862.
Hill, Chandler, W., promoted Corporal, lost arm July 30th, 1864, at Crater.
Holmes, Alex. T., detailed in Quartermaster's Department, 1862, captured October 27th, 1864.
Hipkins, Richard, wounded August 30th, 1862, Second Manassas, and detailed in Quartermaster's Department, February 18th, 1864.
Hardy, Thomas A., enlisted in company Sept. 14th, 1864, captured October 27th, 1864.
Jones, John S., promoted Captain on General Garnett's staff and wounded July 3d, 1863, at Gettysburg.
Kerr, Edward.
King, J. Barry, promoted Sergeant Major 6th Va. Regiment May 25th, 1863, promoted Captain and Quartermaster Lightfoot's Artillery Battalion.
Langhorne, Wm. W., detached August 12th, 1864, in Lynchburg.

Lawson, Adrian S., transferred to Company A, 5th Virginia Cavalry, December 9th, 1864.
Marsden, B. A., captured September 14th, 1862, at Crampton Gap, exchanged and promoted to 2d Lieutenant P. A. C. S.
Merritt, John B., mortally wounded August 30th, 1862, Second Manassas, and died in hospital at Warrenton.
Moore, Walter S., promoted Sergeant Major 61st Virginia Regiment March 22d, 1863, promoted Ensign, 1863.
McPhail, Charles H., killed July 1st, 1862, Malvern Hill.
McKenny, Wm. N., detailed in Army Intelligence Office, July 1st, 1862.
Murray, John, furnished substitute and discharged.
Myrick, David, wounded July 1st, 1862, Malvern Hill, and died in hospital.
Pentz, George McK., transferred to Maryland line, 1862.
Reid, James T. S., promoted 1st Lieutenant Ordnance on General Loring's staff.
Reynolds, Henry S., detailed in Commissary Department, November 21st, 1862, discharged 1864.
Robinson, Wm. C., killed October 14th, 1863, at Bristoe Station.
Robinson, Wm., wounded August 30th, 1862, at Second Manassas, transferred to 32d North Carolina Regiment.
Robertson, Cary, promoted Sergeant Major, August 21th, 1864, killed at Hatcher's Run, February 7th, 1865.
Robins, Geo. S., died in hospital, 1862, Richmond.
Rosenburg, Mich., detailed in hospital, October 7th, 1862.
Rowe, Stephen D., transferred to Company A, 5th Virginia Cavalry, August 17th, 1862.
Rowland, John H., captured September 14th, 1862, at Crampton Gap, exchanged and transferred to Company D, 20th Virginia Battalion Heavy Artillery, December 9th, 1862.
Ridley, Wm. G., killed August 30th, 1862, Second Manassas.
Seal, John R., discharged for disability December 27th, 1862.
Seal, Wm. B., appointed Hospital Steward, October 30th, 1862.
Smith, Jonathan K., killed July 1st, 1862, Malvern Hill.
Segar, John, transferred to Company H, 38th Virginia Regiment, October 8th, 1862.
Segar, Arthur S., promoted Lieutenant in another regiment.
Shipp, John S.
Smith, Henry.
Smoot, Wm., detailed October 20th, 1862, discharged for disability, December 24th, 1862.
Southgate, Lewellyn, captured September 14th, 1862, Crampton Gap, appointed Sergeant Major in Colonel Godwin's command.
Stone, David B., captured May 12th, 1864, at Spotsylvania C. H.
Thomas, Richard S., detailed July 1st, 1862, in Army Intelligence Office, Richmond.
Todd, Geo. M.
Umstadter, M., furnished substitute and discharged.
Voss, Albert C., killed August 30th, 1862, Second Manassas.
Ward, Josiah J., wounded August 30th, 1862, at Second Manassas.
Whiting, Wm. N., captured July 30th, 1864, at the Crater.
Whitehurst, Frank M., promoted 1st Lieutenant Company B, September 9th, 1863.
Williams, John N., discharged for disability, April 6th, 1863.
Wise, Wm. M. B., wounded June 21st, 1862, transferred to Company A, 46th Virginia Regiment, December 13th, 1862.
Walke, Richard, Jr., promoted Ordnance Officer Mahone's Brigade, December 1st, 1862.
Wicker, D. H. C., substitute for John Murray, died in hospital February 15th, 1863.
Walsh, Wm. V., killed July 1st, 1862, Malvern Hill.
Young, Thos. A.

COMPANY F, COMPANY G, SIXTH VA. REGIMENT. 275

TRANSFERRED AND DISCHARGED.

The following men who enlisted in the company at the beginning of the war were transferred to other commands or honorably discharged while the company was stationed on Craney Island:

Beale, Brooke, appointed sub-officer in the navy.
Collier, Jas. M., assigned to Medical Department Aug. 30th, 1861.
Cannon, Douglas C., transferred to Signal Corps March 31, 1861.
Cason, Benj. F., promoted 2d Lieutenant Company B, 9th Va. Regiment.
Freeman, Jos. N., appointed Engineer in the navy.
Foreman, Columbus W., transferred to Company B, 5th Va. Cavalry, March 23d, 1862.
Guyot, Robert S., appointed Ordnance Sergeant 9th Va. Regiment and killed Aug. 28th, 1862, at Warrenton Springs.
Gwynn, T. P., appointed Lieutenant in the Marine Corps C. S. Navy.
Hunter, W. W., appointed Q. M. Sergeant 8th North Carolina Regiment, Dec. 2d, 1861.
Hudgins, W. R., discharged for disability, 1862.
Hyman, F. M., transferred to Signal Corps March 31st, 1862.
Jacquimon, A. H., discharged 1862, over age.
Keeling, Solomon S., transferred to Medical Department, Oct. 12th, 1861.
Mapp, Richard A., transferred to Signal Corps, March 31st, 1862.
Milhado, A. G., transferred to Signal Corps, March 31st, 1862.
Marsden, James B., promoted Lieutenant in Bridgford's Provost Guard and killed.
Morris, Jesse S., promoted in Medical Department, October 9th, 1861.
Mallory, Chas. O'C., promoted Sergeant Major 55th Va. Regiment, Dec. 12th, 1861.
Portlock, Robert G., promoted Sergeant Major 9th Va. Regiment, Dec. 1st, 1861.
Saunders, Palmer, appointed Midshipman in the navy and killed at the capture of the Underwriter by the Confederates.
Stokes, Montford N., promoted Lieutenant Company D, and killed at Bristoe Station.
Sharp, Jas. H., promoted 2d Lieutenant P. A. C. S., Sept. 2d, 1861.
Stone, Geo. F., discharged for disability, 1862.
Taylor, Walter H., made 2d Lieutenant P. A. C. S., promoted Adjutant General on staff of General R. E. Lee.
Tunstall, Alex., promoted Sergeant Major 6th Va. Regiment, May 6th, 1861, and later promoted Adjutant.
Taylor, Robertson, appointed Quartermaster Sergeant 6th Va. Regiment, promoted Adjutant 6th Regiment and Adjutant General Mahone's Division and wounded at Wilderness May 6th, 1864.
Todd, H. S., elected Lieutenant Company B, 9th Va. Regiment.
Urquhart, J. W., transferred to Company H, 5th Va. Cavalry, March 17th, 1862.
Urquhart, A. B., transferred to Company H, 5th Va. Cavalry, March 17th, 1862.
Wise, Wm. B., promoted Lieutenant in a North Carolina Regiment.
Walker, R. P., appointed 2d Lieutenant P. A. C. S.
Walker, Geo. B., transferred to Sussex Cavalry Aug. 10th, 1861, and killed.
Wilkerson, Henry D., promoted 2d Lieutenant Company B, 9th Va. Regiment, and mortally wounded July 3d, 1863, at Gettysburg, died in prison on Johnson's Island.
Williams, Thos. A., appointed Sergeant Major 6th Regiment, promoted Lieutenant in Company K.
Walke, Isaac T., transferred to N. L. A. Blues, March 26th, 1862, promoted Lieutenant of Ordnance Fitz Lee's Cavalry Division, and killed in 1864 at Woodstock.
Williamson, Captain Henry W., promoted Lieutenant-Colonel 6th Va. Regiment, lost an arm at the Crater.
Killed and died—26.

CHAPTER XXXVII

THE INDEPENDENT GRAYS, COMPANY H, SIXTH VIRGINIA REGIMENT.

At the beginning of hostilities in April, 1861, this company was well equipped, well drilled, and in a very efficient condition, so that it responded promptly to the call of the governor for volunteers, and was mustered into service on the 19th of April, 1861, under the following officers:

Captain, Richard C. Taylor.

First Lieutenant, Wm. G. Wilburn; 2d Lieutenant, Josiah H. Smith; 3d Lieutenant, David Wright.

First Sergeant, Henry D. Reynolds; 2d Sergeant, Geo. Hogwood; 3d Sergeant, Wm. F. Wood.

First Corporal, Walter A. Edwards; 2d Corporal, Henry W. Hill; 3d Corporal, Isaac Seldner; 4th Corporal, Wm. N. Beak.

The Greys were among the first troops sent to Craney Island to take charge of the batteries which were being erected there, and had charge of a section of heavy guns. Life on Craney Island was very monotonous. The Confederates built strong earthworks there and manned them with heavy guns. They built bomb proofs and furnaces for heating shot but the enemy's vessels kept at a respectful distance, and the Grays had no opportunity while there to test their efficiency. While on the Island, the company was attached to the 6th Virginia Regiment, as Company H, but remained on the island until its evacuation on the 10th of May, 1862, when it joined the regiment upon its arrival at Petersburg. Captain Taylor was promoted to Major, commanding an artillery battalion in the entrenched camp back of Norfolk, and at the reorganization of the Grays in April, 1862, Lieutenant David Wright was elected Captain, Josiah H. Smith 1st Lieutenant, Wm. G. Wilbern 2d Lieutenant and Henry S. Reynolds 3d Lieutenant. Lieutenant Smith was mortally wounded at the battle of Manassas, August 30th, 1862, and died at Aldie on the 8th of October. Lieutenant Reynolds was discharged on the 23d of January, 1863, and Thos. A. Gatch was elected 1st Lieutenant in 1864, and remained with the company until the surrender at Appomattox. Captain Wright was killed at the battle of the Crater on the 30th of July, 1864.

One of the most gallant events of the whole war was a charge made on the enemy's entrenchments near Chancellorsville, May 2d, 1862, by companies B, C and H, of the 6th Regiment. General Mahone, in his official report of the affair says: " It was during this service of the brigade that the advance line of skirmishers of the 6th Virginia Infantry, under command of Captain W. Carter Williams, charged over the enemy's abatis near the Plank Road, fired upon them in their rifle pits, captured there prisoners from four different regiments, and the colors and color bearer of the 107th Ohio Regiment, returning to his position with his handful of men, with the loss of an officer as prisoner. This gallant and successful sortie was made a little after dark Saturday, May 2d, when General Jackson's fire was heavy, and it was in fighting over the same ground the next morning that the valliant Williams fell mortally wounded."

The charge was made for the purpose of ascertaining the position of the enemy. The officer captured was Captain Crawley, of Company C, and the manner of his capture was somewhat amusing. He had captured a Federal soldier, and when the company retired he thought he was following it, but in the darkness of the night and the thickness of the woods, he mistook his proper course and went towards the enemy's lines instead of his own. The prisoner he had with him told him he was taking the wrong direction and, if he kept on, they would soon be inside the Federal lines, and the condition of affairs would be reversed. He said he did not wish to return to his own lines just then, but would like to be captured, so that he could get a short holiday while waiting to be exchanged, and therefore he warned Captain Crawley that he was taking the wrong direction, but Captain Crawley thought he knew best, and kept on until, sure enough, he found himself in the hands of the enemy. His former prisoner then took him a prisoner and turned him over to the provost guard.

The company was a small one, but its losses were heavy compared with its numbers. Nearly one-third of those who left Norfolk with it and did service in its ranks were either killed or wounded. First Sergeant Seldner was killed May 3d, 1863, and Walter A. Edwards was promoted to fill the vacancy. He was present with the company in every battle in which it was engaged except two, and escaped without a wound. He was captured at Cumberland Church April 7th, 1865, two days before the surrender at Appomattox Court House.

Below will be found the roll of the company after it left Norfolk, together with the list of casualties:

Captain David Wright, promoted Captain May 1st, 1862, killed July 30th, 1864, Crater.
First Lieutenant Josiah H. Smith, wounded Aug. 30th, 1862, 2d Manassas, died Oct. 8th.
First Lieutenant Thos. A. Gatch, elected 1864, surrendered at Appomattox.
Second Lieutenant Wm. G. Willern.
Third Lieutenant Henry S. Reynolds, discharged Jan. 23d, 1863.
First Sergeant Isaac Seldner, captured Sept. 11th, 1862, exchanged and killed May 3d, 1863, at Chancellorsville.
Second Sergeant H. W. Hill, appointed Ordnance Sergeant June 29th, 1862, captured on retreat from Petersburg.
Third Sergeant Walter A. Edwards, promoted 1st Sergeant May 8th, 1863, captured at Cumberland Church April 7th, 1865.
Fourth Sergeant Geo. Hogwood.
First Corporal Alex. M. Smith, promoted color bearer 6th Regiment, wounded Aug. 30th, 1862, at 2d Manassas.

Second Corporal Jas. A. Wirmington, promoted Sergeant May 8th, 1863.
Third Corporal Walter R. Wellons, wounded Aug. 30th, 1862, at 2d Manassas and July 30th, 1864, at the Crater.
Fourth Corporal John L. Simmons, wounded Aug. 30th, 1862, at 2d Manassas, wounded May 2d, 1863, at Chancellorsville, and died May 3d.

PRIVATES.

Anderson, John T., wounded May 6th, 1864, at Wilderness, and disabled.
Abdell, Wm. H., wounded May 3d, 1863, at Chancellorsville, disabled and detailed in Richmond postoffice.
Boush, John T., detailed as wagon driver Dec. 4th, 1862.
Brown, Henry F., wounded Sept. 14th, 1862, lost arm May 8th, 1864, Shady Grove.
Barnes, James, killed March 23d, 1863, by Provost Guard, Petersburg.
Bonfanti, John, promoted Corporal.
Beane, Wm. W., wounded May 12th, 1864, at Spotsylvania.
Crockett, Geo. wounded July 30th, 1864, at Crater, died Aug. 6th.
Dashields, Jas. J., killed May 12th, 1864, at Spotsylvania C. H.
Dunbar, John T., appointed Sergeant May 8th, 1863.
Dunn, Wm. F., promoted Corporal, wounded June 22d, 1864, captured April 5th, 1865, at Cumberland Church.
Dunn, Wm. A., died in hospital, Dec. 8th, 1863.
Ferris, James.
Gray, Wm.
Gillerlain, Peter J., killed July 30th, 1864, at Crater.
Higgins, Francis C., wounded July 30th, 1864, at Crater.
Ironmonger, L. M., promoted Sergeant May 5th, 1864, captured June 16th, 1864.
Johnson, Wm. B.
Johnson, Jacob T., died in hospital Aug. 7th, 1864, Richmond.
Jacobs, Julius, wounded May 12th, 1864, Spotsylvania C. H., and supposed to have died.
Laylor, Geo.
Lewis, Geo. E.
Mordecai, Phillip M.
Mannix, W. R., died in hospital, Aug. 19th, 1862, Danville.
Mitchell, Edward F., detailed and not with the company.
Nottingham, W. W., wounded May 12th, 1864, Spotsylvania C. H.
Plummer, Joshua.
Peck, Wm. N., killed July 1st. 1862, Malvern Hill.
Ross, John R.
Roberts, Wm. J., killed July 30th, 1864, at Crater.
Reynolds, Wm. C., transferred to navy Sept. 3d, 1863.
Shirley, John, died in hospital, June, 1862.
Smith, Andrew.
Smith, John E., promoted Corporal, transferred to navy Sept. 3d, 1863.
Smith, Wm. J., wounded and captured May 12th, 1864, Spotsylvania.
Stubbs, Wm. J., detailed in Army Provost Guard.
Stryker, Martin, captured Oct. 27th, 1864, at Burgess' Mill.
Sykes, Wm. A.
Scott, Wm. T., wounded May 12th, 1864, at Spotsylvania C. H.
Tomlinson, Geo., transferred to navy April 8th, 1863.
Wise, H. A., wounded July 30th, 1864, at Crater.
Westbrook, D. A.
Wise, Geo. W., wounded September 14th, 1862, lost arm May 6th, 1864, Wilderness.
Winhall, Hiram, captured September 14th, 1862, and May 12th, 1864, Spotsylvania C. H.
Wyatt, John L.
Wood, Wm. F., wounded Sept. 14th, 1862, at Crampton Gap, and died in hospital July 14th, 1863.
Killed and died—16.

CHAPTER XXXVIII.

THE SIXTH VIRGINIA REGIMENT MAHONE'S, WEISIGER'S BRIGADE, HUGER'S, ANDERSON'S, MAHONE'S DIVISION.

Having given brief sketches of the five Norfolk companies which were in this regiment, their history would not be complete without telling the part which the regiment played in that great drama which was marked by so many deeds of noble heroism. Of the fifty companies composing the five regiments in Mahone's Brigade, Norfolk county, including the cities of Norfolk and Portsmouth, contributed sixteen, or one-third of the whole. Of those sixteen, six were from Norfolk city, six from Norfolk county, three from Portsmouth, and one from Portsmouth and the county jointly, while in another, Company B, 6th Regiment, Norfolk and Portsmouth were both liberally represented, though the bulk of the company was from Princess Anne county. The 6th Regiment was organized almost immediately upon the beginning of hostilities and was composed of the following companies:

Company A, of Norfolk city, Captain W. N. McKenney.
Company B, of Princess Anne, Captain W. Carter Williams.
Company C, of Norfolk city, Captain Wm. Lamb.
Company D, of Norfolk city, Captain John R. Ludlow.
Company E, of Portsmouth, Captain John H. Myers.
Company F, of Princess Anne, Captain George T. Rogers.
Company G, of Norfolk city, Captain Henry W. Williamson.
Company H, of Norfolk city, Captain Richard C. Taylor.
Company I, of Manchester, Captain Louis Bossieux.
Company K, of Chesterfield, Captain David M. Goode.

The officers of the regiment were:
Colonel—Wm. Mahone.
Lieutenant-Colonel Thos. J. Corprew.
Major Wm. T. Lundy.

These officers were assigned to the regiment by Governor Letcher. First Lieutenant Robert B. Taylor, of Company A, was detailed as Adjutant, and Alex. Tunstall, of Company G, was appointed Sergeant Major. Subsequently Quartermaster Sergeant Robertson Taylor was appointed Adjutant. Companies G and H were detached and placed on duty on Craney Island, and Company I was stationed at the Naval Hospital battery. The seven other companies were together in the entrenchments near Norfolk. On the 1st of September, 1861, Company E was disbanded by orders from headquarters, and the Nansemond Guards, Captain Williams, became Company E. Some time in the fall of 1861 the 6th, 12th, 16th and 41st Virginia Regiments were organized into a brigade, and on the 16th of November, 1861, Colonel Mahone was promoted to Brigadier General. This occasioned the promotion of Lieutenant-Colonel Corprew and Major Lundy, and Captain George T. Rogers, of Company F, was elected Major.

On the 10th of February, 1862, upon the fall of Roanoke Island, which occurred on the 8th, the seven companies which were with the regiment were ordered to Coinjock, or Currituck bridge, at the North Carolina terminus of the Albemarle and Chesapeake Canal, to protect that work should the enemy put in an appearance there, and also to cover the retreat of General Wise with such troops as he might have saved from the wreck at Roanoke Island. There was a battery of three 32-pounder guns at Currituck bridge. General Wise reached Currituck bridge on his retreat and, ranking Colonel Corprew, took command and ordered a retreat to Great Bridge, where General Huger found the regiment. General Wise was transferred to another department, and affairs at Great Bridge were turned over to General Mahone. The regiment remained in that section until General Huger received orders to evacuate Norfolk, when it was marched to the city, reached there May 10th, crossed the Eastern Branch on the draw-bridge and took the Norfolk and Petersburg railroad cars for Petersburg, where it was joined by Companies G, H and I. On the appearance of the Federal fleet, composed of the Monitor, Galena, Naugatuck and Aroostook before the fort at Drury's Bluff on the 15th of May, Companies G and I were sent to the Bluff to act as sharpshooters, and every man on the vessels who exposed himself became a mark for their fire. They were very efficient aids to the fort. They were scattered along the Bluff lower down the river than the position at which the fort was located. The next day the regiment was ordered to Chaffin's Bluff and remained there until after the battle of Seven Pines, in which the other regiments of the brigade took part.

At the reorganization of the regiment in April, prior to the evacuation of Norfolk, the following officers were elected:

Colonel—George T. Rogers.
Lieutenant-Colonel—Henry W. Williamson.
Major—Robert B. Taylor.
Adjutant—Alexander Tunstall.

Adjutant Robertson Taylor was appointed by General Mahone Adjutant General of the brigade when the latter received his appointment as Brigadier General. The field officers of the regiment were peculiarly fortunate, for, though they did their duty well and faithfully, only one of them received a wound during the war. Lieutenant-Colonel Williamson lost an arm at the battle of the Crater, on the 30th of July, 1864. Colonel Rogers and Major Taylor escaped unhurt.

After the battle of Seven Pines the regiment rejoined the brigade and remained with it until the close of the war. On the 21st of June a very unfortunate affair occurred with the regiment. A report reached the lines that a regiment of Federals was advancing up the Charles City Road, and the first battalion of the 6th Regiment was ordered to advance and intercept them. It was understood also that the 41st Regiment would take part in the movement. Two small private roads ran parallel with the Charles City Road, one on each side, and the 41st Regiment took the right hand one and the detachment of the 6th the other. The detachment was under Colonel Rogers, and the idea was that the expedition would proceed until they came up with the enemy and then close in on their rear and capture them. The batallion of the 6th passed through the outer line of Confederate pickets and these mistook Company I, who were uniformed with light blue pantaloons, for Federals, and fired on them, wounding one man. After proceeding about two miles down the road, a single musket shot was fired from the rear and wounded three men in the detachment. A halt was then made and the men were ordered to retire into the woods and lie down. After waiting a few minutes for the appearance of an enemy or a repetition of the shot, and there being no indication of either, the line was again formed in the road and the march resumed. It was then getting towards dusk, and some of the men of the first battalion, looking to the rear, noticed the second battalion of the regiment following them, and only about a hundred yards behind. The second battalion was under command of Major Taylor, and was ordered out after the first battalion had left camp, and just as it was noticed from the first battalion, the men in the second battalion began firing upon the first, mistaking it for the enemy. Some of the men in the first battalion returned the fire until the voice of Major Taylor was heard and recognized, ordering his men to fix bayonets, and the firing on both sides ceased. The regiment was united, and having passed the point at which the enemy was reported to have been seen, without seeing anything of them, it returned to camp. In this unfortunate affair twenty-eight men were killed or wounded in the two detachments. It was in this affair that Dr. Wise, now a practicing dentist in Norfolk, lost his leg, and James N. Bell, afterwards Sergeant Major of the regiment, lost a portion of his hand. Some of the men in the first battalion recognized their comrades in the second before the firing began, and it was through them that it was brought to a stop just about the time that Major Taylor's voice was recognized when he gave the order to fix bayonets.

The 41st Regiment, failing to find the enemy, likewise returned to camp, but without having had any mishaps. Nothing of interest occurred in camp until the 25th of June. There was, in the meantime, an occasional skirmish with the enemy, but the 6th Regiment did not take part in any of them. They were confined principally to Wright's and Armistead's Brigades, but the action of the 25th seems to have been considered by General McClellan as of some importance. This was the first battle with the enemy in which the 6th Regiment was engaged, and was known as the battle of Oak Grove. It was an initiatory move on the part of General McClellan to advance his left wing nearer towards Richmond. The attack was made upon Huger's Division, and fell principally upon the brigades of Generals Wright and Mahone, though a portion of Ransom's Brigade was engaged quite heavily, and a portion of Armistead's Brigade slightly. All four brigades suffered some loss. The enemy was successfully repelled along the whole line of attack. On the 30th the 6th Regiment was exposed to a very heavy artillery fire and had three men killed and two wounded. In the action of the 25th the enemy was handsomely repulsed in front of Wright's Brigade, but one of the regiments, (Hill's) of Ransom's Brigade, had been forced to give way. Its place was occupied by the 12th Virginia and the 1st Battalion of the 6th, while the 49th and 41st Virginia Regiments and the 2d Battalion of the 6th attacked the enemy on his flank and rear, causing a precipitate retreat.

At Malvern Hill, fought on the 1st of July, 1862, the 6th Regiment was very heavily engaged, and lost ten men killed, thirty-three wounded and eight missing.

After Malvern Hill, General Lee pushed on towards Manassas after Pope, and came up with him upon the old battle ground of the year before. The 6th Regiment was in the midst of the magnificent charge which was made by Mahone's Brigade upon the enemy on the 30th of August, and contributed its share towards achieving that brilliant victory, one of the most important in its results of any during the entire war. Then followed the invasion of Maryland, the investment of Harper's Ferry and the battle of Sharpsburg. Mahone's Brigade, as a part of Anderson's Division, was under Jackson's command at Harper's Ferry and to it was assigned the duty of holding Crampton Gap, to keep the enemy in check until the consummation of Jackson's plans, and the surrender of that town. An account of this engagement will be found elsewhere in this work. [See Chapter XIII.] On the 14th of September Franklin's Corps of 17,000 men attacked Mahone's Brigade of four regiments, numbering 800 men, and was held in check for four hours. The brigade did noble work there and paid a heavy penalty for it in the loss of one-half of its numbers, but its gallant stand gave time for Jackson to capture Harper's Ferry. Among the killed in this engagement was the venerable Dr. Thos. Newton, of Norfolk, who, though long past the military age, was serving as a private in Company F, 6th Regiment, the Seaboard

Rifles of Princess Anne county. At Sharpsburg the brigade had been reduced by its losses at Manassas and Crampton Gap, and its fatiguing march after the fall of Harper's Ferry, to a mere skeleton, scarcely as large as one of its companies at the beginning of the war, but this remnant made a brave stand and assisted in repelling the last attack of the enemy upon the left and left center of the Confederate lines. All four of the regiments in the brigade were present with their colors, but as the numbers in the ranks were small, their general and most of the field officers wounded, they were consolidated into one regiment, under Lieutenant-Colonel Parham, of the 41st, the senior officer, and attached to Pryor's Brigade. One set of colors was retained and the others were sent to the rear with a detail to take care of them. In this battle a portion of the 6th Regiment and a few Georgia troops, under command of Lieutenant W. W. Chamberlaine, of Company G, 6th Virginia, got possession of a piece of artillery which had been abandoned by the battery to which it belonged for want of horses to haul it, and served it with effect upon the enemy.

The battle of Sharpsburg was fought on the 17th of September and McClellan's repeated assaults were driven back along the whole line from right to left with terrible slaughter, and after waiting all day on the 18th, for a renewal of the attack, which never came, General Lee retired into Virginia to recuperate his tired troops, and in November the 61st Virginia Regiment was added to Mahone's Brigade. The battle of Fredericksburg took place on the 13th of December, and the Confederates achieved another brilliant victory. The 6th Regiment was in line of battle and exposed to a heavy artillery fire, but was not actively engaged. The brigade was on the left of the line and the enemy made their attacks upon the right and centre. A season of rest followed after the battle of Fredericksburg until April, 1863, when General Hooker began his movement across the Rapidan river, which culminated in his crushing defeat at Chancellorsville. A detail of three officers and thirty-five men from Mahone's Brigade was at work building a bridge at Germanna Ford on the 29th, when they were surprised by the enemy's advance in force, and nearly all captured. Hooker then crossed at Germanna and Ely's Fords, which are higher up the river than United States Ford, where Mahone's Brigade was stationed, and advanced down the river towards Fredericksburg, his route taking him in the rear of Mahone and that officer withdrew from United States Ford and formed line of battle, with his own and Posey's Brigades, near Chancellorsville, to check Hooker's advance until General Lee could be apprised of the condition of affairs and take steps to meet it. In the advance and battle of May 1st, Mahone's Brigade was in front driving back the enemy opposed to it, and taking up a position which it held until the consummation of General Jackson's flank movement against Hooker's right. On the night of the 2d General Lee was very anxious to ascertain the exact position of the enemy's lines in his front, so that he could prepare an attack for the next day in connection with Jackson's corps, and three companies of the 6th Regiment, B, C and H, under command of Captain W. Carter Williams, of Company B, were ordered to advance for that purpose. The advance was gallantly made, the enemy's rifle pits were carried by storm, prisoners belonging to four different regiments were captured, as were also the color bearer and colors of the 107th Ohio Regiment. In this affair, though so much was accomplished, the three companies suffered no loss except the capture of Captain Crawley, of Company C, who became separated in the darkness from his men, and mistaking his direction, walked into the enemy's lines. On the 3d the regiment moved with the brigade to Salem Church to check the advance of Sedgwick, who was moving upon General Lee's rear from the direction of Fredericksburg, and while taking up a position on the left of the line, the 6th Regiment was fired upon very unexpectedly by the enemy upon its flank, but, with the coolness of veterans, it formed its line under fire without disorder, and then drove back the attacking party. The regiment was under command of Colonel Rogers, and in the fighting around Chancellorsville it lost eight men killed, thirty-three wounded and six missing.

The success at Chancellorsville induced General Lee to invade Pennsylvania, and the Gettysburg campaign followed. The 6th Regiment was present on the battle field on the 2d and 3d of July, exposed to the enemy's fire, but most of the time supporting other troops which were in front, and therefore not very actively engaged, though it lost a number of men. It returned to Virginia with the brigade, was actively engaged in the fall campaign of 1863, the important features of which were the engagements at Bristoe Station, October 14th, and Mine Run, December 2d, after which it went into winter quarters, and was undisturbed by the enemy until 1864, when General Grant began his overland campaign towards Richmond. Gee Lee thrust himself across Grant's front in the Wilderness and forced him to turn aside. Mahone's Brigade was on the extreme right of Longstreet's Corps when he made his celebrated movement to turn Grant's left, and had made a brilliant charge, sweeping the enemy before it. The 6th Regiment was on the left of the brigade, and next to it came the 16th. The position of the brigade was nearly at right angles with the line of battle, and in advance of the line. Longstreet with his own and Jenkins' staff at the head of Jenkins' Brigade, was riding down the turnpike which passed in front of the position held by Mahone's Brigade, and when opposite the left of Mahone's line was seen through the thick woods and smoke and mistaken for the enemy. Firing began and Longstreet was wounded, thus putting a stop to the flank movement which he was directing, and which had already yielded such important results. Whether the shots which produced the disaster came from the 6th or 16th Regiment will perhaps never be definitely settled, but the clearest accounts of the affair locate it as having occurred in front of the left of the brigade. This subject and the battle of the Wilderness are discussed more particularly in the history of the 61st Regiment, chapter XXIV.

The 6th Regiment fought through the whole of the campaign of 1864, was at Shady Grove, Spotsylvania Court House, Cold Harbor, North Anna River, Hanover Court House, Cold Harbor, Turkey Ridge and Second Frazier's Farm, crossed over the James river and interposed between Grant's army and Petersburg, took part in the brilliant victories at Wilcox's Farm, June 22d, Gurley House, June 23d, and the Crater, July 30th. This last will rank with the world's most famous battles and has been made the theme of the artist's brush. The larger portion of the 6th Regiment was on picket duty when the news was received that the enemy had broken through the lines, and there was not time to call them in. Eighty-five men were in camp, and these fell in with the rest of the brigade, and hurrying to where the breech had been made, took part in the charge upon the enemy, and of the eighty-five men with the regiment, thirteen were killed, fifty wounded and twelve were missing. Ten escaped uninjured but they inflicted a loss upon the enemy of ten for one. It was in this battle that Lieutenant-Colonel Williamson lost his arm. Ensign Howard S. Wright was mortally wounded; Captain Wright, of Company H, and Lieutenant Spratt, of Company C, were killed, and Captain Coke, of Company F, Captain Goode, of Company K, Lieutenant Hopper, Company A, Lieutenant Cornick, of Company F, and Lieutenant Flournoy, of Company K, were wounded.

After the Crater came the battles of Reams' Station, Burgess' Mill and Hatcher's Run, and when the final crash came and the army retreated from Petersburg, Mahone's Brigade preserved its organization and courage to the last, and, on the retreat it fought two battles and repulsed the enemy in both. At Cumberland Church, only two days before the surrender at Appomattox, Mahone's men and G. T. Anderson's Brigade of Georgians, captured an entire brigade of Federal troops with their officers and colors. Virginia has reason to be proud of Mahone's Brigade, with its five regiments of Virginia soldiers, the 6th, 12th, 16th, 41st and 61st. One-third of them came from Norfolk county, including the two cities, while Princess Anne, Nansemond, Southampton, Isle of Wight, Sussex, Greenville, Chesterfield and Petersburg furnished the rest. One company from Richmond, the Grays, was in the 12th Regiment.

The following members of the 6th Regiment were present with the command at the surrender at Appomattox, April 9th, 1865:
Colonel George T. Rogers.
Major Robt. B. Taylor.
Adjutant Alex. Tunstall, Jr.
Surgeon T. P. Temple.
Assistant Surgeon J. T. Wilkins.
First Lieutenant and Ensign G. E. Ferebee.
Ordnance Sergeant Henry W. Hill.
Hospital Steward Jas. L. D. Butt.

COMPANY A.

1st Sergt. Wm. H. Whitehurst,
Corporal Jas. Costen,
   Stokely Dyer,
Private Wm. G. Arthur,
  A. F. Beckner,
  Thos. D. Frith,
Private Israel Ingram,
Ivy Lee,
John Shrively,
Michael Snyder,
Benj. F. Wyatt.

COMPANY B.

Captain Wm. F. White,
Sergeant John W. Moore,
Private John A. Bartlett,
  R. R. Daughtrey,
Private B. C. Davis,
Wm. A. Ellison,
Wm. Warden.

COMPANY C.

Sergeant Lemuel Pumphrey,
Private Peter M. Gayle,
  Ed. A. Johnston,
  Jos. Sigman,
Private John H. Shepherd,
Geo. W. Turner,
John W. Wray.

COMPANY D.

Captain John R. Ludlow,
Lieutenant E. H. Flournoy,
Sergeant Wm. H. Swift,
  Robt. Moreland,
Private Thos. S. Adams,
Francis Morris,
Geo. T. Wiles.

COMPANY E.

Captain Euclid Borland,
Sergeant Henry Ashburn,
Corporal John Smith,
Private Wm. Wynn,
Jas. Holland,
S. J. Nelms.

COMPANY F.

Lieutenant Jno. S. Cornick,
Sergeant John C. Gornto,
Corporal W. T. Brock,
Private John E. Absolem,
  Jas. G. Braithwait,
  Wm. T. Brewer,
  H. W. Capps,
Private John T. Dawes,
Geo. E. James,
Southey Mills,
Elias A. Parsons,
Wm. H. Seneca,
Cary Williams,
Henry E. Whitehurst.

THE SIXTH VIRGINIA REGIMENT. 287

COMPANY G.

Lieut. Duncan Robertson, Jr.,
Corporal Chandler W. Hill,
    Robt. A. Archer,
Forage Master G. K. Goodrich,
Private Daniel A. Beach,
    Thos. A. Hardy,

Private Richard Hopkins,
    Edward Kerr,
    R. H. Robinson,
    Geo. M. Todd,
    J. J. Ward,
    Wm. N. White.

COMPANY H.

Captain Thos. A. Gatch,
Corporal John Bonfanti,
Private R. D. Bryant,
    Geo. E. Lewis,
    Benj. W. Martin,
    Robt. O. Metts,

Private Jas. W. Phaup,
    John R. Sampson,
    Wm. S. Stubbs,
    R. H. Willard,
    Jas. E. Warrington.

COMPANY I.

Captain Jno. S. Whitworth,
Lieutenant E. J. Mann,
Sergeant W. D. Craig,
Corporal Robt. T. Conway,
    Thos. Wormack,
Private J. D. Brockwell,
    Wm. E. Browder,

Private Thos. W. Browder,
    R. H. Fuqua,
    Parker Hardgrave,
    Abner Seymour,
    Dev'x Montgomery,
    Edward W. Perkinson,
    Wm. M. Walthall.

COMPANY K.

Captain David M. Goode,
Lieutenant T. A. Williams,
Musician Chas. Fisher,
Courier Jas. B. Goode,
    Wm. H. Pinchbeck,
Private Wm. H. Crutchfield,

Private A. A. Ford,
    M. W. Ford,
    Joshua Moseley,
    E. T. Osborne,
    C. R. Dancette,
    J. B. Wilkinson.

Total commissioned officers.............................. 17
       Non-commissioned staff............................ 2
       Enlisted men..................................... 90

                                                 109

It will be seen from a comparison of the above list with the rolls of the Norfolk companies in the regiment, that there are some names here which are not on the company rolls. Those names are men who joined the regiment after it left Norfolk, and not being Norfolk men, were purposely omitted. Some of them were conscripts and some volunteers.

CHAPTER XXXIX.

THE NORFOLK JUNIORS, COMPANY H, TWELFTH VIRGINIA REGIMENT.

This company dates its organization back to the year 1802 and was therefore the oldest volunteer organization in Norfolk before the war. It took part in the war of 1812 between the United States and Great Britain, and was on duty in the vicinity of Norfolk. It was on duty with the other Norfolk companies on the night of the 19th of April, 1861, when the powder in the magazine at Fort Norfolk was seized and a guard from the company was placed on the schooner James Buchanan with the powder, and accompanied it to Richmond. The officers of the company at that time were:

Captain, F. F. Ferguson.

First Lieutenant, Alex. F. Santos; 2d Lieutenant, Jno. Holmes; 3d Lieutenant, Joel C. White.

First Sergeant, Henry C. Woodhouse; Sergeant, Wm. P. Ashley; Sergeant, Robt. J. Barrett; Sergeant, Chas. L. Beale.

First Corporal, John R. Robins; Corporal, John Baldry; Corporal, Luther Walker; Corporal, James Gray.

There were also ninety-five privates mustered into service, making the total effective strength of the company one hundred and seven. On the morning of the 21st of April, the day after the United States authorities set fire to the Gosport Navy Yard, the company was sent there, and with two fire engines, assisted in subduing the flames, and on the 29th was ordered to Boush's Bluff to assist in building a battery at that point. The company was at Boush's Bluff on the 19th of May, when the Monticello made her attack upon the battery at Seawell's Point, and a detachment under command of Lieutenant Holmes was sent down to reinforce the garrison. The men fought with the deliberation of veterans, and were highly complimented in the official report of Captain Colquit, of the Columbus, Georgia, Light Guard, who commanded the post. A full account of this affair will be found in chapter XXXI, ante.

Upon the organization of the 12th Virginia Regiment, the Juniors were assigned to it as Company H, but remained on detached service at Boush's Bluff until the evacuation of Norfolk, on the 10th of May, 1862, when it joined the regiment in the entrenched camp near Norfolk, and was carried by rail to Petersburg. The Juniors carried from Norfolk, in its ranks, more men than any other company from that city, and its losses were heavier than any other. One company, the Blues, was recruited after the evacuation and became a larger company than the Juniors, but the men were not with it at the evacuation. In April, 1862, there was a re-election of officers and a reorganization of the company, and an entire change was made in the roll of the commissioned officers. All of the original officers were dropped and the following were elected:

Captain, Thomas F. Owens.
First Lieutenant, Henry C. Woodhouse; 2d Lieutenant, Chas. Dashiell; 3d Lieutenant, Chas. L. Beale.
First Sergeant, Wm. H. Ramsey.

Captain Owens was wounded at the second battle of Manassas, August 30th, 1862, but recovered, rejoined the company and was with it until the end. Lieutenant Woodhouse was captured at Germanna Ford on the 29th of April, 1863, was subsequently exchanged, rejoined the company and received a wound at Shady Grove, May 8th, 1864, which so disabled him that he was not able to again be with the company. He was still in hospital when the army surrendered at Appomattox. Lieutenant Dashiell was wounded and captured at Crampton Gap, September 14th, 1862, was exchanged, rejoined the company, but was unfit for duty and was discharged on the 5th of April, 1864. Lieutenant Beale was wounded at the battle of the Crater, July 30th, 1864, but remained with the company and was killed on the 19th of August, at the battle of Davis' Farm, on the Petersburg and Weldon railroad. Orderly Sergeant Ramsey was wounded at the second battle of Manassas and died from his wound in a hospital. After the death of Lieutenant Beale, Sergeant John F. Sale was elected lieutenant, and was mortally wounded at Hatcher's Run, February 6th, 1865, and died February 12th. The company was very unfortunate in its commissioned officers, for of the five whom it had after the evacuation of Norfolk, two were killed and the three others were wounded, two of these receiving wounds which incapacitated them from further service.

Before the evacuation of Norfolk a number of the members of the company were transferred to other commands, and their names will appear with those organizations. Privates Charles Reynolds and Jesse Knight got into a difficulty with some members of the 3d Alabama Regiment, in Norfolk, on the 12th of July, 1861, and were so badly wounded that they were discharged as unfit for further military duty, and Thaddeus S. Gray was detailed on special secret service for the government, and subsequently appointed master's mate in the navy. Of the ninety-two men who left Norfolk with the company, thirty found graves on the battle fields of Virginia and never returned. The record of the company was good all through the war. It participated in the following engagements, or was present in line of battle:

Seawell's Point, May 19-21, '62. Oak Grove, June 25th, 1862. Seven Pines, June 1st, 1862. Malvern Hill, July 1st, 1862.

Second Manassas, August 30th, 1862.
Crampton Gap, September 14th, 1862.
Sharpsburg, September 17th, 1862.
Fredericksburg, December 13th, 1862.
Zoah's Church, April 30th, '63.
McCarthy's Farm, May 1st, '63.
Chancellorsville, May 2d and 3d, 1863.
Salem Church, May 3d, 1863.
Gettysburg, July 2d and 3d, 1863.
Bristoe Station, October 14th, 1863.
Mine Run, December 2d, 1863.
Wilderness, May 6th, 1864.
Shady Grove, May 8th, 1864.
Spotsylvania C. H., May 12th, 1864.

North Anne River, May 21-23, 1864.
Hanover C. H., May 28th and 29th, 1864.
Atlee Station, June 1st, 1864.
Cold Harbor, June 2d and 3d, 1864.
Turkey Ridge, June 4th to 13th, 1864.
Frazier's Farm, June 13th, '64.
Wilcox's Farm, June 22d, '64.
Gurley House, June 23d, 1864.
Crater, July 30th, 1864.
Davis' Farm, August 19th, '64.
Reams' Station, August 25th, '64.
Burgess' Mill, October 27th, '64.
Hicksford, December 9th, 1864.
Hatcher's Run, February 6th, 1865.
Amelia C. H., April 5th, 1865.
Cumberland Church, April 7th, 1865.

Appomattox Court House, April 9th, 1865.

The first battle of importance in which the company took part was Seven Pines, June 1st, 1862, and from that time until and including the second battle of Manassas, fought August the 30th, it lost eleven men killed. In addition to the thirty members of the company from Norfolk who lost their lives, two men who joined when the regiment was around Petersburg, were killed. They were William Spencer, from near Richmond, and —— Christian.

In addition to the battles enumerated above, in which the company was engaged with the regiment, it had quite a serious affair of its own on the 19th and 20th of June, 1862. The company was sent by itself on a scout down the Charles City road, near Richmond, for the purpose of ascertaining the position of the enemy, and while on that duty had a spirited engagement with the enemy, in which it had two men, Thos. L. Connor and John Carlon, killed and a number wounded. General Mahone's report of the battle of Malvern Hill compliments the 12th Virginia Regiment very highly, and his report of the Chancellorsville battle says:

" The enemy's cavalry advance on the Ely's Ford road made its appearance, and after a precipitate advance upon our pickets, (capturing several) he subsequently came upon our rear guard, the 12th Virginia Infantry, Lieutenant-Colonel Field commanding— was repulsed so effectually as to leave us free from any further annoyance during our change of position," and further on he says "the 12th Virginia, Lieutenant Colonel Field commanding, for its rigid and efficient resistance to the superior force of the enemy while covering the formation of our line of battle on the turnpike Friday, May 1st, deserves high commendation." On many other occasions the conduct of the regiment was very highly complimented. At the battle of the Crater, July 30th, 1864, in which Mahone's Brigade achieved one of the most brilliant victories of the war, the 12th Regiment carried about one hundred and fifty men in the fight, of whom twelve were killed and twenty-six wounded. Of these two of the killed and three wounded were in Company H.

The following men left Norfolk, May 10th, 1862, with the company:

Captain Thos. F. Owens, wounded August 30th, 1862, 2d Manassas, surrendered at Appomattox.
First Lieutenant Henry C. Woodhouse, captured April 29th, 1863, exchanged, wounded May 8th, 1864, at Shady Grove.
Second Lieutenant Chas. Dashiell, wounded Sept. 14th, 1862, Crampton Gap, discharged April 5th, 1864.
Third Lieutenant Chas. L. Beale, wounded July 30th, 1864, Crater, killed Aug. 19th, Davis' Farm.
First Sergeant Wm. H. Ramsey, wounded Aug. 30th, 1862, 2d Manasas and died in hospital.
Second Sergeant Luther Walker, captured Sept. 14th, 1862, wounded May 2d, 1864, Spotsylvania C. H.
Third Sergeant John R. Baldry, wounded July 1st, 1862, Malvern Hill, killed July 30th, 1864, at Crater.
Fourth Sergeant John F. Sale, promoted Lieutenant Oct., 1864, wounded Feb. 6th, 1865, at Hatcher's Run, and died Feb. 12th.
First Corporal Geo. T. Keefe, wounded June 25th, 1862, detailed Courier Aug. 25th, 1863.
Second Corporal S. F. Jordan, promoted Sergeant, wounded Aug. 19th, 1864, Davis' Farm, surrendered at Appomattox.
Third Corporal John M. Dashiell, died in hospital, November 4th, 1862, Winchester.
Fourth Corporal E. W. Shelton, wounded June 25th, 1862, and Aug. 19th, 1864, Davis' Farm.
Musician Wm. Gale, discharged Aug. 25th, 1864.

PRIVATES.

Atkinson, Junius A.
Anderson, Chas., transferred to Huger Battery May 1st, 1862.
Bew, Geo. W., wounded Aug. 30th, 1862, 2d Manassas.
Bunge, F., wounded June 1st, 1862, Seven Pines, died June 25th in hospital, Richmond.
Buis, John H.
Braithwait, Thos., promoted Corporal, killed July 1st, 1862, at Malvern Hill.
Bryan, Fred. P.
Brockett, Wm., appointed Engineer in Navy May 1st, 1862.
Brownley, Wm. M., surrendered at Appomattox.
Bracey, Geo., wounded Aug. 30th, 1862, captured Sept. 14th, 1862, and never rejoined the company.
Charlton, Jos., died in hospital, Dec. 14th, 1862, Lynchburg.
Cusick, Thos., killed June 1st, 1862, Seven Pines.

Charlton, Cary, killed Sept. 14th, 1862, Crampton Gap.
Connor, Thos. L., killed June 19th, 1862, Charles City Road.
Carroll, H. W., wounded May 8th, 1864, Shady Grove.
Carlon, John, killed June 20th, 1862. Charles City Road.
Connor, James.
Carter, John B., captured Sept. 14th, 1862.
Dozier, Thos L.
Davis, Thos. H., wounded Aug. 30th, 1862, 2d Manassas, and died Oct. 31st in Warrenton.
Davis, Wm. H., surrendered at Appomattox.
Diggs, James, discharged July 29th, 1862, over age.
Dobbs, Andrew J., surrendered at Appomattox.
Dashiel, F. S., discharged July 29th, 1862, over age.
Edmonds, Wm., wounded April 29th, 1863, Germanna Ford.
Fitzgerald, Wm. H., wounded July 1st, 1862, Malvern Hill, appointed Master in the Navy Oct. 7th, 1863.
Gray, Jas. R., killed June 1st, 1862, Seven Pines.
Griffin, A. J., wounded July 30th, 1864, Crater.
Griffin, John, died in hospital, July 6th, 1862, Richmond.
Harris, Wm., surrendered at Appomattox.
Hall, John P., transferred to Huger Battery May 1st, 1862.
James, Wm. E., wounded Aug. 19th, 1864, Davis' Farm, died Aug. 25th.
Johnson, J. Cave, transferred from Company D, May 1st, 1862, surrendered at Appomattox.
Kellum, W. P. M., wounded July 1st, 1862, Aug. 30th, 1862, and disabled and discharged.
Lovett, Edward J., wounded and captured October 27th, 1864, at Burgess' Mill.
Lewis, Thos. J.
Lewis, Wm. killed Aug. 30th, 1862, 2d Manassas.
Longworth, James, captured June 22, 1864, Wilcox Farm.
Lufsey, Jas., surrendered at Appomattox.
Moore, John A.
Marks, R. A., died in hospital, June 27th, 1862, Richmond.
Moreland, Jas., killed May 12th, 1864, Spotsylvania C. H.
Moreland, Thos., died in hospital, Sept., 1864, Richmond.
Mayer, Lewis, killed July 1st, 1862, Malvern Hill.
Murray, Jas. T., wounded July 30th, 1864, at Crater, and Aug. 30th, 1862, at 2d Manassas.
Mayer, Wm., discharged July 17th, 1862, disability.
McNamara, John R., detailed 1863 to work for Government.
Norfleet, Nathaniel, discharged for disability.
Norwood, John W., surrendered at Appomattox.
Nunnaly, E. J., wounded August 30th, 1862, killed July 2d, 1863, Gettysburg.
Owens, Wm. T., captured Sept. 14th, 1862, exchanged and detailed in Gen. Anderson's Pioneer Corps.
Peed, W. A., captured Sept. 14th, 1862, detailed on ordnance duty March 3d, 1863.
Randolph, N. B., captured Sept. 14th, 1862, exchanged and died in hospital 1863, in Fredericksburg.
Randolph, R. G., captured Sept. 14th, 1862, exchanged and surrendered at Appomattox.
Rogers, John M., wounded July 2d, 1863, at Gettysburg.
Robinson, John R., promoted Sergeant, killed Aug. 30th, 1862, Manassas.
Rose, J. H., detailed as Teamster.
Shepherd, John S., discharged for disability.
Simons, Geo. W.
Stone, Wm., wounded Aug. 30th, 1862, Manassas, died Sept. 16th.
Scribner, Jas. D., killed May 12th, 1864, Spotsylvania C. H.
Shipp, Josiah P., transferred to Company G, 1862, wounded May 6th, 1864.

Simcoe, Augustus, discharged Aug. 30th, 1862, over age.
Taylor, Wm. E., appointed Hospital Steward Nov. 6th, 1862.
Tompkins, E., killed Aug. 30th, 1862, 2d Manassas.
Vaden, W. L., wounded accidentally, 1862.
White, Caleb D., promoted Corporal, wounded May 6th, 1864, at the Wilderness.
Williams, Thos. T., died in hospital, 1862, Richmond.
Walker, Wm. H., wounded and captured Aug. 19th, 1864, Davis' Farm.
Ward, Mathias, captured Sept. 14th, 1862, wounded May 12th, 1864, captured Oct. 27th, 1864.
Wilkinson, Samuel D., wounded Aug. 30th, 1862, Manasas.
Wilkins, Henry H., wounded May 12th, 1864, Spotsylvania C. H.
Woodhouse, W. S., wounded July 30th, 1864, at Crater, and died August 15th.
Williamson, John T., captured Oct. 27th, 1864, Burgess' Mill.
White, Wm. J., captured Oct. 27th, 1864, Burgess' Mill.
White, J. J. P., captured Sept. 14th, 1862, surrendered at Appomattox.
White, Ed. J., killed July 30th, 1864, at Crater.
Whitehurst, Leven.
Killed and died—30.

The company surrendered one commissioned officer and eighteen enlisted men at Appomattox Court House. The following is the list:

Captain Thos. F. Owens,
Sergeant S. F. Jordan,
Private *W. J. Branch,
 Wm. M. Brownley,
 Wm. H. Davis,
 *A. A. Delbridge,
 *Jos. Delbridge,
 *Robt. Delbridge,
 A. J. Dobbs,
 Wm. Harris,

Private R. S. House,
 *Jas. Hough,
 J. C. Johnson,
 J. W. Lufsey,
 *J. W. Manning,
 J. W. Norwood,
 R. J. Randolph,
 *T. W. Rawlins,
 J. J. P. White.

*Joined the company after it left Norfolk.

CHAPTER XL.

THE ATLANTIC ARTILLERY, EIGHTEENTH VIRGINIA BATTALION, HEAVY ARTILLERY.

This company was organized and uniformed by Captain J. Hardy Hendren, and mustered into service on the 9th of March, 1862, in Norfolk, with the following officers:

Captain, J. Hardy Hendren.

First Lieutenant, Wm. C. Marrow; 2d Lieutenant, W. Roy Roberts; 3d Lieutenant, John H. Sale, Jr.

First Sergeant, Beverly K. Taylor.

Lieutenant Marrow was promoted to Quartermaster in the Army of Northern Virginia and Lieutenant Roberts was assigned as A. A. G. to the staff of General Pemberton, commanding the batteries around Richmond. First Sergeant Taylor was promoted to Lieutenant.

When the company was mustered into service, it was ordered to the entrenched camp near Norfolk, and was armed with muskets. It remained there until the 7th of May, when it was ordered to Petersburg and attached to the 18th Virginia Battalion Heavy Artillery. After a stay of three or four days the company was sent to Richmond, and assisted in building earthworks and mounting heavy guns. It remained in the batteries around that city until the close of the war, with an occasional expedition to head off raiding parties of the enemy's cavalry. It was sent to Gordonsville with General Fitzhugh Lee's Cavalry against Stoneman's raid; was in the trenches in front of Richmond when Kilpatrick came there with his troopers on the 1st of March, 1864, and at the battle of Drury's Bluff, on the 16th of May, 1864, participated as light artillerists, having charge of a battery of five field pieces. In the fall of 1864, the company was sent down to Chaffins' Farm, and remained there, facing the enemy in Fort Harrison until the evacuation of Richmond by the Confederates, in April, 1865, when it fell back with the troops under General Ewell, and took part in the battle of Saylor's Creek. It was extremely fortunate, and, though always ready for service, escaped the battles and dangers to which most of the other troops were exposed. It lost only one man killed in battle, and four died in hospital from sickness. The following were the casualties in the company:

Charles Pinkham, killed at Saylor's Creek.
W. A. Griffin, died in hospital, Richmond.
Armistead Haughton, died in hospital, Richmond.
Nathaniel Wilkins, died in hospital, Richmond.
James Young, died in hospital, Richmond.
David Mathias, wounded at Saylor's Creek.
J. W. Buchanan, wounded at Saylor's Creek.

Below will be found a list of the men who left Norfolk with the company:

Captain J. Hardy Hendren.
First Lieutenant Wm. C. Marrow.
Second Lieutenant W. Roy Roberts.
Third Lieutenant John H. Sale, Jr.
First Sergeant Beverly K. Taylor.
Second Sergeant Judson Hendren.
Third Sergeant Henry Thompson.
Fourth Sergeant David Mathias.
Fifth Sergeant Armistead Haughton.
Sixth Sergeant Thos. C. Joynes.
First Corporal Samuel Gordon.
Second Corporal John M. Wells.
Third Corporal Thos. R. White.
Fourth Corporal Wm. Leary.

PRIVATES.

Ashton, Wm.
Butt, Niemeyer.
Buford, Jabez.
Buchanan, J. W.
Callis, Wm.
Dozier, Tully F.
Evans, Arthur.
Flannigan, Fletcher.
Griggs, Geo. D.
Griffin, W. A.
Harris, Abraham M.
Higgins, John H.
Kisk, Richard.
Krouse, John H.
Lambert, Henry.
LeDoyne, John H.
Mathias, Henry B.
Patterson, John H.
Pinkham, Chas.
Richardson, Wm.
Scott, Robert.
Sharpley, John J.
Thompson, David S.
Totten, Samuel.
Taylor, John G.
Timberlake, David.
Thayer, Stephen B.
Vellines, John A.
Winslow, Joseph.
Whitehurst, Nathan.
Williams, James M.
Wilkins, Nathaniel.
Young, James.

CHAPTER XLI.

THE UNITED ARTILLERY, COMPANY A, NINETEENTH VIRGINIA BATTALION, HEAVY ARTILLERY.

This company was composed of most excellent fighting material and was commanded by as cool and determined a soldier as there was in General Lee's Army, and, though always ready to respond to the call of duty, and though the men were exposed to danger and death on numerous occasions, an over-ruling Providence seemed to watch over them, and their casualties were insignificant. One man was killed in battle, one killed by accident, and one died in hospital from sickness. Five were wounded.

The company was organized in Norfolk several days before the burning of the Navy Yard by the Federal forces in April, 1861, but at the beginning of hostilities was not uniformed or armed. It was called into service on the 19th of April, to take part in the capture of the powder in Fort Norfolk. A detail was made to capture the gunner, Mr. Oliver, to prevent him from signaling to the Navy Yard, what was being done. The detail sent to capture Mr. Oliver was under command of Lieutenant W. Carter Williams, and the rest of the company landed at the wharf at the fort, in barges. The officers of the company at that time were:

Captain, Thomas Kevill.

First Lieutenant, James E. Barry; 2d Lieutenant, Wm. Carter Williams; 3d Lieutenant, Thaddeus E. Eisenbiess.

The company took its name from the old United Fire Company, of which most of its men were members. A long habit of contending with the flames had inured them to dangers. Upon being mustered into service the company was stationed at Fort Norfolk and was furnished with muskets, and also was placed in charge of four light guns and drilled both as infantry and artillery. They also had charge of a battery of heavy guns, so that, during the year the company was at Fort Norfolk, the men became experts in all branches of the service except the cavalry.

In July, 1861, Lieutenant Williams was elected Captain of a company from Princess Anne county, which was attached to the 6th Regiment as Company B. Lieutenant Eisenbiess was promoted to 2d Lieutenant and Edward Lakin was elected 3d Lieutenant. Upon the organization of the 41st Virginia Regiment of infantry the United Artillery company was attached to it as Company E.

When the iron-clad Virginia (Merrimac) was ready for service it was found that she lacked thirty-one men of having a full crew, and Captain Kevill was applied to for volunteers to make up the deficiency, but the men were not willing to serve under the command of the naval officers and declined to volunteer unless one of their own officers was on board the ship to take charge of them. This was reported to the Secretary of War and by him communicated to the Secretary of the Navy, and the result was that the services of the company were accepted, with Captain Kevill as their commander. The Captain then called for thirty-one volunteers, and the whole company stepped to the front. Selecting thirty one men whom he thought best qualified, by physical strength, to do the heavy work which was required of them, he reported to the Commandant of the Navy Yard on the 7th of March, 1862, and was assigned, with sixteen men, to one of the 9-inch broadside guns. During the engagement the fifteen other men were distributed among guns which were short in their crews. During the second day's engagement, the 9th of March, a piece of metal was knocked off the muzzle of the gun, but the men continued to load and fire it until the close of the battle. The next time the ship went down to Hampton Roads Captain Kevill was again with his men, but on the third trip, May 8th, Lieutenant Lakin had command of the detachment. Two men belonging to the company, A. J. Dalton and John Capps, were wounded by musket balls coming through the port holes in the first day's battle, March 8th.

On the 10th of May, 1862, before sunrise, the company was marched from Fort Norfolk to the entrenched camp and placed in charge of a battery of heavy guns, and remained there until early in the afternoon, when it was marched to the Norfolk and Petersburg railroad depot in Norfolk and took the cars for Petersburg. It remained eight or ten days on Dunn's Hill, near the city, when it was sent to Richmond and ordered to report to Colonel Rhett, commanding defences of the city. While the United Artillery were in Petersburg and General Lee was making arrangements to defend Drury's Bluff from the anticipated attack of the Federal iron-clads, he wrote to General Huger, commanding the Department of Petersburg, that the battery was a very important one, that it should be well defended, and recommended that the United Artillery company be sent there. He told General Huger that he understood this was one of the best companies in the service.

Upon reporting to Colonel Rhett the company was assigned to two two-gun batteries or redouts, one on each side of the Virginia Central railroad, and in two days built platforms for the guns, mounted them and built a magazine. The guns were mounted on heavy army carriages. The company remained in this battery until after the battles around Richmond, when it was moved to battery No. 8 and attached to a battalion commanded by Major Atkinson. Shortly afterwards it was detached from Major At-

20

kinson's command, ordered to Drury's Bluff, and still attached to the 19th Battalion of heavy artillery, reported to Captain S. S. Lee. Subsequently Major Frank Smith, of Norfolk, became commander of the battalion and was killed on the retreat from Richmond to Appomattox. His battalion was on both sides of a road, and each mistaking the other for the enemy, began firing, and in endeavoring to stop it Major Smith was killed. The company remained in the battery at Drury's Bluff until the 16th of May, 1864, when as an infantry company it took part in the battle fought there that day. In June, 1864, when Butler's troops were driven back to the lines of Bermuda Hundreds by Pickett's Division the United Artillery Company was sent to the Howlett House and took charge of a fortification known as Battery Dantzler, after Colonel Dantzler, of the 22d South Carolina Regiment, and when Butler began digging the Dutch Gap Canal the company was moved to Battery Wood, in front of Dutch Gap, where it was constantly engaged shelling the enemy's working parties. Here it took its place regularly with the other troops on the lines, taking its turn at picket duty as an infantry company, but still manning the heavy guns.

During the interval between the battle of Seven Pines and the Seven Days' battles a detachment of the company, under command of Lieutenant Barry, operated a heavy gun which was put upon a railroad flat car, protected with iron, on the York River railroad, but it did not prove very effective, on account of the difficulty in moving it along the track towards and from the enemy. While at Drury's Bluff the men frequently volunteered to take part in naval expeditions which were gotten up by Captain John Taylor Wood and other officers to cut out detached vessels of the enemy.

Lieutenant Barry's health broke down in the winter of 1864-5, and he became unable to do duty. Therefore, by the advice of the post surgeon, which was concurred in by Captain Kevill, he tendered his resignation and was discharged from the company. In September, 1864, Lieutenant Lakin received an appointment in the Navy, and Daniel Knowles was elected Lieutenant. Lieutenant Eisenbiess was killed in 1863 by an accident upon the Richmond and Petersburg railroad. Upon the evacuation of Richmond the United Artillery formed part of the forces under General Ewell, and under the command of Captain Kevill participated in the battle of Saylor's Creek, where it had one man killed and three wounded. Thus it happened, very singularly, that the company met with casualties only in its first and last engagements with the enemy. The following is a list of its losses:

Lieutenant T. E. Eisenbiess, killed accidentally, 1863.
John Belote, died in hospital at Drury's Bluff.
Emanuel Lacoste, killed at Saylor's Creek, April 5th, 1865.

John T. Bullock, wounded at Saylor's Creek.
Fred. S. Clarke, wounded at Saylor's Creek.
John Capps, wounded on the Virginia, March 8th, 1862.
A. J. Dalton, wounded on the Virginia, March 8th, 1862.
Hezekiah Wells, wounded at Saylor's Creek.
A. C. Griswold, captured August 6th, 1864, at Howlett's.
George Smith, captured August 6th, 1864, at Howlett's.
Eugene Solomon, captured August 6th, 1864, at Howlett's.
A. J. Dalton recovered from his wound received on the Virginia (Merrimac) and was transferred to a cavalry company in Morgan's Brigade, was wounded and captured at Dublin in 1864, in the fight with Crook's and Averill's cavalry.

Below will be found the roll of the company:
Captain Thos. Kevill.
First Lieutenant James E. Barry.
Second Lieutenant Thaddeus E. Eisenbiess.
Second Lieutenant W. Carter Williams.
Second Lieutenant Edward Lakin.
Second Lieutenant Daniel Knowles.
First Sergeant Adam Bamn.
Second Sergeant Fayette F. Porter.
Third Sergeant W. F. Coston.
Fourth Sergeant Richard Nelson.
Fifth Sergeant W. H. Cosby.
Sixth Sergeant W. H. Carr.
Ordnance Sergeant John T. Bullock.
First Corporal Alphonse M. Bullock.
Second Corporal John Carstaphan.
Third Corporal John Gillis.
Fourth Corporal Geo. J. Allen.
Musicians Eugene Solomon and Emanuel Lacoste.

PRIVATES.

Applewhite, A.
Albright, Chas. W.
Bell, Miles K.
Burns, W. A.
Belote, John.
Betts, W. M.
Bisby, Henry T.
Bowers, Geo.
Baker, Wm.
Bisby, W. J.
Bunting, John.
Black, John T.
Capps, John.
Croker, Rufus K.
Clarke, Alex.
Clarke, Fred. S.
Cameron, Chas.
Cook, Edward.
Colonna, W. B.
Chestnut, Nicholas.
Cain, Richard C.
Cornell, J. R.
Duke, W. F.
Duncan, Jas.
Dalton, A. J.
Diggs, Wm. J.
Deane, John.
Dudley, Wm. F.
Fisher, Chas.
Fowler, John.
Flynn, John.
Griswold, A. C.
Glennan, Wm.
Georgan, Michael.
Hitchings, Ed. T.
Hundley, Jas.
Hoggs, Geo. W.
Hogan, Eugene.
Jones, John W.
Kevill, John P.
Knight, Geo.
Land, Geo. W.
Lovely, Geo.
Lawrence, David.
Murray, John T.
McCarty, Neal.
Manning, A. J.
Mars, John.
Murray, Geo.
Maloye, Jack.
Morris, John.

Miller, Redman.
Parker, Geo.
Pitt, W. P.
Robinson, F. J.
Richardson, B. A.
Rhea, Geo. W.

Rollins, Wm.
Reid, Chas.
Scultatus, Geo.
Solon, Thos.
Smith, Geo.
Smith, John D.

Stokes, Jas.
Snider, John.
Sharp, Chas.
Scott, Wyatt W.
Thompson, Geo.
Wells, Hezekiah.

The official muster roll shows the following members of the United Artillery Company who were surrendered and paroled at Appomattox Court House:

Captain Thos. Kevill.
Second Lieutenant Adam Baum.
First Sergeant John T. Bullock.
Sergeant Alphonso Bullock.
Sergeant Wm. F. Coston.
Sergeant John Gillis.
Corporal George J. Allen.
Corporal M. Georgan.

PRIVATES.

Wm. Colonna.
Wm. Dudley.
J. H. Deane.
Jas. Duncan.
John Fowler.
Chas. Fisher.
John Flynn.
Geo. Land.

Wm. Morgan.
Redman Miller.
John Morris.
John P. Kevill.
Wm. P. Pitt.
Geo. T. Parker.
F. J. Robinson.
Chas. Reid.

Geo. Scultatus.
Jas. Stokes.
John Stare.
Geo. Thompson.
John Thomas.
R. O. Vaughan.
Jas. B. Yarborough.

At the surrender the company was classed as unattached.

CHAPTER XLII.

YOUNG'S HARBOR GUARD, THIRTEENTH VA. ARTILLERY BATTALION.

This company was raised in the latter part of April, 1861, by Captain John J. Young, as a heavy artillery company, and was recruited principally in Norfolk, a few of the men being from Norfolk county and Portsmouth. Captain Young uniformed the company at his own expense, and also contributed, out of his private funds, towards the erection of an earthwork at Boush's Bluff, to which point the company was ordered immediately upon its organization, for the purpose of throwing up fortifications. The work was armed with 32-pounder ship guns from the navy yard, and Captain Young fired the first shot at the enemy which was fired in this vicinity. On the 18th of May, 1861, the steam tug Kahukee landed a force of workmen at Seawell's Point for the purpose of building fortifications there, and was chased back to Norfolk by the steamer Monticello, which fired a shot at her. As soon as the Monticello came within range of Captain Young's guns he sent a thirty-two pound shot at her, which had the effect of stopping her course, and she turned about and steamed towards Hampton Roads.

Complaint having been made to General Huger that Union sympathizers in the vicinity of Norfolk were in the habit of communicating with the enemy at Fortress Monroe, Captain Young's Company, being composed of seafaring men, was changed into a company of Harbor Guards, whose duty it was to patrol the lower harbor at night, and for that purpose was furnished with four large launches, each armed with a boat howitzer, and also a number of small boats. The men were armed with muskets also. The officers of the company were:

Captain, John J. Young.
First Lieutenant, John E. Winder; 2d Lieutenant, Henry Roberts; 3d Lieutenant, John Lewis.

The company entered upon their new duties in July, 1861, and their work was performed very satisfactorily, and what had previously been a source of information to the enemy was very effectually stopped. An occasional "intelligent contraband" succeeded in making his escape to the Federal lines, but those escapades became very rare and very risky.

The company remained at Boush's Bluff until the 10th of May, 1862, when Norfolk was evacuated by the Confederate forces. Early that morning, the tug J B. White, which was under orders of Captain Young, and employed in his department, landed some stores at Boush's Bluff for the company, and instead of returning to Norfolk, steamed past the Seawell's Point batteries and kept on to Fortress Monroe. The captain and owner of the tug was a Northern man, and the Confederate authorities very unwisely retained him in charge of it. The information which he conveyed to the enemy hastened the movements of the Confederates. That afternoon at 2 o'clock, the men in Captain Young's Company embarked in their barges and rowed past Craney Island to Pig Point and up the Nansemond river to Suffolk, where they destroyed their boats, placed their howitzers on the cars and carried them to Richmond. The Virginia (Merrimac) was lying near Craney Island, and her presence there deterred the Federal vessels from making any effort to interfere with the boats while they were being rowed up Hampton Roads towards Pig Point.

Upon arriving at Richmond the company was sent to Chaffin's Bluff, on James river, and attached to the 13th Virginia Artillery Battalion, under Major W. H. Gibbs, and remained there until the summer of 1863, when it was sent to Harper's Ferry, and met the army returning from Pennsylvania. It returned to Richmond as guards for the prisoners captured in Pennsylvania, and was again stationed in the fortifications near Fort Harrison, on Chaffin's farm. When Butler advanced from Bermuda Hundreds in 1864, the company was moved over to the south side of James river with its four howitzers, and took part in the battle of the 16th of May. It then returned to Chaffin's farm, and was there on the 29th of September, 1864, when the enemy captured Fort Harrison, which was garrisoned by only one company. This company, with a small handful of troops, made a very gallant stand against Butler's Corps, and held the rest of the lines until reinforcements arrived.

When the company was in the fortifications around Richmond, its name underwent a change, and it became known as Young's Howitzers. It did service also at Dutch Gap for a short while, and upon the evacuation of Richmond, was attached to the troops under General Custis Lee, and took part in the battle of Saylor's Creek, just before the surrender at Appomattox.

Captain Young's health failed in 1863, and he was granted a sick leave. Lieutenant Roberts resigned August 25th, 1863, and was appointed a Lieutenant in the Navy, and Lieutenant Lewis resigned June 29th, 1864. Sergeant John C. Murray was elected Lieutenant July 4th, 1864, and in 1865, Walter Young was promoted to First Sergeant.

The following were the casualties of the company. Those reported prior to February 28th, 1865, are from the official reports of the commanding officer, those since that date have been supplied from the recollections of the survivors, but may be relied upon as correct:

Corporal Ezekiel Taylor, died in hospital Sept. 12th, 1862, Richmond.
Corporal Andrew Edmonds, died in hospital April 1st, 1864, Richmond.
Private John Crockett, accidentally shot himself and died Oct. 6th, 1862.
Private Wm. E. Etheredge, died in hospital Nov. 25th, 1862, Richmond.
Private James Gilbert, died in hospital April 5th, 1864, Richmond.
Sergeant John F. Richardson, supposed killed at Saylor's Creek, April, 1865.
Private Ed. E. Holt, died in hospital March 17th, 1863, Richmond.
Sergeant Walter Young, wounded at Saylor's Creek.
Corporal John Sadler, wounded Saylor's Creek.
Private Thos. Aydlott, wounded Sept. 29th, 1861.
Private John Griffin, wounded Sept. 29th, 1864.
Private Jas. Hamilton, wounded Saylor's Creek.
Private John Reid, wounded Saylor's Creek.
Private Benj. Ward, wounded Saylor's Creek.
 Killed and died—7.

 The following is the roll of the company for May 31st, 1862:
Captain, John J. Young.
First Lieutenant, John E. Winder.
Second Lieutenant, Henry Roberts.
Third Lieutenant, John Lewis.
First Sergeant, W. H. Pagaud.
Second Sergeant, John F. Richardson.
Third Sergeant, John C. Murray.
Fourth Sergeant, Wm. Trower.
Corporals, Ezekiel Taylor, Andrew Edmonds, Geo. Sadler, Augustus Godfrey.

PRIVATES.

Abdell, Jos.	Crockett, Jno.	Kirsh, John H.
Allen, Wm. A.	Davis, Jno.	Martin, Jno.
Aydlott, Thos.	Everett, Lemuel.	Morrison, Jos.
Baker, Geo. W.	Etheredge, Wm. E.	Murphy, Thos.
Benson, Geo.	Gilbert, Jas.	Robbins, Asher.
Conoway, Ed. J.	Griffin, Jno.	Reid, Jno.
Colonna, Geo. M.	Hamilton, Jas.	Ward, Benj.
Colonna, Wm.	Hansel, Warren.	White, Wm.
Corbett, Thos. H.	Holt, Ed. E.	Wynn, Wm.
Curtis, Edward.	Hyller, Thos.	Young, Walter.

 Detachments from the company took part in several naval boat expeditions. Private Wm. A. Allen was transferred to a light artillery company and lost a leg in battle.
 Only six men in the Harbor Guard were left at Appomattox. Those were:
  T. L. Blanton,   W. W. Mathews,
  J. Dorsett,   J. T. Pollard,
  T. R. Gary,   W. White.
 At that date the company was not attached to any regiment or battalion. All of the names above except Wm. White were assigned to the company after it left Norfolk.

CHAPTER XLIII.

THE SIGNAL CORPS.

This company was organized by Major James F. Milligan in Norfolk in March, 1862. It was composed originally of men detailed for the service from other commands, but not being able to supply the requisite number from that source, and the members being liable at any moment to be ordered back to the companies in which they were enlisted, it was determined to organize the Signal Corps as an independent command, to enlist men regularly in it, and to transfer to it permanently those who had been detailed to it. As the service required men of considerable intelligence, its members were selected with care. There were men in the organization from every State from which troops were on duty around Norfolk. The officers of the command were:

Major James F. Milligan, of Norfolk, Chief Signal Officer.
Captain—Nathaniel W. Small, of Norfolk.
First Lieutenant—Simon C. Wells, of Salem.
Second Lieutenant—Douglass C. Cannon, of Norfolk.
Third Lieutenant—Joseph B. Woodley, of Portsmouth.
First Sergeant—Francis R. Benson, of Portsmouth.
Second Sergeant—C. W. Young, of Portsmouth.
Third Sergeant—Richard A. Mapp, of Norfolk.
Fourth Sergeant—A. G. Millado, of Norfolk.
Fifth Sergeant—Andrew J. Flanner, of New Orleans.
First Corporal—John Emmerson, of Portsmouth.
Second Corporal—John C. Saunders, Jr., of Norfolk.
Third Corporal—Edward Rooney, of New Orleans.
Fourth Corporal—F. M. Hyman, of Norfolk.

At the evacuation of Norfolk one hundred and twenty-seven men were on the muster roll, and of these forty-one were from Portsmouth. Their names will be found in the lists of the various companies which entered the Confederate service from that city, and in chapter XXV. After leaving Norfolk the command was moved to Petersburg and there perfected in the code of signals, after which two chains of posts were established, with their bases at Bermuda Hundreds and City Point. One extended up the Appomattox river to Petersburg, and the other up the James river to Drury's Bluff, where it connected with a telegraph system to Richmond. Later a chain of posts was established down James river to the vicinity of Smithfield, where a considerable force of the company was located under command of Lieutenant Joseph R. Woodley. This detachment was mounted, and was also provided with a couple of swift row boats, with which they frequently crossed over to the north side of James river at night, inside the lines of the enemy, and gathered information of the movements of troops and vessels. In fact, it was to this source mainly that the Confederate Government relied for its information concerning movements of the Federal fleet in James river and Hampton Roads, and of troops near Fortress Monroe. Several of the members of the corps were afterwards placed on blockade runners, which frequented Wilmington and Charleston for the purpose of signaling the forts, to prevent the vessels from being fired on by mistake.

The following men enlisted in the corps in Norfolk, and, though at this late day it is not practicable to separate them, it is believed that all, or nearly all, of them were residents of that city. All of them lived through the war:

Captain, N. W. Small.
Second Lieutenant, D. C. Cannon, transferred from Company G, 6th Virginia Regiment.
Second Sergeant, A. G. Millhado, transferred from Company G, 6th Virginia Regiment.
Second Corporal, John C. Saunders, Jr.
Fourth Corporal F. M. Hyman, transferred from Company G, 6th Virginia Regiment.

PRIVATES.

Adams, Wm. D.
Averett, Thos. H.
Barnes, V. H.
Boush, Isaac F.
Beach, Wm. F.
Berwick, Wm.
Freer, Geo. H.
Forbes, Robert A.
Greenwood, Fred.
Hastings, Wm. T.
James, Wm. A.
James, Rowland F.
Lathrop, Wm. B.
Lyell, Geo. E.
Marable, Wm. H.
Norsworthy, Jos. C.
Ricks, James R.
Seabury, Wm. H.
Walldren, Thos.
White, Alphens A.
Wiles, Samuel.
Windsor, C. H.

Of these the following were at the surrender at Appomattox:
Lieutenant D. C. Cannon.   Private Geo. H. Freer.
Sergeant F. M. Hyman.   Private Fred. Greenwood.

CHAPTER XLIV.

FIELD AND STAFF, &C., NORFOLK.

Norfolk was represented in the Confederate Army by the following field and staff officers:

Brigadier General Richard L. Page, Page's Alabama Brigade.
Colonel Thos. J. Corprew, 6th Virginia Infantry.
Colonel V. D. Groner, 61st Virginia Infantry.
Colonel Wm. Lamb, 36th North Carolina Infantry.
Colonel Edward E. Portlock, Jr., 21st Arkansas Infantry.
Colonel A. W. Starke, commanding artillery.
Colonel Francis Mallory, 55th Virginia Infantry, killed at Chancellorsville.
Lieutenant Colonel John S. Saunders, Battalion of Artillery.
Lieutenant-Colonel Walter H. Taylor, Adjutant General on staff of General Robert E. Lee.
Lieutenant-Colonel Henry W. Williamson, 6th Virginia Infantry.
Lieutenant-Colonel Arthur Sinclair Cunningham, 10th Alabama Infantry.
Major Edmond Bradford, Inspector General and Mustering Officer Huger's Division.
Major James F. Milligan, commanding Independent Signal Corps and Scouts.
Major Francis Smith, Heavy Artillery Battalion, killed April, 1865, on the retreat from Richmond.
Major Wm. E. Taylor, Norfolk Infantry Battalion and General Gwynn's staff.
Major Robt. B. Taylor, 6th Virginia Infantry.
Major John Saunders Taylor, Provisional Army C. S., killed at Sharpsburg.
Major Richard C. Taylor, Artillery Battalion.
Major Robertson Taylor, Adjutant General on General Mahone's staff.
Major Chas. B. Duffield, Adjutant General on General Wise's staff.
Captain W. W. Chamberlaine, staff of General Walker, Chief of Ordnance 3d Corps A. N. Va.
Captain John D. Myrick, A. A. G. Loring's staff.
Adjutant W. A. S. Taylor, 61st Virginia Infantry.
Adjutant Alexander Tunstall, 6th Virginia Infantry.
Adjutant W. T. Walke, 39th Virginia Cavalry Battalion.
Captain Robert G. Portlock, A. A. General Fagan's Cavalry Brigade.
Captain Richard Walke, Ordnance Officer, General Mahone's staff.
Lieutenant Isaac Walke, Ordnance Officer, Fitzhugh Lee's Cavalry Division, killed at Woodstock August, 1864.

Brigadier General Richard L. Page, was born in Norfolk and entered the United States Navy as a Midshipman on the 1st of March, 1824, and passed through the intervening grades to that of commander, which position he occupied at the beginning of the war, having been promoted on the 14th of September, 1855. His last duties in the United States Navy were as commander of the sloop of war Germantown, on the East India Station. Upon the secession of Virginia he resigned his commission in the United States Navy and was appointed in the Virginia Navy, and subsequently transferred to the Confederate Navy. He was on duty at the Gosport Navy Yard the first year of the war, and after the evacuation of Norfolk, was assigned to the command of the naval depot at Charlotte, N. C. From Charlotte he was transferred to Mobile, and on the 7th of March, 1864, was appointed Brigadier General in the Confederate army, and assigned to the command of Fort Morgan, at the outer defences of Mobile Bay. His brigade was composed of the 21st Alabama Infantry, 1st Battalion Alabama Heavy Artillery, 1st Battalion Tennessee Heavy Artillery, five companies of the 7th Alabama Cavalry and a portion of the 1st Regiment Alabama regulars. He was in command of Fort Morgan on the 5th of August, 1864, when the Federal fleet, under Admiral Farragut, ran by it, and succeeded in sinking one monitor, the Tecumseh, with a torpedo, and a wooden gun boat, the Phillippi, with his batteries. On the 9th of August the Federals landed a force of infantry and began a regular investment of Fort Morgan, and after a very gallant defence, in which his guns were all dismounted and his ability to resist any longer had ceased, he surrendered the fort on the 23d. His garrison amounted to about four hundred men, and they very bravely seconded his efforts to hold the fort, which was really untenable after the fleet had succeeded in passing it.

COLONEL THOS. J. CORPREW was in the volunteer service of the State before the war as captain of one of the Norfolk companies, and at the beginning of the war was appointed by Governor Letcher, Lieutenant-Colonel of the 6th Virginia Regiment. Upon the promotion of Colonel Wm. Mahone to the command of the brigade, he became Colonel of the regiment. He was not re-elected at the reorganization of the regiment in May, 1862.

COLONEL V. D. GRONER, from early youth, evinced a fondness for a military life, and was an officer in one of the volunteer companies of Norfolk before the war. At the beginning of hostilities he received an appointment in the Adjutant General's office in the Confederate States War Department, but desiring to take a more active part in the struggle which was going on, accepted the position of Lieutenant-Colonel of the 4th North Carolina Cavalry in the summer of 1862, and was actively engaged with the enemy in the Blackwater River section. His command drove back several gunboat expeditions, and had a successful engagement with Spiers' Cavalry, driving them back and capturing a number of prisoners. In October, 1862, he was elected Colonel of the 61st Virginia Regiment, by the officers of the regiment. He was severely wounded at the battle of Spotsylvania Court House, May 12th, 1864, and did not rejoin the regiment until August, and, while still on crutches, commanded it at the battle of Davis' Farm, August 19th. His wound, however, compelled him to again retire and he was not able to rejoin his command until just before the retreat from Petersburg. He commanded the regiment at the battles of Amelia Court House and Cumberland Church and surrendered at Appomattox. He was in command of the regiment in the following battles also: Fredericksburg, Chancellorsville, (May 1st, 2d and 3d) Salem Church, Gettysburg, Bristoe Station, Wilderness, Spotsylvania C. H., Davis' Farm, and numerous other smaller engagements.

COLONEL WM. LAMB was quite prominent in politics, though young in years, before the breaking out of the war, and entered into that struggle at its beginning, as Captain of the Woodis Riflemen. He took part in the engagements at Seawell's Point, May 19th and 21st, 1861, between the shore battery and the United States steamer Monticello, and his conduct was very highly complimented by Captain Colquit, commanding the post. Having received authority from the Secretary of War to raise an independent battalion, of which the Woodis Riflemen was to be one of the companies, he went to work in Princess Anne and Norfolk counties and raised two companies, but the Secretary assigned the Woodis Riflemen to the 6th Regiment as Company C, and his Princess Anne Company to the same regiment as Company B. Not relishing this treatment, Captain Lamb resigned, and was appointed by the Governor of North Carolina to the position of Colonel of State troops, and was assigned to duty on the staff of General Joseph R. Anderson, commanding in that State. When the 32d North Carolina Regiment was organized Colonel Lamb was elected its colonel, with headquarters at Fort Fisher, at the entrance to Wilmington harbor. His command extended for twenty miles north from Fort Fisher, and was really that of a Brigadier General. When Fort Fisher was captured, January 15th, 1865, Colonel Lamb was severely wounded and fell into the hands of the enemy. He was appointed a Colonel in the C. S. Provisional Army, and his promotion to Brigadier General had been approved by General Lee before the end came, while Colonel Lamb was in prison.

COLONEL ALEXANDER W. STARKE was an officer in the Marine Corps, U. S. Navy, at the beginning of the late war, and was attached to the sloop of war St. Marys, on the East India Station. The ship returned to the United States in March, 1862, landing at San Francisco, whereupon he resigned his commission, came through the lines without being captured, received an appointment as Captain in the Confederate army and was assigned to ordnance duty. He was subsequently promoted to Major, Lieutenant-Colonel and Colonel of volunteers, and assigned to the command of a battalion of artillery. His command varied from five to eleven companies, and did general service. He was slightly wounded at Fort Harrison on the 29th of September, 1864. At the time of the evacuation of Richmond, April 1st, 1865, his command was stationed on the Nine Mile Road near Seven Pines. He fell back with General Ewell's Division, was in the battle of Saylor's Creek, fell back towards Appomattox, and surrendered with the remnant of the army on the 9th of April.

COLONEL FRANCIS MALLORY was a Captain in the United States army at the breaking out of the war, and received a similar appointment in the Confederate regular army. Upon the organization of the 55th Virginia Regiment he was assigned to it as Colonel. The regiment was attached to Heth's Brigade of A. P. Hill's Division. Colonel Mallory served gallantly with his regiment in every engagement in which it participated until he met his death, on the 2d of May, 1863, at Chancellorsville. His regiment was a part of Jackson's corps, with which he made his celebrated movement to turn Hooker's right, and Colonel Mallory fell in the moment of victory, while leading his regiment in the charge.

COLONEL EDWARD E. PORTLOCK, JR., was born in Norfolk, received a military education at the Norfolk Military Academy, and at the breaking out of the war received an appointment in the War Department in Richmond, was appointed Lieutenant in the regular army, and at the request of General Roane was assigned to his staff in the trans-Mississippi Department, was elected Lieutenant-Colonel and then Colonel of the 24th Arkansas Regiment, was captured at the fall of Arkansas Post, but exchanged and recommended for promotion to Brigadier General. His commission as such had been made out when Richmond fell, but did not reach him. He was in a number of engagements, frequently commanding his brigade, but escaped without a wound.

LIEUTENANT COLONEL JOHN S. SAUNDERS was a Lieutenant in the United States army at the beginning of the war, resigned and enlisted in the Confederate army, and was promoted to Major of Artillery. He was appointed to command a battalion composed of Grimes' Battery of Portsmouth, Huger's Battery of Norfolk, and Moorman's Battery of Lynchburg. The battalion was disbanded shortly after the battle of Sharpsburg. Captain Grimes was killed, his men were divided between the two other companies, and Moorman's Battery was changed to horse artillery and transferred to Fitzhugh Lee's Cavalry Division. Major Saunders was assigned to ordnance duty in Richmond and promoted to Lieutenant-Colonel.

LIEUTENANT-COLONEL WALTER H. TAYLOR was one of the best known officers in the army of Northern Virginia. At the beginning of the war he was a Lieutenant in "Company F," of Norfolk, but before the company was regularly mustered into service received an appointment as Lieutenant in the Provisional Army of the Confederate States and was assigned to duty with General Robert E. Lee. He continued with General Lee as his Adjutant General until the close of the war, was prompt and efficient in the discharge of his duties, and enjoyed the confidence of the Commander-in-Chief. After the war Colonel Taylor published an admirable work, entitled "Four Years with General Lee," in which he gave to the world for the first time, from official sources, the great difference in the numbers of the Northern and Southern armies in the various battles in Virginia.

LIEUTENANT-COLONEL HENRY W. WILLIAMSON was elected Captain of Company F at the beginning of the war and was stationed with it on Craney Island until May, 1862. He was re-elected Captain at the reorganization of the company in April, 1862, and the following month, when the election was held for field officers of the 6th Virginia Regiment, to which his company was attached, Captain Williamson was elected Lieutenant-Colonel, and held that position until the close of the war. He was with the regiment in nearly all of the battles in which it was engaged, and at the battle of the Crater, fought on the 30th of July, 1864, lost an arm.

MAJOR JAMES F. MILLIGAN was a First Lieutenant in the United States Revenue Service before the war, resigned on the 17th of April, 1861, and received an appointment in the Virginia navy. He was assigned to the command of the steamer Empire, which was subsequently changed into a gunboat, given a new name and sent to the North Carolina Sounds. Subsequently Captain Milligan was transferred to the army, and in March, 1862, under or orders from the Secretary of War, organized the "Independent Signal Corps and Scouts," and originated a code of signals. In 1863 the company was enlarged into a battalion of two companies, and Captain Milligan became Major. His corps was very useful to the War Department in gathering information of the movements of the enemy and transmitting it rapidly to Richmond. They picketed James river from Drury's Bluff to Burwell's Bay until Grant crossed over to Petersburg, and made frequent incursions into the enemy's lines in the neighborhood of Newport News and Old Point in search of information.

LIEUTENANT-COLONEL A. S. CUNNINGHAM was a Lieutenant in the regular army, was appointed to a similar post in the Confederate army and assigned to ordnance duty. He was promoted to Lieutenant-Colonel of Volunteers, and during the Seven Days' battles around Richmond was assigned temporarily to the command of the 10th Alabama Regiment, receiving a severe wound while in the discharge of this duty. Upon recovering from his wounds he returned to his duties as an officer of ordnance, and later in the war commanded the 10th Virginia Regiment temporarily.

MAJOR FRANCIS SMITH was Commander of the 19th Battalion Virginia Heavy Artillery, stationed at Drury's Bluff, and upon the retreat from Richmond fell back with Ewell's Division. During the night of April 5th his battalion became separated into two parts, and each mistaking the other for the enemy, began firing. Major Smith endeavored to put a stop to it, but received a wound from which he died.

CAPTAIN ROBERT G. PORTLOCK enlisted in Company F at the beginning of the war and was on duty with it at Craney Island when he was promoted to Sergeant Major of the 9th Virginia Regiment. After the evacuation of Norfolk he became Captain of the President's Guard and did provost duty in Richmond. Subsequently he was tranferred to the trans-Mississippi Department and appointed to a position on the staff of General Fagan, commanding cavalry. He was wounded at the battle of Poison Spring and his promotion to Major was approved at the War Department, though the war ended before he received his commission. He surrendered with the army in Arkansas after the fall of the Confederacy.

MAJOR WM. E. TAYLOR, though not so commissioned in the Confederate army, deserves mention in this connection. Previous to the war the different volunteer companies of Norfolk composed a battalion, of which Major Taylor was commander, and when hostilities began and the battalion was enlarged into a regiment he naturally expected to be made its Colonel, but Governor Letcher appointed Colonel Mahone to command it and offered Major Taylor the position of Lieutenant-Colonel. This, however, he declined and withdrew from the regiment. He served for a while on the staff of General Gwynn, commanding the defences of Norfolk, and in that capacity hoisted the State flag of the Columbus Light Guard of Georgia over the battery at Seawell's Point on the 19th of May, 1861, when the Monticello made her attack upon it. Though well advanced in years and having two grown sons in the army (one of them Major R. B. Taylor, of the 6th Regiment), he was not willing to remain an idle spectator of events, but enlisted as a private in the Seaboard Rifles of Princess Anne county, Company F, 6th Virginia Regiment, and carried his musket until 1863, when his health and strength broke down and he was discharged on account of old age and physical disability. His discharge was obtained for him by friends without his knowledge.

MAJOR ROBERT B. TAYLOR was a son of Major Wm. E. Taylor. He entered the service at the beginning of the war as 1st Lieutenant of Company A, 6th Virginia Regiment, and on the 22d of August was elected Captain of the Woodis Riflemen, Company C. At the reorganization of the regiment, in May, 1862, he was elected Major, which position he held until the surrender at Appomattox. The regiment was a part of Mahone's Brigade, and participated in about thirty-seven engagements, in most of which Major Taylor was present and yet fortunately escaped without a wound.

MAJOR JOHN SAUNDERS TAYLOR was an officer in the United States navy when the war began, but resigned upon the secession of Virginia and entered the Confederate army as a Captain. He was present as an advisory ordnance officer at the battle of Roanoke Island, and as commander of the heavy artillery in Fort Huger distinguished himself in its defence. He was captured with the garrison. He was subsequently exchanged, promoted to Major commanding a battalion of light artillery, and killed at Sharpsburg September 17th, 1862.

MAJOR RICHARD C. TAYLOR entered the service at the beginning of the war as Captain of the Independent Grays, Company H, 6th Virginia Regiment, and was ordered to Craney Island with his company, but was shortly afterwards promoted to Major of Artillery and ordered to the entrenched camp near Norfolk to command the battalion of artillery which was on duty there. He was there until the evacuation of Norfolk, in May, 1862, when, after serving a short while on General Mahone's staff, he was ordered to Chaflin's Bluff. On the 29th of September, 1864, General Butler appeared before Fort Harrison, near Chaflin's Bluff, which was at the time without a garrison. Major Taylor hastened there with one company and directed others to follow, but before reinforcements could arrive the attack had been made and the fort carried by assault. Major Taylor made a gallant fight with the one company and inflicted a heavy loss upon his assailants, but his numbers were too small for an effectual resistance. He was severely wounded and fell into the hands of the enemy.

THE MEDICAL CORPS.

Dr. John C. Baylor, Surgeon Camp Winder Hospital.
Dr. Richard D. Bagnall, Assistant Surgeon 3d Georgia Regiment.
Dr. James D. Galt, Surgeon Pig Point Battery and afterwards with 18th Virginia Infantry.
Dr. W. J. Moore, Surgeon in Charge hospitals at Liberty and Richmond.
Dr. Herbert M. Nash, Surgeon 9th Virginia, Surgeon 61st Virginia, and Chief Surgeon Artillery, 3d Corps.
Dr. Wm. Selden, Surgeon hospitals at Richmond and Liberty.
Dr. Robert Southgate, Inspector of Hospitals and Medical Examiner-General Medical Staff.
Dr. T. B. Ward, Surgeon Mahone's Brigade, 6th Va. Regiment.
Dr. James H. Southall, Surgeon Archer's Brigade.
Dr. F. A. Walke, Surgeon 46th Virginia Regiment.

QUARTERMASTERS AND COMMISSARIES.

A. B. Cooke, Major and Q. M. Southwest and trans.Mississippi Departments.
O. H. P. Corprew, Captain and A. Q. M. Mahone's Brigade.
George Chamberlaine, Captain and A. C. S. 9th Virginia Infantry.
J. Wiley Grandy, Major and Q. M. Army Northern Virginia.
James Barron Hope, Captain and A. Q. M. Lawton's Brigade.
J. Barry King, Captain and A. Q. M. Lightfoot's Battalion Artillery.
Joseph Walters, Major and A. Q. M.
John W. Moore, Captain and A. Q. M.
W. C. Marrow, Major and A. Q. M. Army Northern Virginia.
Tazewell Thompson, Major and Commissary.
George C. Reid, Captain and A. Q. M. Colonel Griffin's Georgia Regiment (62d.)
James Y. Leigh, Captain and A. Q. M.
A. Meade Smith, Major and Commissary Rosser's Cavalry Brigade.

CHAPTER XLV.

IN THE NAVY—NORFOLK.

Norfolk city was represented in the navy by the following officers, whose residences were in the city at the beginning of the war. They are arranged alphabetically and not by grade:

CAPTAINS.

Samuel Barron,	John R. Tucker,	Wm. C. Whittle.

COMMANDERS.

Jas. L. Henderson,	Chas. F. McIntosh,	C. F. M. Spottswood,
Chas. H. Kennedy,	Robt. B. Pegram,	Geo. T. Sinclair,
Benj. P. Loyall,	Arthur Sinclair,	R. D. Thorborn.
	Wm. A. Webb.	

LIEUTENANTS.

Sam'l Barron, Jr.,	Chas. K. King,	Wm. Sharp,
Otey Bradford,	Patrick McCarrick,	Thos. L. Skinner,
Chas. Borum,	Chas. B. Oliver,	John Wilkinson,
A. M. DeBree,	Wm. H. Parker,	Wm. H. Ward,
Thos. L. Dornin,	Henry Roberts.	Wm. C. Whittle, Jr.,
J. Pembrook Jones,	Arthur Sinclair, Jr.,	W. L. Winder.

SURGEONS.

Geo. Blacknall,	F. L. Galt,	W. B. Sinclair,
Jas. Cornick,	Lewis D. Minor,	Jno. DeBree, Jr. (asst.)
Richard Jeffry,	W. F. McClenahan,	R. J. Freeman, (asst.)

PAYMASTERS.

John DeBree.	Rich'd Taylor (asst.),	L. B. Reardon (asst.)

MASTERS.

Richard Evans,	Jas. W. McCarrick,	Wm. B. Whitehead,
John R. Gibbs,	Wyndham R. Mayo,	Henry Wilkinson,
Lemuel Langley.	Lewis Parrish.	

MIDSHIPMEN.

H. S. Cook,	Virginius Newton,	Geo. T. Sinclair,
F. B. Dornin,	Jas. W. Pegram,	W. H. Sinclair,
C. K. Mallory,	L. M. Rootes,	Joshua C. Wright,
P. H. McCarrick.	Palmer Saunders,	W. W. Wilkinson,
	W. B. Sinclair.	

CHIEF ENGINEERS.

Wm. P. Williamson,	Virginius Freeman,	H. A. Ramsey,
Engr.-in-Chief,	Thos. A. Jackson,	Henry X. Wright.

ASSISTANT ENGINEERS.

Jas. Carlon,	James F. Green,	Chas. W. Jordan,
J. T. Doland,	E. G. Hall,	John R. Jordan,
J. M. Freeman, Jr.,	Wm. F. Harding,	John C. Johnson,
W. J. Freeman,	M. P. Jordan,	John T. Tucker.

GUNNERS.

Benj. A. Barron,	B. F. Hughes,	Stephen Schisano.
Crawford Gormley,	E. R. Johnson,	

BOATSWAINS.

W. T. Smith,   Peter Taff.

MASTERS' MATES.

A. G. Corran,	Arthur Freeman,	Wm. McBlair,
Robt. Freeman,	Wm. H. Fitzgerald,	Chas. R. McBlair,
	T. S. Gray,	W. W. Skinner.

MISCELLANEOUS.

Marine Corps—First Lieutenant T. P. Gwinn.
Acting Naval Constructor—Wm. A. Graves.
Sailmaker—Samuel V. Turner.
Total—98. Killed and died 5.

CAPTAIN SAMUEL BARRON was appointed Midshipman in the United States Navy by special act of Congress on the 1st of January, 1812, at the age of four years, and made his first cruise to the Mediterranean at the age of eight years, the youngest naval officer afloat. He was commissioned a Captain on the 14th of September, 1855, and at the secession of Virginia resigned and was appointed in the Virginia navy. He was subsequently commissioned in the Confederate navy, and had command of Fort Hatteras in August, 1861, when it was captured by the Federals. Subsequently he was sent abroad on duty for the Confederate Government.

CAPTAIN JOHN R. TUCKER made quite a name for himself as commander of the steamer Patrick Henry in the battles of the 8th and 9th of March, 1862, in Hampton Roads. He entered the United States navy on the 1st of June, 1826, was promoted Commander September 14th, 1855, and at that grade entered the Confederate navy. He was promoted to Captain in the Confederate navy for gallant and meritorious services. History has not done credit to the officers and men on the wooden vessels in that famous engagement in Hampton Roads. The novelty of the ironclad Virginia has served to attract attention to her and away from her equally as gallant and much more exposed companions. Captain Tucker subsequently commanded the Charleston squadron and contributed materially towards keeping the Federal squadron out of that harbor.

CAPTAIN WM. C. WHITTLE was born in 1805, and entered the United States navy May 10th, 1820. He was promoted to Commander August 4th, 1850, and held that rank at the beginning of the war. He entered the Virginia navy and was subsequently transferred to the Confederate navy. His first duty with the Confederacy was in command of the defences of York river, where he superintended the erection of a battery at Gloucester Point. He relieved Captain Hollins in command of the naval station at New Orleans, and was filling that position in April, 1862, when the city fell into the hands of the enemy.

COMMANDER BENJAMIN P. LOYALL entered the United States navy March 5th, 1849, and was appointed Lieutenant on the 28th of January, 1856. His last duty in the United States navy was on the sloop-of-war Constellation on the African station. He returned home, resigned and entered the Confederate service on the 26th of November, 1861, and was assigned to duty at Roanoke Island with the rank of Captain in the army. He was present and participated in the battle there, and was very favorably mentioned by Colonel Shaw in his official report, and also in the official report of Major G. H. Hill, who commanded Fort Bartow. Lieutenant Loyall fell into the hands of the enemy upon the surrender of the island, but was subsequently exchanged. He served the Confederacy in various capacities in the line of his profession, and was second in command of the boat expedition under Captain John Taylor Wood, which captured the United States steamer Underwriter at Newberne, N. C., at 2 o'clock a. m. on the 1st of February, 1864. The Underwriter was manned with one 6-inch rifle gun, one 8-inch, one 12-pounder rifle, and one 12-pounder howitzer. Lieutenant Loyall commanded the second division of boats and was the first to board the vessel. She was captured after a desperate defence on the part of her crew. Lieutenant Loyall was promoted to the grade of Commander for gallantry on this occasion and was assigned to the command of the iron-clad gunboat Neuse, on the upper waters of the Neuse river. It was in the attack upon the Underwriter that Midshipman Palmer Saunders of Norfolk was killed by a blow on the head from a cutlass. Midshipman H. S. Cook of Norfolk also took part in this engagement and displayed marked courage. After the capture of the vessel she was set on fire by the Confederates and destroyed.

COMMANDER CHARLES F. McINTOSH was born on the 24th of October, 1813, entered the United States service November 1st, 1828, and was promoted to Commander March 2d, 1857. At the beginning of the war he was commanding the Naval Rendezvous at Norfolk, and immediately tendered his resignation and entered the Virginia navy. He was ordered to the Naval Hospital Point and superintended the erection of the batteries there. He remained there, as commander of the post, with the rank of Lieutenant Colonel in the army, until April, 1862, when he was ordered to New Orleans and assigned to the command of the unfinished iron-clad Louisiana. While at the Hospital battery Commander McIntosh was very popular with the officers and men of the garrison, his genial disposition, kind heart and thorough familiarity with the working of heavy guns were qualifications which at once won their esteem, and they regretted his departure to another field of duty. The Secretary of the Navy, Mr. Mallory, has been censured for the delay in the completion of the Louisiana, and also of the iron-clad Mississippi, but as a Congressional investigating committee exonerated him from blame, that report will be accepted by the general historians as conclusive, but there is no reason to question that, though Mr. Mallory displayed great energy, he also displayed a lack of judgment. This was fully illustrated in the testimony of Engineer-in-Chief William P. Williamson before the committee, page 235. He says the contract to make the main shaft of the Mississippi was made with the Tredegar Iron Works in Richmond, and it required two months for that establishment to make preparations to commence work, while at the Gosport Navy Yard there were ample facilities for it without any additional preparations. The shafts of the steamer Glen Cove were used for the purpose. Thus, in this particular, two months of valuable time was lost and the vessel was not ready when the Federal fleet made the attack. On the 24th of April, 1862, Admiral Farragut ran past Forts Jackson and St. Philip. The Louisiana, with her machinery unfinished, was moored to the bank of the river above Fort St. Philip. She was covered with railroad iron and mounted sixteen guns. She was under command of Commander McIntosh, and was also the flagship of Commodore Mitchell, commanding the squadron. Farragut ran past her also, and a large Federal vessel becoming temporarily unmanageable on account of the disarrangement of a portion of her machinery, was carried by the current alongside of the Louisiana. Captain McIntosh, apprehending an attack by boarders, rushed upon the upper deck, followed by a portion of his crew, to repel the anticipated attack, and it was while there that he received his death wound. He lingered until the 28th, when he died, and on that day, by order of Commodore Mitchell, the Louisiana was set on fire and abandoned. It looks now as if both of those vessels would have been finished and Farragut's fleet defeated had the efforts of the Navy Department been concentrated upon them instead of being distributed where they were not so necessary. Had this been done Captain McIntosh might have lived to have rendered additional service to the Southern cause. In the early part of the war Secretary Mallory's efforts were directed mainly towards having built in Europe one or more sea-going iron clads to keep the Federals away from the Southern coast, but he found himself unable to do so, and in a report to Congress, dated November 20th, 1861, he said he " has found it impracticable to purchase abroad such vessels as we require, and the Department has commenced the construction of iron-clad vessels in our own country, and has stimulated the supplies of coal and iron for this purpose." Here is where Mr. Mallory made his mistake. When he finally decided to build the iron-clads at home he found himself without engines for them and without iron to cover them, and the Southern ports were blockaded. Had he taken advice which was given him early in the war to import armor iron and steam engines before the Southern ports were closed, the results would have been very different, and many men whose lives were lost in endeavoring to defend untenable positions might not have been sacrificed.

COMMANDER ROBERT B. PEGRAM entered the United States navy February 2d, 1829, and was appointed a Lieutenant September 8, 1841. His last service in the United States navy was at the Gosport Navy Yard. At the beginning of the war he resigned and was ordered by Governor Letcher on the 18th of April, 1861, to take command of the naval station at Norfolk and organize a naval force. He was relieved on the 22d by Commodore Forrest and ordered to superintend the building of a battery at Pig Point, at the mouth of the Nansemond river, and was in command of that post on the 5th of June, when the Harriet Lane made an attack upon it. He was afterwards assigned to the command of the Nashville, with which he ran the blockade and crossed over to Europe. This vessel was originally intended to carry Messrs. Mason and Slidell to Europe, but it was subsequently decided that they should take another route. He returned from Europe on the Nashville, and was a member of the naval court to investigate the charges against Commodore Tatnall of having destroyed the Virginia unnecessarily. In 1864 he was in command of the iron-clad Virginia, one of the vessels in the James river squadron at Richmond, armed with two 6 and two 8-inch rifle guns and plated with six inches of armor on her sides and eight inches on her ends, but was never given an opportunity to engage the enemy.

COMMANDER W. A. WEBB resigned from the United States navy as a Lieutenant and entered the Confederate service. His first duties with the Confederacy were at Fernandina, Florida, where he superintended the erection of a number of batteries. He was subsequently assigned to the command of the gunboat Teazer, in James river, and commanded her in the naval engagement in Hampton Roads on the 8th and 9th of March, 1862. On the 19th of February, 1863, he was ordered by Secretary Mallory to take charge of a boat expedition to board the monitors off Charleston harbor and capture them or sink them by torpedoes, but nothing came of it, and later he was ordered to command the iron-clad ram Atlanta, at Savannah. On the 17th of June, 1863, he proceeded to Warsaw Sound to attack the monitors Weehawken and Mohawk, but the Atlanta got immovably aground and was surrendered to the enemy. The Federals sent her to Philadelphia, repaired damages, and the following February sent her to Fortress Monroe to operate against the Confederates in Virginia.

The eighteen Lieutenants whom Norfolk contributed to the Confederate navy rendered efficient service.

LIEUTENANT THOMAS L. DORNIN was wounded in Battery Buchanan, near Fort Fisher, during the attack on that work, in January, 1865. He was a Lieutenant on the Chicamauga, but volunteered to defend the fort and worked like a private soldier, sponging one of the two 7-inch rifle Brooke guns until it burst. He then transferred his sponge to the other and served until that burst also. He was severely wounded by a piece of shell from the Federal fleet.

LIEUTENANT J. PEMBROOK JONES served early in the war at Savannah in command of the armed tug Resolute, and was afterwards promoted to command the iron-clad Georgia. In May, 1864, he was captain of the iron-clad gunboat Raleigh, at Wilmington, and on the 6th of that month steamed outside the Cape Fear river and scattered the fleet of blockaders, but on returning unfortunately ran aground on the bar and the back of the vessel was broken. She proved a total loss.

LIEUTENANT CHARLES B. OLIVER served as a warrant officer on the Virginia, and was promoted for gallant and meritorious services on that and other occasions.

LIEUTENANT W. H. PARKER was promoted to Commander for gallant services. He was in the battle of Roanoke Island in command of the gunboat Beaufort, and also in the fight in Hampton Roads, March 8th and 9th, 1862, in command of the same vessel. His services in the navy were varied and valuable, and in 1864 he commanded the iron-clad steamer Richmond, at Richmond. Since the war he published a book, " Recollections of a Naval Officer," which has been regarded as high authority upon the subjects of which it treats. It embraces his own personal observations.

LIEUTENANT HENRY ROBERTS was a Lieutenant in Captain John J. Young's harbor guard, and was appointed a Lieutenant in the navy in 1864.

LIEUTENANT WM. SHARP was a Lieutenant in the United States navy and was stationed at the Gosport Navy Yard at the breaking out of the war and entered the Virginia navy. He was on duty at the Naval Hospital batteries and also on Craney Island in April and May, 1861. In July, 1861, he was ordered to North Carolina as aid to Commodore Barron, and was severely wounded at the fall of Fort Hatteras, April 29th, and fell into the hands of the enemy. He was exchanged later in 1862, and ordered to the Patrick Henry. He was on her during the engagements of March 8th and 9th, 1862, in Hampton Roads, and was shortly afterwards assigned to the command of the gunboat Beaufort, and was also on her on the 11th of June, when the Virginia and other Confederate vessels made their second visit to Hampton Roads. In 1864 he was on duty in North Carolina supervising the building of the gunboat Neuse, and when the war closed had charge of the naval ordnance stores at Charleston.

LIEUTENANT JOHN WILKINSON was promoted to Commander for meritorious services. His first duty in the Confederate service was rendered in April, 1861, when he supervised the erection of a battery at Fort Powhatan, on James river. In May he was sent to Aquia Creek on similar duty. He commanded the steamer Jackson at New Orleans in 1862, and was Executive Officer of the Louisiana when Captain McIntosh was killed, after which he commanded the vessel. He was captured upon the fall of New Orleans, and after being exchanged was sent to Europe to purchase a vessel. He commanded the expedition to release Confederate prisoners on Johnson's Island. He commanded several blockade runners, among them the R. E. Lee. He also commanded the cruisers Chicamauga and Tennessee. With this last vessel, he ran out of Wilmington on the 24th of December, 1864, while the Federal fleet was bombarding Fort Fisher, and was at sea when the war ended.

LIEUTENANT W. H. WARD was a Lieutenant in the United States navy. He entered the service February 17th, 1849, and was appointed Lieutenant September 9th, 1856. His services in the Confederate navy were valuable to the Government. He commanded the boat expedition which removed the troops from Morris' Island, Charleston harbor, in 1864, was second in command of the cruiser Tallahassee when, under Captain John Taylor Wood, she made her successful cruise against the Federal commerce, and afterwards was in command of the same vessel under the name of the Olustee, made a successful cruise on her and returned safely to Wilmington. He afterwards commanded the Chicamauga at Wilmington and took part in the defence of Fort Fisher, in January, 1865. From there he was ordered to Richmond, was with the naval brigade on the retreat from Richmond, and took part in the battle of Saylor's Creek. He was second in command of a boat expedition which left Drury's Bluff February 10th, 1865, to destroy, with torpedoes, the Federal iron-clads at City Point, and which failed on account of the treachery of one of the officers of the expedition. The circumstances of this affair are somewhat peculiar, and are detailed in an article by Master W. F. Shippey, of the C. S. Navy, in Vol. XII, page 416, of the Southern Historical Society Papers. It seems that after the failure of Commodore Mitchell's squadron at Richmond to engage and destroy the Federal iron-clads at City Point a boat expedition left Drury's Bluff to accomplish that object by means of torpedoes. The expedition numbered one hundred and one officers and men, and was under command of Lieutenant C. W. Read of the navy, with Lieutenant W. H. Ward second in command. The expedition had several boats, mounted on wheels and drawn by mules. It was also supplied with long booms with arrangements at the ends for fastening torpedoes. The plan was to move at a distance around the left of Grant's army, then in front of Petersburg, and reach James river in Surry county or Prince George and remain concealed on the shore until an opportunity might present itself of capturing one or more tugs passing up or down the river, then to fit the torpedo booms on them, ascend the river to City Point and sink the Federal iron-clads anchored there. The expedition left Drury's Bluff on the 10th of February, 1865, and Lieutenant Lewis was sent ahead as a scout to reconnoiter. He was to rejoin the party at a ford of the Blackwater river and pilot them from there to the James river. Lewis is said to have been a Northern man, and was at Norfolk at the beginning of the war. He enlisted in the Confederate army and served faithfully with his company until June 29th, 1864, when he was appointed a Lieutenant in the volunteer navy and enjoyed the confidence of his brother officers. Everything went well with the expedition for the first three days. Grant's army was successfully turned without discovery, and on the afternoon of the third day, when near the ford of the Blackwater the party sought temporary shelter from a severe storm of rain and sleet. While engaged in drying their clothing a young Confederate soldier made his appearance and informed them that he had just escaped from the Federal lines, where he had been as a prisoner of war, that Lewis had deserted to the enemy and betrayed the expedition, and was then at the Blackwater ford with a regiment of infantry, lying in ambush, waiting for their approach, and that just before he succeeded in making his escape he overheard Lewis and the Federal commander talking the matter over. Lieutenant Read halted his command where it was and went forward alone to examine the river and rejoined his men the next day, having ascertained the correctness of the report of the young soldier. The party succeeded in getting back to Drury's Bluff with whole skins but disappointed hopes. Several bodies of Federal cavalry were scouring the country in search of them, but Lieutenant Read succeeded in eluding them.

LIEUTENANT WM. C. WHITTLE, JR., was an officer in the U. S.

Navy and entered the Confederate Navy as Lieutenant, June 11th, 1861. He was one of the Lieutenants on the iron-clad Louisiana under Captain McIntosh, at New Orleans, was 2d Lieutenant on the cruiser Nashville, when she sailed for Wilmington under Captain R. B. Pegram, and was 1st Lieutenant of the cruiser Shenandoah, under Captain Waddell, which destroyed an amount of Federal commerce second only to that destroyed by the Alabama.

LIEUTENANT PATRICK McCARRICK was captain of the steamer Northampton, plying between Norfolk and the Eastern Shore of Virginia, when the war began, and brought to Norfolk the first information that the Pawnee was coming up the harbor to reinforce the Navy Yard. He volunteered in the navy of the State of North Carolina, and was appointed 1st Lieutenant and afterwards commander of the steamboat J. E. Coffee, which was converted into a gunboat, and named the Winslow. While in command of this vessel he made frequent trips outside of Hatteras Inlet, and captured a number of prizes, among them several West India schooners loaded with molasses and fruit. He lost his vessel by running on a sunken wreck in Ocracoke Inlet, November 4th, 1861, just after gallantly rescuing the officers and crew of the French corvette Prony, which was ashore on the beach near that place. This was a brave rescue, and was successfully made after the United States fleet had left the Frenchmen to their fate. Captain McCarrick was the recipient of a very cordial letter of thanks from the French Vice-Consul at Norfolk. In June, 1861, he was transferred to the Confederate Navy as master, and on the 18th of March, 1862, was promoted to Lieutenant. After the loss of the Winslow he was assigned to the command of the gunboat Seabird, Commodore Lynch's flag-ship, in the North Carolina sounds. He was in the naval engagements at Roanoke Island, and Elizabeth City, and fought his vessel until she went to the bottom. He was captured at Elizabeth City, but was exchanged, and went out with Captain John Wilkinson from Wilmington as first officer of a blockade runner, and was also with him in the expedition to release the Confederate prisoners on Johnson's Island, which failed to accomplish anything through the thoughtlessness of one of the Confederate agents, by whose inadvertence the affair became known.

SURGEON GEORGE BLACKNALL resigned from the United States Navy at the beginning of the war, and was assigned to the charge of the Naval Hospital at Portsmouth, where he died on the 21st of January, 1862.

MASTER JAMES W. McCARRICK was appointed a Master's Mate in the Navy, subsequently promoted to Master, and was recommended for promotion to a Lieutenancy, but the close of the war prevented it. He was on the gunboat Seabird in the battles of

Roanoke Island and Elizabeth City in February, 1862, and was captured at the latter place. A few days subsequently he was released on parole and returned to Norfolk. Quite an amusing incident occurred in connection with his exchange. Most of the officers captured at Elizabeth City had been exchanged, but Mr. McCarrick still remained on parole, for the reason that the Confederates had not captured an officer of his grade, Master's Mate, to exchange for him, and when the Virginia (Merrimac) went down to Hampton Roads on the 8th of March to fight the Federal fleet, she was accompanied by the gunboats Raleigh and Beaufort. Attached to the Beaufort was Midshipman Chas. K. Mallory, of Norfolk, and as she was about to move off Mr. McCarrick called to him: "Charley, bring a Yankee Master's Mate back with you so that I can be exchanged for him." When the Congress struck her colors, Midshipman Mallory was one of the first to jump on board of her, and seeing a man with the uniform of a Master's Mate on, took him prisoner and transferred him to the Beaufort. The next day, upon their return to the Navy Yard, Mr. McCarrick was on one of the lower wharves in Norfolk to see them pass by, and being noticed by Midshipman Mallory, and being within hailing distance, that young tar called to him and informed him that he had brought back a Master's Mate for him, and it so happened that Mr. McCarrick was exchanged for that very man. He afterwards served on the Tuscaloosa, and was Master on the Tennessee, Admiral Buchanan's flag-ship, at Mobile.

MASTER WYNDAM R. MAYO entered the Confederate service as a Midshipman, on the 8th of July, 1861. He was at the Naval Academy at Annapolis at the beginning of the war, having entered there on the 21st of September, 1860. He was promoted to Master and took part in the defence of Battery Buchanan in January, 1865, as one of the crew of the Chicamauga.

MIDSHIPMAN CHAS. K. MALLORY was attached to the Beaufort in the battles in Hampton Roads, March 8th and 9th, 1862, and was said to have been the first Confederate to board the Congress. He lost his life on board the gunboat Chattahoochee in Florida, on the 1st of June, 1863, when she exploded her boiler.

MIDSHIPMAN P. H. MCCARRICK was a son of Lieutenant Patrick McCarrick. He was attached to the gunboats Raleigh and Teazer and died from sickness.

MIDSHIPMAN PALMER SAUNDERS enlisted in Company G, 6th Virginia Regiment, (old Company F,) and was subsequently appointed a midshipman in the navy. He lost his life in the capture of the Federal gunboat Underwriter at Newberne, on the 1st of February, 1864, from a cut over the head with a cutlass.

CHIEF ENGINEER WM. P. WILLIAMSON entered the United States service October 20th, 1842, and was made a chief engineer March

15th, 1845. At the beginning of the war he was the senior engineer in the navy, and was appointed Engineer in Chief in the Confederate Navy, a position corresponding to that of Chief of the Bureau of Steam Engineering in the United States Navy.

CHIEF ENGIGEER H. A. RAMSEY was Chief Engineer on the Virginia when she had the engagements in Hampton Roads, and was attached to her in that capacity until her destruction by order of Commodore Tatnall.

MASTER'S MATE ARTHUR FREEMAN was a member of a company of youths in Norfolk, who did provost duty in the city the first year of the war, and upon the evacuation of Norfolk, the company having disbanded, he went to North Carolina and became Orderly Sergeant of a Company of Junior Reserves, and was on duty at Goldsboro. He was subsequently appointed a Master's Mate in the navy, was stationed at Savannah, and was with the boarding party which captured the United States gunboat Water Witch in Ossabaw Sound, on the 3d of June, 1864.

CHIEF ENGINEER VIRGINIUS FREEMAN resigned from the U. S. Navy and joined the Confederate Navy, was Chief Engineer of the steamer McCrea at New Orleans, and afterwards superintended the preparation of the machinery of the Mississippi and Louisiana in that city. He was Chief Engineer of the Palmetto State when Captain Ingraham attacked the blockading fleet off Charleston, and was attached to the expedition to release the Confederate prisoners at Point Lookout, which failed because information of it was conveyed to the enemy.

CHAPTER XLVI.

IN OTHER COMMANDS.

There were a large number of Norfolk men attached to commands which were organized in other localities, and on account of the long lapse of time since the close of the war many of them cannot be recalled to memory, but the author, after diligent search, has been able to rescue the following from oblivion. He feels, however, that there is an unavoidable omission of many names which should be found here:

Burgess, T. J., Sergeant Co. A, 7th Georgia Cavalry.
Beall, Edward, private Otey Battery of Lynchburg.
Brown, George, private Fayette Artillery, Richmond.
Baker, John C., Lieutenant North Carolina Junior Reserves.
Broughton, Thos. B., hospital steward.
Bullock, W. H., private Company F, 15th Virginia Cavalry.
Bluford, Geo. W., private Co. D, 1st Virginia Reserves.
Camm, Robt. J., private New Orleans Cadets, killed at Shiloh, April, 1862.
Corprew, John B., private Co. F, 15th Virginia Cavalry.
Fletcher, Hannibal, private Company I, 15th Virginia Cavalry.
Fatherly, Matthew W., Lieutenant 8th North Carolina Regiment.
Foster, W. E., Major and Ordnance Officer Custis Lee's Brigade, local defence troops.
Grandy, P. H., Major 1st North Carolina Regiment, killed at Gaines' Mill.
Grandy, A. H., Lieut. Co. B., 8th North Carolina Regiment.
Glennan, M., commissary sergeant of post at Fort Fisher.
Ghiselin, Jas. W., private, killed at Shiloh, April, 1862.
Harris, Hunter, private Daring's Cavalry.
Henderson, Thos. W., courier headquarters Army Northern Virginia.
Johnston, Chas. H., courier Gen. Pemberton's headquarters.
Johnston, Geo. W., Co. I, 15th Virginia Cavalry.
Johnston, James V., private Co. F, 15th Virginia Cavalry.
Leigh, Roscoe, private Co. I, 15th Virginia Cavalry.
Martin, Geo. G., private Co. A, 3d Virginia Reserves.
Mayer, John F., sergeant Co. A, 3d Virginia Reserves.
Marsden, F. C., private Richmond Howitzers.
McKenney, Jas. M., private Richmond Howitzers.
Moore, Walter S., ensign 61st Virginia Regiment.
Newton, Thos., private Co. F, 6th Virginia Regiment, killed Sept. 14th, 1862, at Crampton Gap.
Parks, Marshall, commissioner for North Carolina and special service.
Pearce, Frank, private 13th Virginia Cavalry.
Reed, Wm. C., private Co. F, 15th Virginia Cavalry.
Rosson, John A., private Co. A, Mosby's Rangers.
Rickhow, Wm. H., purser's steward C. S. Navy.
Rogers, W. F., Captain Revenue Marine, detailed with the navy.
Smith, Peter, private North Carolina Regiment.
Selden, Wm., Captain of Engineers C. S. Army, killed at Roanoke Island, Feb. 8th, 1862.
Sharp, John H., private Otey Battery, Lynchburg.
Saunders, Hunter, private Richmond Howitzers.
Santos, Alex., private Richmond Howitzers.
Todd, Westwood A., private Co. E, 12th Virginia Regiment, promoted ordnance officer Weiseger's Brigade, wounded Aug. 30th, 1862, at Second Manassas.

Turner, Robt. G., seaman C. S. Navy.
Tucker, John S., Captain, lost an arm at Corinth.
Taylor, Washington, Adjutant Scott's Battalion, local defence troops, Richmond.
Thomas, J. W., Jr., Lieutenant Artillery Corps C. S. A.
Walke, W. T., private Co. I. 15th Virginia Cavalry, promoted Adjutant 39th Virginia Cavalry Battalion.
Webber, John S., sergeant Co. A. 38th Battalion Virginia Artillery.
Wyatt, John, sergeant North Carolina Regiment.
Williamson, John G., sergeant Co. A, 3d Virginia Reserves, surrendered at Appomattox.
Williams, Wm. Carter, Captain Co. B, 6th Virginia, killed at Chancellorsville.
Worrell, Ed. W., sergeant Co. C., 6th North Carolina Cavalry.
Killed and died—5.

DETACHED ROLLS AT APPOMATTOX.

The following men belonging to detached commands are recorded as having been paroled at Appomattox.

FROM NORFOLK COUNTY.

B. A. Armistead, Sergeant Company I, 13th Virginia Cavalry.
Lloyd Bunting, private Company C, 13th Virginia Cavalry.
John T. Griffin, captain and assistant civil engineer.
Geo. N. Halstead, Assistant Surgeon C. S. Navy.
Geo. W. Wallace, private Signal Corps.
Wm. H. Halstead, private Signal Corps.

FROM NORFOLK CITY.

Lieutenant Jos. T. Allyn, attached to ordnance.
Assistant Surgeon Richard D. Bagnall, 3d Georgia Regiment.
Lieutenant F. E. Goodridge, ordnance duty, Pickett's Division.
Captain and A. Q. M., O. H. P. Corprew, Mahone's Division.
Surgeon F. L. Galt, C. S. Navy.
Chaplain Robt. Gatewood, Starke's Artillery Battalion.
Lieutenant Chas. K. King, C. S. Navy.
Quartermaster Wm. C. Marrow.
Lieutenant B. A. Marsden, Co. D, 1st Va. Battalion.
Surgeon Herbert M. Nash, Artillery, 3d Corps.
Private W. Hunter Saunders, Richmond Howitzers, General Long's headquarters.
Lieutenant-Colonel John S. Saunders, attached to ordnance.
Lieutenant-Colonel A. W. Starke, commanding artillery battalion.
Courier John H. Sharp, headquarters artillery, 1st corps General E. P. Alexander.
Master's Mate Wm. Smith, C. S. Navy.
Surgeon J. H. Southall, 55th Virginia Regiment.
Lieutenant-Colonel Walter H. Taylor, Adjutant General, staff of General R. E. Lee.

FROM PORTSMOUTH.

Tudor F. Brooks, Commissary Department, Mahone's Brigade.
W. T. Fentress, Lieutenant Light Artillery, on detached service.
Frank T. Foster, private Signal Corps.
Nat. C. Gayle, Carpenter C. S. Navy.
Leroy C. Godwin, private Signal Corps.
Wm. R. Hanrahan, Sergeant Signal Corps.
Samuel Hoffler, Ordnance Sergeant, Mahone's Brigade.
Wm. L. Hatton, private Signal Corps.
J. M. Hudgins, Captain and A. C. S.

Wm. H. Hughes, Lieutenant Lee Battery.
John A. Lovitt, Gunner C. S. Navy.
Richard B. Levy, private Signal Corps.
E. Newton Mahoney, private Richmond Howitzers.
Wm. R. Minter, private Naval Brigade.
F. M. Moore, private Signal Corps.
Jos. T. Owens, Captain Co. D. 26th Va. Regiment.
R. H. Parker, Assistant Surgeon 32d N. C. Regiment.
O. J. Peters, private Signal Corps.
Jas. Parrish, Surgeon Beale's Cavalry Brigade.
Thos. Scott, private Signal Corps.
T. J. Savage, private Signal Corps.
O. V. Smith, 4th Corporal, 3d Company, Richmond Howitzers.
G. S. Vermillion, private Signal Corps.
Luther Williams, private Naval Brigade and Company K, 9th Virginia Regiment.
T. H. Wingfield, Medical Inspector Army of Northern Virginia.
Jas. H. White, private Signal Corps.
E. M. Watts, Surgeon Simms' Brigade.
C. M. Young, Sergeant Signal Corps.

The following anecdote of General Robert E. Lee, which has perhaps not been in print before, shows how that great leader could preserve his cheerfulness even amid the confusion of disaster and defeat. It was the morning after the retreat began from Petersburg. Miss Jennie Riddick, of Nansemond county, Virginia, accompanied by Captain J. T. Griffin, of Norfolk county, and Rev. W. B. Wellons, a chaplain in the army, were in a covered wagon searching for Miss Riddick's brother, who had been wounded a short time before and sent to a hospital. He was Captain of Company C, 13th Virginia Cavalry, and it was her intention, if successful in finding him, to take him with her in the wagon to prevent him from falling into the hands of the enemy. Presently Generals Lee and Longstreet, accompanied by their respective staffs, rode up, and, being an acquaintance, General Lee spoke to Miss Riddick. She asked him the shortest route to North Carolina, and he told her that his intention was to try to get across the river and follow the line of the railroad, and advised her to pursue the same route, then, happening to look into the wagon and noticing Captain Griffin and Rev. Mr. Wellons, and remembering that North Carolina was the Gretna Green for runaway couples from Virginia, a sly twinkle came into his eye as he remarked: " You needn't go there; here are the preacher and the young man convenient, and you can get married right here," and calling to a member of his staff, he said : " Come here, Major, we are about to have a marriage." The marriage, however, did not come off. Miss Riddick presented General Lee with a handsome boquet, but he requested her to keep it for him. Momentous events were following each other very rapidly then, and he never had an opportunity to call for the flowers.

CHAPTER XLVII.

THE FIRST IRON CLAD—THE "VIRGINIA" (MERRIMAC.)

No subject of general interest connected with the late war has been more discussed than the Confederate iron-clad Virginia, formerly the United States frigate Merrimac, and no two descriptions of her are said to agree. The author was in a position to know many facts connected with the origin of the vessel as an iron-clad, and, in addition to his own knowledge, has had access to the original drawings and specifications in the possession of her projector, and is therefore in a position to write advisedly, and, as the vessel was the result of the inventive genius of Portsmouth and Norfolk marine architects and the mechanical skill of Portsmouth and Norfolk workmen, it is appropriate that her full history and description, together with the circumstances which led to her building as an iron-clad, should be recorded in this work and fully established in the interest of history.

In 1846 the United States Government decided to build, at Pittsburg, Pennsylvania, an iron steam sloop of war, the Alleghany, for the purpose of testing, on a large scale, a plan of submerged propellers, invented by Lieutenant W. W. Hunter, of the navy, and Mr. John L. Porter, of Portsmouth, was ordered there, as Acting Constructor in the navy, to superintend her building, and, while engaged upon this work, Mr. Porter conceived the idea of an iron-clad vessel which would be able to go to sea and still be shot-proof. His plan contemplated an iron vessel, to draw nineteen feet of water, and all of the vessel above the water line and to a depth of four feet below it, was to be of a sufficient thickness of metal to render her shot-proof. His idea was that, with the ordnance in use at that time, three inches would be sufficiently thick for the armor if placed on an incline.

Mr. Porter made copies of his plan and forwarded them to the Navy Department at Washington, with the view of having the Government adopt them, but the times were not far enough advanced for iron-clads, and the Navy Department took no further notice of them than to acknowledge their receipt, but Mr. Porter transferred them to his book of naval designs, which he retained and still has in his possession. The sides were inclined at an angle of 45 degrees, and the vessel was to have had a width, over all, of forty feet. The kunckle of the ship was to be two feet below the water line, and her gun deck three feet above that line. The gun deck extended the entire length of the ship, three feet above the water line, and the shield, in which her battery was located, was built in the middle of the ship. The ends beyond the shield were constructed upon the same incline (as to their sides) as the shield, and the deck forward and aft of the shield, was protected with armor plate. The appearance of the vessel upon the water would have been similar to that of the Ericsson iron-clads of 1862, except that, instead of the sides of the vessel being perpendicular, they would have been inclined at an angle of 45 degrees, and instead of the upright turret amidship, there would have been the shield with inclined sides. The ports were to have been closed with wrought iron port shutters, and the resisting surface was to have been entirely of iron. Mr. Porter showed his plans to Lieutenant Hunter, who suggested as an improvement, an iron protective deck, to be built below the gun deck, to prevent a plunging shot from going through her bottom, should it penetrate the shield. This was added, by Mr. Porter, to the drawings, before he forwarded them to Washington, and appears also in the drawings in his sketch book. It may be seen in the above plan, figure 1. This was ten years before England and France began thinking on the subject of iron-clads, and as far as Mr. Porter was concerned, was the result of his own ideas, without assistance from any one. The drawing in his sketch book is arranged with Lieutenant Hunter's propellers attached. Below will be found a cross section of his vessel, taken amidship:

FIGURE 1—Scale, 1-inch 15 feet.

But, as has already been said, the Navy Department in 1846, was not impressed with the idea of an iron-clad vessel, and Mr. Porter retained his own copy of his plans, waiting an opportunity to put them into practical operation. That opportunity arrived at the breaking out of the war between the North and South, but the limited means of construction at the command of the South, compelled him to modify somewhat his original idea, and for want of rolling mills capable of rolling out broad iron plates, he was compelled to use narrow plates and fasten them on a backing of wood.

Mr. Porter was a constructor in the United States Navy at the beginning of the war, and up to that time, had superintended for the Government the building of the Alleghany, Powhatan, Constellation, Colorado, Seminole, Pensacola and other vessels. He was stationed at the Gosport Navy Yard in April, 1861, and witnessed its destruction by the Federal authorities, resigned his commission in the United States Navy, tendered his services to Governor Letcher, and was retained on duty at the Navy Yard. Believing that war was inevitable, and knowing that the South was not able to cope with the United States upon the water, his mind reverted to the iron-clad which he had conceived in Pittsburg in 1846, and he went to work, so modifying it, as to bring it within the power of the Southern Confederacy to build, and, at the same time, to adapt it to the defence of the harbors of the South. The result was a vessel, the hull of which could be built in a few months. He prepared his plans and specifications, made drawings of the vessel and had a model made at the Navy Yard. Virginia had not then transferred her army and effects to the Southern Confederacy. Below will be found a cross section of Mr. Porter's model of 1861.

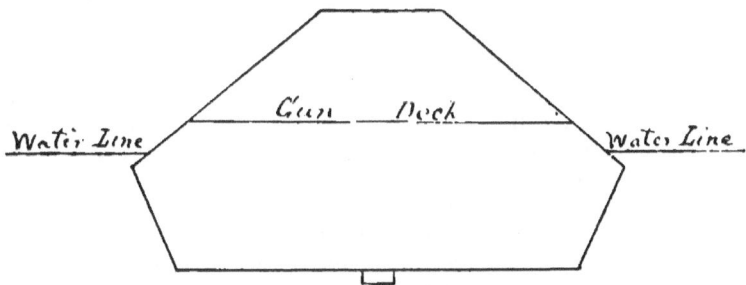

FIGURE 2.—Scale, 1 inch 15 feet.

At that time Commodore Marshall Parks, President of the Albemarle and Chesapeake Canal Company, had been appointed by the State of North Carolina, to act in conjunction with Commander Muse (formerly of the United States Navy), as commissioner to purchase and fit out vessels for the North Carolina Navy, to protect the waters of Albemarle and Pamlico Sounds, and, visiting the Gosport Navy Yard upon business connected with his office, was shown this model by Mr. Porter, and was so impressed with it that he went to Raleigh and informed the Governor and members of the Legislature of the plan, and suggested that some small iron-clads be built for the defense of the North Carolina sounds. He was directed to prepare a "Bill" to authorize the Governor to have some vessels built on the plan, and it was passed immediately. The State of North Carolina, soon after this, decided to join the Confederacy, and Commodore Parks was directed to go to Richmond and turn over all the steamers he had purchased and fitted out, to the Confederate States Navy Department, and therefore the iron-clads were not built. Virginia also joined the Southern Confederacy, and Mr. Porter received an appointment as Constructor in the Confederate States Navy.

The shield, which was on his Pittsburg model of 1846, is retained, but, while that vessel was designed for sea service as well as for harbor defense, his new model was designed for harbor defense mainly, and would not have been a good sea boat in rough weather. The original drawings are in the possession of the author. The vessel was to have been one hundred and fifty feet long on deck and one hundred and forty-four feet on the keel; was forty feet beam at the knuckle and thirty-three feet across the bottom amidships. She was to have been built sharp at the bow and with flat bottom. Her draft of water was eleven feet, and she was fitted with a nine foot propeller. Her knuckle was nine feet perpendicular from the bottom of her keel and her water line was two feet above her knuckle, so that the eaves of the vessel were submerged two feet below the water line. The shield covered the entire length of the vessel, was arranged at an angle of forty degrees, and was made circular at each end. The shield was to have had a thickness of wood and iron, of two and a-half feet, and the ends of the iron, or in other words, the eaves or knuckle of the ship, were to be two feet below the water line, just as he had planned in his Pittsburg ship. The armament was to consist of six 11-inch smooth bore guns, four broadside and one at each end. The end guns were to be pivot guns and have a range out of three port holes, and the broadside guns were on pivots also, and could fire out of each side. While the bow of the vessel was to be sharp, there was sufficient flare in her nine feet of depth from keel to knuckle, to take in the circular end of the shield. Mr. Porter's Pittsburg model was built with sides inclined at an angle of forty-five degrees, but the angle of inclination of this vessel was forty degrees. Mr. Porter made this change because the ordnance in use in 1861 was heavier than that of 1846, and the lower the angle of resistance the greater the ability to resist. With a good engine she would have made seven or eight miles an hour.

Mr. Mallory, Secretary of the Confederate States Navy, called the attention of the House Committee on Naval Affairs to the subject of iron-clads before the seat of government was removed from Montgomery to Richmond. England and France were then experimenting on the subject, and Mr. Mallory thought it would be desirable for the Southern Confederacy to own one or more of a sea-going character, but an effort to purchase two such vessels in Europe failed, and nothing of a practical character was done. On the 22d of June, 1861, Naval Constructor Porter received orders to report to the Navy Department at Richmond. The orders did not state the object for which he was to report, but he took advantage of the occasion to carry his model to Richmond for the purpose of submitting it to the Secretary. This was the model he had previously shown to Commodore Parks, and which has just been described. He went to Richmond June 23d (Sunday), called at the Secretary's office the next day, and showed him his model. The Secretary immediately ordered a board consisting of Mr. Porter, Chief Engineer Williamson and Lieutenant Brooke to consider it. Messrs. Williamson and Brooke were at that time in Richmond.

Thus far, in this account, the author has been writing of what passed within his own personal knowledge, but was not at the meeting of the board, and as to what took place there must rely upon the statements of the members of the board, for only those three gentlemen were present and no one but them could speak advisedly of its proceedings. The board met on the 25th of June, the day after Secretary Mallory ordered it to assemble, and Mr. Porter's model, which had been in the Secretary's office since the preceding morning, was submitted to it, and, according to the statements of Messrs. Williamson and Porter, there was nothing before the board or considered by it except that model. The board decided to recommend the building of a vessel after that plan, and, preparatory to making their report, began discussing the length of time it would take to complete her. Mr. Williamson remarked, "It will take at least twelve months to build her engines unless we can utilize some of the machinery in the Merrimac." Mr. Porter asked, "Why can't you use it all? I can adapt this model to the Merrimac and utilize her machinery in her." Mr. Williamson replied, "I can." It was therefore decided at once to recommend that the Merrimac be converted into an iron-clad. Neither of the members of the board seems to have had any idea of making an iron-clad of that vessel previous to their assembling. Messrs. Williamson and Porter say the board was ordered to meet to consider Mr. Porter's model, and this statement is borne out by Mr. Brooke's testimony before the Congressional investigating committee in February, 1863. Mr. Brooke says: "The Secretary directed Constructor Porter, Chief Engineer Williamson and myself to meet him in my office here, and this model was examined by us all and the form of the shield adopted."

Up to that time Mr. Porter was the only member of the board who knew the condition of the Merrimac or how much of her was left. Mr. Brooke had not seen her since the destruction of the Gosport Navy Yard, when she was burned to the water's edge. She had been raised by the Baker Wrecking Company on the 30th of May, and Mr. Porter, as Constructor at the Navy Yard, had her put in the dry-dock and made a thorough examination of her. Mr. Williamson's duties were not such as to familiarize him with the condition of the vessel, so there is every reason to believe their version is correct, and that it was Mr. Porter who suggested that his shield be placed on the Merrimac. Mr. Brooke says Mr. Williamson first made the suggestion.

But, having come to the conclusion to adapt Mr. Porter's model to the Merrimac, the board prepared the following report, which they submitted to Secretary Mallory for his approval:

NAVY DEPARTMENT,
RICHMOND, VA., June 25th, 1861.

SIR- In obedience to your order we have carefully examined and considered the various plans and propositions for constructing a shoot proof steam battery, and respectfully report that, in our opinion, the steam frigate Merrimac, which is in such condition from the effects of fire as to be useless for any other purpose without incurring a heavy expense in her rebuilding, can be made an efficient vessel of that character, mounting ten heavy guns; two pivot guns, and eight broadside guns of her original battery, and for the further consideration, that we cannot procure a suitable engine and boilers for any other vessel without building them, which would occupy too much time, is would appear that this is our only chance to get a suitable vessel in a short time. The bottom of the hull, boilers and heavy and costly parts of the engine, being but little injured, reduce the cost of construction to about one-third the amount which would be required to construct such a vessel anew. We cannot, without further examination, make an accurate estimate of the cost of the projected work, but think it will be about one hundred and ten thousand dollars, the most of which will be for labor, the materials being nearly all on hand in the yard, except the iron plating to cover the shield. The plan to be adopted in the arrangement of her shield for glancing shots, mounting guns, arranging the hull and plating, to be in accordance with the plans submitted for the approval of the department.

[Signed]   WM. P. WILLIAMSON,
Chief Engineer.

JOHN M. BROOKE,
Lieutenant.

JOHN L. PORTER,
Naval Constructor.

When it is considered that Mr. Brooke had not seen the Merrimac nor the Navy Yard since the beginning of hostilities, that the Naval Constructor was the only member of the board who knew that what was left of the vessel would carry a shield large enough to cover ten guns, or how much it would cost to make the alterations in her hull, and that Chief Engineer Williamson was an expert upon the cost of machinery, it would be reasonable to suppose that the constructor and engineer prepared the report, and that the other member of the board signed it through confidence in their judgment. In fact Secretary Mallory took this view of it at the time. On the 18th of July, 1861, he submitted a report to the Confederate Congress, in which he said: "The cost of this work is estimated by the constructor and engineer in charge at $172,523, and as time is of the first consequence in this enterprise, I have not hesitated to commence the work, and to ask Congress for the necessary appropriation." Mr. Mallory totally ignored " the board," and took into consideration only the views of the constructor and engineer. He seems, at that time, not to have considered Mr. Brooke at all, not even in connection with the cost of her ordnance.

The report of the board speaks of having considered the various plans and propositions for constructing an iron-clad, &c. Messrs. Williamson and Porter say this had reference to whether they would recommend the building of a new vessel after Mr. Porter's model or apply his plan to the Merrimac. " The plans to be adopted in the arrangement of her shield for glancing shots, mounting guns, arranging the hull and plating," were not submitted simultaneously with the report, as it was necessary for Mr. Porter to return to the Gosport Navy Yard and make an accurate measurement of the vessel, so that he could calculate her displacement and prepare the plans. Engineer Williamson also went to the Navy Yard to superintend the preparation of the machinery, and Mr. Brooke remained in Richmond. Mr. Porter measured the vessel without assistance from any one, except a laborer to hold the end of the tape line.

Having completed his measurements, and calculated for everything which was to go in her, he found that he would have sufficient displacement and about fifty tons to spare, upon a depth of twenty-one feet, of which nineteen feet would be of her original hull and the remaining two feet would be the distance he proposed submerging the eaves of her shield, but when he drew a line at the height of nineteen feet from the bottom of her keel, he found it cut one foot into her propeller, and this would have decreased the size of her propeller and diminished her speed, besides consuming time in additional work. He therefore raised the line one foot at the stern and cut her down on a straight line running from a height of nineteen feet forward to twenty feet aft, so that, when completed, she drew twenty-one feet forward and twenty-two feet aft. This additional displacement increased her buoyancy about two hundred tons and had to be overcome by pig iron, or kentlege, which was placed on her deck ends and in her spirit room to bring her eaves to the proper depth below the water line.

Mr. Porter drew the plans for converting her into an iron-clad, and put on her the identical shield which was on his model, and also on his Pittsburg iron-clad of 1846, with the exception that he lengthened it out to nearly one hundred and eighty feet, so as to cover all of her deck where there was sufficient width for the shield, and, as he had a width of fifty-one feet on the Merrimac, he lowered the angle of inclination of her shield to thirty-five degrees. The great width of the ship enabled him to do this and still have room under the shield to work the guns. This width also made it necessary to have separate guns for each side. Finding too, that he had displacement enough to support a heavier armor, he recommended that she be plated with four inches of iron instead of three inches, as originally intended. This recommendation was approved by Secretary Mallory, and was carried out in her construction. The arrangment of her shield, inside and out, was identical with the plan proposed in the vessel the model of which he carried to Richmond, and which the board was called to consider. The original drawings of both vessels are in the possession of the author, and they are identical, except that one was arranged for six guns and the other for ten. The port holes were about four feet high, with straight sides and circular at the top and bottom. She had no boat davits. Her boats rested in chocks on her sides and were hauled out of the water.

Mr. Porter completed his drawings on the 10th of July, without having consulted any one, took them to Richmond the next morning, and submitted them to Secretary Mallory, who immediately approved them, without re-convening the board or calling in the advice or opinion of anyone, and wrote with his own hand, the following order, which he handed to Mr. Porter for delivery to Commodore Forrest, commanding the Gosport Navy Yard:

NAVY DEPARTMENT,
RICHMOND, VA., July 11th, 1861.

Flag Officer F. Forrest:

SIR—You will proceed with all practicable dispatch to make the changes in the Merrimac, and to build, equip and fit her in all respects, *according to the designs and plans of the Constructor and Engineer, Messrs. Porter and Williamson.* As time is of the utmost importance in this matter, you will see that the work progresses without delay to completion.

S. R. MALLORY,
Secretary Confederate States Navy.

Did Mr. Mallory, at the time he issued that order to begin work on the vessel, have any doubts as to whose plans he had approved and was ordering to be carried out? Mr. Porter returned immediately to the Gosport Navy Yard, appointed Mr. James Meads

Master Ship carpenter, and commenced work on the vessel in the dry-dock. The burned part was cut away, and a deck built from one end to the other. Inside the shield the deck was covered with plank, on beams, but outside the shield, at both ends, it was built of solid timber, and covered over with iron one-inch thick. Figure 3 represents the shape of a cross section amidship.

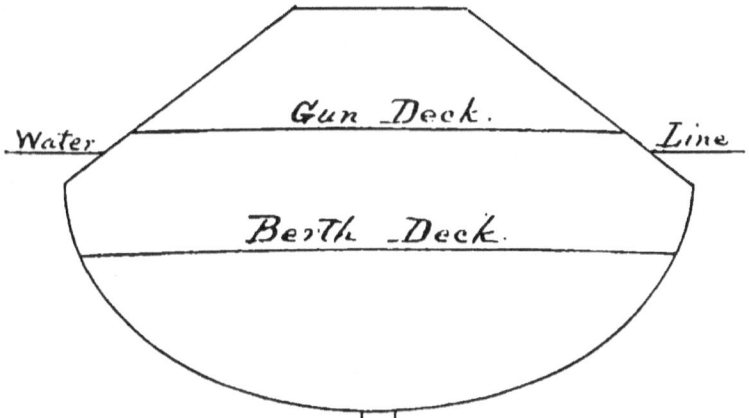

FIGURE 3 — Scale 1 inch 15 feet.

The ship had only two decks, gun and berth decks, and her boilers and engine remained in their original positions. She was fitted with four inch, hammered iron, port shutters on her four quarter ports, but had no shutters to her other ports. They were made in two pieces and closed like a pair of shears. She made her first fight, however, before they were put on her. Her rudder chains were let into the outside after deck flush under the iron, and passed up through the shield in pipes until they came above the water line and were then conducted on rollers to the steering wheel. The ship was 262 feet and 9 inches long from her stem to the after side of the stern post, and from the stem to the forward part of the shield was 29 feet, 6 inches. From the tiller to the after part of the shield was 55 feet, and the length of the shield was 178 feet, 3 inches. The neat length on the gun deck, under the shield, was 167 feet, 7 inches. The rafters of the shield were of yellow pine fourteen inches thick, and were bolted together and were placed at an inclination of thirty-five degrees. Outside of this, a course of four-inch pine planks was fastened, fore and aft, and outside of this there was a course of four-inch oak plank placed up and down. All three of these courses of timber were caulked. Upon the outside of the oak planks was placed a course of rolled iron bars, eight inches wide and two inches thick, running fore and aft, and upon this was another course of similar iron, running up and down, the whole securely bolted, through and through, and held with nuts on the inside. The length of the sides was twenty-four feet, and the perpendicular thickness was twenty-two inches of wood and four inches of iron, but horizontally, it was about four feet. The deck, or top of the shield, was fourteen feet wide and was protected by an iron grating made of two inch square iron with meshes two inches square. The pitch of the gun deck was seven feet. There were three hatchways in the top grating, with pivot shutters. In the original drawings of the ship it was contemplated to build a pilot house at the forward part of the shield, to be covered like the shield, but Mr. Porter subsequently had two cast iron conical shaped pilot houses made and put one at each end. These were cast hollow in the middle and about twelve inches thick, with four loop holes for observations. They were not used by Commodore Buchanan during the engagement in Hampton Roads. He stood in one of the hatchways above referred to and communicated his orders to the wheelsman from that position. As the work progressed, Secretary Mallory became very urgent for its speedy conclusion, and on the 19th of August, a little more than a month after it was begun, he wrote the following order:

CONFEDERATE STATES NAVY DEPARTMENT,
Richmond, August 19th, 1861.

Flag Officer F. Forrest, Commanding Navy Yard, Gosport:

Sir. The great importance of the service expected of the Merrimac, and the urgent necessity of her speedy completion, induces me to call upon you to push forward the work with the utmost dispatch. Chief Engineer Williamson and Constructor Porter, severally in charge of the two branches of this great work, and *for which they will be held personally responsible,* will receive therefore every possible facility at the expense and delay of every other work on hand if necessary.

S. R. MALLORY,
Secretary Confederate States Navy.

In order to protect her rudder and propellor from being run into, Mr. Porter built a heavy, solid deck, or fan tail, extending over them, and it would have been necessary to have broken through this before either of them could have been reached by a colliding vessel. He had a cast iron prow, or beak, made, which weighed about 1,500 pounds. This he fastened on her stem and bolted through it, but the ship struck the Cumberland a glancing blow and it was broken off. When the beak was put on her Mr. Porter was apprehensive that, as the ship was not built originally with a view to making a ram of her, it would not be safe to do so, but Captain Buchanan decided to take the risk, and sunk the Cumberland without materially injuring his own vessel. As a safeguard to protect the hull, a course of iron one inch thick was fastened all around her, three feet down from the knuckle. Her armament consisted of two 7-inch rifle guns, on pivot, one at each end, with a range out of three port holes, and eight smooth bore 9-inch Dahlgren guns of her original battery. The 7-inch rifle guns were made at the Tredegar Iron Works in Richmond under the supervision of Lieutenant Brooke. The armor plate was rolled there also. The gun carriages were made in the Navy Yard. In the engagements on the 8th and 9th of March two of her broadside guns were injured by having pieces knocked out at their muzzles, and they were replaced by two 6-inch rifle guns made at the Tredegar Works. Some of the officers of the vessel have informed the author that they were of the opinion that the two 6-inch rifle guns were on board during her first engagement, but others, and members of the crew, with whom he has conversed coincide with his account. Naval Constructor Porter's notes say the recommendation of the board was carried out, as to her battery, and that the eight broadside guns were 9-inch Dahlgrens. The reports of the commanders of the Federal vessels engaged in the battle of March 8th, 1862, mention the 7-inch rifle and 9-inch smooth bore guns, but make no mention of any 6-inch rifles. Captain Van Brunt of the Minnesota speaks of the mainmast of that vessel having been struck by a 6-inch rifle shell from the battery at Seawell's Point.

The work on the Merrimac was hastened with all possible dispatch, and the workmen employed on her evinced a very patriotic spirit. She was a novel kind of a vessel, and they felt a pride in her as the invention of a Portsmouth man, and a desire to see how she would perform the duty expected of her, and, in order to expedite the work, the blacksmiths, machinists and bolt drivers signed a voluntary proposition to work until 8 o'clock every night without extra pay. The following names were signed to the paper:

Jas. A. Farmer, M. S.,
John Askew,
Wm. T. Butt,
Thos. Bloxom,
Anthony Butt,
Thos. Bourke,
Elias Bridges,
E. H. Brown,
Wm. Gray,
Thos. Guy,
Smith Guy,
Anderson Gwinn,
Hillery Hopkins,
Wm. Hoffler,

Samuel Hodges,
Wiley Howard,
Jos. Ricketts,
H. Reynolds,
Southey Rew,
Wm. Reynolds,
John B. Rooke,
John Rhea,
Thos. L. Rooke,
Harvey Barnes,
Frederick Bowen,
Geo. G. Bear,
John Cain,
Michael Connor,

John Curran,
Geo. Collier,
Sam'l. Davenport,
John Davis,
Alex. Davis,
Joshua Dailey,
Thos. Dunn,
Lewis Ewell,
Lawson Etheredge,
Miles Foreman,
Thos. Franklin,
Jas. Fleming,
Wilson Guy,
John Green,

Lawrence Herbert,	James Moran,	H. Tatem,
Henry Hopkins,	Patrick Parks,	Walter Thornton,
Opie Jordan,	Jas. Pattison,	John West,
Wm. Jones,	Wm. Perry,	Jas. Wakefield,
Thos. Kirby,	Thos. Powell,	E. Woodward,
Jesse Kay,	Wm. Pebworth,	David Wilkins,
Jas. Larkin,	Chas. Snead,	Jas. Wilbern,
Lemuel Leary,	Patrick Shanasy,	Walter Wilkins,
Wm. Leary,	Wm. Shepherd,	Jas. Watson, Jr.,
Hugh Minter,	John Stokes,	Jos. West,
Jas. Mitchell,	Chas. Sturtevant,	John Wilder,
John Moody,	Wm. Shipp,	Edward Walker.
Julius Moran,	Calder Sherwood,	

Various were the comments by visitors and others at the Navy Yard while the ship was in process of construction, and the prevailing opinion seemed to be that she was top heavy and would turn bottom up, and many spoke of Mr. Porter as a visionary. He says that, among the officers stationed at the yard or ordered to the ship, only one, Captain Fairfax, gave him any encouragement, and when she was completed, and he reported to Captain S. S. Lee, executive officer of the yard, that he would turn the water into the dock the next day and float her, Captain Lee asked him, seriously: "Mr. Porter, do you really think she will float?" and the next morning, when the water was actually turned into the dock, the officers present, who were ordered to her, stood upon the edge of the dock to see whether or not she was going to sink. Mr. Porter says Lieutenant Catesby Jones, who was ordered to her as executive officer a short time before she was completed, was among those who expressed a want of faith in her ability to float.

After her engagements on the 8th and 9th of March, 1862, she returned to the Navy Yard and Mr. Porter put her in the dry-dock and made a thorough examination of her. There were about a hundred indentations in her armor where she was struck, and of these about twenty were from the guns of the Monitor. These could be told from the others by their larger size. Six of the outer plates were cracked and were replaced by new ones. None of the plates in the under course were broken, nor were any of her timbers injured. No repairs were necessary to be done to them. The broken plates were occasioned by shots from the Monitor. There were numerous shot holes through her smoke stack, which, however, was not carried away. Her iron beak, or prow, was broken off. This was originally made wedge shaped, projected about two feet from the ship, and was slanting on top. A new beak was made to replace this. It was made of steel and wrought iron, extended back about thirteen feet from the stem, and was securely bolted. The two damaged broadside guns were replaced by two 6-inch rifle guns, steel pointed solid shot were made for her guns, and her sides, for three feet below her knuckle, were covered with an additional course of two-inch iron plates placed up and down, and the top end clasped over the knuckle, to prevent the starting of the ends of the side armor on the shield from the effects of shot. This additional weight was neutralized by removing a portion of the pig iron which had been placed on her originally, so that her depth of water remained the same as when she made her trip to Hampton Roads on the 8th of March.

Various statements have been published, both from Confederate and Federal sources, as to the injury done the vessel in her engagements in Hampton Roads, but the above embraces all the injury she actually sustained. There was an almost imperceptible leak in her bow where her prow was broken in ramming the Cumberland, but it really amounted to nothing. Captain S. S. Lee, in his testimony before the Congressional committee appointed to investigate the Navy Department, page 231, says: "She was not severely damaged at all. She was not materially injured." The repairs were made by Constructor Porter under Captain Lee's supervision, and Mr. Porter's notes say that none of her wooden backing was broken, that none of her second course of iron was broken or removed, that none of her first course of iron was knocked off, and only six of those plates were broken.

A most inaccurate account of the Virginia was written by Lieutenant Catesby Jones and published in the Southern Historical Society Papers, Nos. 2-3, Vol. XI, pp. 65-76. It is unfortunate that so many errors should go forth to the world as history. Among other mistakes, he says:

First.—"Her rudder and propellor were unprotected." The facts are that the fan tail of solid timber which was built out over them made them safer than any other portion of the vessel, outside her shield, and a blow which would have cut through to her propellor would have crushed in the side of the ship.

Second.—He says "there were many vexatious delays attending the fitting of the ship. Many of them arose from the want of skilled labor," &c. The mechanics of Portsmouth and Norfolk will hardly accept that as correct.

Third.—He says he, "by special order, selected her battery." How could he have done this when her rifle guns were made at the Tredegar Works in Richmond under the supervision of Lieutenant Brooke, and her broadside guns were at the Navy Yard? Her battery had been selected by the board which recommended her conversion into an iron-clad, and was specified in their report of June 25th, 1861, which was approved by Secretary Mallory.

Fourth.—He says "The lower part of her shield forward was immersed only a few inches instead of two feet, as was intended." It was two feet under water, covered with kentlege, which was also under water.

Fifth.— He says "had the fire of the Minnesota, Cumberland and Congress been concentrated on the water line we would have been seriously hurt." The vessel was as strong at the water line as she was anywhere else. Her shield ran down into the water a distance of three feet and a half below the water line.

Sixth.— He says "the loss of our prow and anchor, and consumption of coal, water, &c., had lightened us so that the lower part of the forward end of the shield was awash." Had he been correct in this the *bow* of the ship would have been *out of the water*, and to have lightened her to that extent would have required the removal of two hundred and seventy-five tons of material from her in the twenty-four hours she was in Hampton Roads. Every inch, in depth, of displacement on her shield was equal to twenty-three tons, and every inch of her hull, below her shield, was equivalent to thirty tons.

Captain John Taylor Wood, who served gallantly on her as a Lieutenant and afterwards made an enviable record for himself by his deeds of daring in the Confederate Navy, was the author of an equally inaccurate description of the ship. It was published in the Century Magazine of March, 1885.

He seems to have accepted Lieutenant Jones' account as to the vulnerability of the vessel at the water line, and the "unprotected" condition of her rudder and propellor, adopts his mistake as to her drawing 23 feet of water, falls into an error about her pilot house, gives her one more deck than she had, carried away her smokestack in the action of March 9th, and says: "When the ship was in fighting trim both ends were awash." Had this been so her draft would have been only nineteen feet forward and twenty aft, and her eaves would have been even with the water. In reality, however, her ends and eaves were two feet below the water line.

The positions occupied by those two gentlemen, and their well known characters, add weight to their publications, hence it is unfortunate, for the correctness of history, that their articles were not given more careful study before publication.

But the Virginia proved a success, and though, while her success or failure was a matter of doubt, no name was connected with her authorship except Messrs. Porter and Williamson; though the Secretary in his order to Commodore Forrest, directed him to convert into an iron-clad after the plans of Messrs. Porter and Williamson, though in another order to Commodore Forrest he proposed to hold those two gentlemen personally responsible for the success of their plans, though in an official report to Congress he referred to them alone in connection with the estimated cost of the vessel, though up to that time no name but theirs had been mentioned in official orders from the Navy Departmens, in the public press or in private conversation, yet, when she had demonstrated her ability to float and to resist the shots of the enemy, a new claimant appeared for the credit of having projected her. The claim was made in an anonymous communication, signed "Justice," which appeared in the columns of the Richmond Enquirer and Richmond Whig of about the 25th of March, 1862, claiming for Lieutenant Brooke that credit. It was subsequently ascertained that the communications was sent to those papers by an employee in Mr. Brooke's office in the Navy Department.

On the 29th of March Mr. Porter wrote a reply, which he submitted to Chief Engineer Williamson for his approval, and then forwarded to the Richmond Examiner, in which paper it was published. He said in concluding his letter:

"Of the great and skillful calculations of the displacement and weights of timber and iron involved in the planning and construction of this great piece of naval architecture, and of her present weight, with everything on board, no other man than myself has, or ever had any knowledge. *If he has, let him show it*, for while public opinion said she never would float, no one save myself knew to the contrary, or what she was capable of bearing. After the Merrimac was in progress some time, Lieutenant Brooke was constantly proposing alterations in her to the Secretary of the Navy, and as constantly and firmly opposed by myself, which the Secretary knows. To Engineer Williamson, who had the exclusive control of the machinery, great credit is due for having so improved the propeller and engines as to improve the speed of the ship three knots per hour. I never thought for a moment that, after the many difficulties I had to encounter in making these new and intricate arrangements for the working of this novel kind of ship, that any one would try to rob me of my just merits, for, if there was any other man than myself who had any responsibility about her success or failure, I never knew it (except so far as the working of her machinery was concerned, for which Chief Engineer Williamson was alone responsible.)

JOHN L. PORTER,
C. S. N. Constructor.

This letter was submitted to Chief Engineer Williamson and approved by him before it was sent to the Examiner for publication, and Lieutenant Brooke failed to make any reply to it or to accept the challenge contained in it, to prove his authorship.

There seems to be some doubt as to what Mr. Brooke really claims in connection with the vessel, but his testimony before the Congressional Investigating Committee, admitting that the board adopted Mr. Porter's shield and stating that Mr. Williamson proposed putting the shield on the Merrimac, would indicate that he had abandoned all claim as the projector of that portion of the vessel and confined himself to the submerged projecting ends feature, and, though the author has personal knowledge of the fact that the plan of the shield of Mr. John L. Porter's iron-clad of 1846, and that of his model of 1861, which he carried to Richmond, and the shield of the Merrimac were identical, and were submerged two feet at their eaves, and that he conceived the idea and developed it in the drawings and specifications of a vessel, (which drawings are to this day in his possession), fifteen years before he ever saw Lieutenant Brooke, and, that he was at the Gosport Navy Yard when he made the drawings applying that shield to the Merrimac, while Lieutenant Brooke was in Richmond; that, in the conception and development of the plan, he was not aided by any ideas which may have been entertained by that gentleman, still as a historian, he has no inclination to suppress anything which Lieutenant Brooke has been able to advance in support of his claim. The main stay of support which he has, is a report made by Secretary Mallory to the Confederate Congress. That report was dated March 29th, 1862, but was not made public until April 4th, when it appeared in the Richmond press. In that report Mr. Mallory says:

"On the 10th of June, 1861, Lieutenant Brooke was directed to aid the department in designing an iron-clad war vessel, and framing the necessary specifications, and, in a few days, submitted to the department rough drawings of a casemated vessel with submerged ends and inclined plated sides, the ends of the vessel and the eaves, to be submerged two feet, and a light bulwark, or false bow was designed to divide the water and prevent it from banking up on the forward part of the shield with the vessel in motion, and also to serve as a tank to regulate the ship's draft. His design was approved by the department, and a practical mechanic was brought from Norfolk to aid in preparing the drawings and specifications.

"This mechanic aided in the statement of details of timber, etc., but was unable to make the drawings, and the department then ordered Chief Engineer Williamson and Constructor Porter from the Navy Yard at Norfolk, to Richmond, about the 23d of June, for consultation on the same subject generally and to aid in the work.

"Constructor Porter brought and submitted the model of a flat bottomed, light draft propeller, casemated battery, with inclined iron covered sides and ends, which he deposited in the department. Mr. Porter and Lieutenant Brooke have adopted for their casemate a thickness of wood and iron, and an angle of inclination nearly identical.

"Mr. Williamson and Mr. Porter approved of the plan of having submerged ends to obtain the requisite flotation and invulnerability, and the department adopted the design, and a clean drawing was prepared by Mr. Porter of Lieutenant Brooke's plan, which that officer then filed with the department.

"The steam frigate Merrimac was burned and sunk, and her engines greatly damaged by the enemy, and the department directed Mr. Williamson, Lieutenant Brooke and Mr. Porter to consider and report upon the best mode of making her useful. The result of their investigation was their recommendation of the submerged ends and the inclined casemates for this vessel, which was adopted by the department."

The following is the report upon the Merrimac. [See ante.]

"Immediately upon the adoption of the plan, Mr. Porter was directed to proceed with the constructor's duties. Mr. Williamson was charged with the engineer's department, and to Mr. Brooke was assigned the duties of attending to and preparing the iron and forwarding it from the Tredegar Works, the experiments necessary to test the plates and to determine their thickness, and devising heavy rifled ordnance for the ship, with the details pertaining to ordnance.

"These gentlemen labored zealously and effectively in their several departments. Mr. Porter cut the ship down, submerged her ends, performed all the duties of constructor, and originated all of the interior arrangements by which space was economized and he has exhibited energy, ability and ingenuity. Mr. Williamson thoroughly overhauled her engines, supplied deficiencies, and repaired defects, and improved greatly the motive power of the vessel.

"Mr. Brooke attended daily to the iron, constructed targets, ascertained by actual tests, the resistance offered by inclined planes of iron to heavy ordnance, and determined interesting and important facts in connection therewith, and which were of great importance in the construction of the ship; devised and prepared the models and drawings of the ship's heavy ordnance, being guns of a class never before made, and of extraordinary power and strength.

"The novel plan of submerging the ends of the ship and the eaves of the casemate, however, is the peculiar and distinctive feature of the Virginia. It was never before adopted. * * * * We were without accurate data and were compelled to determine the inclination of the plates and their thickness and form by actual experiment. The department has freely consulted the three excellent officers referred to throughout the labors on the Virginia, and they have all exhibited signal ability, energy and zeal."

This report of Secretary Mallory was made from his recollections of what took place nearly a year before. How he obtained his information of what took place in the meeting of the board of June 25th, 1861, does not appear, nor does it coincide with the recollections of Mr. Williamson and Mr. Porter, or with the report made by the board, or the orders of the Secretary himself to proceed with the work. Memory is not always reliable after a lapse of time.

First. After speaking of Mr. Brooke's efforts to design an iron clad and his failure to accomplish anything, even after a practical mechanic had been sent from the Navy Yard to assist him, he says: "The department ordered Chief Engineer Williamson and Constructor Porter from the Navy Yard at Norfolk, to Richmond, about the 23d of June, (1861), for consultation on the same subject generally and to aid in the work."

It is unfortunate that that order was not found. Messrs. Porter and Williamson denied that they were summoned to confer about any plans of Lieutenant Brooke, and the order could have determined the matter if it was among the Navy Department records. It was not produced. The 23d of June, 1861, was Sunday, and the Department was not "open for business" on that day.

Second. The Secretary says: "Constructor Porter brought and submitted the model of a flat-bottomed, light draft, propeller, casemated battery, with inclined iron-covered sides and ends, which he deposited in the Department. Mr. Porter and Lieutenant Brooke have adopted for their casemate a thickness of wood and iron, and an angle of inclination almost identical."

Hence, from the Secretary's recollection of Mr. Brooke's *rough drawings* they were similar to Mr. Porter's *model*, then in his office, as to the shield of the vessel. Mr. Porter's model was tangible and practical. Mr. Brooke's "rough drawings" were ideal and imaginative. Can any one draw from this a conclusion that the board directed that the Merrimac be changed into an iron-clad after the rough drawings of Mr. Brooke and not the matured model of Mr. Porter.

Third.—The Secretary says: "Mr. Porter originated all of the interior arrangements, by which space has been economized, and has exhibited energy, ability and ingenuity."

It seems, therefore, even from the recollections of Secretary Mallory, that Mr. Porter not only carried to Richmond with him a model of a vessel with the Merrimac's shield on it, but he originated all of the interior arrangements of the vessel

Fourth. The Secretary says: "Mr. Porter cut the ship down, submerged her ends," &c.

Her ends were submerged by the Federal authorities who burned her. There was no submerging of her ends as contemplated in Mr. Brooke's idea of water-tight tanks to regulate her draft. She was built upon a straight line from stem to stern.

Fifth.- He says the Department directed Mr. Williamson, Lieutenant Brooke and Mr. Porter to report upon the best mode of making the Merrimac useful. The result of their investigations was the recommendation of the submerged ends and the inclined casemates for this vessel, which was adopted by the Department."

Their report, which is published in full in this chapter, contains nothing of that character. It speaks for itself and contradicts the Secretary. When the question of the consideration of the Merrimac was submitted to the board does not appear, and all three of the members of the board have stated that the conversion of the Merrimac into an iron clad was purely accidental, and the result of circumstances, not of original design.

Sixth. The Secretary says: "We were compelled to determine the inclination of the plates by actual experiment."

The Secretary's memory is greatly at fault here, too. The angle of inclination of the plates was marked in Mr. Porter's drawings when he submitted them to the Secretary at the time the order was given to begin the work, and was not altered. Those drawings are now in the possession of the author, and are an unquestionable proof that the angle of inclination was designed by Mr. Porter, from his own judgment, when he prepared the drawings of the vessel, and not as the result of any experiments made by Lieutenant Brooke subsequent to that date. The shield was built upon an angle of 35 degrees, just as is delineated in the original drawings which were submitted to Secretary Mallory July 11th, 1861.

Seventh.—The Secretary says: "Mr. Brooke's plan was adopted by the Department." Well, suppose the Department did adopt Mr. Brooke's plan, which, up to that time, consisted only of some rough drawings, that plan was not considered by Mr. Williamson and Mr. Porter, and was not in the mind of the Secretary himself when he ordered the work to be commenced on the Merrimac, for he wrote an autograph order to Commodore Forrest directing him to proceed with all practicable dispatch to make the changes in the Merrimac, and to build, equip and fit her in all respects *according to the designs and plans of the Constructor and Engineer, Messrs. Porter and Williamson.*

These discrepancies between Secretary Mallory's report and certain facts which have been so well established as to become axiomatic, are referred to simply to show the unreliability of an official report which is based upon memory, without regarding cotemporaneous documents.

Lieutenant Brooke has borne testimony in behalf of Constructor Porter. At the session of Congress of 1862-3 a joint committee of the Senate and House of Representatives was appointed to investigate Mr. Mallory's management of the Navy Department, and on the 26th of February, 1863, Lieutenant Brooke testified before the committee. See their published report, page 410. He said:

"The Constructor brought with him a model. I should have said the name of the Constructor was J. L. Porter. This model is one of the models now in the Secretary's room. It consisted of a shield and hull," &c. * * * "The Secretary directed the Constructor, Chief Engineer Williamson and myself to meet him at my office here. We met there and this model was examined by us all, and the form of the shield was approved. It was considered a good shield, and for ordinary purposes a good boat for harbor defence." * * * "Mr. Williamson proposed to put the shield on the Merrimac. Mr. Porter and myself thought the draft was too great, but were nevertheless of the opinion that it was the best thing that could be done with our means." Mr. Brooke further says, after telling of the adoption of Mr. Porter's shield, "the Secretary then called the attention of Mr. Porter and Mr. Williamson to the drawing giving a general idea of the vessel I proposed."

Therefore, from Lieutenant Brooke's own testimony, the shield of the Merrimac was Mr. Porter's shield, and it was at Mr. Williamson's suggestion that it was put on that vessel, and furthermore, the shield was adopted before his plans were submitted to the board. How, then, could the vessel have been converted into an iron-clad after Mr. Brooke's plans? Was there anything about her pertaining to an iron-clad except her shield? Was there anything about her except her shield which could be dignified into the name of a *plan?*

The article previously referred to, written by Lieutenant Catesby Jones, has been referred to by friends of Lieutenant Brooke as a proof of his claim. Lieutenant Jones said:

"The Merrimac was raised and on June 23d following the Hon. S. R. Mallory, Confederate Secretary of the Navy, ordered that she should be converted into an iron-clad on the plan proposed by Lieutenant John M. Brooke, C. S. N."

Following the same views expressed by Lieutenant Jones, Captain John Taylor Wood wrote to the Century Magazine:

"During the summer of 1861 Lieutenant [George John] M. Brooke proposed to Secretary Mallory to raise and rebuild this ship as an iron-clad. His plans were approved and orders were given to carry them out."

Those two gentlemen give Lieutenant Brooke more credit than he claims. He testified under oath before the Congressional committee that the proposition to make an iron-clad of the Merrimac first came from Chief Engineer Williamson, and that he himself opposed it. Nor were any orders ever issued by Secretary Mallory to make an iron-clad of her after Mr. Brooke's plans. The order to make her an iron-clad distinctly specified "the plans of the Constructor and Engineer, Messrs. Porter and Williamson," and an order issued six weeks later proposed to hold those two officers "personally responsible" for their success. The order was issued July 11th, 1861, and not (on Sunday) June 23d, 1861. Lieutenant Jones seems to have had no authority for his version,

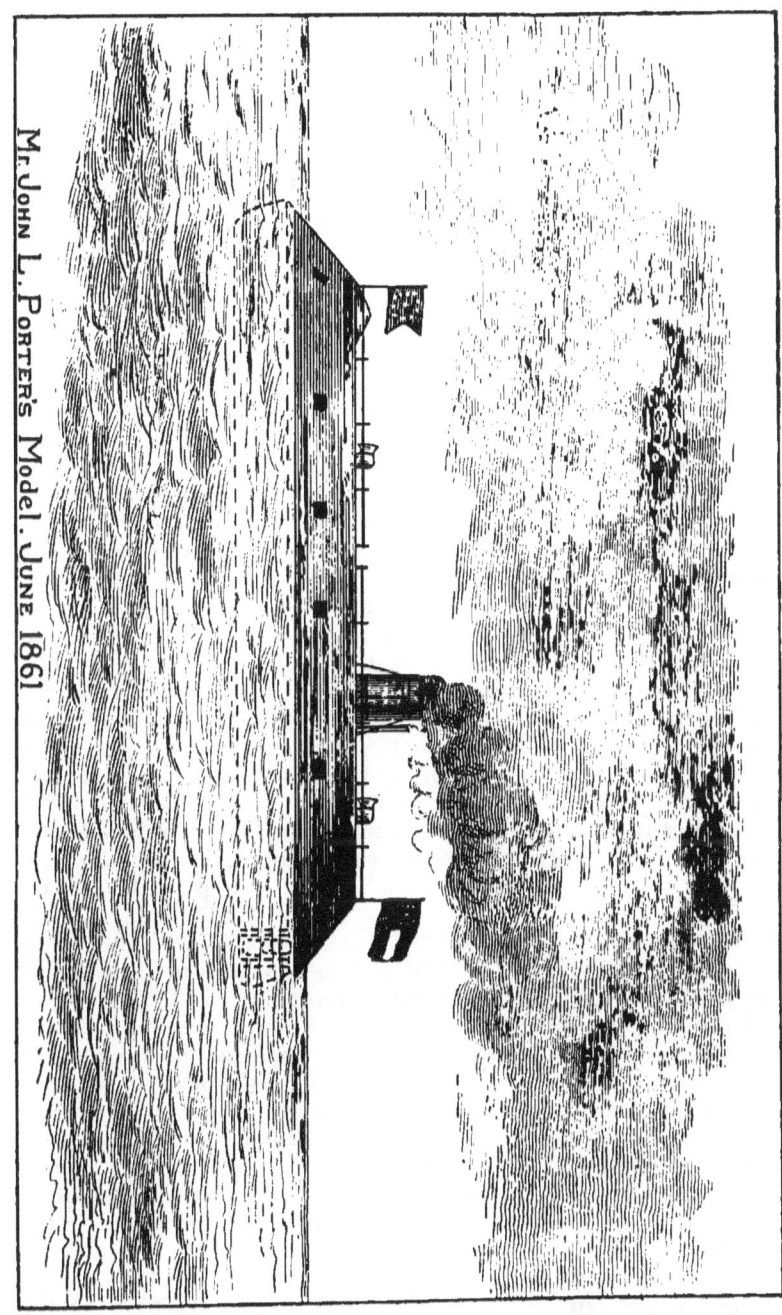

nor could he produce any such order as he refers to, and Captain Wood seems to have based his article upon Lieutenant Jones'. But such is history!

As soon as the report of Secretary Mallory was made public Constructor Porter, with the sanction of Chief Engineer Williamson, replied to it as follows through the Richmond Examiner:

NAVY YARD, GOSPORT, April 8th, 1864.

To the Editor of the Examiner:

Sir. I find in the Examiner of the 4th instant a report of the Secretary of the Navy to Congress, giving a detailed statement of the origin of the iron-clad Virginia. I feel sorry to have to reply to this report, inasmuch as it is published over the signature of the Secretary, * * but justice to myself requires that I should reply to it.

The report commences by stating that "on the 10th of June Lieutenant Brooke was directed to aid the Deparment in designing an iron-clad war vessel and framing the necessary specifications, and in a few days submitted to the Department rough drawings of a casemated vessel with submerged ends and inclined plated sides, the ends of the vessel and the eaves to be submerged two feet." I do not doubt the statements of the Secretary, but no such plans were submitted to the board, and, from the fact that the master carpenter had returned to this yard without completing any plans, and myself being sent for immediately, and from the further fact that the Secretary presented us no plans from this source, I stated in my last communication that Lieutenant Brooke failed to produce anything, after a week's trial, and I am still of that opinion, so far as anything tangible is concerned. The report states that "the practical mechanic who was brought up from Norfolk was unable to make the drawings for Lieutenant Brooke, and that the Department then ordered Chief Engineer Williamson and Constructor Porter from the Navy Yard at Norfolk to Richmond about the 23d of June, for consultation on the same subject generally and to aid in the work."

I do not understand this part of the report exactly, but if it is intended to convey the idea that we were to examine any plan of Lieutenant Brooke I never so understood it, neither did we act in accordance with any such idea, as our report will show.

The report next refers to my model, which I carried up with me, the shield and plan of which is carried out on the Virginia, but the report seems to have lost sight of the fact that the eaves and ends of my model were submerged two feet, precisely like the Virginia. The ship was cut down on a straight line fore and aft, to suit this arrangement, and the shield extended over her just as far as the space inside would admit and leave room to work the guns. A rough breakwater was built on it to throw off the water forward.

The report states that I "made a clean drawing of Lieutenant Brooke's plan, which that officer then filed with the Department." The only drawing that I ever made of the Virginia was made at my office in this Navy Yard, and which I presented to the Department on the 11th of July, just sixteen days after the board adjourned. This drawing and plan I considered my own, and not Lieutenant Brooke's. As soon as I presented this plan the Secretary wrote the following order while everything was fresh in his mind concerning this whole matter:

NAVY DEPARTMENT,
RICHMOND, July 11th, 1861.

Flag Officer F. Forrest:

Sir. You will proceed with all practicable dispatch to make the changes in the Merrimac, and to build, equip and fit her in all respects *according to the designs and plans of the Constructor and Engineer, Messrs. Porter and Williamson.* As time is of the utmost importance in the matter, you will see that the work progresses without delay to completion.

S. R. MALLORY,
Secretary Confederate States Navy.

What, I would ask, could be more explicit than this letter, or what words could have established my claim stronger, if I had dictated them?

The concluding part of this report says: "The novel plan of submerging the ends of the ship and the eaves of the casemate, however, is the peculiar and distinctive feature of the Virginia." This may all be true, but it is just what my model calls for, and if Lieutenant Brooke presented "rough drawings" to the Department carrying out the same views it may be called a singular coincidence, and here I would remark that my model was not calculated to have much speed, but was intended for harbor defence only, and was of light draft, the eaves extending over the entire length of the model and submerged all around two feet, end and sides, and the line on which I cut the ship down was just in accordance with this, but if Lieutenant Brooke's ideas, which were submitted to the Secretary in his rough drawings, had been carried out, to cut her ends down low enough to build tanks on to regulate the draft of the vessel, she would have been much lower than my plan required, for all the water which now covers her ends would not alter her draft three inches if confined in tanks. All of the calculations of the weights and displacements, and the line to cut the ship down, were determined by myself, as well as her whole arrangements.

That Lieutenant Brooke may have been of great assistance to the department in trying the necessary experiments in determining the thickness of the armor, getting up her battery and attending to the shipping of the iron, &c., I do not doubt, but to claim for him the credit of designing the ship is a matter of too much interest to me to give up. Engineer Williamson discharged his duties with great success. The engines peformed beyond his most sanguine expectations, and these, with the improvements in her propeller, increased her speed three miles per hour. * * The Secretary of the Navy has not only been my friend in this Government, but was a true and serviceable one under the U. S. Government, and has rendered me many acts of kindness for which I have always esteemed him, but the present unpleasant controversy involves a matter of so much importance to me that I shall be excused for defending my claim, not only as the constructor, but the originator of the plan of the Virginia.

JOHN L. PORTER,
Confederate States Naval Constructor."

There seems to have been a difference of recollection as to what became of Lieutenant Brooke's rough drawings. He says Secretary Mallory laid them before the board. Messrs. Williamson and Porter say they were not before the board, or considered by it, and Mr. Mallory is silent on the subject. He says the board adopted Mr. Brooke's plan of submerged ends, but does not say how he obtained the information, nor does he claim to have been present at the conference.

Messrs. Williamson and Porter say the plans of Mr. Porter were adopted, and that it was decided to build a new vessel after his model and Mr. Porter first made the proposition to adapt them to the Merrimac, after finding out the impracticability of getting an engine for a new boat. Mr. Brooke says Mr. Porter's shield was adopted and Mr. Williamson first proposed to apply it to the Merrimac.

Chief Engineer Williamson gave to Mr. Porter a letter certifying to the fact that the Merrimac was converted into an iron-clad after his plans and not after plans of Mr. Brooke. That letter was burned up in Mr. Porter's office in Richmond, but there are witnesses living at this writing who have read it. There are witnesses too, living who were on intimate terms with Chief Engineer Williamson, and to whom he expressed himself freely on the subject of the Merrimac, and to those he always said Mr. Porter was her projector. Mr. Williamson's death prevented Mr. Porter from getting a duplicate of his letter, but its contents and his views upon the subject can be substantiated by living witnesses. The following letters will bear out what has been said on this subject. The first was sent to the author by Captain Wm. R. Singleton:

THE "VIRGINIA" (MERRIMAC) 351

VIRGINIA (MERRIMAC)

WASHINGTON, D. C., June 15th, 1891.

DEAR SIR - * * In 1857, when I was constructing engineer in charge of the Pensacola Navy Yard, Mr. John L. Porter was the naval constructor and Lieutenant John Newton, (since then General and Chief Engineer) was in charge of Forts Pickens, McCrea and Barrancas. As we were, all three, from Norfolk and Portsmouth, Virginia, and, in early days, school boys together, we frequently met at the Navy Yard. On one occasion in my office, the conversation turned upon defences of harbors, &c. Mr. Porter explained to us by diagrams, his method of constructing a vessel, which he said originated with him at the time he was constructing the naval ship at Pittsburg, in 1846. * * I can remember the sketches made at the Pensacola Yard in 1857. The Merrimac was altered to suit the broad idea so far as she could be in her then condition. I believe subsequently the Richmond was constructed from the beginning, as was his original idea.

Hoping that Mr. Porter will get the credit to which I always insisted that he was justly entitled, I am,

Very respectfully yours,

WM. R. SINGLETON,
Late Constructing Engineer U. S. Navy.

Chief Engineer Schroeder, in the following letter, bears testimony to the existence and character of Mr. Porter's iron-clad, designed in Pittsburg in 1846, and also to the views of Chief Engineer Williamson as to the projector of the Virginia:

NORFOLK, VA., January 8th, 1892.

DEAR SIR—During the late war my duties took me frequently to the Bureau of Steam Engineering in Richmond, and I often heard, while there, Major Wm. P. Williamson, the Engineer in Chief, say that the design of the Merrimac's shield was that of Mr. John L. Porter, who was the Chief Constructor of the C. S. Navy. Major Williamson was a member of the board which recommended making an iron-clad of the Merrimac. I distinctly remember sketches and plans, similar in design to the shield of the Merrimac, which Mr. Porter had made in Pittsburg years prior to the war.

Yours truly,

CHAS. SCHROEDER.

These two letters, together with the plans of the vessel in Constructor Porter's sketch book of naval designs, establish very clearly the fact that in 1846, fifteen years before Mr. Porter ever saw Lieutenant Brooke, he designed an iron-clad vessel in Pittsburg, the shield of which was of the same design as the shield he put on the Merrimac. This was ten years before England and France began experimenting on the subject of iron-clads, hence there is no good reason to question that the first iron-clad vessel ever designed, was the work of a native and citizen of Portsmouth.

That Chief Engineer Williamson, over his own signature, has certified that Constructor John L. Porter was the projector of the vessel, will be seen from the following letter:

NORFOLK, VA., January 9th, 1892.

SIR—During the late war I was chief clerk in the office of Chief Constructor John L. Porter, Confederate States Navy, corner of Main and Eleventh streets, Richmond. The office of Chief Engineer Wm. P. Williamson, of the Bureau of Steam Engineering, was in an adjoining room, and scarcely a day passed without his coming in Mr. Porter's office for consultation. We frequently talked on the subject of the Merrimac, and he told me repeatedly that she was made into an iron-clad after the plans of Mr. John L. Porter, and that there was no ground whatever for the claim which Lieutenant Brooke had set up to being her projector. I also remember having read a letter to that effect which Mr. Williamson gave to Mr. Porter, and which was, in all probability, burned with the other papers in Mr. Porter's office, at the evacuation of Richmond by the Confederates in April, 1865. Mr. Porter was, at that time, absent from Richmond, having gone to North Carolina on business for the Navy Department, and the building in which his office was located, was burned in the general conflagration.

Very respectfully,

JNO. W. BORUM.

Commodore Marshall Parks, an intimate friend of Chief Engineer Williamson, had many opportunities to learn from him the history of the Merrimac, and has furnished the author with the following testimonial, both as to the character of the model Constructor Porter took with him to Richmond and as to Chief Engineer Williamson's statement of what took place at the meeting of the board on the 25th of June, 1861.

NORFOLK, VA., January 9th, 1892.

DEAR SIR—In reply to your communication I will state that when I was appointed by the Governor and Council of North Carolina as commissioner with Commander Muse (who had resigned from the United States Navy) to establish her navy, I had to visit the Gosport Navy Yard frequently to obtain supplies for the gunboats we had purchased and were fitting out at Norfolk. I well recollect on one of those visits Naval Constructor John L. Porter exhibited to me a model of an iron-clad which was identically the same plan which was afterwards applied to the Merrimac.

He subsequently carried it to Richmond, and orders were given to carry out his plan. I went to Raleigh and informed the Governor and members of the Legislature of the plan, and suggested that some small iron clads be built for the defense of the North Carolina sounds. I recollect that the plan so impressed me and them, that I was directed to write a "Bill" to authorize the Governor to have some vessels built on the plan, and it was passed immediately.

The State of North Carolina soon after this decided to join the Confederacy, and I was directed to go to Richmond and turn over all the steamers we had purchased and fitted out to the Confederate States Navy Department. I have had a life-long acquaintance with Major W. P. Williamson, who was the senior engineer of the United States Navy, and during and since the war he always expressed himself to me that the Merrimac was converted into an iron-clad after the plans of Mr. John L. Porter, and that Lieutenant John M. Brooke had nothing to do with her except to superintend the preparation of a portion of her guns.

Very respectfully, your obedient servant,

MARSHALL PARKS.

As all of Naval Constructor Porter's *original drawings* are still in existence, subject to the inspection of any one who has any desire to look at them, and, as they speak for themselves, and as the foregoing letters are from gentlemen and officials who were in positions to know the facts of which they write, there can be but one conclusion drawn from them and that is that the Merrimac was converted into an iron-clad after the plans of Naval Constructor John L. Porter. The evidence may be summed up briefly.

Mr. Porter invented an iron-clad in 1846, the plan of which submerged the eaves too feet below the water line. In May, 1861, he had a model made at the Gosport Navy Yard, changing somewhat the shape of the hull of his Pittsburg boat, but retaining the features of her shield and submerged eaves. She was submerged all around, eaves and ends.

In June, 1861, Lieutenant Brooke was in consultation with Secretary Mallory on the subject of iron-clads and Mr. Joseph Pierce, Master Ship Carpenter of the Gosport Navy Yard, and afterwards a Naval Constructor in the Confederate Navy, was sent to Richmond to help him develop his idea, but nothing was developed and no vessel was designed, no specifications drafted.

On the 23d of June Mr. Porter went to Richmond and took his model with him, and on the 25th, by order of Secretary Mallory, Messrs. Williamson, Brooke and Porter met in Mr. Brooke's office in the Navy Department and that model was laid before them. The form of the shield was adopted (even Mr. Brooke admits this) and, according to Mr. Brooke's recollection, Mr. Williamton suggested that it be adapted to the Merrimac, but Messrs. Williamson and Porter say the proposition first came from Mr. Porter. Mr. Williamson could not have made the suggestion for he did not know that the Merrimac could carry the shield, but be that as it may, the shield which was on Mr. Porter's model was, according to the statements of all three members of the board, directed to be adapted to the Merrimac, because there were no facilities to build a new engine for a new boat, and Mr. Porter returned to the Navy Yard in Portsmouth to measure the remains of that vessel, and prepare the plans. He made the plans unassisted by anyone, originated all of the interior arrangements, decided how long her shield would be, fixed the angle of inclination at 35 degrees, and cut her down so that the ends of her iron plating, or eaves, would be two feet under water, just as was contemplated in his Pittsburg vessel of 1846, and in the model which he carried with him to Richmond.

Lieutenant Brooke's idea of submerging the ends of an iron clad, according to Secretary Mallory's report, contemplated the building of water tight tanks on them to regulate her draft of water, and Mr. Porter shows that, had she been cut down in conformity with Mr. Brooke's idea she would have been cut down much lower than was actually the case, for all of the water which was over her ends would not have affected her draft three inches if confined in tanks. Therefore she could not have been cut down to suit Mr. Brooke's idea.

Messrs. Porter and Williamson were very explicit as to the part Mr. Brooke performed, namely, that his connection with the plan of the ship consisted in superintending a portion of her battery; and it will be remembered there were only three members of the board, and no one but those three gentlemen were competent to speak of what took place at their meeting.

But Mr. Porter completed the plans for the hull, took them to Richmond and submitted them to Secretary Mallory on the 11th of July, 1861, just sixteen days after the meeting of the board. Lieutenant Brooke's rough drawings, such as they were, and the plan proposed therein, whatever it was, must have been fresh in the Secretary's mind. If they made any impression upon him there had not been time for it to have been eradicated, especially as he and Mr. Brooke had been talking the matter over between themselves from the 10th to the 25th of June, but while everything was fresh in his mind, if it had been Mr. Brooke's plan which he approved, would he have written his order to Commodore Forrest "to make the changes in the Merrimac, and to build, equip and fit her in all respects, *according to the designs and plans of the Constructor and Engineer, Messrs. Porter and Williamson?*"

There is no mention in this order of Lieutenant Brooke or his plans, nor was there in Mr. Mallory's report to Congress of July 18th, 1861, nor in his order to Commodore Forrest of Aug. 19th, declaring his purpose of holding Messrs. Porter and Williamson personally responsible for the success of their plans. Charity to Mr. Mallory would say his report of March 29th, 1862, was the result of a defective memory.

Had it been practicable Mr. Porter would not have submerged

the ends of the Merrimac at all, but would have raised them out of the water like the ends of his Pittsburg model, and like he did the iron-clads which were subsequently built for the Confederate navy, but too much of her had been burned off for that, and, on account of the manner of the construction of the hulk, it would have been impossible to have built up and protected her ends above the water without the expenditure of a great deal of time and money, even if there had been enough of her left for that purpose, hence he was compelled to arrange her after the plans of his model, which was submerged all around, caves and ends, the model he took to Richmond, and which, according to Messrs. Williamson and himself, he was directed to apply to the Merrimac. The Merrimac was not selected as the result of any plan, but simply because she had an engine in her which could be utilized where it was, and the Confederates lacked the facilities for building a new engine for a new boat. The burned portion of her was cut away and the weight of her armor, armament, &c., submerged the remainder so that only her shield was out of water. It is not probable that Constructor Porter would have built a new vessel with her ends extending out under water beyond her shield. He converted the Merrimac into an iron-clad after that style through necessity, and not from choice. They were the weak points of the ship, the crew had no place for recreation and were kept in the casemate, the ends were liable to spring aleak, and being hidden from sight, confused the pilot in steering, besides retarding the vessel. The shield was extended as far forward and aft as the sharpness of her ends would permit.

It was a well known fact that pig iron was put on the Virginia to sink her deeper in the water, and various writers have endeavored to account for this. Lieutenant Brooke, in his testimony before the Congressional investigating committee, which has gone forth to the world as history, says: "After the vessel was launched Mr. Porter stated to me that he had accidentally omitted in his calculations some weights which were on board the ship, in consequence of which she did not draw as much water when launched as he anticipated." Mr. Brooke evidently made a mistake here. Mr. Porter could hardly have told him that, for if he had omitted in his calculations any of the weights in the ship she would have drawn *more* instead of *less* water than he calculated. The facts are, Mr. Porter had to give her more draft than was necessary to prevent cutting into her propeller, which was already in the ship, and this was the displacement which had to be overcome by the pig iron. Mr. Porter could hardly have told Mr. Brooke that the ship was launched. She was built in the dry-dock, and when finished the water was turned in and she was simply floated off the blocks. She was not launched.

The cuts which are published of the Virginia, and also of the vessel contemplated in Mr. Porter's model which he carried with him to Richmond and submitted to the board, are very positive evidence that they were identical in plan, and Mr. Brooke admitted in his testimony before the Congressional investigating committee that this shield was adopted by the board before his own rough drawings were submitted to it. The converting of the vessel into an iron-clad consisted in putting the shot proof shield on her. That is all of an iron-clad nature there was about her, all there was of a plan. All of the rest of her was the result of accident, and not design, and if any one is entitled to the credit of submerging her ends beyond her shield, it was Commodore Paulding of the United States Navy, who ordered the Gosport Navy Yard to be burned, in consequence of which the Merrimac was burned to the water's edge. The deck plan of the Virginia shows for itself, that the shield was extended fore and aft as far as the conformation of the ship would permit, and was there stopped from necessity. When Constructor Porter drew the plans by which she was converted into an iron-clad he followed precisely the plan which he had mapped out in his model, submerged her eaves and ends two feet all around, and would have extended her shield her entire length had she not been too sharp at the bow and stern, and therefore he stopped it where the vessel became too narrow to admit its being built any further. He did not desire any assistance from Mr. Brooke's undeveloped idea or unmatured plans. The plans upon which he converted the Merrimac into an iron-clad were his own, and were fully matured, delineated and calculated before he ever saw Mr. Brooke. No better proof can be adduced of this than the original drawings of the three boats, which are still in existence.

Subsequent to the publication of the report of Secretary Mallory Lieutenant Brooke applied to the Confederate Patent Office and obtained a patent for "an iron-clad with submerged ends, projecting beyond her shield," and it has been claimed for him that this is an evidence that he was the author of the plans upon which the Virginia was built into an iron-clad. There might be some grounds for this claim if the matter had been contested and judicially decided when the patent was granted, but Naval Constructor Porter had no knowledge that the patent was being applied for, and therefore no opposition was made to it, and it was issued as a matter of course. After it was granted it was not worth contesting. No naval architect would construct a vessel in that manner from choice. The Virginia grew out of the necessities of the Confederacy and the want of facilities to build a new engine for a new vessel. No iron-clads were subsequently built with submerged projecting ends. Mr. Porter did not then foresee that this patent would, in future years, be appealed to as evidence to deprive him of the credit of his invention. The claim set forth in the patent seems to be solely for submerged ends, and not for the iron-plated shield.

CHAPTER XLVIII.

THE BATTLE OF HAMPTON ROADS.

When the water was turned into the dry-dock and the Merrimac was floated, her name was changed by order of the Secretary of the Navy to "The Virginia," and though not really completed, Captain Buchanan, who had been assigned to her as her commander, decided to proceed with her to attack the Federal vessels in Hampton Roads, and on the 8th of March, 1862, a little before noon, she steamed slowly away from the Navy Yard. Both banks of the river were lined with spectators, and the troops stationed at the various batteries around the harbor cheered her as she passed. She appeared on the water like a sunken house with nothing but the roof above the tide. Her officers were:

Captain, Franklin Buchanan, of Maryland.

Lieutenants, Catesby ApR. Jones, of Virginia; Chas. C. Simms, of Virginia; Robert D. Minor, of Virginia; Hunter Davidson, of Virginia; John Taylor Wood, of Louisiana; J. R. Eggleston, of Mississippi, and Walter R. Butt, of Virginia.

Midshipmen, R. C. Foote, of Tennessee; H. H. Marmaduke, of Missouri; H. B. Littlepage, of Virginia; W. J. Craig, of Kentucky; J. C. Long, of Tennessee, and L. M. Roots, of Virginia.

Paymaster, James Semple, of Virginia.

Surgeon, D. B. Phillips, and assistant, A. S. Garnett, both of Virginia.

Captain of Marines, R. T. Thom, of Alabama.

Engineers—Chief, H. Ashton Ramsay, of Virginia; assistants, John W. Tynan, of Virginia; London Campbell, of Virginia; Benjamin Herring, of North Carolina; E. V. White, of Georgia; E. A. Jack, of Virginia, and Robert Wright, of Virginia.

Boatswain, Charles H. Hasker; Gunner, Charles B. Oliver; Carpenter, Hugh Lindsay; Clerk, Arthur Sinclair, Jr.; Volunteer Aide, Douglas F. Forrest; Commandant United Artillery, Captain Thomas Kevill, all of Virginia.

Pilots, Wm. Parrish, Wm. Clarke, Hezekiah Williams and George Wright, all of the Virginia Pilots' Association.

Her crew was made up of about three hundred men, some of whom were seamen, but the larger portion were landsmen, who volunteered from the army, but for such service as was expected on the Virginia, landsmen were as good as seamen. No record has been kept of the names of the crew. Some of the men were obtained from General Magruder's army on the Peninsula, some were from Norfolk county and Portsmouth, and thirty-one men from the United Artillery Company of Norfolk, under Captain

Kevill, volunteered to make up her complement. Sixteen of that number manned the forward gun on the starboard side and the rest were distributed among the other guns' crews.

In order to guard against any accident to her machinery, her engines were worked very slowly until she reached Hampton Roads. Chief Engineer Ramsey is reported as having said "he had little confidence in it," but it worked very well during the engagement. After passing Seawell's Point the pilot took the south channel for Newport News, where the frigate Congress and sloop-of-war Cumberland were lying at anchor. While the Virginia was heading for Newport News the United States steam frigate Minnesota started from Old Point by the north channel to the assistance of her consorts, and was soon followed by the steam frigate Roanoke and the sailing frigate St. Lawrence. The Minnesota grounded about a mile and a half from Newport News, and the Roanoke and St. Lawrence, seeing the result of the battle with the Congress and Cumberland, retired to Fortress Monroe, not, however, before the latter had received a 7 inch shell from the Virginia.

While the Minnesota was moving up from Fortress Monroe she passed within range of the rifle guns in the Confederate batteries at Seawell's Point, manned by the Jackson Grays, Captain Wm. H. Stewart, of Norfolk county, Company A, 61st Virginia Regiment, and they opened fire upon her. She returned the fire, but without effect. Several shots from the battery struck the ship, and one of them lodged in her mainmast. The officers of the Minnesota took this for a shell from a six-inch Armstrong gun.

The Virginia was accompanied by the gunboats Raleigh, Lieutenant J. W. Alexander, mounting one rifle 32-pounder gun, and Beaufort, Lieutenant Wm. H. Parker, mounting one rifle 32 pounder and one 24-pounder. The lookouts on the Congress and Cumberland sighted the Virginia as soon as she passed Craney Island and both ships prepared for action. Moving slowly towards the enemy, Captain Buchanan gave the order to fire the bow gun at the Cumberland when about a thousand yards from her. The gun was a seven-inch rifle, and it was so well aimed that the shell passed through the Cumberland, raking her fore and aft and doing fearful execution. The captain of the gun was named Cahill. He was from New Orleans, and volunteered from one of the Louisiana regiments at Yorktown to serve on the Virginia. Mr. Richard Curtis, formerly of Portsmouth, but now of Norfolk, was also at this gun. He entered the Confederate service in one of the Hampton companies which was attached to General Magruder's command, and, like Cahill, volunteered to serve on the Virginia. The course the Virginia pursued brought her abreast of the Congress before reaching the Cumberland, but passing the former vessel with a broadside, Captain Buchanan stood for the Cumberland and passed word down to his crew to stand fast, that he was going to ram her. True to his purpose, he struck her on the starboard side, knocking in her a large hole, from which she filled and sank in about fifteen minutes. The Congress and Cumberland both opened their guns upon the Virginia, but the shots glanced harmlessly from her shield. As the Cumberland careened over from the blow of the Virginia the men on the Virginia saw her bulwarks lined with sailors and marines armed with cutlasses and muskets to repel an attack of boarders, her commander thinking that was the purpose of the Virginia in coming so near without firing upon her. Almost immediately after the impact the bow gun of the Virginia was fired a second time into the Cumberland, and the sponger, in his enthusiasm, leaped into the port hole to sponge out the gun. As he did so he was killed by a musket ball from the Cumberland, which entered his forehead. His name was Dunbar, and he, too, was from New Orleans. Passing beyond the Cumberland, which soon went down bow foremost, with her colors flying and guns firing, the Virginia kept on until she found room to turn around, when she returned to engage the Congress. This vessel was run ashore by her commander to escape the ramming power of the Virginia, but was soon disabled, her decks strewn with dead and wounded and the vessel on fire in three or four places. After about an hour's firing she hoisted a white flag in token of surrender. The Beaufort and Raleigh steamed alongside of her and took possession. Two of her officers, Lieutenants Smith and Pendergrast, went on board the Beaufort and surrendered their swords, after which they asked permission to return to the Congress to assist in removing the wounded to the Beaufort, as the Congress was on fire. The permission was granted, but they availed of it to make their escape to the shore and never returned to the Beaufort. The enemy kept up a constant fire of musketry and artillery from the shore to prevent the Confederates from taking possession of the vessel, and a number of men on the Raleigh and Beaufort were killed and wounded, among them some of the Federal prisoners from the Congress. Lieutenant Minor, of the Virginia, while rowing to the Congress in the Virginia's launch was also wounded. This determined Captain Buchanan to destroy her. He accordingly set her on fire with hot shot from the Virginia. She burned until about midnight, when, the fire having reached her powder magazine, she was blown up. During the engagement Captain Buchanan stood in one of the hatchways in the top of the Virginia's shield, and, from that position, directed the movements of the vessel, but desiring to return the fire from the shore, he called for a musket, and getting above the shield, so that he could take better aim, he exposed nearly his whole body, and his thigh bone was broken by a musket ball from the shore. The wound disabled him, and the command of the vessel devolved upon Lieutenant Jones. Captain Buchanan's leg was subsequently amputated. Lieutenant Jones now directed his attention to the Minnesota, which was still aground, and separated from the Virginia by the "middle ground," or shoal. Before the Congress surrendered the Confederate vessels had been reinforced by the James river squadron, composed of the Patrick Henry, twelve guns, under Captain John R. Tucker, the Thomas Jefferson, two guns, under Lieutenant J. M. Barney, and the Teazer, two guns, under Lieutenant W. C. Webb. These vessels ran past the shore batteries at Newport News without suffering any material injury, except that the Patrick Henry received a shot through her boiler, which disabled her temporarily. The escaping steam scalded four men to death. The Thomas Jefferson towed her out of action, and, after a delay of about two hours repairing damages, she returned and played a prominent part in the battle. These vessels being of lighter draft than the Virginia, succeeded in getting much nearer to the Minnesota than the iron-clad could. The Minnesota was very badly cut up, and Captain Van Brunt, her commander, says it was more from the fire of the gunboats than from the Virginia. The engagement was kept up until darkness prevented a proper aim, when the Confederate vessels retired to Seawell's Point, with the intention of renewing the battle in the morning.

During the night efforts were made to get the Minnesota afloat, but they were unsuccessful, and in the morning she was lying almost exactly where she grounded the day before. About 7 a. m. on the 9th the Confederate flotilla again advanced against her for the purpose of completing her destruction. A new antagonist, however, appeared upon the scene and offered battle. This was a Federal iron-clad which had arrived during the night, and proved to be the Ericsson Monitor. It consisted of a hull, sharp at both ends, standing about eighteen inches out of the water, and amidships on the deck was a round turret of iron, nine inches thick, in which were two eleven-inch Dahlgren guns. When the Monitor first made her appearance from behind the Minnesota she looked like a raft to the people on the Virginia, and Lieutenant Davidson remarked, "The Minnesota's crew are leaving her on a raft," but the raft started towards the Virginia and showed fight. The details of this combat are very interesting in marking a new era in naval warfare. For the first time in the history of the world two iron-clads were contending for the mastery. They were made upon different plans—that of the Virginia, with inclined sides, was the better plan of the two, and has since been adopted by the United States Government in the construction of its later war vessels, but the greater mechanical facilities at the disposal of the United States enabled that Government to build the better war vessel upon an inferior plan. The Virginia's great length, deep draft of water and inferior machinery were disadvantages as compared with her antagonist's greater speed, lighter draft and ability to turn in a shorter space. The armor of the Monitor was five inches thicker than that of the Virginia, and was made in large plates without the wooden backing, but, being perpendicular, had to resist the shots of the Virginia by main strength, while the inclined sides of the Virginia caused the shots of the Monitor to glance off without imparting their full momentum.

When the iron clads became engaged the Confederate wooden vessels retired from the contest to await the result of the battle. For several hours, part of which the two ships were almost touching each other, they continued pouring broadside after broadside into each other without any apparent effect. The Monitor fired both solid shot and shell, while the Virginia had nothing but shell. These were not heavy enough to penetrate the Monitor's armor, while the heavy projectiles from that vessel glanced harmlessly from the Virginia's inclined sides. Both seemed to be invulnerable. At one time during the action the Virginia got aground, and the Monitor took up a favorable position for attack, but she soon floated again and attempted to run down the Monitor; the latter, however, partially avoided the blow, which glanced from her side. It has been claimed by Confederate authority that, but for a mistake made at this time on the part of the Virginia, she would have forced the Monitor under water. It is said that while her bow was pressing against the Monitor's side that vessel was being badly careened, and that a few more forward turns of the Virginia's propeller would have forced her under the water, but the Virginia's engines were reversed and the two vessels separated. Finally a shell from the Virginia struck the pilot house of the Monitor and disabled her commander, Lieutenant John L. Worden, who had taken up his position there. The Monitor then withdrew from the fight and steamed away towards Fortress Monroe. The Virginia again turned towards the Minnesota as if to complete her destruction, and Captain Van Brunt was considering the propriety of setting her on fire to prevent her falling into the hands of the Confederates when, very much to his surprise, as well as to his delight, the Virginia changed her course and steamed for Seawell's Point, whence she continued on to the Navy Yard. No satisfactory reason has been given why the Virginia left the Roads without first destroying the Minnesota. The Monitor had withdrawn from the fight and the Minnesota lay there a helpless prey, unable to move. The reported leak on the Virginia's bow, caused by the breaking off of her beak when she rammed the Cumberland, was an insignificant affair at best, and had been stopped by Mr. Hasker, the boatswain. The machinery of the vessel was working very well, the tide did not necessitate her return, for she remained in the Roads until dark the day before, and there was no necessity for her immediate return to the Navy Yard. The only inconvenience which resulted from the action was the perforation of her smokestack with numerous shot holes, but the withdrawal of the Monitor left the Virginia in a position to have had those stopped up temporarily, and with little loss of time. As it was, her returning to the Navy Yard without first destroying the Minnesota has enabled the Northern historians to lay claim to a victory for the Monitor. Captain Van Brunt, commander of the Minnesota, in his official report of the action, says the Monitor was the first to withdraw. He says:

"The Merrimac, finding that she could make nothing of the Monitor, turned her attention once more to me, and now, on her second approach, I opened upon her with all my broadside guns and ten-inch pivot gun, a broadside which would have blown out of the water any timber-built ship in the world. She returned my fire with her rifled bow gun with a shell which passed through the chief engineer's state room, through the engineers' mess room amidships, and burst in the boatswain's room, tearing four rooms into one, in its passage exploding two charges of powder, which set the ship on fire, but it was promptly extinguished by a party headed by my First Lieutenant. Her second went through the boiler of the tugboat Dragon, exploding it and causing some consternation on board my ship for the moment until the matter was explained. This time I had concentrated upon her an incessant fire from my gun deck, spar deck and forecastle pivot guns, and was informed by my marine officer, who was stationed on the poop, that at least fifty solid shot struck her on her slanting side without producing any apparent effect. By the time she had fired her third shell the little Monitor had come down upon her, placing herself between us, and compelled her to change her position, in doing which she grounded, and I again poured into her all the guns which could be brought to bear upon her. As soon as she got off she stood down the bay, the little battery chasing her with all speed, when suddenly the Merrimac turned around and ran full speed into her antagonist. * * * The Rebels concentrated their whole battery upon the tower and pilot house of the Monitor, and soon after the latter stood down for Fortress Monroe, and we thought it probable she had exhausted her supply of ammunition or sustained some injury. Soon after the Merrimac and the two other steamers headed for my ship, and I then felt to the fullest extent my condition. I was hard and immovably aground, and they could take position under my stern and rake me. * * * After consulting my officers, I ordered every preparation to be made to destroy the ship after all hope was gone to save her. On ascending my poop deck I ascertained that the enemy's vessels had changed their course and were heading for Craney Island."

Thus it is apparent that, had the Virginia remained ten minutes longer in Hampton Roads, the Minnesota would have been destroyed by her own crew.

The Virginia returned to the Navy Yard and was docked. A new and stronger prow was put on her, and a course of two-inch iron, extending four feet down from the knuckle, was placed all around her, wrought iron shutters were fitted to her four quarter ports and solid shot were cast for her guns. The holes in her smokestack were patched and a half a dozen pieces of armor plate were removed and replaced by new ones. These alterations consumed nearly a month's time, and it was the 8th of April before she came out of the dry-dock. Commodore Tatnall had in the meantime, succeeded Captain Buchanan as her commander, and on the 11th of April, accompanied by the Patrick Henry, Thomas Jefferson, Raleigh, Beaufort, Teazer and a wooden tug or tender from the Navy Yard, he steamed down to Hampton Roads prepared to engage and capture the Monitor. Each of the small steamers was manned with a boarding party. There were three divisions on each boat, and it was expected that some of them would be sunk by the Monitor before reaching her, but if any one boat succeeded in boarding her the enterprise promised to be successful. One division was directed to cover the pilot house with tarpaulins to prevent the wheelsman from seeing; another was to drive iron wedges between the turret and deck to prevent it from revolving, and the third was to ignite combustibles, such as turpentine, &c., and throw them down the funnel into the turret, and then cover the turret over with tarpaulins to smother the crew. The Virginia found the Monitor under the guns of Fortress Monroe, and Commodore Tatnall, apprehending torpedoes and shoal water, approached her as close as he thought advisable and then lay to, challenging her to come out and fight. The challenge was not accepted, and, noticing two brigs and a schooner anchored off Hampton bar, Commodore Tatnall ordered the Thomas Jefferson to capture them. The capture was effected without any resistance, and, hoisting their flags with the Union down, to tempt the Monitor to come to their rescue, the Jefferson took them in tow and carried them to Craney Island, whence they were taken to the Navy Yard. The brigs were the Marcus, of Stockton, New Jersey, and the Sabout, of Providence, Rhode Island, and were loaded with hay for the United States army. The schooner was the Catherine T. Dix, of Accomac county, Virginia, and was in ballast. Finding the Monitor would not fight, the Virginia returned to Seawell's Point and anchored. This affair was witnessed by a couple of English and French men-of-war which were anchored in the Roads, and which, expecting a fight, moved up towards Newport News, to give the combatants room.

It is more than probable that, had the Monitor come out to fight the Virginia, she would have been captured.

She had another opportunity to fight the Virginia on the 8th of May, but again declined. On that day, a little before noon, the Federal fleet, consisting of the Monitor, Naugatuck, Minnesota, Dacotah, Seminole and San Jacinto, moved over to Seawell's Point and began bombarding the Confederate batteries. The Virginia was at the Navy Yard, and steamed down to the assistance of the batteries. As she turned Lambert's Point she came within sight of the Federal fleet about six or seven miles lower down the river, and the entire fleet retired to Fortress Monroe. Commodore Tatnall pursued until he reached the vicinity of the Rip Raps, when he returned to Seawell's Point.

On the first of May the order came to evacuate Norfolk and Portsmouth, and the proper disposition to be made of the Virginia became a question of considerable moment. Commodore Tatnall requested Naval Constructor Porter to have a set of wooden port-bucklers made for her, to keep the water from coming in her port holes. He said he knew a port in Georgia where there was sufficient depth of water for her, and he intended taking her there. The bucklers were make, but were never taken out of the carpenter shop at the Navy Yard. The fear of torpedoes at Fortress Monroe and the fact that the Virginia was not a safe sea boat in stormy weather, when the waves would be liable to wash over her, induced Commodore Tatnall to change his mind about taking her to Georgia, and he commenced lightening her, for the purpose of carrying her up James river. The pilots informed him that they could carry eighteen feet over the principal bar in the river, and he desired to lighten her to seventeen feet. Paymaster Semple inquired of Naval Constructor Porter if the vessel would have stability on a draft of seventeen feet, but did not volunteer any information as to the object of his inquiry. Mr. Porter replied that she would. To have lightened her to that draft, however, would have necessitated the removal of almost everything in her, even to a part of her machinery. But the Commodore began on the morning of the 10th to throw overboard everything moveable, and, having brought her hull out of water, and not having succeeded in reducing her depth sufficiently to have carried her over the bar, and having no means of again settling her in the water, he determined to set her on fire and destroy her. Accordingly the match was applied and about daybreak on the morning of the 11th she was blown up, the fire having reached her magazine. Thus perished by the hands of her own commander this famous vessel, which the most powerful engines of war in the possession of her enemies were unable to injure. How much more glorious would have been her end, and how much higher her name would have stood in history, had her commander, instead of setting her on fire, ran past Fortress Monroe and destroyed or dispersed McClellan's fleet of war ships and transports which were lying outside the fort and in York river. The guns of Fortress Monroe were as powerless to injure her as were those of the Monitor, Minnesota, Cumberland and Congress. The enemy gained everything and lost nothing by her destruction, and her late antagonists, who were kept at bay by the terror of her name, steamed boldly up to the twin cities which she had so thoroughly guarded. Her crew marched to Suffolk and took part in the defence of Drury's Bluff later that month.

Whether or not Commodore Tatnall was justifiable in destroying the Virginia will remain a matter of discussion. A naval court of inquiry exonerated him from all blame, but his defence of himself was marred by an attempt to blacken the good name of the Virginia pilots and to fasten upon them the imputation of being deficient in personal courage.

The Federal Government had a wholesome fear of the Virginia and offered rewards and promotion to any one who would destroy her. The Navy Department ordered the Potomac river to be blocked with vessels loaded with stone, to prevent her coming to Washington. These preparations were kept up for several weeks, until it was ascertained that her draft of water was too great to enable her to ascend the river. General Wool was authorized by a dispatch from Washington, dated March 9th, at 1 p. m. (after the Monitor had retired from the fight), to evacuate Newport News, but to hold Fortress Monroe at all hazards. President Lincoln issued orders that the Monitor be not too much exposed; he was afraid to risk the consequences of another battle with the Virginia, and on the 14th day of March, five days after the battle between the two iron-clads, Quartermaster General M. C. Meigs of the United States army, wrote to Captain Dahlgren, commanding the Washington Navy Yard, as follows:

"Your telegram relative to barges received. I have ordered eight more sent down. I have seen nothing yet to satisfy me that in the next engagement the Monitor will not be sunk."

These barges were to block up the Potomac river, and General Meigs was correct. Had the Monitor come out to fight on the 11th of April, when the Virginia was prepared for her, she would have been sunk or captured. General Wool, commanding the department at Fortress Monroe, in a letter of the 14th of March to Secretary of War Stanton, expressed the fear that the Monitor would be overcome in the next engagement and that Newport News would have to be abandoned, and on the 15th, the Secretary, having no faith in the ability of the Monitor to successfully contend against the Virginia, proposed to make a contract with Mr. C. Vanderbilt to destroy her, but what the utmost exertions of the United States Government were powerless to do was done by her own commander, and the first and most famous of iron-clads passed out of existence.

Mahoneyville Distilling Company,

ALEXANDRIA, VA.,

Main Office, Nos. 11 and 13 High Street. · PORTSMOUTH, VA.

DISTILLERS OF

Arlington Pure Rye and Cameron Springs Whiskey
AND RYE MALT GIN.

ALSO

J. & E. MAHONEY,

RECTIFIERS AND WHOLESALE DEALERS IN

Foreign and Domestic Wines and Liquors.

PROMPT ATTENTION GIVEN TO ALL ORDERS.

PORTSMOUTH BARGAIN HOUSE,

B. F. HOWELL,

Dealer in Furniture, Carpets, Dry-Goods, Notions, Clothing, Trunks, Stoves, Boots, Shoes, Glass, Crockery and Tinware.

Cor. High & Washington Streets, Portsmouth, Va.

Carrying the line of goods that I do, enables me to beat all competition. The Cheapest Goods in this Section. Goods sold on installments.

JNO. N. HART. WM. F. HART.

JNO. N. HART & BRO.,
Lumber, Shingles and Laths,

Cor. High and Chestnut Streets,

Adjoining Godwin's Factory. Portsmouth, Va.

R. B. DAUGHERTY,

DEALER IN IMPORTED AND DOMESTIC

Canned Goods & Groceries

508 CRAWFORD STREET,

PORTSMOUTH,   VIRGINIA.

JOS. F. WEAVER,

DEALER IN

DRUGS, MEDICINES,

Chemicals, Patent Medicine, Perfumery
Fancy and Toilet Articles.

51 SOUTH STREET,   - -   PORTSMOUTH, VA.

Prescriptions Carefully Compounded.

NIEMEYER & CO.,

115 & 117 HIGH ST., PORTSMOUTH, VA.

Coal, Lime, Cement and Building Material,

AND COMMISSION MERCHANTS.

CITY STOVE HOUSE.

ALEXNDER & POWELL,

DEALERS IN

Cooking & Heating Stoves

Ranges, &c., Tinware and House Furnishing Goods,
Gas Fitting and Plumbing.

517 and 519 CRAWFORD ST.,   PORTSMOUTH, VA.

☞ Established 1865.

W. C. NASH,
—DEALER IN—

Dry Goods and Notions,

CLOAKS, CASSIMERES, OILCLOTHS,

MATTINGS, LADIES' UNDERWEAR, &c

Kirn Building, 229 High St., Portsmouth, Va.

OWENS BROS.,
Wholesale ∴ Fancy ∴ Grocers

119 AND 121 HIGH STREET, PORTSMOUTH, VA.

— DEALERS IN —

Fruits, Vegetables, Candies. Cakes, Crackers, Cigars, Tobacco, &c.

Agents for Price & Lucas' Cider and Vinegar and Skillman's Fancy Cakes.

WILLIAM H. STEWART,
ATTORNEY AT LAW.

COMMISSIONER IN CHANCERY

For the Court of Hustings for the City of Portsmouth and for the Circuit Court of the County of Norfolk.

Office, No. 407 Court Street.   Residence, No. 517 North Street.

W. B. JOHNSON,
Funeral Director and Embalmer,

Office, - - - - - 502 County Street.

Residence, - - - 700 County Street.

PORTSMOUTH, - - - **VIRGINIA.**

The Bank of Portsmouth,
PORTSMOUTH. VA.
ORGANIZED FEB. 9TH, 1867.
The Oldest Bank in Portsmouth or Norfolk.

Capital paid in, $100,000; surplus and undivided profits, $31,500.
LEGH R. WATTS, President;   J. L. BILISOLY, Cashier.

DIRECTORS.

LEGH R. WATTS, President, General Counsel Seaboard Air Line.
O. V. SMITH, Vice Pres't., Traffic Manager Seaboard Air Line.
JOHN M. ROBINSON, President Seaboard Air Line, Old Dominion Steamship Co., Bay Line, etc., etc.
JOHN H. HUME, of R. G. Hume & Bro.
W. V. H. WILLIAMS, Secretary and Treas. of Portsmouth Ins. Co.
E. N. WILCOX, of Hume & Bro.
THOMAS SCOTT, Furniture Dealer.
EDWARD MAHONEY, Retired Capitalist.
GEO. L. NEVILLE, Contractor.

CORRESPONDENTS.

Chicago, Continental National Bank; Boston, National Revere Bank; New York, Importers and Traders National Bank; Richmond, State Bank of Virginia; Baltimore, Merchants' National Bank; Washington, National Metropolitan Bank; Philadelphia, First National Bank, Independence National Bank, Corn Exchange National Bank.

Our connections North, East, West and in Virginia and North Carolina enable us to offer the best facilities for collections, which we make at reasonable rates.

JOHN T. GRIFFIN, President.   J. H. TOOMER, Cashier.

CITY DEPOSITARY.
Merchants and Farmers Bank
PORTSMOUTH, VA.

Incorporated under the Laws of the State of Virginia. Commenced business December 1st, 1885.

Capital Stock, $51,500; Surplus and undivided profits, $35,000.

Transacts a general banking business. Accounts of farmers, merchants and others solicited.

W. V. H. WILLIAMS, Secretary.   O. V. SMITH, President.

Portsmouth Insurance Co.,
INCORPORATED 1852.
The Only Home and the Oldest Fire Insurance Office in Eastern Virginia.

Represents the Liverpool and London and Globe, Imperial, of London; Mutual Life, of New York; Travelers, of Hartford.

The Leading Life and Accident Companies of the World.

Union Agency for sale of Railroad and Steamboat Tickets.

Office: Company's Building, 217 High St., - - - - Portsmouth, Va.

R. G. HUME & BRO.,
224 High Street, Portsmouth.

BOOKS, ∴ STATIONERY.
SCHOOL SUPPLIES OF ALL KINDS.

State Agency Weber, Wheelock Pianos,
Wilcox & White, Needham Organs

JOHN R. NEELY.
(Successor to R. J. Neely & Co.)

WHOLESALE AND RETAIL DEALER IN

DOORS, SASH, BLINDS,
Mouldings, Brackets. Wood and Slate Mantles, Paints, Oils, Varnish. and Builders' Hardware, White Pine, Walnut, Ash and Oak Lumber, Hot-bed Sash, &c.

Cor. Queen and Water Sts., — PORTSMOUTH, VA.

JOHN C. EMMERSON,
WHOLESALE AND RETAIL DEALER IN

LUMBER, SHINGLES and LATHS,
White Pine and Poplar a Specialty.

☞ **STEAMBOATS SUPPLIED WITH WATER.** ☜

MAIN OFFICE, S. W. COR. LONDON & WATER STREETS,

PORTSMOUTH, — — VIRGINIA.

THOMAS SCOTT.
317 High Street, Portsmouth, Va.

The Oldest Furniture House
IN EASTERN VIRGINIA.

Beautiful Lines of Furniture, Carpets, Mattings, Oilcloths, Rugs, Mattresses, &c., always in stock.

Will be pleased to wait on his friends.

J. S. CRAWFORD,
Furniture, Carpets, &c.,

Desks, Pictures, Oil Cloth and Matting, Feathers, Springs, Mattresses and Pillows, Lace Curtains, Portiers and Wall Paper. Country Orders Solicited. Northern Prices Duplicated. Largest Furniture and Carpet House in the City.

Crawford Building, 221, 223 High Street,
PORTSMOUTH, VA.

G. M. REYNOLDS & CO.,
Insurance, Real Estate & Rental Agents,
AUCTIONEERS.

335 and 337 High Street. PORTSMOUTH, VA.

ESTABLISHED IN 1881.
W. J. BRENT,
General Contractor and Builder,
1309 and 1311 GREEN STREET.

Improved Facilities for Conducting the Business in all its Branches. Estimates furnished on application. All work promptly attended to.

H. B. WILKINS.
DEALER IN
⇒COAL & WOOD.⇐
1213 Washington St., Portsmouth, Va.

Has always on hand a full stock of First Class Pine and Hard Wood, also the Best Grades of Hard and Soft Coal. Delivered to any part of city or county.

www.ingramcontent.com/pod-product-compliance
Lightning Source LLC
Chambersburg PA
CBHW020218240426
43672CB00006B/347